"The discipline of daily Bible-reading is one that is always in danger of become routine or a chore. That is where a good devotional guide can be helpful in keeping the familiar stories and teachings of Scripture fresh and thought-provoking. Alistair Begg has produced one such volume. Like Spurgeon's *Morning and Evening*, this is not a guide to extended passages of Scripture but a series of reflections on particular verses touching particular aspects of the faith. Each one is designed to make the Christian think more clearly, love God more fervently, and act in ways that are more godly. For those looking for a book that will reinvigorate their devotions, this book might well be it."

CARL R. TRUEMAN, Professor of Biblical and Religious Studies, Grove City College, PA; Author, *The Rise and Triumph of the Modern Self*

"A good daily devotional is a wonderful aid to a daily habit of reading and meditating on Scripture. And this one, as you would expect from Alistair Begg, is pure gold. With the skill of a spiritual surgeon, he carefully dissects both the Scriptures and our hearts. A daily devotional dose of wisdom from one of the finest preachers of our time. How could this possibly be anything but life-giving nourishment for the mind and heart?"

DEREK W.H. THOMAS, Senior Minister, First Presbyterian Church, Columbia, SC; Teaching Fellow, Ligonier Ministries; Chancellor's Professor, Reformed Theological Seminary

"I found these daily devotions by Alistair Begg to be a huge help to daily Bible reading—a critical barometer of our spiritual health. Time and again I was made to think freshly about a passage and then given another chapter which made me reflect more deeply on the verses that the commentary had opened up. A very timely gift to aid discipleship in the church."

RICO TICE, Founder, Christianity Explored Ministries; Author, *Faithful Leaders* and *Honest Evangelism*

"If you are looking for wise and perceptive guidance to help you see and experience the deep impact of God's words in Scripture, you will love this devotional. Each day's reflection is a gem, focusing the light of the chosen Scripture text onto our thinking, our affections and our behaviour. I cannot imagine it being read without benefit!"

JOHN WOODHOUSE, Former Principal of Moore Theological College, Sydney, Australia

"These daily reflections from Alistair Begg are simple but profound, short but meaty, challenging but encouraging. They offer truth for all of life, truth to consecrate a life, truth to transform a life. Together, they make an ideal devotional resource for individuals, couples, and families alike."

TIM CHALLIES, Blogger; Author, *Visual Theology* and *Seasons of Sorrow*

"Here speaks a pastor who knows both his Bible and his people. He not only understands the Scriptures but lovingly applies them like medicine for the soul. These daily devotions will do that. They will help you get to know the Bible better and how it fits together. They will stretch your mind with deep, bracing theology expressed with accessible clarity. They will warm and nourish your heart because they breathe the beauty of Christ. I have been struck by the freshness and variety of the devotions, from every part of the Scriptures, and by the pastor's heart that beats through them. There is rich nourishment here for the soul, the fruit of many years of mining the Scriptures and caring for people."

CHRISTOPHER ASH, Writer-in-Residence, Tyndale House, Cambridge, UK;
Author, *Zeal Without Burnout* and *Married For God*

"In this rich resource, Alistair Begg provides what we've come to expect from him—solid biblical truth presented with clarity, winsomeness, and a focus on the person and work of Christ."

NANCY GUTHRIE, Host, Help Me Teach the Bible podcast;
Author, *Even Better Than Eden* and *Saints and Scoundrels*

"These devotions will help you praise when you are celebrating, will comfort you when you are struggling, will encourage you when you are doubting, and will be a balm when you are hurting. Each day, Alistair points to the glory and goodness of God as He reveals Himself to us in His word. Whoever you are, there is rich treasure for you in this book."

KEITH & KRISTYN GETTY, Hymn Writers; Founders of Getty Music
and the Sing! Conference

TRUTH FOR LIFE

365 DAILY DEVOTIONS

VOLUME ONE

ALISTAIR BEGG

1

Truth For Life: 365 Daily Devotions (Volume One)

Reprinted 2021 (twice), 2022 (three times), 2023, 2024

Published by:
The Good Book Company

thegoodbook.com | thegoodbook.co.uk
thegoodbook.com.au | thegoodbook.co.nz | thegoodbook.co.in

Published in association with the literary agency of Wolgemuth & Associates.

Cover design by Faceout Studio, Molly von Borstel
Design and art direction by André Parker

ISBN: 9781784985851 | JOB-007749 | Printed in India

INTRODUCTION

God's word is a glorious gift. Our Father has given it to us in order that we might know His Son and that we might live in the power of His Spirit, in obedience to His truth.

It is worth pausing to consider this reality: when we read the Bible, we're dealing with the words of the Creator of the universe, spoken to His creation. It is impossible for us to understand ourselves, our world, or anything else without His word. As we read a newspaper, as we try to make sense of our society, and as we look to our history and to our future, it is the Bible we need if we are to get a handle on it all. God's word is the truth that you and I need to navigate every day of this life, and to point us to the one in whom we find the life that really is life.

So in this devotional, by far the most important words on each page are the ones at the top, just under the date and title. Those are the words of the living, reigning, eternal God. My aim in the comments below those divinely inspired words is simply to explain them, to encourage you from them, and to reflect on how they inspire and equip us to enjoy living for Christ in every area of our lives. God's word says of itself that it is able to "make you wise for salvation through faith in Christ Jesus" and that these God-breathed words are "profitable for teaching, for reproof, for correction, and for training in righteousness, that the man of God may be complete, equipped for every good work" (2 Timothy 3:16-17).

This is a *daily* devotional, because man does not live by bread alone but by every word that comes from the mouth of God (Matthew 4:4). That is, God's word sustains us each day and is as necessary to our spiritual health as food is to our physical health. On some days you may find reading God's word a delight, and on other days it may be done more out of duty, but every day it is essential. Think of it like exercise. If you're a runner, there are times when you're running around the track and it feels amazing; and there are others when it feels like an effort and you need to push on and push through. Most of us will not tumble out of our beds each morning thinking how fantastic our time in God's word is going to be. If we approach the Scriptures thinking that we need to be stirred as we read them, or that we ought to "get a blessing" whenever we open them, then we will either be intermittent or disappointed Bible readers. There will be times of delight and excitement and feeling something as you read and meditate on God's word—but do not worry if those times do not come every day, or even most days. Make a commitment to turn to the Bible every day (and if you realize you have fallen out of the habit of doing so, simply jump back in), for God's word is living and active, and it will be going to work in you in ways far deeper and more profound than your feelings can intuit.

And the Scriptures will—or they should—make a difference to our minds, to our hearts, and to our lives. Therefore, at the bottom of each devotion you will see three icons: . These are a prompt to say to yourself, *Now that I have read and considered these verses...*

- *how is God calling me to think differently?*
- *how is God reordering my heart's affections—what I love?*
- *what is God calling me to do as I go about my day today?*

It may be that God's word does not speak to all three of those areas each day; but learning to ask yourself these questions will ensure that you are open to what God's Spirit may be saying about your mind, heart, and life. And they will be helpful prompts to pray in response to what you have read, too.

Beside those icons you will see a passage that is linked in some way to what we have been considering; if you have time, turn up that passage and enjoy going deeper into God's word. I have also found it very profitable to read through the whole of the Scriptures from start to finish in a year, and so, at the very foot of each page, you'll see a Bible-reading plan that enables you to do just that.

God's words are the words that we need. And so I am praying for you: that, in taking you to those words each day, this book would be life-changing for you, God's beloved child, as His Spirit works through His word to show you His Son. Why not make that your prayer too? You could begin each day by using the words of my friends Keith Getty and Stuart Townend and praying:

Holy Spirit, living breath of God,
Breathe new life into my willing soul.
Let the presence of the risen Lord,
Come renew my heart and make me whole.
Cause Your word to come alive in me;
Give me faith for what I cannot see,
Give me passion for Your purity;
Holy Spirit, breathe new life in me.[1]

1 Keith Getty and Stuart Townend, "Holy Spirit, Living Breath of God" (2005).

JANUARY 1

KING OF CREATION

"In the beginning, God created the heavens and the earth." GENESIS 1:1

There was never a time when God did not exist. Before there was time, before there was anything, there was God. And since His nature is unchanging, so He has also always existed in the Trinity—God the Father, God the Son, and God the Holy Spirit.

When reading the Bible, we discover that each member of the Trinity was involved in creation: God the Father took the initiative, God the Spirit is described as "hovering over" the proceedings, and God the Son was the agent of creation in all that was made (Genesis 1:2-3; John 1:3).

"All things bright and beautiful, all creatures great and small"[2] should leave us in awe; they were all fashioned by God's command. And He is not only the Creator of all; He is also the Lord of all that He has created. All of nature is in His hands, under His control. As we see waves crashing against the shoreline, it's wonderfully encouraging to know that each one is there as a result of God's sovereign rule. He hasn't stepped away from His creation, nor will He ever.

It's important to remember that God is also transcendent. He is on His throne, above, beyond, and distinct from all that He has made. This is what distinguishes Christianity from pantheism, the idea that the natural world is a manifestation of God and therefore everything is somehow a part of Him. With this belief, we dare not kill a fly or step on an ant because those insects are divine. Similarly, we should not chop down a tree or eat meat, because these too are "parts of God." Teachings like these are mistaken and misguided and tend to lead to idolatry. Scripture makes it clear time and time again that people will choose to worship "the creature rather than the Creator" (Romans 1:25). When we see a great painting, we rightly admire and enjoy the painting, and then we praise the painter. All of creation is God's canvas, and all of it speaks of "his invisible attributes, namely, his eternal power and divine nature" (v 20).

Only God is to be worshiped, for creation exists by His power and for His glory. His existence knows no beginning or end, and He will reign forever. He is the King. Today, exalt Him as He alone deserves. Go for a walk or look out of the window and praise Him as you see His beauty displayed in what He has made. Praise Him as He continues to rule over His creation, holding you in His sovereign hand.

REVELATION 4

2 Cecil F. Alexander, "All Things Bright and Beautiful" (1848).

JANUARY 2

BEHOLD YOUR GOD!

"Go on up to a high mountain, O Zion, herald of good news; lift up your voice with strength, O Jerusalem, herald of good news; lift it up, fear not; say to the cities of Judah, 'Behold your God!'" ISAIAH 40:9

During the prophet Isaiah's lifetime, God's people had been taken captive into a foreign territory. They were dejected, unable even to sing songs of praise to the Lord (see Psalm 137:1-4). Yet while they were in that state of exile, God came to His people with words of comfort (Isaiah 40:1)—comfort found only in the fulfillment of His promise: that the glory of the Lord would be revealed, not only to Israel but to all mankind.

These good tidings were nothing to be quiet about. God's people were meant to give a triumphal shout, captivating each other with the glory of their hope. Once described as "people who walked in darkness," they now saw "a great light" (Isaiah 9:2).

The distinction between the darkness of this fallen world and the light of heaven is a striking picture that runs all the way through Isaiah, and indeed through the whole Bible. Darkness is a result of disinterest in God, rebellion against Him, and unwillingness to do what He says. There is but one message that shines light into such darkness, refreshing hearts and minds: "Behold your God!"

This message is just as relevant to God's people today as it was in Isaiah's time. The darkness often feels very heavy and the light sometimes looks very dim. Yet often the message of hope also dawns during uncertain times. God promised, "The glory of the Lord shall be revealed, and all flesh shall see it together, for the mouth of the Lord has spoken" (Isaiah 40:5). Ultimately, God fulfilled this promise when He took on flesh and established His presence among us.

When John wrote his Gospel, he looked back on the same scene to which Isaiah had been looking forward, saying, "The Word became flesh and dwelt among us, and we have seen his glory, glory as of the only Son from the Father, full of grace and truth" (John 1:14). Here was—*He* was—the Light of the world, and "the light shines in the darkness, and the darkness has not overcome it" (v 5). Isaiah was describing the one who would come—but we, like John, are able to reflect upon the completed work: the promised glory that has now been revealed.

God has come to us, breaking through our darkness and bringing salvation. You can behold your God in a manger, on a cross, walking out of a tomb, and now reigning on high. It is not hard to see the darkness—but we must nevertheless look to the light, for there we find hope that casts out fear and good news that is worth heralding. Today, behold your God!

ISAIAH 40:1-31

JANUARY 3

EVERY PROMISE FULFILLED

"The book of the genealogy of Jesus Christ, the son of David, the son of Abraham." MATTHEW 1:1

The beginning of the New Testament may not immediately strike us as inspiring. In fact, if someone were reading through the Bible for the very first time and reached the end of Malachi, which points forward with anticipation, their excitement might falter when the next book begins with… a genealogy. They (and we!) might even be tempted to skip Matthew and begin with another Gospel altogether.

Keep in mind, though, that the promises God made to His people in the Old Testament all looked forward to their fulfillment. As we read through the New Testament, we realize that in fact it couldn't open in a more fitting manner, since the genealogy in Matthew draws the line from Abraham to David and at last to Jesus as the one who fulfills all these promises.

Similarly Mark, throughout his Gospel, reaches one hand back to the prophets who pointed forward to the one who was yet to come. Mark uses the Old Testament to set the stage for this striking reality, his second sentence beginning "As it is written in Isaiah the prophet…" (Mark 1:2). And the first words he records Jesus as saying are, "The time is fulfilled, and the kingdom of God is at hand" (v 15). Jesus' disciples had the privilege of witnessing what prophets and kings had longed to see (see Luke 10:24)—a privilege that even now continues through the illuminating work of God's word.

The New Testament shows us that the means by which God's promises are fulfilled can be summed up in two words: *Jesus Christ.* God made His promises to Israel using terminology and categories that they understood—words like *nation* and *temple*. Christ's coming redefined Old Testament concepts in light of the gospel: Old Testament prophecies, we discover, are all fulfilled christologically—by and in the person of the Christ. Therefore, instead of looking for a new temple in the state of Israel, we meet with God through His Son, the Lord Jesus; enjoy His presence in each of us by His Spirit; and look to the reality of Christ's reign to transform our lives both now and forevermore.

The coming of the Son of God breaks the boundaries of Old Testament categories. This is not meant to be unsettling for God's people; it is meant to be thrilling! Christ is the perfect fulfillment of all God's promises. He is the reality of all God's great assurances. Wait no more, then, to see how God will fulfill His every promise. We know now that each one was, is, and ever will be satisfied through Christ. He has promised to be with you, to work for you and through you, and to bring you to an eternal kingdom of perfection. There are times when it is hard to hold on to those promises. When those times come, we look back to a man born of Abraham and David's line, conceived of the Spirit, who was able to announce, "The time is fulfilled, and the kingdom of God is at hand" and who hung on a cross and rose from the grave so that all God's promises would become "yes" in Him.

MATTHEW 1:1-18

◇ Bible Through The Year: Genesis 7–9; Romans 3

JANUARY 4

CONTENTED IN CHRIST

"I have learned in whatever situation I am to be content. I know how to be brought low, and I know how to abound." PHILIPPIANS 4:11-12

We live in a society permeated by discontent. Commercials condition us to be envious. The real issue, though, is not so much the society we live in but the state of our own hearts and minds. We're drawn away from contentment by so much which clamors for our attention: titles, possessions, influence, or fame. Yet all of these and more seek to rob us of any sense of joy in what God has given us, persuading us that it will never be enough. The chase is never-ending.

Paul, though, could say not only that he was content but that he could be content "in whatever situation I am." This is what everyone is searching for! What was the secret, then? It was to ground his sense of self and his outlook on life in the sufficiency of the Lord Jesus Christ. Paul didn't champion a stiff upper lip in the face of hardship or offer a false gospel of self-sufficiency. No, his contentment was the result of bowing his heart and mind to God's will, no matter what conditions he faced.

Not everyone has lived on both sides of the street. Not everyone knows how the other half lives. But Paul did. He knew what it was to be warm and fed, and he knew what it was to be cold and naked. If he had derived contentment from his circumstances, his life would have been a constant roller-coaster ride, leaving him intoxicated by wonderful luxuries one minute and overwhelmed by their absence the next. Such a fickle spirit would have neutralized Paul, making him unable to serve Christ.

Paul was a normal man with normal needs. In a letter to Timothy from a dungeon in Rome, Paul wrote, "Do your best to come to me soon ... Bring the cloak ... the books, and above all the parchments" (2 Timothy 4:9, 13). He had been deserted by others and lacked certain possessions. Yes, Paul wanted things like clothing, books, and company—but he knew he would be fine without them, for his peace rested in something greater.

Like Paul, your contentment can and should ultimately be grounded in your union with Jesus. Refuse any ambition other than belonging to Him and remaining entirely at His disposal. When you know Christ and how wonderful He is—that He is your all in all, more precious than silver, more costly than gold, more beautiful than diamonds, and that nothing you have compares to Him[3]—the way you view your circumstances and the measure of your contentment will be completely transformed.

PSALM 73

3 Lynn DeShazo, "More Precious Than Silver" (1982).

JANUARY 5

OUR GREAT HIGH PRIEST

"Every high priest chosen from among men is appointed to act on behalf of men in relation to God, to offer gifts and sacrifices for sins ... No one takes this honor for himself, but only when called by God, just as Aaron was. So also Christ did not exalt himself to be made a high priest, but was appointed by him who said to him, 'You are my Son, today I have begotten you'; as he says also in another place, 'You are a priest forever, after the order of Melchizedek.'"

HEBREWS 5:1, 4-6

The concept of priesthood and the sacrificial system is far removed from our contemporary Western world, but understanding it is fundamental to Christian living. The practice of animal sacrifice in Old Testament Israel was not a man-made system created as a futile attempt to reach God and make humans acceptable to Him. Rather, it was meant to help God's covenant people understand His character, His expectations, and the wonder of His plan of redemption (and it can still help us in this way today). In all of its nuances, God was pointing His people toward the finished and perfect work of the Lord Jesus Christ, who would come both as His people's Great High Priest and as the one perfect sacrifice offered on their behalf.

Historically, Israel's high priest would have come from the line of Aaron, Moses' brother, and would have been considered "chief among his brothers" (Leviticus 21:10). This individual would have experienced the same societal conditions, pressures, and trials as the men and women he was representing, which would have helped him to be a more compassionate advocate on their behalf.

Long before the arrival of Jesus, however, the historical pattern of high-priestly appointments had been corrupted by Herod the Great and other rulers, who chose the high priest for themselves. They didn't understand that the high priest's role was not an honor to be bestowed by man but ultimately a call from God, as it had been for Aaron. High priests were not to represent the political establishment; they were to represent God's people to God Himself.

That is one of the factors that makes Jesus the very best high priest: He did not take upon Himself the glory of becoming a high priest; rather, He was appointed by the Father. He acknowledged, "If I glorify myself, my glory is nothing. It is my Father who glorifies me, of whom you say, 'He is our God'" (John 8:54). He perfectly endured the same hardships we face. He has gone before Almighty God for our sins even though He was sinless. With a spirit of gentleness, Jesus spurs us toward righteousness. Because He offered the perfect sacrifice—indeed, because He was the perfect sacrifice—you and I can enjoy God's presence both now and forevermore. No sin or suffering, no disappointment or despair, makes this glorious reality any less true: that you have a priest, forever, and therefore you have a place with Him, forever.

HEBREWS 4:14 – 5:10

JANUARY 6

CHERISHING GOD'S WORD

"My son, keep my words and treasure up my commandments with you; keep my commandments and live; keep my teaching as the apple of your eye; bind them on your fingers; write them on the tablet of your heart." PROVERBS 7:1-3

I find it a dangerous thing to go grocery shopping when I'm hungry. I find myself tempted to buy food that under normal circumstances would not appeal to me at all. I am not alone, according to King Solomon: "One who is full loathes honey, but to one who is hungry everything bitter is sweet" (Proverbs 27:7).

This same principle can be applied to our pursuit of purity. There is a real danger in going through our days spiritually hungry because we have not fed well upon the word of God.

If we are going to make any meaningful attempt at maintaining our purity, it is imperative that we not only read God's word; we must also *cherish* it. Solomon—the king of Israel to whom God gave wisdom that surpassed anyone else's (1 Kings 3:3-14)—uses language that gets at the notion of cherishing God's word when he tells his son to "keep" his words, to "treasure" them, to keep them "as the apple of [his] eye," to "bind" them, and to "write" them on his heart.

To relate to God's word this way requires us to get beyond using the Bible merely as a textbook to study, a book of proof texts for arguments, or a promise book to which we occasionally turn. Cherishing God's word requires us to seek the perspective of the psalmist who, distancing himself from the proud and the scoffers of his day, says of the man who is walking with God, "His delight is in the law of the Lord, and on his law he meditates day and night" (Psalm 1:2).

There is a direct correlation between delighting in God's word—allowing it to control and guide our lives—and maintaining a zeal for purity. If we fail to cherish Scripture, the question is not *if* we will stumble in the matter of purity but *when*.

Every one of us can keep our way pure by hiding God's word in our hearts (Psalm 119:9). Do you have a plan for memorizing Scripture? Let me challenge you to make a commitment to memorize a verse of the Bible, whether it's every other day, every day, every week, or whatever it might be. Make a plan, and stick with it.

Feast on God's word and be satisfied. Cherish the Scriptures and be pure.

PSALM 119:1-16

JANUARY 7

THE GOSPEL DISPLAYED

"Only let your manner of life be worthy of the gospel of Christ." PHILIPPIANS 1:27

The way we dress, the way we smile or scowl, the way we carry ourselves, the tone and content of our speech… Every day, we are always making statements to those around us about what really matters and what life truly consists of.

For Christians, such statements should be in harmony with the gospel.

So Paul called the Philippians to close the gap between their beliefs and their behavior—between the creed they professed and the conduct they displayed. Christ's call to us today is no different. Even so, however mature we are in our faith and however much we close the gap, there always remains more to do.

Paul's phrase "let your manner of life" comes from the Greek verb *politeuesthe*, which the NIV translates as "conduct yourselves." The root of this word comes from *polis*, which means "city," and gives us other words like *police* and *politics*. In a very real sense, Paul is concerned with Christian citizenship and conduct. As we understand ourselves to be members of the city of God, we learn what it means to live as strangers and ambassadors in that other city, the city of man. When we close the gap between belief and behavior, others will get a foretaste of heaven through their interactions with us.

So what kind of statement should our actions make? Simply this: the gospel of Christ is a gospel of love. We see this in the words of John: "In this is love, not that we have loved God but that he loved us and sent his Son to be the propitiation for our sins. Beloved, if God so loved us, we also ought to love one another" (1 John 4:10-11). In other words, just as God loves us, so we should love those around us—even those whom we, or others, tend to see as unlovely or unlovable—and we should do it with hope and joy! This message of love is the challenge that Paul gives us.

Not merely in the words you say,
Not only in the deeds confessed,
But in the most unconscious way
Is Christ expressed.[4]

So pause to think about how you will dress today, when you will smile and when you will scowl today, how you will carry yourself today, and the tone and content of your speech today. What kind of statements are you making to the world? Let them be ones that are worthy of the gospel of love.

1 JOHN 4:7-21

4 Attributed to Beatrice Cleland, "Indwelt," in, for instance, *Our Aim: A Monthly Record of the Aborigines Inland Mission of Australia* 68, no. 7 (17 March, 1955), p 1.

JANUARY 8

BATTLING BITTERNESS

"Now the Syrians on one of their raids had carried off a little girl from the land of Israel, and she worked in the service of Naaman's wife. She said to her mistress, 'Would that my lord were with the prophet who is in Samaria! He would cure him of his leprosy.'" 2 KINGS 5:2-3

Suffering in and of itself does not lead a person into a deeper relationship with God. As with those who hear the word of God yet do not respond to it with faith, suffering divorced from faith and hope will actually embitter us as our hearts grow harder rather than softer toward God. In other words, suffering will either make us run to God or away from Him. In the midst of trials, we must ask ourselves, "Is this trial making me bitter and callous, or is it making me loving and gentle?"

In the midst of the book of 2 Kings, among the stories of monarchs and prophets, we find an extraordinary picture of gentleness and humility in the face of great heartache through the example of a little Israelite girl. The Syrians had captured this young girl during a raid; they had carried her away from her family and from Israel and had forced her to work in the service of Naaman, a commander in the Syrian army. What an unfathomable tragedy for a young child and her family!

Yet in the midst of her great suffering, we catch a glimpse of her tender heart: upon learning that her master suffered from leprosy, this child told Naaman's wife how he could be healed. If she had allowed herself to become embittered, then, when the word went around the house that her master was sick, she might have concluded, *Well, it's nothing more than what he deserves.* But she didn't. She wanted the best for her enemy, rather than hoping for the worst. This is remarkable. How could she do this? Because presumably, in the face of her emptiness and the sadness of being separated from her family, she had turned time and time again to her loving God and His promises.

As we journey through our own suffering, and as we seek to minister to those who are in deep affliction, we must not forget to cultivate a tender and open heart. Will it be easy? By no means! But God's faithfulness is so vast, so comprehensive, that it is able to sustain us, even in our deepest pain. So turn to God in every circumstance and take comfort in His faithfulness and provision. When you do, then you "may be able to comfort those who are in any affliction, with the comfort with which we ourselves are comforted by God" (2 Corinthians 1:4).

2 CORINTHIANS 5:6-21

JANUARY 9

THE INVITATION OF ALL INVITATIONS

"Come to me, all who labor and are heavy laden, and I will give you rest."
MATTHEW 11:28

Whenever you receive invitations, you probably find yourself asking the same sorts of questions: Who is it from? Who is it for? Why does it matter? This verse presents one of the loveliest invitations in the whole of the New Testament—but to understand it best, we must ask those same questions.

First, this is a personal invitation. It is not an invitation to a program, nor is it an invitation to a religion or philosophy to be included alongside Hinduism, Buddhism, Confucianism, New Age-ism, humanism, or any other "ism" that may be found among today's worldviews. It is an invitation from Jesus Himself. He is bidding each of us, "Come to me."

The significance of the invitation lies in who is issuing it. In the Gospels, Jesus declares who He is: the Messiah, the Savior of the world, the Son of God (see John 4:25-26; 1 John 4:14). By virtue of this identity, Jesus could command a response—but instead, He extends an invitation. And who does He invite to come? "All who labor and are heavy laden." This invitation is all-inclusive. It doesn't single out a certain group among a larger group but describes all of humanity. Each of us needs to hear these words, because there's not one person who isn't figuratively pushing around a wheelbarrow filled with all the cares, responsibilities, fears, and failures that make up his or her life.

Why does all this matter? Jesus invites us to find "rest for your souls." He's speaking in eternal terms of a rest that never fails. He's beckoning us towards a banquet, and He doesn't even ask us to provide the clothes. We show up for the banquet just the way we are. God takes all the "Here are my good deeds" clothes that so many of us like to dress up in, calls them rags, and tosses them aside. He takes all the "I'm so bad and messed up that there's no hope" clothes and tosses them aside too. In their place, He covers us over with "the robe of righteousness" (Isaiah 61:10), which is provided by Jesus Christ Himself. We can rest from our striving to make something of ourselves or to earn heaven for ourselves when we come to Jesus and receive all we need, and could ever need, from Him.

This is the invitation of all invitations. Today, for the first or the thousandth time, bring your burdens to Him. Receive His rest.

Just as I am, without one plea
But that Thy blood was shed for me
And that Thou bidst me come to Thee—
O Lamb of God, I come, I come.[5]

MATTHEW 11:25-30

5 Charlotte Elliot, "Just As I Am, Without One Plea" (1835).

JANUARY 10

MUCH IN COMMON

"All who believed were together and had all things in common." ACTS 2:44

One of the greatest attractions of the early church in the eyes of the surrounding pagan world was its communal lifestyle. What was it that united such diverse people—Gentiles and Jews, circumcised and uncircumcised, barbarians and Scythians, slaves and free men (Colossians 3:11)? Jesus Christ. There was no real explanation for the commonality of these Christians' lives together apart from Him.

From those days until now, the church has always been united in a unique fellowship marked by several commonalities. First is its common *faith*. The early church did not gather on the basis of ethnicity, education, interests, or anything else; instead, they brought all of their diverse lives under a shared faith in Jesus Christ as their Savior. Today, Communion remains an eloquent expression of this same unity; there is one loaf and one cup for us to partake from as one body. Jesus is the Bread of life, who sustains and unites us.

Second, we have a common *family*. When we believe in Jesus as our Savior, we are welcomed into His family with other believers, having the same heavenly Father. This familial bond transcends that of even earthly families, because the family of faith is eternal. As such, we should look after the interests of our spiritual brothers and sisters. For us as believers not to love one another would be not only sad but contradictory: "Whoever loves God must also love his brother" (1 John 4:21).

Third, by God's grace, the true church also experiences common *feeling*. We see a lesser version of this at sporting events: each individual fan is different, but together they share a common feeling, conviction, and goal. Sometimes they are lifted up together and sometimes they are deflated together. Similarly, as members of one family, we share in each other's joy, peace, pain, and sorrow. "If one member suffers, all suffer together; if one member is honored, all rejoice together" (1 Corinthians 12:26). Paul's metaphor in that chapter is of the church as a body: as believers we are different, and we have varying strengths and weaknesses, and so we make up a body that works better together than apart. My weaknesses are complemented by your strengths, and vice versa.

All families have their difficulties and struggles, and we are all sinners; so it is easy to forget the privilege of belonging to the people of God. When was the last time you thanked your Father for your church family? When was the last time you looked round on a Sunday at your brothers and sisters gathered together and allowed yourself to be buoyed by knowing that this is what you are, by grace, a part of?

Our world, just as in the days of the apostles, is full of division and loneliness. People are fragmented, fearful, and lost. But we, the united body of Christ, can offer to this world a deep fellowship and an eternal, hope-filled future. You have the opportunity to become the very hands and feet of your heavenly Father, reaching into people's lives as you invite them into His family. Will you seize it?

COLOSSIANS 3:5-17

JANUARY 11

PRAISE IN THE DARKNESS

"Then Job arose and tore his robe and shaved his head and fell on the ground and worshiped. And he said, 'Naked I came from my mother's womb, and naked shall I return. The LORD gave, and the LORD has taken away; blessed be the name of the LORD.' In all this Job did not sin or charge God with wrong."
JOB 1:20-22

Job is perhaps the greatest biblical example of endurance in hardship. Despite being a blameless and upright man, in just one day he experienced the death of his children and the loss of nearly all his possessions. Yet one of his first reactions was to acknowledge God's sovereignty both in plenty and in poverty, in bringing joyful circumstances and in bringing grievous ones. As chaos, disappointment, and pain descended upon him, he shaved his head, put on his torn robe, and fell to the ground, not only in anguish but also in worship.

Remarkably, in the darkness of this pain "Job did not sin or charge God with wrong." Instead, in his tears, he trusted in God's providence. In other words, he recognized that God knows what He is doing in every circumstance. God is worthy of our praise even in the hardest situations. Job knew that his times were in God's hands (Psalm 31:15).

Most of us have lived through cries of anguish and pools of tears. We know how hard it can be to acknowledge God's sovereignty and goodness in the middle of a storm. We wonder where He is. In our human response to pain, we're inclined to find statements about God's providence stale or clichéd—but they aren't. In fact, with the passing of time or the changing of circumstances, we can look over our shoulders and recognize that there is no tragic situation that God has not sovereignly permitted. He allows all things to pass through His hands, and they do not take Him by surprise.

We must not make light of each other's pain or offer easy answers. Instead, we are called to spur each other on to Christlikeness during times of hardship, reminding one another that God has granted us eternal life and steadfast love and that His care has preserved our spirits (Job 10:12). And, of course, we can look back in history and see that our God has entered the darkness of this world and plumbed the depths of suffering. He is a God who knows what it is like to be us. He is a God who has set before us a future where there is no pain or crying.

Even in the difficulties of life and the depths of pain, the fatherly providence of God permits all things for our good and His glory. He has proved that He knows what He is doing. For that, we can still praise Him in the darkness.

PSALM 22

JANUARY 12

POWER AND PURITY

"After six days Jesus took with him Peter and James, and John his brother, and led them up a high mountain by themselves. And he was transfigured before them, and his face shone like the sun, and his clothes became white as light."
MATTHEW 17:1-2

As John Lennon and Paul McCartney once suggested, there are places we'll remember all of our lives.[6] Surely Peter, James, and John would have regarded this mountainside, where they saw Christ's transfiguration, as one of those places. Certainly Peter never forgot it (2 Peter 1:17-18).

What was involved in the transfiguration? To begin with, it changed Jesus' appearance. His face "shone." Clearly this was not a matter of cleanliness but of supernatural transformation. There was a radiant glow to His face that Matthew could only describe as "like the sun." His clothes were dazzling white—whiter than you or I have ever seen—signifying the matchless purity of heaven.

One of the ways in which the Old Testament describes God is that He wraps Himself "with light as with a garment" (Psalm 104:2). And that is how Jesus looked at the top of His mountain. Who does such a thing? Only God! It was no coincidence, but a clue that the transfiguration was a revelation not only from God but of God Himself. In this scene, Christ revealed Himself as God in an unprecedented way. Scripture tells us that Jesus is "the radiance of the glory of God" (Hebrews 1:3). Yet when He entered our world, God's glory was veiled in Christ's humble humanity. The transfiguration was what John Calvin referred to as "a temporary exhibition of his glory."[7] It was a little pulling back of the curtain—a little flash up on the mountainside and into the minds of these three disciples. God was making it possible for Peter, James, and John to get a taste of what they could not yet fully comprehend but would one day enjoy eternally.

In Scripture, when there is a display of God's majesty people often react by falling on their faces. The disciples were no different, responding with terror. But Jesus graciously said to them, "Rise, and have no fear" (Matthew 17:7).

Do you and I approach Christ in similar awe of His perfect holiness and transcendence? Or is there a possibility that our view of God is at times too small? Come before Him in such a way that you find yourself on your face as you consider His power and His purity. Then hear Him, in His mercy, say, *Get up. You don't need to be afraid.* That is the way to live in awe and joy today and every day, until you gaze on our glorious Lord for yourself.

MATTHEW 17:1-9

6 John Lennon and Paul McCartney, "In My Life" (1965).

7 *Commentary on the Harmony of the Evangelists Matthew, Mark, and Luke,* trans. William Pringle (Calvin Translation Society, 1845), Vol. 2, p 347.

JANUARY 13

TRUE FRIENDSHIP

"A man of many companions may come to ruin, but there is a friend who sticks closer than a brother." PROVERBS 18:24

No one likes to feel alone and without a friend. We all recognize the priceless gift that a true friend can be. Deep friendship is the standard which the Bible holds up to us. Solomon says that a true friend is always loyal, regardless of circumstances: "A friend loves at all times" (Proverbs 17:17). We see our friends exactly as they are, and we still remain consistent in our loyalty to them. Further, sincere friends are prepared to wound in order that their friends might become all that God intends them to be: "Faithful are the wounds of a friend" (27:6). We may not particularly like it, but each of us is in need of friends who will hold us accountable when we err—and each of us is called to be that kind of friend, too. We must also consider our use of language: as Paul says, "Let no corrupting talk come out of your mouths, but only such as is good for building up ... that it may give grace" (Ephesians 4:29). You can break a heart with just a word, and it can take a lifetime to repair it.

People who take these principles seriously may find themselves asking, "Is there really any friend who embodies such characteristics—who is always constant, who rebukes me in love, who will show grace and sensitivity in all of their dealings with me?" And the answer to those questions is found, ultimately, in the person of Christ. The scope of the Lord Jesus' friendship is amazing! He befriended the strangest individuals—stopping under a tree to speak with a tax collector, asking for water from an immoral woman, reaching out to a leper. He was consistent in His love; He was prepared to speak words of truth, however challenging; He built others up. Supremely, He is the one who loved His friends enough to lay down His life for them (John 15:13). He is the friend of sinners:

What a friend we have in Jesus,
All our sins and griefs to bear!
What a privilege to carry
Everything to God in prayer![8]

Jesus' friendship is the golden standard for ours. We are called to love and befriend others as He did: "You are my friends if you do what I command" (John 15:14). Seize every opportunity to share this friendship with those who are friendless and forlorn.

We live in a world where acquaintances are often countless and "Facebook friends" are many. But that is not true friendship. Do you have friends who are constant, close, and Christlike? If you do, cherish them. If you do not, pray for some. And today, be that kind of friend to others. You may just be the answer to someone's loneliness or the protection from someone's ruin.

JAMES 5:13-20

8 Joseph Medlicott Scriven, "What a Friend We Have in Jesus" (1855).

JANUARY 14

FREEDOM FROM OURSELVES

"He asked them, 'What were you discussing on the way?' But they kept silent, for on the way they had argued with one another about who was the greatest. And he sat down and called the twelve. And he said to them, 'If anyone would be first, he must be last of all and servant of all.'" MARK 9:33-35

Rivalry is part and parcel of life. On a team, friendly rivalry can be a means of spurring each other on, helping the team members to become faster or stronger. But when rivalry becomes the occasion of selfishness and jealousy, it undermines unity.

On the way to Capernaum, Jesus had been teaching the disciples, saying, "The Son of Man is going to be delivered into the hands of men, and they will kill him. And when he is killed, after three days he will rise" (Mark 9:31). Perhaps as Jesus walked ahead of them, He heard snippets of conversation from the disciples jostling their way along behind Him. Their discussion was filled with jealous rivalry over their own greatness.

That's a bad topic of conversation on any occasion, but especially in this context. How incongruous that when Jesus was giving them instruction concerning His own suffering and death, they were preoccupied with their own status and greatness!

Jesus asked them about their conversation to use it as an opportunity for instruction. In the span of a sentence, He turned human ideas of greatness completely upside down. True greatness in His kingdom lies in putting yourself last and acting as servant to everyone else. This is, after all, how the King of that kingdom lived, and lives, for He "came not to be served but to serve, and to give his life as a ransom for many" (Mark 10:45).

If we're honest, when we consider this scene we see our faces in those of the disciples. We hear our voices echoing theirs. We find ourselves scrambling for position as they did. Selfish rivalry rises to the surface often and in the most unlikely places. Yet the antidote is always the same: humility. We all need the kind of humility, writes David Wells, that is a "freedom from our self which enables us to be in positions in which we have neither recognition nor importance, neither power nor visibility, and even experience deprivation, and yet have joy and delight … It is the freedom of knowing that we are not in the center of the universe, not even in the center of our own private universe."[9]

This is a difficult lesson to learn. Yet despite our rivalry, despite the absence of our humility, Jesus does not abandon us. To see our faces in this scene is to be reminded that we're constantly in need of God's grace as we walk along the pathway of discipleship. Only the grace of God can get your focus off of yourself and set you free from yourself. Only gazing at the one who left the glories of heaven to die for you on a cross can change your heart so that you seek to serve, not to be served, and care less about your prestige than you do about the good of others. Jesus is calling you today to serve, even as He serves you.

ROMANS 12:3-13

9 *Losing Our Virtue: Why the Church Must Recover Its Moral Vision* (Eerdmans, 1998), p 204.

JANUARY 15

THE TRIUMPHANT KING

"Grace to you and peace from him who is and who was and who is to come, and from the seven spirits who are before his throne, and from Jesus Christ the faithful witness, the firstborn of the dead, and the ruler of kings on earth."
REVELATION 1:4-5

What do you do when your Christian convictions and the circumstances of your life appear to declare two different truths?

This was the conundrum facing the first readers of the book of Revelation. The last book in our Scriptures was not written to confuse but to bless (Revelation 1:3). We ought not to regard it as if it were a collection of riddles or some theological Rubik's Cube. Rather, we must understand that John was writing to readers in a historical context—first-century believers who were being buffeted and persecuted by the authorities of their day—in order to offer hope and assurance.

The gospel was being preached, and the people of God were absolutely convinced that even as Jesus had gone, so He would return. They believed that, as the ascended Lord and King, Jesus was fully in control of all circumstances and His will was being established throughout the whole earth. That was their conviction. But when they looked at their circumstances, these did not seem to square with those convictions. None of the things that they affirmed to one another and shared with their friends and neighbors appeared to be happening. Mockers abounded. In fact, the apostle Peter had already warned the believers, "Scoffers will come in the last days," and they would ask, "Where is the promise of his coming? For ever since the fathers fell asleep, all things are continuing as they were from the beginning of creation" (2 Peter 3:3-4).

While the church was small and beleaguered, the empires of man were growing in strength and significance. Persecution was increasing in its intensity, and the Evil One doubtless came and insinuated to these suffering Christians that they had bought into a great delusion. They needed Jesus to come and give them His perspective so that their troubles would not discourage, perplex, or overwhelm them. They needed to understand simply this: that Jesus was still the triumphant Lord and King. His resurrection from the dead had declared His authority and His integrity. He could be trusted with His people's lives and futures.

In a world that continues to oppress God's people, the book of Revelation is exactly what the church today needs. While economic gloom, material deprivation, and issues of morality and personal identity threaten to unravel the minds of men and women, John's message reminds us that our Christian faith is sufficient for the challenges and questions that confront us. Do your circumstances suggest to you that perhaps your convictions about your faith might be mistaken? Rest in this assurance: Jesus rose, Jesus reigns, and ultimately, Jesus wins.

REVELATION 1:1-8

JANUARY 16

REFRESHMENT FOR HARDER DAYS

"'It is enough; now, O Lord, take away my life, for I am no better than my fathers.' And [Elijah] lay down and slept under a broom tree. And behold, an angel touched him and said to him, 'Arise and eat.'" 1 KINGS 19:4-5

All of us have surely found ourselves in a spiritual valley when we expected to be on a mountaintop. Perhaps when we least anticipated it, physical fatigue set in, or we received discouraging news, or a besetting sin returned to plague us. Troubling circumstances in our lives often converge, precipitating a change from faith to fear.

The prophet Elijah found himself hiding in the wilderness largely because his focus had changed: he had started to look at God through his circumstances rather than looking at his circumstances through God. He had magnified his life's difficulties, and it paralyzed him. As he began to walk by sight instead of faith, his peace was disrupted and his spiritual prosperity was eroded.

Elijah had fallen into the "self" trap. Focusing on the many failures of the Israelites towards God, he had fallen prey to the notion that he was the only one who was serving God (1 Kings 19:10). His faith and hope were replaced by discontent and a lack of peace. In self-pity, he ran away to the desert, lying down on the job under a broom tree, praying to die. Yet instead of judging him or chastising him, God came to Elijah and refreshed him with food and drink, preparing him for the journey ahead. With a gentle whisper, the Lord then revealed Himself afresh to His downcast servant and reinstated him, giving him a whole new list of duties to perform (v 4-16).

During trying times, we often allow self-pity to settle in. We begin to think we are the only one who is facing such trials. Some of us may relate to Elijah's experience; the Lord used us greatly, and we had influence for the gospel in the past, but, for whatever reason, we're now a long way from that mountaintop. God may let us get so low—but he never leaves us there. As the angel was with Elijah when he was in his valley, so God's Spirit is with us in ours.

If you find yourself in the desert, don't just find a broom tree to lie down under. Don't assume your best days lie behind you. God has a purpose for you and me. He completes what He begins (Philippians 1:6). Be refreshed by the reminder of God's presence and press on in the work He has called you to.

2 CORINTHIANS 4:7-18

JANUARY 17

THERE CAN BE HOPE IN GRIEF

"We do not want you to be uninformed, brothers, about those who are asleep, that you may not grieve as others do who have no hope. For since we believe that Jesus died and rose again, even so, through Jesus, God will bring with him those who have fallen asleep." 1 THESSALONIANS 4:13-14

Sooner or later, you will face grief as a loved one leaves this life. The question is not whether you will grieve; the question is *how*.

Some of the Thessalonians were confused about the return of Jesus Christ and the resurrection of the dead. Their lack of understanding was causing distress. How were they supposed to think about fellow Christians who had died before Jesus returned? Where were these Christians now, and what would become of them? In answering, Paul begins by reminding believers of the distinction between God's people and the rest of mankind, "who have no hope." We were once like everyone else; we should "remember that [we] were at that time separated from Christ … having no hope and without God in the world" (Ephesians 2:12). Now, though, we have been redeemed and transformed. We have been brought from hopelessness to hope. This change ought to be a great encouragement to us. It is this living personal faith that distinguishes us from the "others."

Additionally, in referring to "those who are asleep," Paul emphasizes the temporary nature of death for the believer; it is not a permanent condition. Yet while the metaphor of sleep helps us to grapple with what will happen to our bodies, it does not explain the totality of what happens to the soul. It is not intended to convey the idea that the soul is unconscious in the interim period between death and resurrection. Jesus plainly taught that after death there would be an instantaneous awareness of happiness or pain (see, for instance, Luke 16:22-24). It is clear in Scripture that death brings the believer immediately into a closer, richer, fuller experience of Jesus (23:42-43; Philippians 1:21-24).

This focus on death's temporary nature informs our understanding of Christian grief. For the grieving unbeliever, death brings only the dreary wail of despair and a deep emptiness that no amount of wishful thinking or resorting to cliché can fill. For the believer, there is genuine, tearful sorrow, but it should always be accompanied by an exalting psalm of hope, for when the Lord returns, He will "bring with him those who have fallen asleep." A Christian's funeral is not a time to say goodbye forever but to say, "See you again." The absence of your loved one is temporary; the reunion will be permanent.

When life's most puzzling questions tempt us to despair, we can find comfort in knowing that God's word is sufficient for all things, including our understanding of death. Take these verses to heart and imprint them on your memory, for the day will come when you need to cling to them. And make this your prayer: "Lord Jesus, help me to become a student of the Book, to no longer live with confusion or uneasiness but to be filled with Your knowledge as one who resides in Your company, that I might live and grieve with hope."

1 THESSALONIANS 4:13-18

◇ Bible Through The Year: Genesis 41–42; Romans 14

JANUARY 18

A COMMITMENT TO PRAYER

"[Daniel] got down on his knees three times a day and prayed and gave thanks before his God, as he had done previously." DANIEL 6:10

Short-term commitment is not too hard. It is disciplined consistency that comes harder to us—yet it is a key to spiritual growth.

The often sporadic nature of our commitment is seen in short-lived exercise programs, Bible memorization, reading plans, and New Year's resolutions. How many of us start something well, only to later abandon it! But equally, you have probably encountered people who are incredibly consistent and disciplined. They walk their dog at the exact same time every day or collect their mail with such precise timing that you could set your watch by it; and when they set themselves to undertake a task or learn a new skill, they do so with a diligence that leaves you in no doubt that they will complete it.

Daniel was a man who exhibited such disciplined consistency when it came to prayer. His life was not marked by bursts of enthusiasm followed by chronic inertia. He clearly prayed whether he felt like it or not. There were probably times when he got up from his knees feeling really blessed and other times when he left feeling really flat, but he kept on. He prayed and he prayed and he prayed, no matter the circumstances. That's discipline!

When a crisis hit, it didn't create Daniel's disciplined lifestyle; it revealed it. After King Darius issued an edict that made it illegal to pray to any god or man other than him for thirty days (Daniel 6:7), Daniel could have rationalized obedience to the king rather than to the Lord. He could have reasoned that because he'd stored up such phenomenal credit on the strength of all his years of prayer, he could be let off for a month. Apparently, though, such a thought never even crossed his mind. Instead, he continued in prayer just "as he had done previously."

Surely there was a link between Daniel's life of prayer and the bravery he showed in obeying the God of Israel rather than the most powerful king in the known world. Our Lord told us, too, that we "ought always to pray and not lose heart" (Luke 18:1). We are not to close prayer down for a while if we don't feel like it or have little spare time for a season. If we want to live for Jesus when we're under pressure, our prayer lives must be consistent. We must regard prayer as a fundamental element of our faith, not merely a nice supplement.

The door is wide open for you to demonstrate the same kind of consistent commitment to prayer as Daniel did. Through regular discipline, prayer can become your natural reaction to every situation in your life. Do you need to set aside a time each day when you will pray and give thanks to your God, come what may? Wherever God takes us, whatever we do, however His plan unfolds, may our prayers be unceasing.

EPHESIANS 3:14-21

JANUARY 19

NO OTHER NAME

"There is salvation in no one else, for there is no other name under heaven given among men by which we must be saved." ACTS 4:12

Near the campus of Northwestern University in suburban Chicago, there is a vast temple erected by the Bahá'í faith. It's a magnificent structure, with nine porticos—one for each of nine major world religions—all leading to one central auditorium. The architecture is meant to signify the many paths to "truth," which Bahá'ís believe cannot be found in any one dogma, person, or entity.

This mindset is not much different from the cultural environment in which the apostle Paul lived. The Roman Empire was very open, very willing to think expansively, and very prepared to absorb all kinds of religions. Indeed, Rome housed a vast collection of idols and gods in its pantheon, paying homage to its belief in multiple avenues to truth.

How, then, could such a pluralistic, open, polytheistic culture also feed Christians to lions in the Colosseum? Why did Emperor Nero target believers, even going so far as to use their bodies as human torches to light his parties?

The answer lies in a simple fact: Roman culture *could* not and *would* not tolerate Christianity because Christians were not prepared to simply add Christ to the imagined pantheon. Rather, they held fast to the truth that, as Peter and John courageously told the same Jewish court that had sentenced Jesus to death, there is salvation in no name other than that of Jesus. In first-century Roman culture, as soon as people professed this belief, they were scorned, and mocked, and sometimes even sentenced to death.

Pluralism cannot abide—indeed, it is often mercilessly intolerant towards—those who reject its view that all paths are equally valid. Some 2,000 years later, we must acknowledge that we are living in an environment not incomparable to the Roman Empire, albeit thankfully less brutal in its persecutions. Biblical Christianity, with a Christ who will come again in glory, an inerrant Bible, and a triune Godhead, is an offense to a pluralistic world.

Despite what the world around us may believe, though, Jesus does not belong on a pedestal next to other false gods or religious figures. He is far more than just another portico that leads to truth. As the Philistine god Dagon fell and was broken before the ark of the Lord (1 Samuel 5:1-4), so all others will be revealed to be nothing compared to Him. That message is not popular, but it is true—and it is wonderful, for if there were no crucified Savior, there would be no way at all to eternal life, for all other ways lead only to death. One day Buddha, Muhammad, and every other false prophet will bow at Jesus' feet and declare that He is Lord, to the glory of God the Father. Until that day, hold fast to the truth and seek to point people to the one who is *the* way, *the* truth, and *the* life that we all need (John 14:6). It was Christians following the example of John and Peter's refusal to give up or stay silent that changed the Roman Empire; by God's grace, we could likewise transform the world today as we follow in their footsteps.

ACTS 4:1-22

◇ Bible Through The Year: Genesis 46–48; Romans 15:14-33

JANUARY 20

NUMBERING OUR DAYS

"Teach us to number our days that we may get a heart of wisdom." PSALM 90:12

In his book *If Only It Were True*, Marc Levy encourages readers to imagine a bank crediting their account with $86,400 each morning. The account can't carry over any balance from day to day, and it deletes whatever remains. What would you do? Draw out every cent, of course!

He then points out that we *do* all have such a bank: it's called time. Every morning we are given 86,400 seconds, and every night we forfeit whatever time we failed to spend wisely. There is no balance or overdraft; we can live only on today's balance and hope to derive the utmost from it.[10]

Although Christians have the certain hope of eternal life, our time on this earth is still limited. That's why in Psalm 90 Moses reminds us, in light of the brevity of our human existence and the eternality of God, to number our days rightly so we may gain a heart of wisdom.

In our busy culture, we can become so preoccupied with living for the moment that we do not recognize the relationship between our mortality and sin. If we have no answer to death and do not want to live fearing it, the best we can do is to ignore it and live as though our days are not numbered.

But in the resurrection of Jesus Christ we do have an answer to death, and we need have no fear of it. Our lives can trust in and attest to God's providential care, which gives substance, foundation, and meaning to our existence. We need God to bring this truth home to our hearts and minds.

Numbering our days rightly is a result of both an inward transformation that God's Spirit effects over time and a conscious effort to use our time in light of eternity. And there's no better day than today to begin numbering our days rightly! We won't stay this age for another moment. When you meet elderly Christian men and women who exhibit deep wisdom and are content with how they spent their lives, it is because of commitments they made in the prime of life. Their examples should inspire us to follow the guidance of Ecclesiastes: "Remember … your Creator in the days of your youth, before the evil days come and the years draw near of which you will say, 'I have no pleasure in them'" (Ecclesiastes 12:1).

Be as determined to avoid wasting time in this life as you are to avoid squandering the money in your bank account. Cherish the mundane and seemingly insignificant moments and ask God to use them to make a difference in your soul and for those around you. Make every second count for Christ.

2 TIMOTHY 4:1-8

10 Marc Levy, *If Only It Were True* (Atria, 2000), p 208.

JANUARY 21

CITIZENS OF SOMEWHERE ELSE

"Many, of whom I have often told you and now tell you even with tears, walk as enemies of the cross of Christ. Their end is destruction, their god is their belly, and they glory in their shame, with minds set on earthly things. But our citizenship is in heaven, and from it we await a Savior, the Lord Jesus Christ, who will transform our lowly body to be like his glorious body." PHILIPPIANS 3:18-21

"We are not from round here." That is what the residents of the first-century Greek city of Philippi—even those who were born there—might have said, for they lived by Roman laws, wore Roman clothes, and wrote their documents in Latin. They were Roman citizens. The whole place looked like Rome—but it wasn't Rome. Citizens of Philippi were in Greece, but living as citizens of Rome.

Being a Christian, Paul told them, is similar: we're living the Christian life while absent from the Christian capital—which, you will be relieved to know, is not Washington, DC, or London! The true "Capitol steps" are far higher and far grander. Our citizenship is in heaven, and when we live as aliens here—as people who don't belong—we'll make a difference in the world around us.

As Christians, our great daily opportunity is to walk out into another day and be different—to be what we are: citizens of heaven, people who are not from round here. We should find people saying, "Hey, I can tell by the way you walk and talk that there is something different about you." This means that when you think about your life, you need to ask yourself some questions: What is the object of my devotion, the thing that makes me tick and drives my existence? Is it my appearance? Is it my portfolio? Is it passion and pleasure? What am I living for?

The Bible warns that if we live to "enjoy the fleeting pleasures of sin" (Hebrews 11:25), eventually they'll eat us up and squeeze the life out of us. Instead, we are to live in expectation of future glory. We are going to be transformed; we will have new bodies "like his glorious body." Our heavenly bodies won't be weakened by sin, by selfish desire, or by disintegration. We are going to be home one day, and it is going to be wonderful!

If people suspect from your life and discover from your speech that you have a citizenship in heaven, that you serve a living God, and that you are looking forward to going home, where your life will be utterly transformed, then sooner or later some of them will ask you to give them "a reason for the hope that is in you" (1 Peter 3:15).

So, remember where you are from. The impact of the gospel, under God, is directly related to your willingness to live like Christ. Allow the wonder of your heavenly citizenship to make you sensitive and compassionate as you move among those who are "enemies of the cross" (Philippians 3:18). Christ will return—and when He does, the day you get home will have arrived. If that proves not to be today, then today is a day of opportunity for you to be different. How will you take that opportunity?

1 PETER 2:9-17

◇ Bible Through The Year: Isaiah 1–2; Mark 1:1-22

JANUARY 22

WHEN STORMS COME

"A great windstorm arose, and the waves were breaking into the boat, so that the boat was already filling … And they woke him and said to him, 'Teacher, do you not care that we are perishing?' And he awoke and rebuked the wind and said to the sea, 'Peace! Be still!'" MARK 4:37-39

Anyone who has lived for much time at all knows that in life storms will surely come. Sometimes, seemingly out of nowhere, we are faced with an unexpected job loss, a grim diagnosis, the painful passing of a loved one, or the sorrow of goodbyes. Like the disciples caught in the storm on the Sea of Galilee, we can feel overwhelmed by these trials, as if our boat were sinking.

Following Jesus does not insulate us from life's storms, but we can take comfort from knowing that God promises to hold us fast through them. He can calm our hearts, and He may even quiet the very storms themselves.

When storms come, we are often tempted to doubt God. The disciples questioned Jesus even though they had seen His miracles firsthand. They looked Jesus in the eye, and they shared meals with Him every day—but when the storm arose, they took to panic stations of unbelief as if they'd forgotten who He was or what He was capable of doing. Don't we often find ourselves there too? As soon as the turbulence hits—as soon as life's winds and waves rise—our doubts and weaknesses burst forth, and we forget who it is who dwells within us and what He is capable of doing.

God does not prevent storms from coming. But He is a God who is both present through them and sovereign over them. Jesus not only stayed with the disciples during the storm, but He displayed His power by calming it. As God, He had created the very sea itself. Why would the sea ever be a problem for Him? For us, too, even circumstances that seem hopeless and insurmountable unfold exactly as He has planned. When difficulties, fear, and pain persist, we can trust Him to give us a peace that "surpasses all understanding" (Philippians 4:7) and bring us through to a place of calm, whether it arrives in this life or only beyond the final tempest of death.

The question, then, is not "Will storms come in my life?" They surely will. Rather, we must ask, "When the storms come, will I believe that Jesus Christ is able to deal with them—and will I let Him do that?" He can lift the clouds of doubt fogging our minds. He can mend broken hearts. He can soothe our longings for love. He can revive weary spirits. He can calm anxious souls.

When you see Jesus as the Creator of the universe, the one who calmed the sea, and the one in whom everything holds together, then you too can experience the calming of the storm.

MARK 4:35-41

JANUARY 23

THE LORD'S WORK

"And whatever you do, in word or deed, do everything in the name of the Lord Jesus, giving thanks to God the Father through him." COLOSSIANS 3:17

Today, you and I have work to do.

In his first letter to the Corinthians, when the apostle Paul instructed the church to welcome Timothy warmly into their community, it wasn't because Timothy was trying to make a name for himself, held some honorific or title, or was seeking to become noteworthy. No, it was simply because Timothy was "doing the work of the Lord" (1 Corinthians 16:10).

The Lord's work is anything on which we might lay our hands or focus our minds that is pleasing to God, as we work for him rather than in order to impress others (Colossians 3:23). This can be within the body of Christ or in service to the world around us.

Paul purposefully includes the phrase "whatever you do" in verse 17. The "whatever" of Christian service means that in all our endeavors, with the help of the Holy Spirit, we should seek to position ourselves to be effectively involved in gospel ministry. Whether we're helping a neighbor, greeting visitors who come through the doors of our church, or volunteering in the community, every type of service is an opportunity to point others to our Savior. What a privilege it is to know that we were placed here on earth to be involved in seeing unbelieving people become committed followers of Jesus Christ!

Within the body of Christ, we should recognize that our spiritual growth is a result of others' service to the Lord. Paul rightly viewed the Corinthians as the result of his labor in Christ's name, writing, "Are not you my workmanship in the Lord?" (1 Corinthians 9:1). The very existence of the church in Corinth was due to the fact that the apostle was doing the Lord's work. Paul was neither irrelevant nor pre-eminent; rather, he was purposefully appointed to a specific responsibility.

As Christians, we are called not simply to sit and learn but to grow and go, to fish and feed. God appoints every believer to particular responsibilities within Christian ministry and service, and those responsibilities include working for Him in whatever circumstances and opportunities come our way today; for they do not come by chance but by divine arrangement. Paul admirably modeled this to us through his obedience to God's call, recognizing that he was "a chosen instrument" who would carry God's name "before the Gentiles and kings and the children of Israel" (Acts 9:15).

The work of the Lord was something Paul took seriously. We should too. We are all called to honor God wherever we are. Consider what might change in how you think and what you do if in every moment you asked yourself, "Now, what would Jesus have me do here? How can I praise His name and bring Him pleasure in this moment?" Today, you have the privilege of having work to do for Him.

PSALM 127

◇ Bible Through The Year: Isaiah 5–6; Mark 2

JANUARY 24

GIVING BACK TO THE GIVER

"But who am I, and what is my people, that we should be able thus to offer willingly? For all things come from you, and of your own have we given you."
1 CHRONICLES 29:14

Some time ago, some of the staff at our church decided to put stickers on everything in the building, announcing that it was "Property of Parkside Church." Initially, I wondered if we really expected that someone wanting to steal a garbage can would turn it over, read the sticker, and suddenly decide to return it. It seemed like a fairly pointless exercise. I soon discovered, though, that I actually quite enjoyed turning things upside down and looking at these little stickers declaring, "This belongs to the church"!

Reminders of God's ownership and gracious provision echo throughout Scripture. When King David was involved in making plans for the temple, he pointed to God's providence with clarity and humility; he knew that as created beings in a created world, we can only give to our Creator what we have already been given by our Creator. In the New Testament, too, the apostle Paul writes, "What do you have that you did not receive? If then you received it, why do you boast as if you did not receive it?" (1 Corinthians 4:7).

David's words were not a new insight for God's people. Generations before, when the Israelites were preparing to build the tabernacle, Moses had instructed the Israelites, "Take from among you a contribution to the LORD" (Exodus 35:5). What did they have among them? Only what the Creator had provided. Only what the Redeemer had granted them in their exodus from Egypt (12:35-36). Only what the Sustainer of their lives had made possible for them to do (35:30-35).

As with the church property that has now been labeled, we might say that everything we have—indeed, everything in creation—is stamped with the seal of God's possession. Abraham Kuyper, an influential theologian who also served as prime minister of the Netherlands at the beginning of the 20th century, said, "There is not a square inch in the whole domain of our human existence over which Christ, who is Sovereign over *all*, does not cry: 'Mine!'"[11]

This viewpoint is vastly different from that of our contemporary culture, which tends toward two false notions: either that we are self-made people or that everything in the earth, including ourselves, is god. Not so, says the Bible: "The earth is the LORD's and the fullness thereof, the world and those who dwell therein" (Psalm 24:1).

God is calling us to walk in humility as we remember that all we have comes from Him. Our very lives should proclaim, "I belong to God!" There is nothing you can offer to God that isn't already in His possession. So give willingly and generously—money, time, talent—as God directs you, in response to His grace.

2 CORINTHIANS 8:1-15

11 Abraham Kuyper, "Sphere Sovereignty," in *Abraham Kuyper: A Centennial Reader,* ed. James D. Bratt (Eerdmans, 1998), p 488 (emphasis added).

JANUARY 25

CONTINUE IN GRACE

"Some of them ... spoke to the Hellenists also preaching the Lord Jesus ... A great number who believed turned to the Lord. The report of this came to the ears of the church in Jerusalem, and they sent Barnabas to Antioch. When he came and saw the grace of God, he was glad, and he exhorted them all to remain faithful to the Lord with steadfast purpose." ACTS 11:20-23

"God moves in a mysterious way, His wonders to perform."[12] In the life of the early church, it was the persecution of the congregations in Jerusalem—the only churches on earth at that point—that caused the gospel message to reach further and faster than would have happened without those first Christians being forced to flee their city. As the believers were scattered throughout the cities of Phoenicia, Cyprus, and Antioch, the gospel was spread to the "Hellenists"—the Greeks—in the region, and many came to believe.

However, when news of these Gentile conversions got back to the church in Jerusalem, it was not immediately welcome. Up until that point, the gospel's expansion had been almost entirely among the Jews. Now the word was coming back that Greeks were becoming Christians too. This confronted the church with a new development that they were not quite ready for. What was happening? Should they smile at it or frown over it? Who could they send to handle an encounter such as this?

It should not surprise us that they chose to send Barnabas. While not everybody in the church can cope with new and different opportunities, Barnabas was an encourager and a man who recognized God's redeeming work in others, even when it was surprising or strange (see Acts 9:26-28). Sure enough, Barnabas recognized that what had happened was the work of the Lord, and he was glad at the display of God's grace, encouraging the new believers with the exhortation we all need: to continue in grace and to remain true to God with all our hearts.

If we have lived our lives attempting to channel the Spirit of God into our own little concrete trenches, having determined that this way or that place is the only one in which God will work, we should reconsider. As God continues to expand His kingdom and pours His Spirit out upon the people we least expect to be included in it, we have the opportunity to respond with the kind of enthusiasm that Barnabas exemplified. While the gospel message is unchanging, our world and times are changing constantly. Yet God continues to call people to Himself "from every nation, from all tribes and peoples and languages" (Revelation 7:9). We should expect Him to surprise us—to work in ways we had not predicted and in a time-frame that is different from ours. And when He does, we need to be ready to be like Barnabas, "full of the Holy Spirit and of faith" (Acts 11:24), rejoicing in the new works of God, ready to be a part of them, and encouraging others to continue in His grace.

ACTS 10:1-48

12 William Cowper, "God Moves in a Mysterious Way" (1773).

JANUARY 26

WHEN THINGS DON'T GO YOUR WAY

"Let all bitterness and wrath and anger and clamor and slander be put away from you, along with all malice." EPHESIANS 4:31

Most if not all of us know what it is like to wake up with the thought that life isn't anywhere near what we would like it to be. Perhaps you felt like that when you woke up today. Physically, emotionally, relationally, financially, and even spiritually, we may be facing especially difficult days, and as a result, we're tempted to become disillusioned. What are we to do?

One helpful place to start is by asking God for His protection from three powerful sources of spiritual trouble: the "silent killers" of bitterness, resentment, and self-pity. These three will slowly strangle our faith and spill over into envy and malice toward those who have what we so want. So in the situations we face, perhaps known only to us and to God, we need His help in responding with soft hearts instead of harsh spirits.

In his letter to the believers in Ephesus, Paul encouraged—in fact commanded—them to put away all bitterness, wrath, and anger. While it's easier said than done, Paul's command itself is that straightforward. In fact, there's never a command in the word of God that we cannot obey, no matter how difficult it seems, for God always empowers what He commands. So if He says, *Get rid of something*, you and I can be certain that He can apply the power of the Spirit within our lives to enable us to do what He's commanded. When we live with bitterness, resentment, or self-pity filling our hearts, then we have only ourselves to blame. Much as I may want to, I can't put the responsibility on God.

One individual who could have argued that her circumstances legitimized these three poisonous feelings is Hannah, whose story we read of at the beginning of 1 Samuel. She must have battled each one as another month passed by without her falling pregnant, and as another day brought the taunts of her husband's other wife and the sight of the children God had given to that woman. But she took her frustrations and sadness and she did something good with them: she prayed. She poured her heart out to God. And, knowing she was heard, she walked away at peace. Although at that point her body remained infertile and her circumstances remained unchanged, her spirit had been freed by her heavenly Father.

God protected Hannah from the silent killers of bitterness, resentment, and self-pity—and He will protect us too. You don't need to stay awake at night, then, trying to ensure that your life works out how you want it to. And you don't need to be dominated by that sinking feeling upon awakening to another day of unwanted circumstances. Rather, you can use those moments to learn the value of leaving your heart's questions and the situations you don't understand in God's care—which, after all, is exactly where they belong.

1 SAMUEL 1

JANUARY 27

HE CAME FOR BRUISED REEDS

"A bruised reed he will not break, and a faintly burning wick he will not quench; he will faithfully bring forth justice." ISAIAH 42:3

The great political leaders of ancient times relied on might to rule. (Many today still do.) Cyrus the Great, king of Persia, was described as trampling people into oblivion and treading on them as a potter might tread on clay (see Isaiah 41:25). Yet at the same time Isaiah prophesied of the Servant to come—one who would be in direct contrast with the rulers of the day.

Jesus, the Servant, is gentle, tender, and kind. Those whom others are tempted to reject and discard He is willing and able to use. What an encouraging word!

In the picture of a bruised reed, we see the significance of Jesus' tenderness towards us. You can't lean on a bruised reed, and neither can you make music with it. Yet Jesus picks up those whom others have cast aside and makes a beautiful melody in and through their lives. Today, you may find yourself feeling horribly downtrodden, damaged by what others have done to you or injured by past mistakes. Perhaps you've been tempted to believe that you're broken and useless. But there is glorious news for you: the Servant picks up bruised reeds, and He does so with care.

Jesus also makes use of smoldering wicks. He doesn't snuff them out; rather, He takes the flickering stump and He makes it a shining light. Maybe you've been led to believe that your best days are behind you; you're a sputtering old candle, a faint and dying flame. If you haven't got it figured out by now, you tell yourself, there's probably no hope for you at all. But once again there is good news: smoldering wicks find hope in this Servant, who has come to rekindle us.

Jesus is phenomenally interested in the no-names—the bruised reeds, the smoldering wicks. He redeems and uses them to bring light to the world and praise to His name. In truth, one way or another we are all bruised reeds and faintly burning wicks. Are we willing to recognize our humble situation so that we can know the gentleness and kindness of the Servant? After all…

He'll never quench the smoking flax,
But raise it to a flame;
The bruisèd reed He never breaks,
Nor scorns the meanest name.[13]

LUKE 7:11-17

13 Isaac Watts, "With Joy We Meditate the Grace" (1709).

JANUARY 28

MORE THAN A NAME

"God said to Moses, 'I AM WHO I AM.' And he said, 'Say this to the people of Israel: "I AM has sent me to you."'" EXODUS 3:14

In some cultures, the meanings behind names don't matter much. We choose a name because we like the sound of it, or because it's precious to our particular family. In other cultures, though, a name itself may carry great significance. Its meaning can establish something about the person who bears it or the hopes of the people who bestowed it.

When Moses encountered God in the burning bush, he asked, "If I come to the people of Israel and say to them, 'The God of your fathers has sent me to you,' and they ask me, 'What is his name?' what shall I say to them?" (Exodus 3:13). The name God shares with Moses is "I AM WHO I AM," which is then abbreviated to "I AM"—YHWH. This word has four consonants with no vowels. Try to pronounce YHWH and you'll find that it's nearly impossible. It is, if you like, an unspeakable name.

What was God doing in answering like this? Moses was requesting a name of authority to give to the people of Israel and to Pharaoh, and God gave him this unpronounceable name. God seems to have been saying, *There is no name that can adequately encapsulate the totality of who I am. So, tell them that I AM WHO I AM has sent you. Tell Pharaoh to watch what I do on behalf of My people. Then he will know who I AM.*

The Bible is the story not only of God's work of salvation but also of the unfolding of God's character. Many of us have become adept at reading our Bibles and asking important questions of application: "How does this relate and apply? What does this mean for me?" These matters are not irrelevant or wrong, but they are not the primary questions to ask. God is the hero of the story and the theme of the book, and so the first question we ask of every passage ought to be this: "What does this tell me about God?" The Bible was written to establish God's dealings, character, and glory.

Many of us believe that what we need from church each Sunday are anecdotal bits and pieces or inspirational lists dealing with our finances, relationships, and any other issues we might be facing. There has never been a time in Christianity's history when more how-to books have been written for believers. Yet how are we really doing? We seemingly know how to do everything, but we don't know who God is!

In order for Moses to do what God had called him to do, he needed to understand who God was (and is). He, like us, needed to know that God is more than just a name.

Lives are transformed when we read the Bible and ask, "What can I discover about God?" It is as we see what God has done and better understand who He is that we grow in our awe and love of Him—and then we will be able to live as He desires, fulfilling His call in our lives. We will never plumb the depths of the glories of our unspeakably awesome God, but we *will* spend eternity seeing more and more of Him. And as we read His word, that can begin today.

EXODUS 3:1-22

JANUARY 29

JUSTICE IS SATISFIED

"If while we were enemies we were reconciled to God by the death of his Son, much more, now that we are reconciled, shall we be saved by his life." ROMANS 5:10

God is not a kindly grandfather or a cosmic Santa Claus who just gives out gifts and who is really not much concerned with anything else. No—He is holy, and He is righteous. So humans, because of our sin, are alienated from God. A hostility exists between humanity and our Creator. This is not a message that you hear very often, and it's certainly not very palatable. But God doesn't overlook that hostility. He never has, and He never will. Scripture is very clear on God's disposition towards sin. Indeed, Paul describes human beings as God's enemies, making clear that sin separates us from God. Paul's language also echoes the psalmist's words, which say of God, "You hate all evildoers" (Psalm 5:5)—a message that is neither pleasant to read nor easy to understand at first glance.

Where, then, is our hope? How can we ever be reconciled to God? How can God punish sin as it deserves yet still pardon sinners?

O loving wisdom of our God!
When all was sin and shame,
A second Adam to the fight
And to the rescue came.[14]

Jesus, by His death on the cross, satisfied God's justice. He took upon Himself both our obligation to perfectly obey God's law and our liability for failing to do so. He then satisfied our obligation through His sinless life and canceled our liability by His sacrificial death upon the cross. When our alienation from God resulted in God's hatred towards our sinful existence, He did not abandon us. Rather, God came and reconciled us through His Son. If this does not sound like the most incredible news of all, we have not properly understood the seriousness of our sin, or the reality of His judgment, or the magnitude of our salvation.

For those of us who have been Christians for a while, it is easy for familiarity to breed, if not contempt, then complacency. But Christ's death is not just the entry point of our faith; it is our faith. So today, pause to see the second Adam, the perfect human, succeeding where the first Adam failed and defeating the devil, reversing the effects of the fall. This is the gospel. Your sins have been pardoned. You have been rescued. You are now a friend, not an enemy. Christ is now your confidence, your peace, and your life.

The reality of being in Christ is not a trivial matter; it is an amazing guarantee. When we were powerless in the face of sin, Christ's power set us free. When we could not afford a debt so great, He bore it on the tree (1 Peter 2:24). You are now seated with Him in the heavens. Your greatest success today will not lift you higher than He has already lifted you; nor can your greatest struggle or failure pull you down from there.

COLOSSIANS 1:15-23

14 John H. Newman, "The Dream of Gerontius" (1865).

JANUARY 30

PROTECTED BY HIS PRESENCE

"The LORD was with Joseph, and he became a successful man." GENESIS 39:2

There's no better place to serve God than the place in which He sets you.

There is no flawless job, no faultless family, no set of circumstances free of troubles. Those of us who constantly search for the ideal life, forgetting that perfection is saved for heaven, set ourselves on a journey that will be marked by frequent disappointment.

It is an understatement to say that the conditions Joseph experienced were less than ideal. After beginning his life as the object of his father's special love, he found himself the object of slave traders' dealings. The security of his family home was replaced with the shackles of enslavement.

Like Joseph, we all see our circumstances change over time. We may move away from our longtime home, our loved ones may face turmoil, or financial hardship or health problems may strike unexpectedly. Few of us, though, will have experienced such a precipitous collapse as Joseph. (And if you have, how encouraging to know that Scripture includes the stories of God's intervention in the lives of people like you!) We might think that Joseph had every reason to run away, to hide, to give up, to become antagonistic—and yet God's presence brought him through each valley.

Joseph wasn't protected *from* his circumstances; he was protected *in* his circumstances. He was protected by the presence of God. There's a lesson in this for us. It's never the believer's resilience, knowledge, or wisdom that guards him or her. Rather, the servant of God is protected by God's very presence. It's natural for us to ask God to change our situations, to take away great difficulties, or to remove us from trials. We look at our surroundings and think, "I never bargained for this!" We start to believe the lie that everything will be ok if we can just get away or if our problems are just taken away. But the fact of the matter is that no matter where we go, problems will come and perfection will be elusive this side of heaven. Our only true refuge, as the psalmist says, is in the Lord (Psalm 11:1).

God could have arranged Joseph's life differently. Instead, He chose to allow events to unfold as they did. He purposed that it would be "through many dangers, toils and snares"[15] that He would bring His servant. The Lord was with Joseph, no less as he walked in the slave train and sat at the slave market than when he rose to respect and prominence in his master's household. And the Lord's presence is with us too. Indeed, He has promised us, "I am with you always, to the end of the age" (Matthew 28:20)—through the valleys as well as on the mountaintops. In what situation has God set you today? And how will knowing He is with you there, and has good work for you to do there, change your view of both the circumstances you would have chosen and those you certainly would not?

PHILIPPIANS 4:4-13

15 John Newton, "Amazing Grace" (1779).

JANUARY 31

DO NOT BE ASHAMED

"Do not be ashamed of the testimony about our Lord, nor of me his prisoner, but share in suffering for the gospel by the power of God, who saved us and called us to a holy calling." 2 TIMOTHY 1:8-9

It's far too easy to be ashamed—to be ashamed of the Master, of the Master's servants, and of the Master's message. Therefore, it is a great challenge to hear how Paul exhorts Timothy, and us, to "not be ashamed."

Vague talk about religion, God, and spirituality is largely tolerable in Western culture; we often hear or read all kinds of ambiguous statements that seem to be loosely aligned with the gospel. What is unacceptable by society's standard, though, is a clear declaration that there is salvation in no one other than Jesus Christ. If we are prepared to claim with Peter that there is "no other name under heaven given among men by which we must be saved" (Acts 4:12), then Paul's word to Timothy here will be a word for us: "Share in suffering for the gospel."

Paul's invitation to join in the privilege of suffering for the gospel is, in one sense, troubling to us. It stands in stark contrast to the Christian triumphalism of our day, which always seeks to present Christian living in glowing colors. So many want only to confirm and affirm God's power to heal, to accomplish miracles, and to lead His people to victory. The Bible and human experience, however, tell us that in the vast majority of cases—and leaving aside death as the ultimate healing—those for whom we have prayed will continue to suffer and live in the midst of difficult days. We must tell the truth: in the words of John Newton, the Christian must pass "through many dangers, toils and snares"[16]—and there are always more trials just over the horizon, especially if we are to remain faithful to the call to preach the gospel to the end of the earth (Acts 1:8).

How, then, are we to persevere in suffering for the gospel? It is the power of God, through the grace of God, that keeps us to the end. Newton's lyrics speak to this reality: "'Tis grace hath brought me safe thus far, and grace will lead me home." A wonderful truth!

God has saved you, and He can hold you fast in the midst of suffering. God has commissioned you, and He can give you courage when you are called to testify to the truth about Him. The truth of His sustaining power is able to stir your heart and transform your life. In the midst of difficult and doubt-filled days, you can cling to this reality as a bastion for your soul. And when you are tempted to shrink back from standing up for the Master, His servants, or His message, you can look to His power, offering up a silent prayer for your witness to be effective as you open your mouth to speak. "Do not be ashamed."

ROMANS 1:8-17

16 John Newton, "Amazing Grace" (1779).

FEBRUARY 1

JOYFUL WORSHIP

"Know that the LORD, he is God! It is he who made us, and we are his; we are his people, and the sheep of his pasture." PSALM 100:3

The book of Psalms has been described as a medicine chest for our souls. In it we can find laments for the downtrodden, cries to God in trying times, and offerings of praise and thanksgiving. Whatever ails you, you will find balm in the Psalter.

Woven throughout the psalms of praise in particular is this foundational truth: the Lord is God and we are His. Our very existence as God's people is an indication of who He is. Once we weren't a people, but now we are a people. Once we hadn't received mercy, but now we receive mercy daily (1 Peter 2:10).

The truth of the matter is that we are not our own. We never were. We are image-bearing creatures formed by a mighty Creator. He is the Potter who fashioned us, and "we are his." Further, we are redeemed sinners, "bought with a price" by a loving Savior (1 Corinthians 6:20). He is the Shepherd who gave His life for us and now tends to us (John 10:11-15), and "we are his." We are twice-bought: in creation and in redemption, we are His.

Therefore, what is now ours in the Lord Jesus Christ is not an occasion for pride but for praise. Knowing that the Lord is God and that we are His will prompt us to praise and thank Him (Psalm 100:3).

Praise is the spontaneous acknowledgment of what is valuable. People naturally praise what they treasure. God is our Maker and our Redeemer, and He is therefore entitled to and worthy of our praise. No one and nothing deserves your praise more than Him.

Even in less-than-ideal circumstances, we still have reason to praise God simply because of who He is. When we bid farewell to a loved one or we lose a job that provides our earthly comforts, we can still choose to praise Him. When our voices are choked with tears, when our hearts fail us, when our circumstances frustrate us, when life seems to let us down—we may still find in God's "steadfast love" that "endures forever" (Psalm 100:5) endless reason for joyful worship and thankful praise. He is never less than your mighty Creator and loving Savior.

A thankful heart is a distinctive mark of the Christian experience. Let it mark you today.

PSALM 148

FEBRUARY 2

THE PRIVILEGE OF PRAYER

"Now Jesus was praying in a certain place, and when he finished, one of his disciples said to him, 'Lord, teach us to pray, as John taught his disciples.'"
LUKE 11:1

Our fellowship with God through the Lord Jesus Christ is principally expressed through our prayers. They give evidence of our relationship with Him. He not only speaks with us through His word but has also entrusted us with the amazing privilege of communicating with Him in prayer.

Scripture provides us with multiple accounts of Jesus' own prayer life. The better acquainted we are with these records, the more we realize that Jesus treated prayer as a holy habit. He regularly prayed in the early-morning hours to lay the day's plans before His Father. Praying in a quiet and solitary place enabled Jesus to then follow His Father's voice over the noise of the crowds and even the requests of His disciples. Prayer formed the context or framework of all the decisions He made.

Jesus' prayer routine prompted His disciples to plead, "Lord, teach us to pray." They were apparently struck by His intensity and focus, which created a hunger in their hearts for similar intimacy with the Father.

In response to their request, Jesus instructed His disciples not to "heap up empty phrases" or to "think that they will be heard for their many words" (Matthew 6:7). In other words, in praying we are not to babble or drone on. Instead, in the example that Jesus then gave—namely, the Lord's Prayer—we discover that God's spiritual children are free to address God simply and directly as their heavenly Father.

And what are we to pray for? To begin with, we are to ask for God's name to be rightly honored, for Him to bring His kingdom in us and around us, and for Him to supply our daily needs. We are to admit our need for daily repentance, the necessity of extending forgiveness to others, and our dependence on God for dealing with temptation. In our prayers, Jesus explained, we are to seek and ask to see God's glory and grace in the midst of everyday life.

In our Christian pilgrimage, there is arguably nothing more important—or more difficult to maintain—than a meaningful prayer life. But here is help. If Jesus, the divine Son of God, needed to pray, then so do you and I. That humbling thought should drive us to our knees. And once there, we can freely employ the Lord's Prayer as an aid in our own prayer. God has given you the great privilege of approaching Him in prayer and addressing Him as Father. He stands ready to listen and to help. Be sure to treat prayer as a holy habit and never as an optional extra.

LUKE 11:1-13

FEBRUARY 3

WE CALL HIM FATHER

"When you pray, say: 'Father, hallowed be your name.'" LUKE 11:2

The moment a child is adopted, her whole life changes; she gets a new name, a new family, and often an entirely new way of life. Yet that legal reality can exist without her feeling an accompanying true sense of belonging to the family. It's one thing for a child to come and live in a home; it's another, deeper reality to fully experience and express the knitting together of a family—to call one's new parents "Mommy" and "Daddy."

The same is true of our spiritual adoption when we profess faith in Jesus Christ. Our adoption changes our status utterly, eternally, and incontrovertibly. But God isn't satisfied with a simple name change, as it were. He wants us to know what it means to be His sons and daughters. He longs for us to have the experiential wonder of thinking of Him as our heavenly Father. To do this, He gives us His Spirit to mold our character and help us see our relationship with Him as that of child and Father. "Because you are sons," Paul told the Galatian church, "God has sent the Spirit of his Son into our hearts, crying, 'Abba! Father!'" (Galatians 4:6).

The Christian experience shouldn't simply be like a legal transaction. It's so much more than dogma or doctrine. Salvation is not just the forgiveness of sins; it is also the welcoming of Spirit-empowered transformation. Christianity is not mechanical but relational. What Jesus accomplished objectively and legally on the cross, the Spirit continues subjectively and experientially in our hearts. We have been rescued, accepted, and loved. With this change, we can anticipate devotion, passion, tears, enlightenment, involvement, and, ultimately, praise.

When we are tempted to forget our new status as God's children, the Spirit stands waiting to testify, *No, you truly are His! You've been bought at the greatest price. You are loved and cherished.* When we haven't done as God would have us do and when we're feeling bruised, broken, and discouraged, the Spirit helps us cry, "O Father, Father, could You please help me?" Such pleas should serve as reminders of the wonder of Jesus' finished work—His redeeming sacrifice and sending of the Spirit to live within our hearts. Without those, there would be no relationship with God other than as our Creator and Judge, and therefore no opportunity for our hearts to cry, "Abba! Father!"

God seals our adoption as sons and daughters not by some peculiar sign or gift but by the persuasive witness of His Spirit. As we talk to Him in prayer, hear from Him through His word, and walk with Him, we grow in awareness of His power and His work within us. Because we have been freed from sin's curse and have been given the blessing of adoption, we can cry out to God as our Father, adoring Him and worshiping Him in spirit and in truth. So Christian, today, whatever else is true of you, here is the greatest reality: you are an adopted child of God. Nothing and no one can change that. So today, whatever else you are feeling, let this truth be what most comforts, grounds, reassures, and motivates you: you are a child of God.

ROMANS 8:12-25

FEBRUARY 4

YOUR KINGDOM COME

"Your kingdom come." LUKE 11:2

The kingdom of God is vastly different from any earthly kingdom that has existed or will exist. Earthly kingdoms are under the sway of sovereigns whose power is limited and will inevitably decline. But God's kingdom is far more than a geopolitical entity or piece of history. It is everlasting, universal, and personal, and His dominion over it will endure throughout all generations (Psalm 145:13).

We must keep these truths in mind when we pray "Your kingdom come." When we follow Jesus' example and pray like this, one of the things we are asking is that God's sovereign rule might increasingly be established in our hearts and lives. We are praying that those who know Christ might live in increasing, joyful submission to His rule.

This is a vastly different worldview from any we're confronted with on a daily basis. Mostly, today's Western culture praises personal achievement and self-sufficiency. We're encouraged to believe that we are in control. But when God's kingdom comes into our lives—when we pray for Jesus to take His rightful place upon the throne of our heart—a revolution takes place. We are no longer slaves to sin. The King of creation resides in our lives and begins conforming us to the image of His Son (Romans 8:29). When we pray in this way, the Holy Spirit ministers to us by establishing God's kingly rule over every dimension of our lives.

And that's not all. When we pray "Your kingdom come," we are also acknowledging that God is King of the nations—that He reigns over all the affairs of time. Isaiah describes God as whistling for the nations to come "from the ends of the earth; and behold, quickly, speedily they come!" (Isaiah 5:26). The King summons the nations as we might call a family dog to come inside. When He whistles, they run to do His bidding.

We need not be panic-stricken or tyrannized, then, by any shift in earthly powers. Instead, we can rejoice in the Lord our King, who is sovereign over all these things.

His kingdom cannot fail,
He rules o'er earth and heav'n;
The keys of death and hell
Are to our Jesus giv'n:
Lift up your heart,
Lift up your voice!
Rejoice, again I say, rejoice![17]

PSALM 2

17 Charles Wesley, "Rejoice, the Lord Is King!" (1744).

FEBRUARY 5

ENOUGH FOR TODAY

"Give us each day our daily bread." LUKE 11:3

If bread has represented anything throughout history, it's daily sustenance. Other foods are certainly pleasant additions to our existence, but when we think of bread, most of us think of one of life's most basic needs being fulfilled.

This kind of thinking is consistent with God's unique provision for His people. In the Old Testament, the Israelites' experience of wandering in the wilderness required their total dependence on God to meet their daily needs. One of the most tangible ways they learned this lesson was through God's provision of manna from heaven.

God made it clear to His people that, each day, He would supply enough manna for one day and one day only. They were not to leave any of it over until the morning (Exodus 16:19). His purpose in supplying one day's worth of bread at a time was to teach His people to trust His provision. Sadly, some Israelites doubted that He would do what He had promised and disobeyed Him, keeping some manna for the next day (for doubting God's promises always leads to disobeying God's commands). They awoke in the morning to be confronted by a stinking, worm-infested mass of leftover manna (v 20). God was teaching them to rely on Him to provide for them. It was a lesson that they would take a long time to learn.

When we take this Old Testament example and consider the words "Give us each day our daily bread," we realize that, in this line of the Lord's Prayer, Jesus is underscoring a timeless reality: in every age, God teaches His people to trust not in the provision itself, which leaves us longing for more, but in the *Provider*, who satisfies our every need.

God desires for us to wake up and discover afresh His daily provision. This is why He instructed the Israelites to keep a small measure of manna for posterity, saying, "Let an omer of it be kept throughout your generations, so that they may see the bread with which I fed you in the wilderness" (Exodus 16:32). In following this instruction, one generation could speak to the next concerning the reality and wonder of His ongoing, daily provision.

The Father, whom we come to know through Jesus, cares about our personal, practical, and material needs. Perhaps you awoke this morning beleaguered by and feeling anxious about ongoing problems or upcoming events in your life. Remember this: you are God's personal concern, and you may approach Him in confidence, asking Him to give you all that is necessary for today. And then you can trust Him to give you exactly what you need today, and then tomorrow, and ever onwards. You can throw the whole weight of your anxieties upon Him, because He cares for you and provides for you (1 Peter 5:7).

EXODUS 16

FEBRUARY 6

A FORGIVING SPIRIT

"Forgive us our sins, for we ourselves forgive everyone who is indebted to us."
LUKE 11:4

At a quick glance, this request may sound like a quid pro quo—that our forgiveness of others somehow earns us the right to be forgiven. If we allow the Scriptures to speak for themselves, however, we will recognize that the opposite is true. God forgives only the penitent—those who feel godly sorrow and repent of their sins. And what is one of the chief evidences of being penitent? A forgiving spirit! In other words, when we forgive one another, we don't earn forgiveness; we show that we have already been transformed by God's forgiving grace.

Jesus taught that it is inconceivable that we who have been forgiven so much should refuse to forgive the debts of others against us (Matthew 18:21-35). Yet we're still tempted to hold grudges, stay angry, to "forgive but not to forget." D.L. Moody is said to have compared that idea to somebody who buries the hatchet but leaves the handle sticking out.

An unforgiving spirit is perhaps the greatest killer of genuine spiritual life. We shouldn't claim to be seeking God if we actively harbor enmity in our hearts against our brothers and sisters. It will extinguish the flame of Christian joy and make it nearly impossible to benefit from the Bible's teaching. It is no surprise, then, that Jesus essentially says, *What I'm saying about a forgiving spirit is a fundamental element of believing prayer. Check your life for it.*

Are you bearing a grudge or replaying someone's wronging of you in your mind? Is there someone you have failed to forgive? Reflect on the forgiveness you have received, and ask God to enable you to forgive—for in your forgiveness of the sins of others against you, you reveal that you understand His grace and have been truly forgiven by Him.

How can Your pardon reach and bless
The unforgiving heart
That broods on wrongs and will not let
Old bitterness depart?
In blazing light Your cross reveals
The truth we dimly knew,
How small the debts men owe to us,
How great our debt to You.
Lord, cleanse the depths within our souls,
And bid resentment cease;
Then, reconciled to God and man,
Our lives will spread Your peace.[18]

MATTHEW 18:21-35

18 Rosamond Herklots, "Forgive Our Sins as We Forgive" (1969).

FEBRUARY 7

VICTORY OVER TEMPTATION

"Lead us not into temptation." LUKE 11:4

The Bible clearly teaches that God is not the author of sin and temptation: He does not tempt anyone (James 1:13). That being the case, why would we pray and ask God not to lead us into temptation? What exactly are we asking God to do, or not to do?

We find our answer in the subtle distinction between testing and tempting. When we pray "Lord, lead us not into temptation," what we're really saying is "God, help us so that we do not let the testing which comes from you become a temptation from Satan to do evil." We are likewise asking Him not to lead us into trials without His presence and power, which are what will keep us walking through them in faith and joy instead of sinking in despair or faithlessness.

This phrase from the Lord's Prayer is therefore important because it reminds us, and necessarily so, of temptation's reality and proximity. In Genesis 4 God warns Cain, "Sin is crouching at your door; it desires to have you, but"—and here comes the exhortation—"you must rule over it" (Genesis 4:7, NIV). Sadly, Cain did not respond by asking God to give him all he needed to rule over it instead of letting it rule, and ruin, him. In the Lord's Prayer, Jesus teaches us not to make the same mistake.

Given sin's propensity to consume us, we cannot simply ask God not to lead us into temptation and then believe the issue is handled. No, our actions must correspond with our prayers. If we are genuinely asking the Lord for help not to violate His holy commands, then we must not put ourselves heedlessly, needlessly, or willfully within sin's reach.

God is both willing and perfectly able to help us battle temptation. He is fully committed in His covenant of love to ensuring that none of His children will fall into sin's grip. There will never be an occasion in our lives when the temptation to sin is so strong that God's grace and power cannot enable us to bear it; as Scripture reminds us, "God is faithful, and he will not let you be tempted beyond your ability, but with the temptation he will also provide the way of escape" (1 Corinthians 10:13). Nor will there ever be a failure to resist temptation that cannot be covered over by the blood of Christ. Therefore, in every situation and in the face of every temptation, remember this: in Christ we're "on the victory side."[19] You can resist, for you have the Spirit to guide and guard you. What regular temptations to disobedience are you facing at the moment? At what places or in what moments do your trials turn to temptations? Ask God for His help right now—for you need it, and He stands ready to supply it.

LUKE 4:1-13

19 Fanny Crosby, "On the Victory Side" (1894).

FEBRUARY 8

OUR HEAVENLY FRIEND

"Which of you who has a friend will go to him at midnight and say to him, 'Friend, lend me three loaves, for a friend of mine has arrived on a journey, and I have nothing to set before him' ... I tell you, though he will not get up and give him anything because he is his friend, yet because of his impudence he will rise and give him whatever he needs. And I tell you, ask, and it will be given to you." LUKE 11:5-9

It's tempting to think that talking about God is the principal expression of our relationship with Him. It's possible, though, for us to talk about God without any intimate knowledge of who He truly is. Evidence of our personal relationship with God is often found not in our public words but in our private prayers—not in what we say *about* Him but in what we say *to* Him. Indeed, as Robert Murray M'Cheyne was said to have observed, "What a man is on his knees before God, that he is—and nothing more."

Therein lies a challenge! Because if we're honest, many of our prayers reflect a static or distant relationship, not the dynamism that should mark a warm friendship. But if this is true of us, then we can be assured that we are not alone. Jesus' disciples also desired to grow in intimacy with their heavenly Father but knew they needed the Lord to teach them how to do so (Luke 11:1)—and by way of answer, Jesus, having outlined what came to be called the "Lord's Prayer," told them a parable about a friend's bold request.

Jesus begins His illustration by establishing the relationship of the two men within His story: they are friends. He then continues to explain how the one man, wishing to show hospitality to a traveling guest, goes to the other's home at midnight to borrow bread. He even risks waking his friend's entire family just to make his request. Because of his bold persistence, Jesus says, the second man rises and gives the first what he needs.

What we need to grasp from Jesus' story is this: if a sincere human friendship produces such a generous response, we can rest assured that God will never refuse us anything we truly need when we come to Him in prayer. The man's request is a bold one, but as demanding as it may seem, it is heard by a friend and answered because of his persistence. How much more, then, can we be absolutely confident that our heavenly Father is prepared to respond when we approach Him with a sincere, humble heart.

Assurance before God is not necessarily presumptuous. Rather, we can have confidence before His throne because of the friendship He has established with us through Jesus. Because of Him, we can speak to our Creator with the "impudence" of a close friend. What a thought! There is no midnight with God, nor will there ever be a moment when He is inconvenienced by our coming to Him as our Friend. All we must do is knock.

EPHESIANS 1:15-23

FEBRUARY 9

PRAYING WITH CONFIDENCE

"Everyone who asks receives, and the one who seeks finds, and to the one who knocks it will be opened ... If you then, who are evil, know how to give good gifts to your children, how much more will the heavenly Father give the Holy Spirit to those who ask him!" LUKE 11:10, 13

When a teenager who has just gotten her driver's license asks her mom or dad for the car keys, it's not typically a vague, half-hearted request. Instead, her mind is engaged and her will is focused: "Please can I have the car keys? I want the car. I'd like to use the car. I'm asking you for it now."

Similarly, the verbs that Jesus uses to teach His disciples how to make requests to God in prayer—ask, seek, knock—convey urgency, consistency, and clarity. It's as if He's saying, *I want you to pray in a way that involves humble, persistent determination. I want you to seek and to go on seeking, and I want you to knock with an urgent sincerity.*

He is inviting you and me to come before our heavenly Father and simply to ask.

We must be careful about *what* we ask for, though. When we present our petitions before the Lord, they need to be tempered by the Spirit through what John Calvin calls the "bridle of the word of God."[20] In other words, the Bible teaches that we can ask in total confidence *for the things that God says are good and right*—things like His help so that we can present our bodies as living sacrifices, grow as witnesses to the gospel, or increase our desire to worship. But we must not think that we can manipulate God, demanding that He gives us whatever will make our life easier or wealthier. It is possible to "ask and ... not receive, because you ask wrongly, to spend it on your passions" (James 4:3).

So we are to ask boldly, but we are also to ask humbly. We are to ask God to do great things, and then we are to accept His answer. There are good reasons why God will not always give us what we ask, even when what we ask is in itself good and godly. Our prayers are not always in accordance with His good and sovereign will. We cannot always determine what's good for us—but God always knows what's best for His children. Therefore, when we bring our requests before God, we must look to His word as our roadmap and remember that He is working to bring about His purposes for our lives and to conform us to the image of His Son.

So come before God and just ask. Your requests can be specific, and bold, and shaped by God's word—and then you can expect, and indeed desire, God to answer them exactly as He sees fit.

COLOSSIANS 1:9-12

20 *Commentary on a Harmony of the Evangelists Matthew, Mark, and Luke,* trans. William Pringle (Calvin Translation Society, 1846), Vol. 3, p 19.

FEBRUARY 10

GOD RESTED

"So God blessed the seventh day and made it holy, because on it God rested from all his work that he had done in creation." GENESIS 2:3

Humanity is the pinnacle of creation. We are not just advanced apes; we alone of all God's creation are made in His image (Genesis 1:27). We are creatures because we were made by a Creator—but we are also unique among all creatures because we were made like God. Mankind possesses inalienable dignity, and God desires that we would respect our Creator and live in relationship with Him.

If man is creation's pinnacle, then rest is creation's end goal. When God completed His creative work, He rested. That doesn't mean that He ceased to be either present or active in His world but that He rested from creating. There was no need for further improvements or additions. Nothing needed unpicking and reworking. And God's grand design—His desire for human beings—is that we too might live with Him in the wonderful, ongoing day of rest.

The creation account in Genesis 1 repeats the phrase "there was evening and there was morning" for each of the first six days. But when it gets to the seventh day, the pattern is broken. The seventh day is, if you like, an ongoing day in which God is pursuing a people for Himself. He is bringing mankind into a relationship with Himself, providing for them, protecting them, giving them fellowship with one another, and allowing them authority over His creation.

Part of the purpose of the Sabbath, as instructed in the Ten Commandments, was to give the Israelites an understanding of this, God's ultimate design for life (Exodus 20:8-11). By rest and reflection, they would ponder all that it might mean to live as God's people under God's rule and blessing.

When Jesus calls people to Himself, He says, "Come to me, all you who labor and are heavy laden, and I will give you rest ... You will find rest for your souls" (Matthew 11:28-29). The writer to the Hebrews takes that idea and declares, "There remains a Sabbath rest for the people of God" (Hebrews 4:9). What was designed in the beauty of Eden and destroyed in the fall will one day be restored when we enter into God's presence. We experience now the rest of bringing our sin to Jesus to be dealt with and our cares to Jesus to find help for. We will experience one day the perfect rest of resurrection life in a restored world filled with the holiness of our perfect God. That is a prospect to fill our gaze and reorient our hearts on our best and our worst days in this world. We truly will one day rest in peace.

As we walk toward this future, the pattern of God should be the pattern we imitate. As God commanded, we are to honor the Lord's Day—and take time to consider all that He desires for us, to enjoy a life of communion with Him, and to join Him as He actively pursues a people to call His own.

PSALM 8

FEBRUARY 11

INHERITING THE KINGDOM

"Do you not know that the unrighteous will not inherit the kingdom of God?"
1 CORINTHIANS 6:9

Nothing defines believers more than our membership in the kingdom of Jesus Christ. That's part of what makes Christians unique. We are now members of a whole new kingdom. We may be black or white, rich or poor, male or female, but what unites us is our allegiance to one King—namely, Jesus. We march to His instructions, we rejoice among His troops, and we are glad to do His bidding.

God's kingdom is a righteous kingdom. His character is perfection, His standards are excellent, and He cannot look on sin. Therefore, those who deny His character and reject His standards, Paul warns, "will not inherit the kingdom of God." A lifestyle marked by wickedness, rebellion, and self-sufficiency is incompatible with Christ's rule—and therefore a decision to spend life in that way is a decision to live outside of the borders of His kingdom.

We must take note that Paul is not referring to isolated acts of unrighteousness. No member of Christ's kingdom lives a sinless life this side of eternal glory. Rather, Paul is referring to someone who persistently pursues or tolerates sin. He has in mind the kind of life that declares, "I don't want God to interfere in my choices, but I do want to live with the notion that I actually belong in His kingdom, and I do want all the benefits of that."

God sets the kingdom borders. It is simply not the case that everybody is in, no matter who they are, what they believe, or what they want! That notion may sound very palatable, but it is simply not what God's word teaches—God, and no one else, decides who is in His kingdom.

God says there will be a day of judgment. Indeed, Jesus will return in His glory, and "before him will be gathered all the nations, and he will separate people one from another" to receive either the kingdom of God or eternal destruction (Matthew 25:32). This kingdom is not an idea that Jesus introduced somewhere along the line to correct a flaw in the system. This was planned from all eternity.

The coming judgment should create a sense of urgency in evangelism, and it should create honesty about and ruthlessness with our sin. We must present to the world—and preach to ourselves—a living Savior in the person of Jesus, who will do exactly what He said He will do. It is only in recognizing our sin and our need for a Savior that we will inherit this everlasting kingdom of God.

LUKE 13:22-30

FEBRUARY 12

THE KEY TO UNITY

"In him you also are being built together into a dwelling place for God by the Spirit." EPHESIANS 2:22

When someone comes to Christ by faith, the transformation of their identity is comprehensive. In the language Paul employs in Ephesians 2, the dead sinner is now alive in Christ; the child of wrath becomes a child of God. But the new identity is not merely individual. We are not each of us alone in Christ; we are in Him *with all of God's people.* This is why Paul, in Ephesians 2, moves from our individual experience of grace to the corporate work that God's grace accomplishes. Paul tells us, "You are no longer strangers and aliens, but you are fellow citizens with the saints and members of the household of God" (v 19). The "one new man" (v 15) that Christ is making is gloriously crowded with fellow heirs of grace. This is not to say that our individual human identity becomes irrelevant. Our background and our makeup—our sex, ethnicity, and personal history—are not obliterated in Christ. We are who we are, made in God's image, fashioned according to His purposes. But what unifies us *in* Christ—our union *with* Christ—transcends everything else.

We must beware the temptation to forget the reason for our unity. No one is immune from turning elements of their identity into barriers—barriers of status, of color, of class, of personality type, or personal preferences. As Christians, we must be prepared to acknowledge how easy it is to get this wrong. We must be prepared, if we find ourselves guilty of such wrong, to repent from and grieve over that which displeases God.

The key to Christian unity is the gospel. Paul recognized that only God can soften hard hearts, only God can open blind eyes, and only God can bring disparate people together and form something truly, gloriously united. God is making "one new man," and He is making that new man in His church. In Christ, God is building a "holy temple" (Ephesians 2:21) that is "being built together into a dwelling place for God by the Spirit." Partiality based on race, class, or status has no place in the place where God dwells by His Spirit. One day you will experience the fullness of your union with Christ and His people for eternity; but that can, and should, begin now. You have the privilege of fostering that unity today in the way you use your time and in the way you think of, pray for, and speak to your brothers and sisters in your church.

We are building day by day,
As the moments glide away,
Our temple, which the world may not see;
Every victory won by grace
Will be sure to find its place
In our building for eternity.[21]

1 CORINTHIANS 13

21 Fanny J. Crosby, "We Are Building" (1891).

FEBRUARY 13

THE ULTIMATE REALITY

"Thus says God, the Lord, who created the heavens and stretched them out, who spread out the earth and what comes from it, who gives breath to the people on it and spirit to those who walk in it: 'I am the Lord. I have called you in righteousness; I will take you by the hand and keep you.'" ISAIAH 42:5-6

In 1932, Albert Einstein observed, "Our situation on this earth seems strange. Every one of us appears here involuntarily and uninvited for a short stay, without knowing the whys and the wherefore."[22] Indeed, you won't have to listen too long before you hear people say that we live in a world of chance, where history merely repeats itself and there is no overarching purpose in the universe. If this is true, it is hard to find significance in life. There is nothing to do but live, and then die.

God speaks into the absence of purpose resulting from this view of reality. He proclaims the ultimate reality that changes everything: Himself. God introduces Himself, revealing His identity: "I am the Lord." God's name (here, "the Lord") is not simply what we call Him; it expresses His being. God's many names in the Bible give significant information about who He is: eternal, self-sustaining, sovereign… and much more!

As God speaks, He also reveals His power. The heavens are His design, and He is the one who spread out the earth and gives form and life to all that comes from it. Creation's stability and productivity are grounded in the Creator. We are not the product of some self-existing evolutionary surge but of the direct act of a Designer. We cannot make sense of our existence apart from God. We were never meant to.

And what is God's purpose now for everything that He has made? To bring about righteousness on the earth through salvation. "I am the Lord; I have called you in righteousness; I will take you by the hand and keep you; I will give you as a covenant for the people, a light for the nations." He is speaking here not to us but to His Son, the Servant whom Isaiah introduces. When we are in need of counsel, in need of friendship, in need of forgiveness, in need of salvation, God has said, "Here is my servant, whom I uphold" (Isaiah 42:1, NIV).

We will never be as satisfied in life as when we discover our ultimate reality in Christ. Flowing from that reality we find our purpose: "to glorify God, and to enjoy him forever."[23] If you wish to know purpose and fulfillment in life, you have only to embrace and rejoice in the Lord's Servant, glorifying God just as Simeon did: "My eyes have seen your salvation that you have prepared in the presence of all peoples, a light for revelation to the Gentiles, and for glory to your people Israel" (Luke 2:30-32).

ISAIAH 42:1-13

22 "My Credo," quoted in Michael White and John Gribbin, *Einstein: A Life in Science* (Free Press, 2005), p 262.

23 Westminster Shorter Catechism, Q.1.

FEBRUARY 14

A DISCIPLE OF CHRIST

"There was a disciple at Damascus named Ananias. The Lord said to him in a vision, 'Ananias.' And he said, 'Here I am, Lord.'" ACTS 9:10

Every day, you are shaping your reputation. And as a Christian, every day you are shaping Christ's reputation too. What do our lives say about Christ as we walk around as His disciples?

Ananias may be a lesser-known Bible character, but he had a profound influence on Paul's life and therefore on all of church history. This resulted from his daily devoted faithfulness as a disciple of Christ. Three traits of his discipleship can help to shape our own character and commitment to Christ as we seek to be used in God's kingdom.

First, Ananias was, as the KJV puts it, "a *certain* disciple" (emphasis added): one who was specifically chosen. Even before bringing Paul (then known as Saul) to Damascus or calling upon Ananias, God sovereignly orchestrated the spread of the church after the day of Pentecost in Jerusalem to reach at least 200 miles north to Damascus, where a group of believers, including Ananias, were then established. Then, out of this group, God specifically chose Ananias to reach out to Paul after his conversion. This profound display of God's sovereignty should inspire and encourage us to trust that God may be working in ways yet unseen to prepare and use us to accomplish His will.

Next, Ananias was a *bold* disciple. He identified himself as a follower of the Lord—part of the very group in Damascus that Paul was on his way to persecute before his conversion (Acts 9:1). Ananias's loyalty wasn't simply to a local church, a denomination, or a theological view but to the Lord Jesus Christ Himself. Similarly, if Jesus has taken hold of our lives and changed us then we cannot keep this life-altering fact to ourselves either. Just as we say no to sin when we receive Christ's salvation, we must also say no to secrecy about our faith. Either our discipleship will destroy our secrecy, or our secrecy will destroy our discipleship.

Finally, Ananias was a *committed* disciple. Later, Paul would remember Ananias as a "devout man according to the law, well spoken of by all the Jews who lived" in Damascus (Acts 22:12). A reputation like this is not gained in five minutes, or even five days, but slowly, in the steady ebb and flow of life. Ananias developed such a reputation by committing his whole life to following God and His word—a commitment that he surely displayed through his daily business and interactions with others.

Ananias's life challenges us to be faithful in seemingly small ways on apparently ordinary days. Perhaps one day we will be called to do something extraordinary for the Lord—but we are not to wait until then before we live wholeheartedly for Him. This is what disciples do: boldly, devotedly, and humbly they pursue God and trust Him completely. Whether you are in the midst of studies, raising children, pursuing a career, or facing retirement and old age, seek to do it all faithfully to the glory of God. Make it your aim to be known simply as Ananias was: as a disciple of Jesus Christ.

ACTS 9:1-19

FEBRUARY 15

THE DAY OF ATONEMENT

"The life of the flesh is in the blood, and I have given it for you on the altar to make atonement for your souls, for it is the blood that makes atonement." LEVITICUS 17:11

When God rescued the Israelites from Egypt, their redemption led to a relationship with Him. Living under God's rule, the people enjoyed His presence in the tabernacle. But from the very beginning, the Israelites could not keep the law of God. This introduced a dilemma: how could a holy God live with a sinful people?

On a specific day of each year—the Day of Atonement—the high priest of Israel was instructed by God to enter the Most Holy Place—the place in the tabernacle where God's presence dwelled—to offer sacrifices for the people's sins. The high priest would take two unblemished goats. The first he would sacrifice as a sin offering for the people and then sprinkle its blood on the atonement cover, also known as the mercy seat. The Israelites deserved death for their sin, but God graciously provided this goat as a substitute to die in their place. The people could live because the animal had died. And the result of that atonement was seen in what happened to the second goat: the priest would place his hands on its head, confess the people's sins over it, and then drive it out far into the wilderness. The high priest was then able to appear before the people, saying, in effect, *Your sins are atoned for. The blood has been shed, and by the shedding of blood there is remission for sin. The other goat I have driven out into the wilderness, and in the same way you need not be concerned about your sins anymore nor bear them as a burden on your back.* In a very specific way, God was establishing this essential truth: *He is willing to do what is necessary to bring sinful people into His presence.* Since His people were (and still are!) unruly, He had to provide a sacrifice for their sinfulness, allowing them to approach Him based on the actions of another. And each sacrifice pointed beyond itself to the perfect sacrifice that Christ would offer by His death on the cross, dealing with sin once and for all. As a result, we can enjoy utter confidence before God. But this confidence is not in ourselves; rather, "we have confidence to enter the holy places by the blood of Jesus, by the new and living way that he opened for us through the curtain, that is, through his flesh" (Hebrews 10:19-20).

When you are tempted to vacillate, doubt, and look at your own works as the basis of assurance, remember those two goats, both pointing you to the work of Jesus on the cross. Your sin has been paid for and your sin has been removed. Your performance neither adds to nor detracts from your status before our holy God. Here is where you find your confidence:

Upon a life I have not lived,
Upon a death I did not die,
Another's life, another's death,
I stake my whole eternity.[24]

HEBREWS 10:11-25

24 Horatius Bonar, "Christ for Us" (1881).

FEBRUARY 16

WHO DO YOU SAY THAT I AM?

"Simon Peter replied, 'You are the Christ, the Son of the living God.' And Jesus answered him, 'Blessed are you, Simon Bar-Jonah! For flesh and blood has not revealed this to you, but my Father who is in heaven.'" MATTHEW 16:16-17

When we read the Gospels, it becomes apparent that when people came into contact with Jesus of Nazareth, they seldom reacted with polite neutrality. His words and deeds inspired deep love and devotion but also fear and hatred. What could possibly account for such a range of responses?

In this conversation on the road to Caesarea Philippi, Peter spoke out—as was often the case—and for more than just himself when he replied, "You are the Christ." The word he used to identify Jesus was *Christos*, which in Greek meant "Messiah" or "Anointed One." Throughout the Old Testament, God had anointed kings, judges, and prophets, but they were all representatives and spokesmen pointing forward to the future Messiah, the Savior, the very Anointed One of God. Therefore, what Peter declared was especially noteworthy. He was saying to Jesus, *You are that one. You are the one of whom the prophets have spoken.*

What is even more astounding is Jesus' explanation for Peter's statement. Peter didn't come to his conclusion because he was smart or had an advanced capacity for logical and rational thinking or because an inspiring preacher had spelled it out for him. His declaration was possible because God the Father had actually revealed it to him.

Peter's confession of faith, like our own, could never have come about by his own strength. Faith is a gift that we are given. This exchange between Peter and Jesus is a concrete example of the Spirit of God taking the word of God and bringing it to someone's mind and heart in a way that causes him or her to declare the messiahship of Jesus.

Like Peter, our ability to declare Jesus as Lord and Messiah is not our own doing; it is "the gift of God, not a result of works, so that no one may boast" (Ephesians 2:8-9). If our faith were the result of our own intellectual capacity or emotional intelligence or moral goodness, we could place confidence—we could boast—in ourselves. But on good days this will leave us proud, and on bad days it will make us brittle. No: our faith rests entirely on God's gift, and so we place our confidence in Him—and we are humble on our best days and confident on our worst. Rejoice with gratitude today, then, because God delights to transform hearts and minds by the truth of His word so that we can join Peter in declaring, "You are the Christ."

EPHESIANS 2:1-10

◇ Bible Through The Year: Exodus 1-3; Mark 15:1-25

FEBRUARY 17

A WORD TO CHILDREN

"Children, obey your parents in the Lord, for this is right. 'Honor your father and mother' (this is the first commandment with a promise), 'that it may go well with you and that you may live long in the land.'" EPHESIANS 6:1-3

On two occasions when Paul gives to his readers a long list of the ugly fruits of godlessness, right in the middle we find one little phrase: "disobedient to parents" (Romans 1:30; 2 Timothy 3:2). Conversely, when you read church history, you discover that at times of spiritual awakening, practical godliness followed—including children's submission to godly parental authority.

Children's obedience to their parents is not merely a suggestion; it is an obligation. Scripture teaches that such obedience is right according to the natural order of God's creation, in accordance with His law, and as a response to the gospel. Parents should not be afraid to call for, and praise, obedience. But Paul doesn't only say obedience is right, but that it is rewarded. In the Lord, there is a blessing that accompanies paying attention to God's commands and promises. And when parent-child relationships are marked by love, trust, and obedience, we don't just create healthy people; we create a healthy society.

Parents would do well to remember five truths that the Bible teaches about our children:

1. "Children are a heritage from the Lord" (Psalm 127:3). They are a gift and a blessing. Thinking of our children should prompt gratitude to the Giver of those children.
2. We don't own our children; they belong to God. They're on loan to us, for a limited time.
3. Children are flawed from conception, guilty of sin and not deserving of eternal life—just like all of us (Psalm 58:3; Romans 3:23).
4. Because they are sinful, children are in need of the commandments of God. As parents, we are responsible for instructing them in God's law from the earliest days.
5. Our children can be saved only by grace. Therefore, we must teach them to look to Jesus alone for salvation.

Many of us live in a culture where these truths are opposed. On the one hand, children are seen as innately good, and their education or health or happiness is held up as the highest good. On the other, they are often the butt of jokes or subject of complaints. Sometimes even within the church itself, there is an absence of clear, biblical statements about parenting. But here is what God says: children growing up in the home are to obey their parents; parents are to raise their children to know God's law and God's grace. If we would raise a generation in our homes and in our churches that is more godly and more zealous than ours, we would do well to nurture our children in the context of God's truth. Many of us are parents with children in our homes. All of us will be members of churches with children in our midst. So what should it look like for you to contribute to the spiritual health of the next generation?

PROVERBS 2

FEBRUARY 18

PURCHASED FOR GOD

"By your blood you ransomed people for God from every tribe and language and people and nation, and you have made them a kingdom and priests to our God, and they shall reign on the earth." REVELATION 5:9-10

I was at Bible college with a Welsh missionary candidate named Mary Fisher. She was studying the Shona language so that she might teach young boys and girls in Zimbabwe. Within a relatively short time after her arrival there, there was a terrorist raid on the school at which she was teaching. Along with many other teachers and children, Mary did not survive; her life was snuffed out in that attack.[25] Yet while her death was tragic, her life had testified to the all-surpassing joy of serving God, not only here but also in eternity.

In the song of the elders gathered around the Lamb in Revelation, we are reminded that the purpose of Christ's death was so we might be ransomed by God. We have been set free from the sin that held us in its grip in order that, having been purchased by His blood, we will live for Him. Our praise is for God. Our service, like that of Mary Fisher, is for God.

As believers in the first century looked around and saw some of their friends taken into captivity for their faith, they tried to make sense of Christ's triumph over death, the victory of His ascension, and the reality of His return. In light of the tribulation they faced, these Christians were able to find encouragement in the reminder that even as Jesus made atonement for our sins, His focus was always on the Father. He purchased us *for God.*

How else do we make sense of the tragedies told in missionary biographies or explain the apparent rampant chaos represented in the death of martyrs? The last recording of Mary Fisher offers clarity. As a singer and guitar player, she was teaching the children in her class lyrics of a song based on Paul's words to the Philippian church: "For to me to live is Christ, and to die is gain" (Philippians 1:21).[26] Walking His path and holding His hand, the song states, is the way of peace and joy.

That song is nothing but empty rhetoric unless Revelation 5 is absolutely true when it tells us that Jesus went to the cross in order to purchase us for God. And Revelation 5 *is* absolutely true; and so, even if all of our breath were to be squeezed out in His service, even if all of our life were to be trampled over for His name's sake, still it would be time and energy and life well spent. You have been ransomed by God so that you might praise Him today and enjoy Him for all eternity. Whatever your day holds, be sure to walk through it with that as your greatest passion and highest purpose.

PHILIPPIANS 1:12-18

25 https://www.nytimes.com/1978/06/25/archives/12-white-teachers-and-children-killed-by-guerrillas-in-rhodesia.html. Accessed February 19, 2021.

26 J. White, "For Me to Live Is Christ" (1969).

FEBRUARY 19

THE COST OF COMPLAINING

"The people complained in the hearing of the LORD about their misfortunes, and when the LORD heard it, his anger was kindled." NUMBERS 11:1

There should be no place for grumbling in the Christian life.

That was a lesson that Israel learned the hard way (and learned slowly). After God freed them from slavery in Egypt, the Israelites received His law, were given His commands, and knew their destination. They eagerly set out to reach the promised land, but they hadn't gone very far at all—barely around the first bend in the road—before they began to complain. They wanted meat to eat instead of manna, and they even wished they were back in Egypt (Numbers 11:4-6). Where once they had thought God's daily provision of manna was a wonderful indication of His love for them, now they complained about having to eat the same old thing.

Grumbling seems to be a small thing, but it is a sign that gratitude is missing. Whenever unbelief and a lack of thankfulness mark the lives of God's children, consequences are inevitable. We may not end up like the Israelites, who wandered in the desert for 40 years, but our own grumbling is not without a cost.

Do you remember when you first felt the excitement of your newfound faith? Maybe you bought your first copy of the New Testament and thought all you were discovering was fantastic. You read it everywhere. Then, perhaps, something happened along the journey; now it seems to be just "the same old Bible," and you wish God would do something more dramatic, something better? Do you remember a time when sharing your faith seemed to be an exciting privilege—but now it feels like a burden and a duty? Do you remember a time when you were overflowing in gratitude for the cross—but now you find you focus more on the ways that God has not led you along the paths or to the places you would have preferred?

When the apostle Paul wrote to the early church, he reminded them of Israel's story as a warning: "We must not put Christ to the test, as some of them did and were destroyed by serpents, nor grumble, as some of them did and were destroyed by the Destroyer. Now these things happened to them as an example, but they were written down for our instruction" (1 Corinthians 10:9-11).

If we have faith in Christ, we've been set free from slavery to sin—even our complaining! We've been liberated by a sacrifice: the shedding of Christ's blood on the cross. And we too have set out on a journey, not to Canaan but to heaven. In light of that, God has given us both wonderful promises and necessary warnings. Do not presume upon His provision or grumble about the route He leads you on, but instead be filled with gratitude for all He has provided materially and spiritually. The cross lies behind you, heaven lies before you, and the Spirit dwells within you. There is no need, or excuse, for grumbling.

PSALM 95

FEBRUARY 20

ANXIETY'S ANTIDOTE

"Do not be anxious about anything, but in everything by prayer and supplication with thanksgiving let your requests be made known to God. And the peace of God, which surpasses all understanding, will guard your hearts and your minds." PHILIPPIANS 4:6-7

If I told you to write down all that you've been anxious about this week, or even today, I imagine you would have a substantial list. I know I would. And yet the word of God says to us, "Do not be anxious about *anything*." How, then, are we to respond when we find ourselves feeling choked in a battle with anxiety?

Paul says that the antidote to suffocating anxiety is prayer and thanksgiving. This response isn't natural. In fact, it goes directly against the tendencies of our sinful hearts. Most of us find it considerably easier to retreat into a corner and complain, or to chew over worrying circumstances in an effort to control them, rather than to bring anxiety-inducing matters before God in prayer. How easy—and how fruitless—it is to choose to sit and stew, allowing anxiety to paralyze us instead of getting down on our knees and crying out to Him.

Prayer swallows up the question "How am I going to cope with this?" by pointing us away from ourselves and to God's provision. Prayer turns our focus toward God, who is totally competent, who knows our needs intimately, and who will give us either what we ask or something better than we can imagine. And a thankful heart helps us confront without bitterness the question "Why has this happened to me?" by helping us remember God's promises. He always acts with purpose, fulfills His plan, and knows exactly what He's doing.

Some of us had parents who would act as our alarm clocks when we lived at home. When we needed to wake up at a certain time in the morning, all we had to do was tell our father or our mother, and we were confident they would wake us. All that was left for us to do was sleep! This is the kind of response Paul wants from us in the face of anxiety. We are to go directly to our heavenly Father and say, "Will you take care of this for me?" And God always answers, *I've got this. Trust Me.*

When we understand that God is in control of all things, we'll bring all of our struggles and challenges to Him. The peace He provides will be a stronghold for our hearts.

Though troubles assail and dangers affright,
Though close friends should fail us and foes all unite,
Yet one thing secures us, whatever betide,
The promise assures us, "The Lord will provide."[27]

So why not write out that list of things you've been anxious about this week? Then pray about them, taking those situations to the throne of heaven and leaving them there. And then next to each item you can write what God says to you: *I've got this. Trust Me.*

1 PETER 5:6-11

27 John Newton, "Though Troubles Assail" (1775).

FEBRUARY 21

NOT SO AMONG YOU

"Jesus called them to him and said to them, 'You know that those who are considered rulers of the Gentiles lord it over them, and their great ones exercise authority over them. But it shall not be so among you.'" MARK 10:42-43

One of the great lies in almost every generation is that God's people will reach their unbelieving neighbors better if they look, sound, act, and live as much like them as possible. The New Testament doesn't support that, nor does church history. Instead, history bears out what the Bible teaches—namely, that God's people are always most effective in an alien culture when, both by their life and lifestyle, they are clearly countercultural (1 Peter 2:11-12).

Just prior to these words of Jesus, James and John, the "Sons of Thunder," went to Jesus to ask a favor: they wanted places of honor in His kingdom (Mark 10:35-45). This desire, however, was not born of loyalty but of raw ambition, similar to that of the Roman rulers during that time, who sought self-promotion.

Jesus didn't pull any punches in His response. His language was radical. The disciples were His followers, and they were to be different. They needed to understand that in God's kingdom, the way up is actually down. Honor is found in giving it, not in receiving it. Greatness is displayed in serving, not in being served. The greatest example of this principle is Jesus Himself, who "did not count equality with God a thing to be grasped, but emptied himself, by taking the form of a servant, being born in the likeness of men. And being found in human form, he humbled himself by becoming obedient to the point of death, even death on a cross" (Philippians 2:6-8).

This is challenging, because we live in a culture that is preoccupied with self-esteem, self-aggrandizement, and self-made status. Yet if we profess to be Jesus' followers, His words here remind us that we are not to be marked by the culture but by Him.

We tend to have an unhealthy preoccupation with being regarded as significant, intellectually sensible, and socially acceptable. When has that ever been an effective strategy for the work of the gospel? The choice is clear: either we're going to do what Jesus says or we're going to do what the culture says.

We must not diminish the force of Jesus' words nor the scale of His challenge. But neither do we need to despair, for we can find encouragement in the fact that John eventually got it right. Near the end of his life, he wrote, "By this we know love, that he laid down his life for us, and we ought to lay down our lives for the brothers" (1 John 3:16). Hear this word of uncomfortable grace—"it shall not be so among you"—and be conformed to the image of Jesus, willing to lay down your rights and your reputation in service and love.

PHILIPPIANS 2:1-11

FEBRUARY 22

KNOWING GOD

"No longer shall each one teach his neighbor and each his brother, saying, 'Know the Lord,' for they shall all know me, from the least of them to the greatest, declares the Lord." JEREMIAH 31:34

In the days of the prophet Jeremiah, God refused to break the covenant He had made with His people. Despite His steadfast love, though, God's people continued to sin. This presented a problem: how could God fulfill the promises He had made to bless His people when they continually demonstrated their unfaithfulness to Him?

As a part of His great plan, God pledged a new covenant—a work of inner re-creation. As the theologian Alec Motyer writes, "When his people could not rise to the height of his standards, the Lord does not lower his standards to match their ability; he transforms his people."[28]

This new covenant is the purpose and promise of God to regenerate hearts through the blood of the Lord Jesus. He takes our hearts and He makes them the perfect shape—like fitting a piece in a jigsaw puzzle—so that His law becomes a delight to us.

In God's declaration of this new covenant, the verb "know" is key. In the original Hebrew, its meaning is clear from the very beginning in Genesis: the straightforward statement that Adam "knew" his wife and they bore children (Genesis 4:1) demonstrates the level of intimacy it conveys. God is saying that when His people come to an understanding of His love, they won't simply be doing Bible studies at arm's length; they'll be people who truly know Him.

What Jeremiah spoke of in the future tense, we are able to enjoy in the present; for in between his prophecy and our time, the Lord Jesus held up a cup of wine the night before He died and announced, "This cup that is poured out for you is the new covenant in my blood" (Luke 22:20). By God's grace, you and I may know the King of Kings and the Lord of Lords. Not only this, but He also knows each of our names, individually; and He knows our needs and is committed to our well-being. Jesus bears our names before the Father—and because of all He is and all He's done, those names are written in the Book of Life.

What kind of King is this? The answer is beyond our ability to fully comprehend. Someday, we will see Him face-to-face and understand far more than we do today. But still, today you can go about with the confidence that comes from knowing that you know the God who redeemed you through His Son, who dwells in and works in you by His Spirit, and in whose throne room you will one day stand.

JEREMIAH 31:31-40

28 *Look to the Rock: An Old Testament Background to Our Understanding of Christ* (Kregel, 1996), p 58-59.

FEBRUARY 23

CONFORMED TO HIS IMAGE

"Those whom he foreknew he also predestined to be conformed to the image of his Son, in order that he might be the firstborn among many brothers."
ROMANS 8:29

It's not uncommon for couples who have been married for a long time to be asked if they are brother and sister because they have taken on so many of each other's characteristics. To some extent, this makes sense, doesn't it? We become like the company we keep.

The same should be true for us in our walk with Christ.

God's purpose for your life is to conform you to the likeness of His Son. Think about that: consider Jesus' human perfections, and realize that you get to become like Him! God is deeply committed to this; it is a work He promises to bring "to completion at the day of Jesus Christ" (Philippians 1:6). What is God doing today? We can summarize it simply as this: He is making us more like Christ.

Many of us are familiar with the guarantee of Romans 8:28 that "for those who love God all things work together for good, for those who are called according to his purpose." But the verse that follows tells us what the "good" is that our almighty God is working towards in all facets of our lives: "to be conformed to the image of his Son."

God is far more concerned with your Christlikeness than your comfort. Often, more spiritual progress is made through disappointment and failure than through success and laughter. While we shouldn't seek out hardship, we can recognize that our Father knows best and that nothing takes Him by surprise. When we experience "unanswered" prayer or when our challenges and pain linger far longer than we wish, we find hope in seeing that God's eternal purpose is at work in and through the lives of His children.

You and I are not the only ones who have experienced significant spells of quiet desperation or ongoing disappointment when we are tempted to ask, "What is God *doing*?" What was He doing when Stephen's persecutors took their jackets off and threw rocks at him (Acts 7:58)? What was He doing when Paul was run out of Damascus, lowered down from the wall in a basket (9:25)? What was He doing when Peter was imprisoned by King Agrippa (12:3)? Hard as it may be to see, He was accomplishing His eternal plan: to make His followers more like Jesus as they walked home towards Jesus.

Here is the source of your hope when you get up in the morning. Come rain or shine, come delight or disappointment, God will definitely accomplish His purposes in your life through the day. Your heavenly Father has a plan and purpose for each one He calls His own. You may be able to see how He is doing it in real time, or a few months afterwards, or perhaps not until you stand with Christ in eternity. But know this: today is another day when your Father will be making you more like His Son.

ROMANS 8:26-39

FEBRUARY 24

HOPE THROUGH THE SILENCE

"Behold, I send my messenger, and he will prepare the way before me. And the Lord whom you seek will suddenly come to his temple; and the messenger of the covenant in whom you delight, behold, he is coming, says the L*ORD of hosts."* MALACHI 3:1

God's people are a waiting people.

After God's people returned from their exile in Babylon, the "minor prophets" Haggai, Zechariah, and Malachi brought God's word to them. Their message was similar to what their predecessors had said before the people went into captivity: *You Israelites are ridiculous! You keep breaking the covenant. And if you keep breaking the covenant, God is going to come in judgment.*

But the minor prophets' message was not *only* one of judgment. There was also hope.

They may have physically returned to the land, but spiritually the people were still in exile. Judah—all that remained of Israel—held on to the hope that God was going to fulfill His promise so that His people might enjoy His blessings. But God's kingdom still had not come in the way that the previous prophets had declared it would—because God's King had not yet come. So the people were waiting for the Lord to return and fulfill all the promises of salvation.

The last of the Old Testament prophets, Malachi, insisted that this King would still appear—but 400 years of silence followed. People were born, went about their business, worked, and died, and on the cycle went. They probably asked one another, "What about those words, 'I will send my messenger, and he will prepare the way before me'? It's been centuries since that promise."

Eventually, a few of those people may have been walking down to the market when a funny-looking character wearing a strange outfit and eating a strange diet appeared in the streets, quoting the Old Testament: "Behold, I send my messenger before your face, who will prepare your way, the voice of one crying in the wilderness: 'Prepare the way of the Lord, make his paths straight'" (Mark 1:2-3). With those words, John the Baptist ended generations of silence. After many long years of waiting, God was faithful in keeping His promises, just as He always is. He sent both His messenger and His King so that all people could experience His blessing—namely, the fulfillment of salvation through Jesus Christ.

In our day, God's people are still looking forward. We know Jesus has come; we also know He is coming. God's kingdom has not yet arrived in all its glorious fullness. So we are a waiting people in a world of instant gratification, an expectant people in a world of rapid disillusionment. Therefore, when it seems that God is taking too long to fulfill His promises in your life, do not lose hope. Generation after generation, He has proven to be faithful—and in sending Jesus, He introduced the fulfiller of every promise. You can rest in His constancy. "Surely," says Jesus, "I am coming soon" (Revelation 22:20). He will do what He has said.

2 PETER 3:1-13

FEBRUARY 25

RUN HARD

"Do you not know that in a race all the runners run, but only one receives the prize? So run that you may obtain it. Every athlete exercises self-control in all things. They do it to receive a perishable wreath, but we an imperishable. So I do not run aimlessly." 1 CORINTHIANS 9:24-26

Athletic competitions mattered in the Greek culture that permeated the eastern Roman Empire at the time of the New Testament. One commentator sums up Corinth as a city whose masses demanded only two things: bread and games.[29]

Smaller, local contests awarded a number of prizes, but in major events there was only one prize—often a laurel or pine crown. Competitors spent months and months of their lives setting themselves apart from all they might otherwise enjoy—all of the relationships, all of the food, all of the leisurely pursuits that would undermine their ability to win—in order to fix their gaze upon a laurel crown. Paul uses this picture to encourage believers to live with eyes set on the eternal prize of glorifying Christ and being united with Him.

In school cross-country races, what begins as one large company often quickly becomes three groups: a small group goes for gold, the great mass of runners in the middle go for "just ok," and the ones that hang behind are typically the cynical, disruptive, disillusioned, sorry souls. The word for "run" that Paul uses in this verse describes running not as a straggler, not as a wanderer, not as a half-hearted participant but as a prizewinner. As Christians, we must say no to running aimlessly. We must go for gold.

To live with a focus on the prize requires sacrifice—specifically, the sacrifice of any desires contrary to God's will. The word "athlete" in verse 25 translates the word *agonizomenos*, from which we get the word "agony." To be an athlete is to choose not to be comfortable. To be a Christian is to choose the same thing. Are we prepared to agonize and sacrifice for Christ, knowing that only then will we experience the joy of winning the prize of a life well-lived for Him?

But how are we to offer such a sacrifice or run with such a focus? It will not be the result of our own strength or self-righteousness. All of that is the soul and substance of false religion. No, only our union with Christ provides the power and the potential for this change. Jesus set the example of willing sacrifice with the eternal prize in mind (Hebrews 12:2). When He underpins our hearts and lives, there is no limit to the extent we will joyfully go to as we run our race for Him and follow on behind Him.

When asked about the race plan that had seen him win gold in the 1924 Olympic 400 meters, the famous Scottish Olympian and missionary Eric Liddell is reputed to have answered, "I run the first 200 meters as hard as I can. Then, for the second 200 meters, with God's help, I run even harder." Today, then, do not run aimlessly or slowly, but with God's help run even harder after the gold, for His sake and His glory.

HEBREWS 12:1-3

29 Erich Sauer, *In the Arena of Faith: A Call to the Consecrated Life* (Eerdmans, 1966), p 30.

FEBRUARY 26

WORDS THAT HARM

"The tongue is a fire, a world of unrighteousness. The tongue is set among our members, staining the whole body, setting on fire the entire course of life, and set on fire by hell ... No human being can tame the tongue." JAMES 3:6, 8

Three things never come back: the spent arrow, the spoken word, and the lost opportunity. What we say cannot be unsaid. What's more, we will be called to account for every word we have spoken—even our careless ones—at the day of reckoning (see Matthew 12:36). As King Solomon put it, "Whoever guards his mouth preserves his life; he who opens wide his lips comes to ruin" (Proverbs 13:3); and "Death and life are in the power of the tongue" (18:21). Our words can serve to encourage, to nourish, and to heal. But they can also cause strife, create dissension, and do harm. Solomon gives us a multifaceted picture of what characterizes such harmful words. He describes words that harm as those that are reckless, as being "like sword thrusts" (12:18). Our words so often spill forth unguardedly, and we become someone who "gives an answer before he hears" (18:13). "When words are many, transgression is not lacking" (10:19).

You will likely have heard the saying that sticks and stones can break our bones, but words can never harm us—but that is dead wrong. Bruises may fade and the marks they made be forgotten. But hurtful words that have been said to us and about us tend to remain with us for a long time. Truer are these lines:

A careless word may kindle strife,
A cruel word may wreck a life,
A bitter word may hate instill,
A brutal word may smite and kill.

It would be difficult to estimate how many friendships are broken, how many reputations are ruined, or the peace of how many homes is destroyed through harmful words. The very source of all such animosity and abusive language, according to James, is none other than hell itself. Yes, our tongue is "a fire," and "no human being can tame the tongue" without the work of God's Holy Spirit.

Stop and think of how many words you have used in the last 24 hours, and how they were used. "Death and life are in the power of the tongue"—so did any of your words cause harm, tearing someone else down in some way? That is a sin to be repented of and turned from. Is that something you need to do, both before God and to the person to whom those words were spoken? Then think of the words you may speak over the next 24 hours. How might they be used to bring life? How might you reflect the one who "committed no sin, neither was deceit found in his mouth"? Rather, "when he was reviled, he did not revile in return ... He himself bore our sins ... that we might die to sin and live to righteousness" (1 Peter 2:22-24).

JAMES 3:2-12

FEBRUARY 27

WORDS THAT HELP

"From the same mouth come blessing and cursing. My brothers, these things ought not to be so. Does a spring pour forth from the same opening both fresh and salt water? Can a fig tree, my brothers, bear olives, or a grapevine produce figs? Neither can a salt pond yield fresh water." JAMES 3:10-12

In the course of our lives we are confronted by unfairness, by unkindness, by disagreeable circumstances, and often by disagreeable people. Before offering a verbal response in these situations, we would do well to recall this truth learned from our Lord: our words reflect our hearts (Matthew 12:34). If our words are not Christlike, we must look first not to our mouths but to our hearts. Equally, it is an indication of our Lord's work within us when we respond to conflict and challenge with words that *help* rather than those that harm.

Our tongues contain immense power, and we may leverage them to help, to encourage, to affirm, to enrich, to reconcile, to forgive, to unite, to smooth, and to bless. It is not by accident that so many of the Old Testament proverbs address the words we speak. According to Solomon, "The mouth of the righteous is a fountain of life" (Proverbs 10:11). He compares this use of words to lovely earrings that adorn the beauty of the wearer and to beautiful ornaments that enhance the loveliness of a home (25:12). Perhaps his most classic statement about the power of speech is his observation that "a word fitly spoken is like apples of gold in a setting of silver" (v 11).

What is it that makes for such life-giving language? How can our mouths be those that bring blessing to others? Words of blessing are marked by honesty, by "speaking the truth in love" (Ephesians 4:15). They are thoughtful, spoken by one who "ponders how to answer" (Proverbs 15:28). They are often few and marked by reason: "Whoever restrains his words has knowledge, and he who has a cool spirit is a man of understanding" (17:27).

And, of course, helpful words will be gentle words. Though it may be hard to remember in the throes of difficult circumstances, it remains true that "a soft answer turns away wrath" (Proverbs 15:1). Indeed, a gentle response wells up from moral strength; it takes far more self-control to respond in gentleness than to give way to unbridled passion and anger.

What will mark your words? Will you commit yourself to using your tongue—that small but immensely powerful member of your body—to bless rather than curse, to give life rather than tear it down, and to help rather than harm?

Resolve today to use your words for the good of those with whom you interact, honoring Christ in your heart and letting His sweet aroma fill your speech. Then humbly acknowledge that you cannot do this yourself (James 3:8), and ask Him to fill you with His Spirit—the Spirit who grows peace, gentleness, and self-control both in your heart and in your speech (Galatians 5:22-23).

GALATIANS 5:16-25

FEBRUARY 28

COMMITTED AND CONSISTENT

"I wholly followed the LORD my God. And Moses swore on that day, saying, 'Surely the land on which your foot has trodden shall be an inheritance for you and your children forever, because you have wholly followed the LORD my God.'"
JOSHUA 14:8-9

Many people get off to a flying start in life only to later lose whatever it was that once made them successful. Perhaps they were well known as a young man or woman. At the age of 40, their life was one of prominence, influence, and status. In the church, we can see such individuals—indeed, we can see *ourselves*—as supremely useful to God. But too often we are then tempted to become masters of yesterday, frequently looking back to the "good years" and grumbling about the way things have become.

Although it's true of so many, this was not at all true of Caleb, who fled from potential apathy and kept on in faith. He spent his middle years in a less than desirable environment. From the age of 40, he was stuck wandering around the wilderness for four decades because the people around him had failed to have faith in God. Yet during this time of frustration and wanderings, Caleb remained free of embitterment and disgruntlement.

In fact, things eventually got so bad that the people began to look for a leader to take them back to the good old days (Numbers 14:4). Yet no one really needs a leader to go backward; you can just go back! We need leaders to push us forward. There is a tomorrow. There are generations yet to come. There are purposes yet to be unfolded in God's plan for our world.

Caleb reveals this spirit. The apparent commitment of his early life was matched by his consistency in the middle years. He was committed and consistent not only at 40 but also at 50 and 60 and 70. Throughout the decades, he "wholly followed the LORD."

For many, marriage, the establishment of a home, business concerns, health issues, and so on are often accompanied by a loss of spiritual ardor and effectiveness. Many are those who have great resources, energy, and wisdom to offer but who decide instead to chill out, leaving the work of ministry to the next generation. Like the Israelites in the wilderness, they settle for disinterest, criticism, and cynicism, failing to see the disintegration in their own spiritual lives.

What about your commitment, your conversations, and your spiritual edge? Are they the same as they once were? There is a great need in the church today, as there was in Israel's wilderness generation, for experienced men and women of faith who live lives marked by consistent commitment, in good times and bad, in season and out, as through the years they walk toward the inheritance that the Lord has promised His faithful followers. What will that look like for you today—and in ten years?

JUDGES 1:1-20

MARCH 1

A BASTION FOR OUR SOULS

"Blessed be the God and Father of our Lord Jesus Christ, who has blessed us in Christ with every spiritual blessing in the heavenly places, even as he chose us in him before the foundation of the world, that we should be holy and blameless before him. In love he predestined us for adoption to himself as sons through Jesus Christ." EPHESIANS 1:3-5

God has loved you for a long, long time.

Paul's striking outpouring of praise at the beginning of his letter to the Ephesians announces to us the wonder of all that God has done for us in Christ. One of the features that makes it so striking is that it begins with God, reminding us that before we ever existed, He took the initiative to draw people to Himself. We may be tempted to believe we need to search for God through human effort; indeed, many world religions teach just that. But from its very beginning, the Bible teaches that it is actually God who reaches out to us.

Our election in Christ is not some kind of historical afterthought; it goes all the way back into eternity past, before creation. Yes, we do decide to follow Christ—but it is so humbling to recognize that we could never have chosen God if He had not chosen us before the creation of the world. You would not be capable of deciding to follow Him if He had not first decided to make you His child.

There is a delicate tension in reconciling the responsibility of man with the sovereignty of God. Many people believe they must choose between the two when, in fact, both ideas are biblical and connected. They are two truths that sit side by side, seemingly irreconcilable in our finite human minds yet both entirely true. We don't need to worry away at them as an intellectual exercise. Instead, we are free to respond by bowing down in wonder over the kindness of Almighty God on our behalf.

The doctrine of election is not a banner under which we march but a bastion for our souls.[30] It makes all the difference to our security and our joy. Once you humbly recognize that your identity in Christ was established the moment He first set His affection upon you, even before the dawn of time, you find freedom and you have confidence. You don't need to seek to come up with some reason in yourself to understand why you have received His amazing grace; you can simply enjoy knowing that He chose you because He loves you. You don't need to live burdened by your sin or crushed because you feel you are making little progress in your Christian life, for His love was never based on your performance or on your promise of doing better. You can walk through the peaks and valleys of this life with the assurance that you are loved by the one who made all things and directs all things—and that because you never had to win His love, you can never lose it.

JOHN 6:35-51

30 Eric J. Alexander, "The Basis of Christian Salvation" (sermon, 1984).

MARCH 2

NOTHING IN MY HAND

"Christ redeemed us from the curse of the law by becoming a curse for us—for it is written, 'Cursed is everyone who is hanged on a tree'—so that in Christ Jesus the blessing of Abraham might come to the Gentiles, so that we might receive the promised Spirit through faith." GALATIANS 3:13-14

As believers in Jesus, we have been delivered from the great curse of sin. The wonder of this deliverance grips us the moment we understand that this curse, which means we are guilty before God and deserve to die, has been lifted from us by Christ.

Having been saved, though, it is easy for the wonder to wear off and the grip to slacken. We can so easily live pleasant, comfortable lives that make it hard to see sin's hold on us. We are so easily prone to believe that if we only try a little harder at our marriages, our jobs, our relationships, and our achievements, we'll be good people, deserving of blessing. We want to be achievers, not believers. We're constantly lured back to the false religion of self-effort.

Such was the temptation for the Galatian church. And so Paul wrote to them and essentially said, *That is not the Christian message.* In fact, it is its opposite! If the gospel is that Jesus came only to add something to our lives that was lacking, the curse of the law would either be of no concern or be beyond remedy. But the curse is real, and it must be dealt with. Why would we be interested in someone who died to take our place unless we first understand that we deserve the curse He bore?

We need only look at the law of Moses to see the effect of its curse (for instance, Exodus 20:1-17). The law reveals how we haven't loved God with all our heart. We haven't obeyed Him, we haven't loved others as ourselves, we haven't always told the truth, we're guilty of coveting. The list goes on. When God's Spirit convicts us and we see our shortcomings, though, we sing with the hymn writer, "Not the labor of my hands can fulfill Thy law's demands."[31] We see the weight of the curse that once rested and should still rest upon us, and then we are able to see Christ in all His glory as our Savior, who came to lift its burden.

This is the very heart of our faith. When we look upon the cross and see how Jesus hung there, we see what He did as something both necessary and voluntary. He took His place where we ought to be. That's grace.

If we were able to put ourselves in the right with God by our own endeavors, there would be no wonder in redemption and no beauty in the prospect of adoption. When we are tempted to look to ourselves and our works, we must remember that Christ has broken the curse. And in that wonder, we can glory. No matter how many days or years it is since you were first gripped by grace, sing anew to yourself right now:

Nothing in my hand I bring,
Simply to Thy cross I cling.

GALATIANS 2:15 – 3:9

31 Augustus Toplady, "Rock of Ages" (1776).

MARCH 3

SOUL REST

"While the promise of entering his rest still stands, let us fear lest any of you should seem to have failed to reach it. For good news came to us just as to them, but the message they heard did not benefit them, because they were not united by faith with those who listened." HEBREWS 4:1-2

Too often Christians are terrific at leisure but lousy at resting. Why? One reason may be because Western culture places a high premium on the relentless pursuit of higher and higher levels of success and prosperity. Even our leisure is full of "pursuits" and a desire to improve and achieve. And underneath this lies the affliction of every culture: our alienation from the God who created us and made us both to work and to rest.

When sin entered the world, rest eluded mankind. Whatever else you might say about humanity, it is undeniable that we are not marked by tranquility or restfulness. Leisure is not rest if you have worked so hard to achieve only a few moments of peace or if you fill your leisure time with things to do. Surely there is something more God desires.

God offers a rest that soothes our souls. Soul-rest flows from a life surrendered to Him in faith. When the dust of death, which came from sin, settled upon humanity, we could no longer enjoy the deeper rest God intended. We need a new creation—and this is exactly what God has provided! "If anyone is in Christ, he is a new creation" (2 Corinthians 5:17). In creation God established the principle of physical rest, and in redemption He established the possibility of perfect spiritual rest. Yet even so, people so often insist on living their lives with a disregard for God. They spurn His invitation to rest their souls, remaining only hearers of the word but not doers (James 1:22), and then they hope to enter into their rest when they die. The Bible holds out no hope for such an approach to life. Just as the Israelites in the wilderness found God's promises of no benefit because they failed to believe them, we similarly can't expect to know God's gift of soul-rest, in this life or in the one to come, if we continue in our own faithless striving.

Thankfully, everything resolves in Jesus. He cuts through the facade of empty religious pretense and desperate worldly striving and offers us a gracious invitation: "Come to me, all who labor and are heavy laden, and I will give you rest. Take my yoke upon you, and learn from me, for I am gentle and lowly in heart, and you will find rest for your souls" (Matthew 11:28-29). This is a rest that we enjoy even as we work, a rest that enables us truly to rest from our work, and a rest that we will one day enjoy fully, finally, and eternally in His presence.

Is your soul at rest today? Or are you anxious about what tomorrow may bring or exhausted by what you feel you must achieve today? The work that satisfies your greatest desire and solves your greatest need—the work of salvation—was finished by Jesus on your behalf at Calvary. He invites you to come to Him: to know that He has taken care of your eternal future and that the tasks that He purposes for you today will all be done—no more and no less. So *believe* Him, and let your soul truly rest.

HEBREWS 4:1-10

MARCH 4

FORGIVEN AND FORGIVING

"Should not you have had mercy on your fellow servant, as I had mercy on you?"
MATTHEW 18:33

A forgiven person should be a forgiving person—and, since forgiveness does not come naturally to us, we need to hear this again and again.

In other words, we forgive because God, through Jesus, forgives us. The Bible makes it perfectly clear that forgiveness doesn't spring from any human merit and isn't the result of our own endeavors to be gracious and forgiving towards others; rather it comes from the grace of God.

One of the chief evidences that someone has truly repented of their sins, therefore, is a forgiving spirit. Conversely, if we continually harbor enmity, grudges, and bitterness in our hearts, we not only harm our own lives and jeopardize our relationships, but frankly we also call into question whether we've ever truly discovered the nature of God's forgiveness at all.

It's impossible to extend genuine forgiveness unless we've experienced it ourselves, and impossible not to do so if we have. It will only flow from our hearts once we have been changed by God's grace and have considered the enormity of our offense against Him. When such a transformation takes place, the sin of others against us will carry less weight as God enables us to forgive as we've been forgiven.

This is the principle behind Jesus' parable of the servant in Matthew 18, who, having been forgiven a debt that was the first-century equivalent of $8 billion, then refused to forgive a debt of $20,000. Jesus wants us to see the unreasonableness of the servant who had been forgiven an enormous debt in refusing to forgive the debt that was owed to him. Viewed on its own, that debt was substantial; set against the amount he himself had been forgiven, it was tiny. Likewise, it is inconceivable that we, who have been forgiven such a vast debt of offense against God, should ever fail to forgive others.

If we have experienced God's mercy, then we must certainly not neglect the exercise of forgiveness. In forgiving others, we enjoy the fullness of God's pardon. Give up the records of sins that you're tempted to hold on to. When this is hard because the wrong you're being called to forgive was serious, look at the debt for which God has forgiven you, and look at what He gave up to do so—and that will enable you to extend mercy in your turn. Surely, if God has forgiven you, He will pour out His grace and mercy to help you walk in harmony with others.

MARK 11:20-25

MARCH 5

GOD IS FOR US

"Let no one say when he is tempted, 'I am being tempted by God,' for God cannot be tempted with evil, and he himself tempts no one." JAMES 1:13

When we come to faith in Jesus Christ and the bonds of sin are broken, a number of things become true of us immediately. We are transferred from death to life and indwelt by God's Spirit. We're placed within His family. We are redeemed, changed, and born again. Sin no longer reigns in our lives.

It does, however, *remain*.

In trusting Christ, we are not living a life of ease whereby we are exempt from attacks from the Evil One or the subtle tendencies of our own hearts. Instead, from the point of conversion through to the point of seeing Christ and being made like Him, the Christian is involved in "a continual and irreconcilable war"[32] against temptation.

Scripture is full of warnings about temptation: that enticement to sin and evil that we all experience. Temptation is not simply the lure of things which are wild and unthinkable, but the impulse to take good things which God has given us and use (or misuse) them in a way that sins against God. In *The Screwtape Letters*, C.S. Lewis alludes to this subtlety of sin when Screwtape urges his apprentice devil to "encourage the humans to take the pleasures which our Enemy [namely, God] has produced, at times, or in ways, or in degrees, which He has forbidden."[33]

Scripture is clear that God is never and cannot be the source of temptation. When James says that "God ... tempts no one," he has built his statement on God's character. God is incapable of tempting others to evil because He Himself is insusceptible to it. Tempting others to evil would require a delight in evil which God does not possess.

The word translated "tempt" can also be rendered "test." So what our fallen nature might turn into a temptation to sin is also a test that can strengthen our faith. When we face a time of testing, which God allows, we should remember that His purpose is not our failure but our benefit. The devil longs for us to fail, but God longs for us to succeed. He is for us, and He is working all things, even trials and temptations, for our good.

So what temptations are you regularly doing battle with (or giving in to)? Learn to see those as temptations but also as opportunities—as moments to choose obedience, to please your Father, to grow to be more like Christ—to gain a victory in your ongoing war. "Resist the devil, and he will flee from you" (James 4:7).

1 PETER 1:13-21

32 The Westminster Confession of Faith 8.2.

33 *The Screwtape Letters* (1942; HarperCollins, 2001), p 44.

MARCH 6

WHERE ARE YOU?

"The man and his wife hid themselves from the presence of the LORD God ... But the LORD God called to the man and said to him, 'Where are you?'"
GENESIS 3:8-9

Across ethnic, linguistic, and geographical boundaries, children everywhere enjoy the fun of playing hide-and-seek. It is a universal and innocent game. But the first game of hide-and-seek in this world was neither fun nor innocent. It was something deadly serious.

After Adam and Eve's disobedience in the garden, they hid from each other behind fig leaves and from their Creator behind the trees of the garden. They attempted a cover-up—and God came seeking them with a simple question: "Where are you?"

This question turns on its head the common assumption that man is looking for God, who is hiding somewhere in or beyond the universe. Instead, we discover the opposite: we are the ones who are hiding, and God is the one who comes seeking.

The question may seem like a strange one for God to ask these first humans. After all, doesn't God know everything already? But God asked where Adam and Eve were not so He could gain new information but because He wanted to help them understand their situation. God came to *draw* them out more than to *drive* them out.

Imagine the many ways God could have reacted in response to Adam and Eve's rebellion. If He had responded strictly in judgment, He could have instantaneously brought about the sentence of death that He had warned them of (Genesis 2:16-17). But it is in God's nature always to have mercy; so He came instead with a single question. This is the first glimpse of God's grace after humanity turned their backs on Him. God did not immediately give them what they justly deserved; rather, out of His immense kindness, He granted what was not deserved: an opportunity to respond and return.

None of us would feel comfortable if those closest to us could see all of our deepest thoughts and previous actions. We may hide the truth from each other, and perhaps even from ourselves. But to hide from God is futile. There is simply no way to hide and nowhere to shift the blame to.

We must not believe the lie that God won't see the "little" sins we keep hidden from others. He sees. Ultimately, He sees into our souls and knows exactly what we have done and where we stand. Wonderfully, we do not need to pretend that we can hide. He comes to us in mercy, not in judgment, for "God did not send his Son into the world to condemn the world, but in order that the world might be saved through him" (John 3:17). Are you burdened by some besetting sin or secret shame? Are you seeking to hide from God what you have been hiding from others? There's never been a better time to stop hiding from Him. Step into the light. Uncover what cannot remain hidden before Him—so that He might cover it with His blood and so that you might know you are both known and forgiven. He is a kind and saving God who desires a relationship with us.

1 JOHN 1:8 – 2:2

MARCH 7

JESUS THROUGHOUT SCRIPTURE

"The eunuch said to Philip, 'About whom, I ask you, does the prophet say this, about himself or about someone else?' Then Philip opened his mouth, and beginning with this Scripture he told him the good news about Jesus."
ACTS 8:34-35

As we journey through the Bible, we recognize that Jesus did not arrive out of nowhere. From start to finish, the Bible is a book about Him. Indeed, even the Old Testament prophets, under the inspiration of the Spirit, wrote about Jesus. If we take our eyes off Christ, then, however well we know Scripture, we will have missed its center, its key, and its hero.

In the Gospels, Jesus pointed people to the Old Testament to help them understand who He was. Early in His ministry, He was once at the synagogue reading from the scroll of Isaiah. As He finished, Luke tells us, He "began to say" to His listeners, "Today this Scripture has been fulfilled in your hearing" (Luke 4:21). Later, speaking to people who were especially interested and versed in the Old Testament Scriptures, Jesus warned them, "You search the Scriptures because you think that in them you have eternal life; and it is they that bear witness about me" (John 5:39). After His death and resurrection, when He encountered some of His dejected followers on the road to Emmaus, Jesus, "beginning with Moses and all the Prophets ... interpreted to them in all the Scriptures the things concerning himself" (Luke 24:27).

In other words, Jesus clearly taught that every part of the Old Testament finds its focus and fulfillment in Him.

When you read the Scriptures, you meet Jesus, because this book testifies to Him. Even if our studies and understanding of Old Testament passages provide us with good, important ethical truths about life, there's great danger of us missing the Truth, Jesus. The purpose of every page of your Bible is for you to meet Jesus, to come to know Him, and to proclaim His great name, all for His glory.

In every sermon you hear, every lesson you study, and every passage of God's word that you read, be asking yourself, "Did it bring me to Christ? Did I discover Jesus in it?" And do not stop listening, studying, and reading until you can answer yes, for it is in Him that the treasures of salvation, truth, wisdom, and comfort are to be found.

PSALM 119:17-32

MARCH 8

ABRAHAM'S HOPE

"No unbelief made him waver concerning the promise of God, but he grew strong in his faith as he gave glory to God." ROMANS 4:20

Before Abraham ever had any children, God promised him that there would be a vast company of people that would be his descendants. Time passed, and it looked as if Abraham and his wife, Sarah, were never going to have any offspring. The promise seemed in danger of failing, so Abraham and Sarah decided to take matters into their own hands. Sarah offered her maid Hagar to bear Abraham a child, and Hagar had a baby, Ishmael. Yet God made it clear that the descendants He had promised were not going to emerge through Ishmael's line. God was showing Abraham and Sarah that if His promise was going to be fulfilled, then only He could do it. Abraham was given one task: to trust in God's promise—a promise that faced overwhelming difficulties and that therefore required an all-powerful God for its fulfillment.

As the years went by, Sarah still didn't conceive. God came to Abraham again, reassuring him that even in her great age, she was going to bear a son. Eventually, at ninety years old, she gave birth to a boy, Isaac, whose name means "he laughs." Abraham, who once laughed with wonder at the prospect of Isaac's birth (Genesis 17:17), was now surely overcome with astonishment.

God keeps His promises. It is impossible for a ninety-year-old woman to give birth, but God is able to make it so. The promise of an heir to this aged couple called for nothing other than the supernatural gift of life. Without God's divine intervention, there would have been no offspring; there would have been no birth. Similarly, there can be no spiritual life without God's intervention. But by His power there can be new life—true life! From the very beginning, God was teaching His people that it takes a miracle for the gospel to take root in any life.

God keeps His promises. And His promises to His people are many, they are stunning, and they are all yes in Christ (2 Corinthians 1:20). Our part is to do what Abraham learned to do: to trust in God's promises, even when they look far distant or impossible. After all, a promise that faces overwhelming difficulties demands an all-powerful God for its fulfillment—and that is precisely the God that you and I call Father.

Is there someone you know who needs to be reminded that God keeps His promises today? Let's be honest: that is a reminder that we all need. Like Abraham, put your hope in God alone. He is able to keep His promises, and it is only by His power that they will be fulfilled. But you already know that God does miracles, just by looking in the mirror, for it took the same divine power that put the stars in place and that sustains the world to awaken your heart, bring you to faith, and give you eternal life.

GENESIS 15:1-21

MARCH 9

AN OPPORTUNITY TO LEARN

"Take my yoke upon you, and learn from me." MATTHEW 11:29

What does a parent ask their children after they come home from school? Some will ask, "Did you learn anything today?" But many more will say something like, "Did you have fun today?"

With regard to schooling, perhaps it does not matter much which question is asked and which priority is therefore being revealed. But the same question is often asked about church: Did we have *fun* at church today? Did we *enjoy* church?

Instead, we should be asking, "What are we *learning* of and from Jesus?"

Jesus gives us the great privilege of having the opportunity to learn from Him. Throughout the Gospels, He speaks in a way that addresses life's big questions: Who am I? Where did I come from? Why am I here? Where am I going? Does life even matter?

Knowing Christ as personal Lord and Savior changes the way someone thinks about these big topics. It transforms their perspective on time, on resources, on career, on the kind of person they want to marry or the kind of spouse they want to be. It does this because to know Jesus truly is to invite Him to be the authority in life. Everything changes as we learn from Him.

Coming to Jesus begins with learning that Christ died for sins once and for all, the righteous (that's Him) for the unrighteous (that's us), to reconcile us to God (1 Peter 3:18)—and responding to that. Simply having a head knowledge of this is not equal to believing it, trusting it, and being happily yoked to the one who offers us all this.

We all know people who are trying to unscramble the riddle of their lives, putting the pieces of the jigsaw puzzle together as best they can, and we've all been in the same position. But until we are willing to learn from God, the pieces will not fit. But now we can truly know God, not because of our intellectual prowess but because God chooses to make Himself known through the truth of His word.

Are you willing to learn from Jesus in every area of your life? Do you see it as a privilege, and not a burden, to follow His teaching and place yourself under His authority? Be sure to seize every opportunity to learn gospel truth, and may it satisfy your heart's longings and transform your life day by day.

EPHESIANS 4:17 – 5:2

MARCH 10

THE LIE OF ISOLATION

"How long, O LORD? Will you forget me forever? How long will you hide your face from me?" PSALM 13:1

People say time flies when you're having fun. But when things shift into a minor key, life seems to move in slow motion. We find ourselves thinking, "I don't know if I'm ever going to get out of these circumstances. And I don't know how I can endure them."

Psalm 13 contains a recurring question: "How long? How long?" David's circumstances aren't described, but he clearly feels forgotten and forsaken—a feeling we all can relate to. It's akin to what we feel when we lose a loved one or when we feel that we must walk through a valley of trial alone.

To be isolated from human relationships is, without question, crushing. But what David writes of here is even more significant. He's expressing a feeling of isolation from God Himself.

This sentiment is shared by many of God's people throughout Scripture. In Isaiah, God's exiled people cry out, "The LORD has forsaken me; my Lord has forgotten me" (Isaiah 49:14). Christian pilgrims—genuine followers and servants of Jesus—do sometimes feel like saying, "I believe the Lord has actually forgotten us. If He has not forgotten us, if He was still with us, how would we be in this predicament? If He truly was watching over us, surely we would not have to endure these trials."

Yet in David's emerging depression, we discover that his perception (as is often the case with our own) does not reflect reality. And David has the spiritual maturity and humility to acknowledge that what he *feels* is true does not align with what he *knows* is actually true. So he reminds himself of God's steadfast love, His salvation, and His generosity—and resolves to rejoice in those things even as he struggles and suffers (Psalm 13:5-6).

This is the hope-filled tension of the Christian life. We ask, "How long, Lord? Where are you, God?" even as we remind our own hearts that God has not stopped loving us, delivering us, or working in us.

Do not believe the lie of abandonment that your emotions can feed you. Rest in God's comforting response to His forgetful people: "Can a woman forget her nursing child, that she should have no compassion on the son of her womb? Even these may forget, yet I will not forget you. Behold, I have engraved you on the palms of my hands; your walls are continually before me" (Isaiah 49:15-16). God's care for His children is like the sun: it's constant. Even when the clouds obscure it, it's still there. It's always there.

Will you trust in God's constancy today? When you are next feeling forsaken, know that God looks at His hands, engraved with each and every one of His children's names, and He says, *There you are. I have not forgotten you.*

PSALM 13

◇ Bible Through The Year: Job 14–16; 1 Corinthians 6

MARCH 11

AS HE PLANNED

"What do you have that you did not receive? If then you received it, why do you boast as if you did not receive it?" 1 CORINTHIANS 4:7

We call it by different names, disguising it in many ways—but jealousy is often one of the "tolerated" evangelical sins. You are unlikely to find it on a "Top Ten" list of sins that a pastor is warning his church against or mentioned very often when believers share their struggles with each other. It is on God's list, though, and it is often mentioned in the Scriptures. In fact, jealousy is found in the midst of some of the most sordid sinful behaviors that the New Testament epistles address, because it is meant to be taken so seriously (see, for instance, Romans 13:13).

Not much has changed since Paul wrote to the Corinthians. The average local church still contends with far too much chaos and division caused by jealousy—and one of the dangers of jealousy can be the way it causes us to doubt that God knows what He is doing in apportioning gifts.

Everything you have, Paul tells these proud, disunited, envious church members, *you received*—and the Giver of the gifts, the Creator of the universe, does not make mistakes. So how could they—and we—walk around arrogantly as if they would make a better job of being in control of creation? Did we determine our height, girth, speed, or any of our abilities? Who made us unique? God! Our DNA is divinely planned. Our circumstances are exactly as God intends, and He does not make mistakes. Envy is a sin because it is the attitude that suggests that God is not good or does not know what would be for our good. Envy is how idolatry feels.

When we are playing piccolo in the orchestra of life, we may find ourselves looking across at a big tuba a few chairs away, being played with deep, loud notes, and be tempted to say to ourselves, "Nobody can hear me. My sound is not good enough." From there flows a sense of bitterness about our place and a sense of envy of the tuba player's. But ours is the piccolo sound for a reason. It is the instrument we were meant to play—so let's play it with joy and excellence!

In our endeavors to use the gifts God has given, why are we jealous of one another? Why do we let discontentment rob us of the joy He has freely offered? Why do we allow what He has done for someone else to blind us to what He has done for us—not least in giving us eternal riches in His presence? Here is the truth that we each need to rehearse: "God gave to me exactly what I require, I am composed exactly as He planned, and all that He has, and has not, given me is for my good and His glory."

Do not allow jealousy to consume you. Instead, live out joyfully the role for which you were created. For you are His workmanship, recreated in Christ Jesus for good works, which He has prepared for and gifted you to do (Ephesians 2:10). Let that be enough for you today.

1 TIMOTHY 6:6-12

MARCH 12

RADICAL REMORSE

"When Judas, his betrayer, saw that Jesus was condemned, he changed his mind and brought back the thirty pieces of silver to the chief priests and the elders, saying, 'I have sinned by betraying innocent blood' ... He departed, and he went and hanged himself." MATTHEW 27:3-5

What happened to Judas after he betrayed Jesus? "He changed his mind." This phrase has also helpfully been translated, "He was seized with remorse" (NIV). Judas's heart was altered, seemingly instantaneously—and with it, so was his perspective.

The Judas we see in the Garden of Gethsemane, leading a procession of armed men to arrest Jesus with boldness and barefaced animosity, is not the Judas we see here, hours later, before the chief priests and elders. His hardened heart was replaced by a spirit of regret that gripped his soul.

Consider Judas's experience for a moment, and let it be a reminder that sin always offers false hope. The moments before we sin very often feel radically different from those that follow. It's the same drastic change that Adam and Eve felt in the Garden of Eden following their disobedience. All they knew in the moment before eating the fruit, all they anticipated in that act of rebellion, became dust in their mouths (Genesis 3:6-8). In the same way, all that seemed so attractive to Judas in handing over Jesus to His enemies quickly became nothing to him.

When we sin, all of the bewitching, intoxicating influences—all that drew us to rebel—passes away in a moment. What glittered turns out to be fool's gold. Only the naked fact remains: *I have sinned against a holy, loving God.*

With such radical remorse, we have a choice: repent and be reconciled to God, or despair and condemn ourselves. Tragically, Judas chose the latter. His guilt was so great that surely every face he saw accused him, every sound he heard pierced him, every reverberation in his soul condemned him. He attempted to alleviate his guilt by returning his payment to the chief priests—yet lifting the weight of the bag of coins off himself wasn't enough to lift the weight from his heart. Feeling isolated and beyond reach, he died a dreadful death.

Maybe today you're also feeling weighed down by your sin. Maybe you've sought to fix matters yourself, but the weight still bears down. If so, know this: Judas's story doesn't have to be yours. You can turn to Christ. He offers freedom and forgiveness: a yoke that is easy and a burden that is light (Matthew 11:28-30). This is what Christ died for—the redemption of sinful betrayers like Judas.

Judas's example stands as a reminder to us next time sin beckons us. What sins are proving particularly tempting to you at the moment? Remember, how they look beforehand is not how they will feel afterward. For moments of temptation, here is help, and for moments of guilt, here is hope. God's forgiveness stands waiting for our remorse and repentance. All you must do is turn to Him.

PSALM 51

MARCH 13

WITH UTMOST PATIENCE

"The signs of a true apostle were performed among you with utmost patience, with signs and wonders and mighty works." 2 CORINTHIANS 12:12

When we think about the period immediately following Christ's ascension, when the apostles flourished in ministry and the church was born, it's easy to imagine the "signs and wonders and mighty works" that were performed—and to wish we had been there to see them, to have our faith strengthened and our ministry furthered by them.

Without question, both the quality and quantity of supernatural events in that time were special and unrepeatable. The apostles were supernaturally gifted in a way that contemporary Christians are not. It is important to notice, though, that the early church did not make these experiences the touchstone of their faith. We can't focus solely on the miracles and lose sight of their context: those who were filled with God's Spirit were immediately concerned to understand and proclaim God's word, which empowered them to have "utmost patience"—or, as some translations say, "great perseverance"—throughout their lives. What built the church was not so much the miracles of the apostles as the faithful, bold endurance of those apostles.

Paul did not want the focus of his ministry to be on the many marvels he performed or the significant trials he endured but on the resolute faith God had given him and the truths he preached. Observing Paul's ministry, seeing his burdens, and hearing the cries of his heart, it's easy for us to see that the signs and wonders God performed through him were not meant to be flashy exhibitions of Christian showmanship. Rather, they were born out of suffering and adversity, they took place in a life that was stretched to the limits, and they underlined the truth of the message that was being preached.

Knowing this context would have caused Paul's followers to ask not so much how he did such miracles but how he could demonstrate such steadfast faith. How could he carry on with "utmost patience" while suffering? Only by his faith in Jesus Christ and his knowledge of God's word.

What enables us to stand up to tests and to face challenges in the Christian life with patient endurance? Is it miracles? Signs? Wonders? No—while God's special favor may be a help to us at some point, it's actually a solid, experiential grasp of basic Christian doctrine that will undoubtedly be the light to our path when all else seems dark (Psalm 119:105), the root of faith that runs deep, the anchor for our souls (Hebrews 6:19). When God's truth settles in our hearts and minds, we can say with confidence, "How firm a foundation, ye saints of the Lord, is laid for your faith in His excellent word!"[34]

What will sustain you is not outer experiences but inner faith. The Spirit's work within you will always be a greater miracle than anything God may do around you. May others look at you and see not just the wonders He works in your life but also your utmost patience through trials and your obedience to the truth of His word.

JAMES 5:7-11

34 Anon. (possibly Robert Keene), "How Firm a Foundation" (1787).

MARCH 14

EXEMPLARY COMMITMENT

"Joshua the son of Nun and Caleb the son of Jephunneh ... tore their clothes and said to all the congregation of the people of Israel, 'The land, which we passed through to spy it out, is an exceedingly good land. If the LORD delights in us, he will bring us into this land and give it to us, a land that flows with milk and honey.'" NUMBERS 14:6-8

On May 3, 1953, an airliner bound for London from Singapore crashed 22 miles northwest of Kolkata, India, with no survivors. Fred Mitchell, who had become the director of China Inland Mission ten years before, was traveling on that aircraft. In his biography, Fred was described as "an ordinary man from a village home with working-class parents, who spent the greater part of his life as a chemist in the provinces—and who walked with God."[35]

Until Caleb the son of Jephunneh became a spy, appointed by Moses to scope out the land that God had promised to give His people, there was nothing to indicate that he was particularly significant or distinguished, either. But it was almost certainly in those ordinary experiences, along the humdrum track of his life, that God forged and developed the character that is revealed in Numbers 14.

Crisis tends to reveal character. When the Israelite spies came back to report on their discoveries in Canaan, they announced that the cities were fortified, and that "we are not able to go up against the people, for they are stronger than we ... we seemed to ourselves like grasshoppers" (Numbers 13:31, 33). And the people responded by accusing God of bringing them to a land where they would be killed (14:3).

Caleb's commitment to God stands out. He was prepared to resist the tide of popular opinion. When the spies recommended not entering the promised land, he stood against them. When everybody was rebelling against God, he would not join them. He, along with his faithful friend Joshua, were the only men to advise courageous obedience to God.

Caleb was certain of what could be accomplished by God's power. He did not deny the truth of what the other spies had to say; he simply looked at it from a different perspective. He was confident not in his ability nor in the ability of the Israelites but in the power of God and the trustworthiness of His character. He was a man of faith in the midst of fear. He knew that a grasshopper helped by God is a grasshopper that can do great things.

Although we may feel that our lives are simply routine, we can always seek God in the ordinary. In the most mundane moments, He will forge our character so that we too can become people of courage in all circumstances. God is not looking for giants through whom to achieve His plans. He is looking for ordinary people who are prepared to trust Him, step out in faith, and courageously obey. There is nothing to stop you being that person today.

NUMBERS 13:25 – 14:25

35 Phyllis Thompson, *Climbing on Track: A Biography of Fred Mitchell* (China Inland Mission, 1953), p 12.

MARCH 15

THE ETERNAL PLAN OF GOD

"Blessed be the God and Father of our Lord Jesus Christ, who has blessed us in Christ with every spiritual blessing in the heavenly places, even as he chose us in him before the foundation of the world, that we should be holy and blameless before him." EPHESIANS 1:3-4

The Bible gives no direct answer as to why God allowed the fall to happen in the Garden of Eden. It simply states that God is in control of all things—even of that.

In Paul's letter to the Ephesians, however, we are given a glimpse into God's eternal plan. We see that God was at work before our world existed and was not caught off guard by the fall. When the kingdom was spoiled as a result of Adam and Eve's rebellion, God already knew it would happen. Before Adam and Eve were created, before they were disobedient, God had already planned the rescue.

When we think about God's rescue mission, which ultimately culminated in the cross, we ought not to see it as something supplied in a moment of crisis. Rather, we should see the cross as grounded in the eternal mind of God, who had determined from all of eternity to call a people to Himself through Jesus and to restore under Him everything that would be spoiled by the fall.

God's purpose in this plan was and is "in accordance with his pleasure and will," and it is "to the praise of his glorious grace" (Ephesians 1:5-6, NIV). The motivation in God's eternal plan was not only a desire to make men and women happy—although men and women *do* become ultimately happy as a result—but a concern for His name. He was determined that everything should be brought under the feet and control of His Son, the Lord Jesus, as it ought to be. Thus, God's eternal plan of redemption is about Him rather than all about us. It concerns us. It transforms us. But it is all about God. Until the gospel moves us to praise Him and live for Him, we have not properly understood it.

God is this world's center. Since the fall, men and women have refused to accept His authority and instead expend their energies in trying to depose Him, with catastrophic results. There is no part of this present life that is not covered with the dust of death, because man has determined that he does not like the idea of God at the center.

Will you readjust your life and acknowledge God's right to oversee every aspect of it? Will you live for His praise rather than yours and for His cause rather than yours? The paradox is this: it is in seeking His glory instead of your own that you will experience the joy that comes from making your life orbit around the Son—joy from living the way that God planned for you and all creation from eternity.

EPHESIANS 1:3-14

MARCH 16

COMFORT FOR A TROUBLED MIND

"By God's power [you] are being guarded through faith for a salvation ready to be revealed in the last time. In this you rejoice, though now for a little while, if necessary, you have been grieved by various trials." 1 PETER 1:5-6

There are two things we need to acknowledge about suffering—namely, that it *does* exist and it *does* hurt. Affliction is a reality in everyone's life at one time or another. Such affliction takes on many forms, not the least of which is mental suffering.

When writing to fellow believers about suffering, Peter recognized that there are many and various ways in which we can be grieved. The specific sorrow that Peter's first readers were burdened by was the mental anguish that comes from enduring hardship—but Peter was fully aware that there are all kinds of trials that buffet our minds and crush our spirits.

Because of the gospel, Peter doesn't have to end on a note of hopelessness and despair. Instead, he gives us promises to which we can cling.

First of all, Peter reminds us that our trials last only "a little while." Now, "a little while" needs to be understood in the light of eternity; even a lifetime is "a little while" compared to forever! Thus, a long period of suffering in this life is still, in God's economy and in the framework of His plan and purpose for His children, "a little while." That is not to say that such suffering will *feel* brief—especially when we are in the midst of it. For many, suffering means that a minute can seem like a day, a day can seem like a year, and a year can seem as if it's never going to end. But we can and must cling to this promise: our current misery is not our eternal end. Suffering may fill your life today, but one day, "in the last time," salvation will.

Secondly, we are able to say with confidence that in every moment of suffering, God is present. In the account of Saul of Tarsus's conversion we find Jesus intimately identifying with His people's suffering: he says, "Saul, Saul, why are you persecuting *me*?" (Acts 9:4, emphasis added). How could Jesus say "me" when He was in heaven? It was because, through the Spirit, Christ was present with His people. He stood in solidarity with them. His Spirit was with them, guarding them as they walked through valleys toward their day of final salvation. He does the same for us.

You have in the Lord Jesus a Great High Priest who is perfectly able to sympathize with your sufferings (Hebrews 4:15). When you're tempted to believe the lies that God has abandoned you or that no one else understands where you've been or what you're going through, you can be confident in this: there's "no throb nor throe that our hearts can know, but He feels it above."[36] And you can be confident in this, too: one day the sorrow will be behind, and only glory will lie ahead. That is a truth in which you can rejoice today, whatever today may hold.

1 PETER 1:3-9

36 William E. Littlewood, "There Is No Love Like the Love of Jesus" (1857).

MARCH 17

DELIVERED BY PRAYER

"I know that through your prayers and the help of the Spirit of Jesus Christ this will turn out for my deliverance." PHILIPPIANS 1:19

Are there people in your life for whom you don't pray because you think they don't need it? With our limited human perspective, it can be easy to overlook those who appear on the outside to have it all together. But the truth is, we all need and benefit from the prayers of others.

When the apostle Paul was in prison, he wrote to the Philippian church and said that he knew his deliverance would be the result not only of the Holy Spirit's help but also of the prayers of God's people. Whether he meant deliverance from his immediate hardships or the ultimate deliverance that would bring him into Christ's presence, Paul wanted his Christian friends in Philippi to know that he was dependent on others' prayers to sustain him during his ministry.

This was not unique to this congregation. When Paul wrote to the Christians at Rome, he said the same thing: "I appeal to you, brothers, by our Lord Jesus Christ and by the love of the Spirit, to strive together with me in your prayers to God on my behalf, that I may be delivered" (Romans 15:30-31). He longed for them to strive together and be refreshed. He desired that his service would be helpful to the saints. He wanted to be delivered. And all of this, he told them, could be accomplished through their prayers! As the great Victorian preacher C.H. Spurgeon once said, prayer is the rope that rings the bell in the belfry of God.[37] Under God's providence, it unleashes His pattern and plan and power.

Cry out to God—that is what Paul is urging us to do. If we want to see the Spirit of God move in a way that can only be described as supernatural, we must first be willing to earnestly, humbly, and continually pray. Paul's words tell us that as we rally with other saints, we can support them in their weaknesses. We can ask that they be granted courage. We can play a role in their deliverance.

So, who do you know who does need your prayers? Will you pray for them—diligently, boldly, and persistently? And who do you know who does not appear to need your prayers? Well, they do! Will you pray for them in just the same way?

PHILIPPIANS 1:3-11

37 *Feathers for Arrows: or, Illustrations for Preachers and Teachers, from My Note Book* (Passmore & Alabaster, 1870), p 171.

MARCH 18

THE CONQUERING LION

"I began to weep loudly because no one was found worthy to open the scroll or to look into it. And one of the elders said to me, 'Weep no more; behold, the Lion of the tribe of Judah, the Root of David, has conquered, so that he can open the scroll and its seven seals.' And between the throne and the four living creatures and among the elders I saw a Lamb standing, as though it had been slain."

REVELATION 5:4-6

As children, many of us heard our parents say, "Did you remember to...?" One example that I remember hearing often when I returned from someone's house was "Did you remember to say thank you?" I didn't need a fresh revelation; I simply needed to remember.

As he watched the vision Jesus gave him of heavenly reality, the apostle John was brought to tears when confronted by the fear that there was no one who could look into the secrets of the world and explain the troubles of his first-century experience. But John did not need new information. He needed to be reminded of what he already knew. He had erred by forgetting the basics.

John was told not to weep but to look to the one who could open the scroll. When he turned, he saw "a Lamb standing, as though it had been slain." The Lamb's wounds were a reminder of Christ's death, by which He has achieved salvation. But this Lamb was standing, representing the triumph of His resurrection. Here, in this vision, we see Jesus, the all-merciful and all-powerful one. He is the Lamb, and He is the Lion. He deserves and demands the worship and obedience of all the world, and He will have it.

Jesus was the solution to John's tears, just as He is to our own tears of fearfulness when we feel the world pressing in against us—when we feel worn down, small, weak, and marginalized, and when we are tempted to believe that this world, rather than being under control, is governed only by chaos.

None of us know what a day will bring or what will happen during a night. These secrets belong to God alone. But what great grace we experience when God gives us a tap on the shoulder and turns us to our Bibles, saying, *Are you forgetting that the Lion of the tribe of Judah has actually triumphed, that He is in charge, that He oversees the future, that He is King?* "Fear not," Jesus had already told John: "I am the first and the last, and the living one. I died, and behold I am alive forevermore and I have the keys of Death and Hades" (Revelation 1:17-18).

So when you feel discouraged or defeated or troubled by the present or the future, the call is simply this: remember what you already know. Look to the Lion of Judah, who is for us the slain Lamb. He is worthy and able to open the scrolls and direct the history of this world to its end: to His return and our entry into glory.

REVELATION 5

MARCH 19

THE TRUE PROPHETIC VOICE

"They have healed the wound of my people lightly, saying, 'Peace, peace,' when there is no peace." JEREMIAH 8:11

When faced with a serious medical condition, none of us want to receive treatment from an incompetent doctor. Imagine going to a physician whose remedy for gangrene is simply to put a nice bandage on it, offer you a sticker for your troubles, and tell you to have a pleasant afternoon. That may make you feel better, but it would not treat the problem—and soon enough you would feel considerably worse!

In the Old Testament era, the prophets' role was to speak God's word and call God's people to obey His covenant. God would put His word into the prophets' mouths, and they would announce what God said—not what they themselves had in mind. And often, their message was *Look out! Judgment's coming*. Not exactly an agreeable declaration!

Because God's message was so challenging, false prophets became numerous—and in a way, they had the best of both worlds. They were known as prophets and could go around making great statements, and yet they could also tell people whatever they wanted to hear. The false prophet was like a bad doctor, telling the people that everything would turn out fine when, in reality, the prognosis was grim. It is marvelous to hear that all is well and that your land is one of peace—unless the enemy is about to appear over the horizon. Then, you need to be prepared.

While true prophets spoke of God's coming judgment, their message also warned the people against complacency and encouraged them against despair. God has always guaranteed His commitment to His people, promising a wonderful future for them. Their only hope in the face of judgment would be in finding refuge not *apart* from God but *in* God.

False prophets still abound in our time. Their words are heard in the flattery of the average commencement speaker: "You are the greatest group of young people this community has ever seen. The future is in your hands. You're ready to soar!" But similarly shallow words are also spoken in far too many churches, with teaching that consists of vague generalities and supposedly inspiring half-truths for the hearers—and a half-truth is also a half-lie. So we need true prophetic voices in our day as much as God's people did in Jeremiah's. Our churches, and our nation and world, need those who have the courage to speak truth, even if it brings mockery and rejection: to speak of sin, to insist that God has ethical standards, to warn of judgment, to announce Jesus' future return, and therefore to be able to point compellingly to the only one who can save.

Ask God to raise up individuals who are prepared to challenge their hearers with God's word and in submission to God's Spirit. Pray that when you hear God's word truly preached through such a voice, you would guard yourself against complacency, be willing to listen, and be ready to take refuge in God, your only hope. And pray that in your neighborhood and your workplace you would be that voice.

1 THESSALONIANS 5:1-11

MARCH 20

GRACIOUS GRATITUDE

"Being strengthened with all power, according to his glorious might, for all endurance and patience with joy; giving thanks to the Father, who has qualified you to share in the inheritance of the saints in light." COLOSSIANS 1:11-12

Almost everyone appreciates a good gift. Family, freedom, leisure, a warm bed, and a refreshing drink all make for a grateful heart, and we're all naturally able to express at least some measure of gratitude for them. "Thank you" is a phrase we learn young.

The American revivalist Jonathan Edwards helpfully distinguished between what he referred to as "natural gratitude" and "gracious gratitude."[38] Natural gratitude starts with the things we're given and the benefits which accompany them. Anybody is capable of natural gratitude. Gracious gratitude, though, is very different, and only God's children can experience and express it. Gracious gratitude recognizes the character, goodness, love, power, and excellencies of God, regardless of any gifts or enjoyments He has given. It knows we have reason to be grateful to God whether it's a good day or a bad day, whether we're employed or unemployed, whether the daily news is upbeat or overwhelming, whether we're completely healthy or facing a terminal diagnosis. Such gratitude is only discovered by grace, and it is a true mark of the Holy Spirit in a person's life. Gracious gratitude enables us to face all things with the awareness that God is profoundly involved in our lives and circumstances, for He has made us special objects of His love.

When Jonathan Edwards died as a result of a smallpox vaccination, Sarah, his wife, wrote to their daughter, "What shall I say? A holy and good God has covered us with a dark cloud." Notice the honesty in that. There's no superficial triumphalism. But her husband was not taken out by chance; it was the overruling sovereignty of God that determined the right time to bring Jonathan home to his eternal reward. And so Sarah continued, "But my God lives; and he has my heart … We are all given to God: and there I am, and love to be."[39]

Amid grief, we will never be able to speak words like these from natural gratitude, which cannot help us in loss. Such reflection can only flow from gracious gratitude. You may be facing difficult or even heartbreaking circumstances at the moment; and if you are not, then that day will come, for this is a fallen world. But in those moments, you can cling to God's love and choose to trust God's goodness, expressed most clearly at the cross. Then, even in the darkest hours, you will know the joy of His presence and always have cause to give thanks to Him. There is strength, dignity, and worship in being able to say, "The LORD gave, and the LORD has taken away; blessed be the name of the LORD" (Job 1:21).

ROMANS 11:33-36

38 "A Treatise Concerning Religious Affections, in Three Parts," in *The Works of Jonathan Edwards,* ed. Sereno Dwight, revised and corrected by Edward Hickman (1834; reprinted Banner of Truth, 1979), 1:276.

39 Sarah Pierpont Edwards to Esther Burr, April 3, 1758, in *Memoirs of Jonathan Edwards* by Sereno Dwight, in Edwards, *Works,* 1:clxxix.

MARCH 21

WHY THE DELAY?

"Long ago, at many times and in many ways, God spoke to our fathers by the prophets, but in these last days he has spoken to us by his Son, whom he appointed the heir of all things, through whom also he created the world." HEBREWS 1:1-2

There are many ways in which to describe the times we live in: 21st-century, post-modern, globalized, technological. But foundationally and fundamentally, we live in the "last days." This phrase can sound very strange or exciting, depending on its familiarity. Indeed, there can be a great deal of confusion surrounding the idea of the "last days."

The New Testament uses this phrase simply to describe the time between the first and second coming of Jesus. Jesus *has* come, and Jesus *will* come, and we live between those two great staging posts in salvation history. His first appearance brought His kingdom to earth and ushered in the "last days" as a present reality. His life, death, resurrection, and ascension all point to God's Spirit at work—and if God's Spirit is at work, Jesus teaches, "then the kingdom of God has come" (Matthew 12:28). Jesus therefore speaks in the present tense when He invites a crowd to "receive the kingdom of God" (Mark 10:15; Luke 18:17). He is talking about an entry not into some future realm but into a present reality—the current rule and reign of Jesus Himself.

So the kingdom is *now*. But the kingdom is also *then*: something that we look forward to in the future, fully inaugurated by the return of the Lord Jesus. At His second coming, Jesus will fully establish His kingdom. At that time, He will welcome believers to "inherit the kingdom prepared for you from the foundation of the world" (Matthew 25:34) and "the earth shall be full of the knowledge of the Lord as the waters cover the sea" (Isaiah 11:9). The kingdom that first arrived with its King in the past will fully come in all its perfection and glory in the future.

The Christian, therefore, lives in this in-between dimension referred to as the "last days." Those who are in Christ belong to the new creation but have not yet received all of that new creation's benefits and blessings. For the time being, believers live in the present age, in a fallen world marked by sin, longing for the age to come.

Why, then, does the time between Christ's first and second comings seem so long? It is because God has deliberately delayed Jesus' return so that more people have the opportunity to hear the words He has spoken, to repent, and to believe (2 Peter 3:9). The last days are the days of opportunity to enter the kingdom before the door is closed.

Since we know in which age we live and whose arrival will bring it to a conclusion, "what sort of people ought [we] to be?" (2 Peter 3:11). Scripture tells us: "Make every effort to be found spotless, blameless and at peace with him. Bear in mind that our Lord's patience means salvation" (v 14-15, NIV). In other words, if "the last days" draw to a close today and the Lord Jesus returns in His glory, make sure that you will be found living in a way that pleases Him and seeking ways to speak words that proclaim Him.

LUKE 17:20-37

MARCH 22

MAJESTIC SURRENDER

"Judas, having procured a band of soldiers and some officers from the chief priests and the Pharisees, went there with lanterns and torches and weapons. Then Jesus, knowing all that would happen to him, came forward and said to them, 'Whom do you seek?' They answered him, 'Jesus of Nazareth.' Jesus said to them, 'I am he' ... They drew back and fell to the ground." JOHN 18:3-6

The Gospel writers all cover similar events from Jesus' life, but each highlights particular details and aspects of Jesus' identity. One of John's intentions was to establish Jesus' supremacy and victory over the very circumstances that were meant to degrade and humiliate Him. Consider Jesus' arrest in the Garden of Gethsemane: He surrendered willingly but authoritatively, revealing His majesty as Savior of the world. Once, people had tried to force a king's crown upon Jesus, and He had withdrawn because He knew that worldly kingship was not His destiny (John 6:15). Here, when the soldiers came to force a cross upon Him, He knew all that would unfold. They were surely expecting to have to search far and wide for this notorious Galilean carpenter. Instead, here He was, willingly surrendering, with a majesty in His voice, a look in His eye, and a bearing about His person that contributed to the magnitude of the moment. No wonder they "drew back and fell to the ground."

When Jesus surrendered Himself to those who would treat Him as a blasphemer and a criminal, He did not deny who He was. In fact, He used language that communicated His divine identity and authority. Jesus used the phrase "I am" not only to tell the soldiers He was Jesus of Nazareth but also to identify Himself as the one who had appeared to Moses at the burning bush (Exodus 3:14). This was the same phrase that had, months earlier, seen Him nearly stoned (John 8:58-59), for it was a clear claim to be the self-existent, living God. Now here is this God, stepping forward to stop His friends resisting and allow His enemies to kill Him. Why? As Christ came forward in the garden, He was not only protecting His disciples but also providing for His people. He stepped forth as the substitute for sinful humans, as the fulfillment of all that had long been anticipated. He knew exactly what He stepped toward: "Christ also suffered once for sins, the righteous for the unrighteous, that he might bring us to God" (1 Peter 3:18).

In His combination of willing surrender and divine authority Christ took the next step toward the cross, where His sacrifice won our salvation. He did not run from the cross but rather walked resolutely toward it. And He did that for you.

It is a thing most wonderful,
Almost too wonderful to be,
That God's own Son should come from heaven,
And die to save a child like me.[40]

JOHN 18:1-14

40 William W. How, "It Is a Thing Most Wonderful" (1872).

MARCH 23

EVERY GOOD AND PERFECT GIFT

"Every good gift and every perfect gift is from above, coming down from the Father of lights, with whom there is no variation or shadow due to change."
JAMES 1:17

Have you ever been shopping for a gift and had no idea what the intended recipient needed or wanted? You didn't know what size or color of sweater to buy or if the child's toy was age-appropriate, so eventually you just threw your hands up in frustration and said, "I'll just buy something! They'll take it back anyway. Who cares?"

Gift giving is not always as easy or joyful as it should be. The fact of the matter is, even the best of us can't give perfect gifts every time because we are flawed. We lack the insight and the knowledge, and sometimes the resources or even the willingness, to give the right gift. In this we are utterly different than God, for God is the giver of perfect gifts, and *only* perfect gifts. He is spontaneously good and overflows with generosity. He gives without expecting anything in return, and He doesn't restrict His goodness based on what the recipients deserve. And no gift from Him ever needs to be returned.

Not only is God perfectly generous, but that generosity never changes. Even the best earthly parents need to be approached at the right time and in the right way because they can be inconsistent. Children learn to choose their moments. As a teen, I found it easy to read my father's body language while he was on hold with the electric company and think, "I'm not sure now is the time to ask for two new tires for my car."

With our heavenly Father, though, we don't need to wonder if it's ok to approach Him. He is neither fickle nor quick to anger. We can be confident that He will always act appropriately. We will never find Him unaware, unable, unavailable, or unwilling. Through Christ, He is accessible and responsive to our hearts' pleas and our daily concerns.

We are children of God, and one of the ways our Father expresses His love for us is in His perfect gifts to us. Therefore, a mark of every one of His children should be gratitude. If we know our Father's character, how can we be anything other than grateful—even when His gifts are not the ones we would have chosen ourselves? So, be careful to count your blessings, daily. Remember that all good things are gifts from Him. Be sure to say to Him:

Great is Thy faithfulness, O God my Father,
There is no shadow of turning with Thee …
All I have needed Thy hand hath provided—
Great is Thy faithfulness, Lord, unto me![41]

PSALM 103

41 Thomas O. Chisholm, "Great Is Thy Faithfulness" (1923).

MARCH 24

THE FOLLY OF FAVORITISM

"Israel loved Joseph more than any other of his sons, because he was the son of his old age. And he made him a robe of many colors. But when his brothers saw that their father loved him more than all his brothers, they hated him and could not speak peacefully to him." GENESIS 37:3-4

Favoritism in relationships is folly.

We see this throughout the story of God's people in the Old Testament, but it is perhaps writ largest in the life of Joseph, for he was the object of his father Jacob's special interest. Joseph "was the son of [Jacob's] old age" and of his great lifetime love, Rachel. So Jacob, whom God had renamed Israel, loved this son more than the others. From this root of partiality sprang much bad fruit in this family.

Jacob expressed his favoritism through a gift, a "robe of many colors" which he himself had made. It was clearly a token of favoritism—one that Joseph obviously enjoyed wearing. This controversial coat provoked intense hostility from Joseph's brothers. From their hostility sprang malice and murderous intent. They eventually went as far as selling their own brother into slavery and faking his death.

If the gift of a coat could incite such a response, then surely the problem was far greater than the coat itself. There must have been deep-seated sin behind the scenes. And that's exactly what we find with Joseph's brothers. Their issue was not so much that the coat was very valuable; it was that it set Joseph in a different class from them. In giving him this gift, Jacob had elevated Joseph above his siblings, and this gnawed away at them. The choice of a favorite always necessitates the implicit choice of a non-favorite, which is a trigger for both arrogance and pride in the one chosen as the favorite and for resentment and bitterness in those who are not. You may have seen around you, or even in your own life, the corrosive effects of either being a favorite or being passed over for that status.

Jacob should have known better for he himself had been the object of undue favoritism—his own mother had preferred him over his brother, Esau, and it had led to chaos. His relationship with Esau, like Joseph's with his brothers, was damaged for years.

Let us not be too quick, though, to distance ourselves from the mindset and actions of Jacob or of his sons, as if we could never be guilty of something similar. We must all beware the folly of favoritism in relationships and the fury which so often accompanies it. Partiality is a common and understandable error, but it casts deep, dark, destructive shadows.

Rather than simply shake our heads at Jacob's foolishness, let's learn from it. Every relationship is a unique gift from God. To the degree that we show favoritism to those around us, for whatever reason it might be, we can be assured that it will fracture and devastate relationships. If, however, we cherish each friend, family member, and neighbor with obvious love and affection, we honor God and encourage the hearts of those He has placed around us.

GENESIS 37

MARCH 25

THINKING CHRISTIANLY

"Finally, brothers, whatever is true, whatever is honorable, whatever is just, whatever is pure, whatever is lovely, whatever is commendable, if there is any excellence, if there is anything worthy of praise, think about these things."
PHILIPPIANS 4:8

In many ways, we are what we think. Our minds are the root of our actions, and it is through our minds that our affections are stirred. Therefore, it is absolutely imperative that we think about the right things and that we learn to think in the right way. In other words, we must learn to think Christianly.

Some people would say that to think Christianly is to have a mind that only contemplates explicitly Christian topics, closing itself to every other notion. But this doesn't fit the description of Christian thinking that we find in Scripture. The Bible teaches that we actually ought to think about *everything*, but that we need to learn to do so from a biblical perspective (2 Corinthians 10:5). We should consider music, engineering, medicine, art, justice, freedom, and love—the whole gamut of human existence—through the lens of the revealed truths of God's word.

The apostle Paul understood this, so he gave us a list of qualities with which to construct the framework of our thinking. As followers of Christ, Paul said, our thoughts ought to be directed and governed by qualities like truth, honor, justice, and purity.

We are, he says, to think about those things in which there is "any excellence." The word he uses for "excellence" is the Greek word *areté*, which is the most comprehensive word in the Greek language for "virtue." In other words, Paul gives us the standard against which we can judge our thought patterns on a regular basis. We can look to God's word and ask, "Is what I am choosing to think about, and the way that I am choosing to think about it, in line with moral excellence? Is it in line with God's approval?"

What a challenge this is! This manner of thinking won't happen in a vacuum or without plenty of effort. If we hope to cultivate it, we must meditate on God's word day and night (Joshua 1:8). As we continually strive to be transformed by the renewal of our minds (Romans 12:2), we will not only glorify God but also be strengthened in our ability to contend for the gospel in our conversations.

So, as you think about your thoughts, here are three questions to ask as you seek to apply this verse in your life:

Is there anything I should think about more?

Is there anything I should think about less, or not at all?

Is there anything I should think about differently?

PSALM 1

MARCH 26

KEEPING OURSELVES IN GOD'S LOVE

"Keep yourselves in the love of God, waiting for the mercy of our Lord Jesus Christ that leads to eternal life." JUDE 21

Even though God is perfectly able to "keep you from stumbling" and cause you to persevere in the faith (Jude 24), He still calls you to play an active role in keeping going in the Christian life—that is, to keep yourself in His love.

Pursuing God's love ought to be a constant in our lives. This is why the Bible has so much to say about it! There is no coasting in the walk of faith; our faith won't be strengthened on its own. What does it look like, then, to keep ourselves in God's love?

First, Scripture teaches us that to preserve our love for God, we must remain in constant hatred of all sin (see Proverbs 8:13; Psalm 97:10; Romans 12:9). Start to play with sin, encourage it, or allow yourself to be excited by it and your love for God will inevitably decay.

Second, we can foster our love for God by delighting in the ordinances He gave the church. Jesus instituted Communion, for instance, as a means of Him meeting with us in a particular way, showing Himself to us that we might know His love and love Him too. It is impossible for us to keep ourselves in a healthy relationship with God while disengaging ourselves from the means of grace that He established.

Third, we need to remember that keeping ourselves in God's love is not only an individual pursuit but also a corporate endeavor. We come to Christ individually, but we do not live in Him solitarily. Like living stones, we are being built up into a spiritual house in order that we might be a holy priesthood of believers (1 Peter 2:5). Cultivating deep and honest friendships with others who love God helps *us* love God. Relationships are seldom neutral. If we desire to grow in our faith, we must seek the company of godly friends.

Growing in our faith demands action and accountability—but it also requires patience as we wait "for the mercy of our Lord Jesus Christ that leads to eternal life." We are meant to pursue a growing relationship with our heavenly Father, turning from sin and enjoying His gifts alongside others who have a new nature and are indwelt with the Holy Spirit, as we eagerly await the redemption of our bodies and the perfect completion of God's purposes (Romans 8:23).

So, "work out your own salvation with fear and trembling, for it is God who works in you" (Philippians 2:12-13). We do not work for our salvation, but we do work it out, in all areas of our life. What sin must you fight? In what way must you pursue deep Christian friendship? Keep yourself in the love of God.

1 JOHN 5:12-21

MARCH 27

SAVED BY SACRIFICE

"The blood shall be a sign for you, on the houses where you are. And when I see the blood, I will pass over you, and no plague will befall you to destroy you, when I strike the land of Egypt." EXODUS 12:13

What happens in Communion? Why do Christians eat the bread and drink from the cup?

As we seek to answer these questions, not many of us think to look back to Moses. If we stand too close to his story, all we'll have is a truncated view of the bulrushes, burning bush, and plagues. But if we step far enough back, we will see and be able to share the glory of God's big picture.

To set in motion the exodus of His people Israel, God, passing through the land in judgment, sent the last of ten plagues on Egypt, and every firstborn Egyptian was killed. The Israelite firstborns also would have died, for they were not innocent of sin, and sin leads to death (Romans 6:23). But God provided a way of escape for them through the Passover. When the Lord saw the blood of a sacrificed lamb on a doorframe, painted up using a hyssop plant (Exodus 12:22), He passed over that household.

In the Old Testament, this passing over was the great act of God's salvation. In and through it, God taught His people a vital principle: *God saves by substitution*. He saved these people because animals were sacrificed in their place. As Moses records, that night in Egypt "there was not a house where someone was not dead" (Exodus 12:30). A son had died, or a lamb had died. God's people deserved death for their sins, but because they trusted in the sacrifice of another, as God had commanded and that God had provided, they were delivered. Every year throughout Old Testament history, God's people looked back to this event and remembered that great truth: God saves by substitution.

All those years and all those feasts underline the significance of the moment when, as John the Baptist saw Jesus coming, he said, "Behold, the Lamb of God, who takes away the sin of the world!" (John 1:29). Here was someone who was God's provision to save His people from sin and set His people free, just like the Passover lamb.

Israel's exodus is a foreshadowing of mankind's great exodus: when men or women, deserving God's judgment, trust in the blood that was shed on their behalf on the cross, they find freedom from sin. Every shackle is broken, just as the Israelites' chains were shed when they were set free from slavery.

Next time you are thinking about Communion, consider the story of Moses, the burning bush, and the plagues. Then connect the dots and remember that the reason we take Communion is because Jesus is our sacrifice. He is the Lamb of God. He is your substitute. You have no judgment to fear, for it lies behind you, paid and dealt with at the cross. You are on the way to the promised land.

JOHN 19:16b-37

MARCH 28

A SOLID DIET

"You have become dull of hearing ... You need someone to teach you again the basic principles of the oracles of God. You need milk, not solid food, for everyone who lives on milk is unskilled in the word of righteousness, since he is a child. But solid food is for the mature." HEBREWS 5:11-14

Imagine visiting your favorite restaurant and noticing that all the patrons are seated at their tables drinking milk from large baby bottles. What a bizarre scene that would be! Yet this is the picture that the writer of Hebrews painted when he urged the Jewish Christians of his day to remain hungry for greater and greater Christlikeness. He knew that many were already becoming complacent in their faith. Those who should have already been teachers instead needed to review their ABCs all over again.

The difficulty for these believers with understanding biblical principles resulted from neither any complex subject matter nor the writer's inability to clearly explain. Rather, they were willfully slow to learn. When the author writes that they were "dull of hearing," the word for "dull" is the same one he uses later when warning them not to be "sluggish" (Hebrews 6:12). There he exhorts his readers, instead of tolerating such a slothful attitude, to be "imitators of those who through faith and patience inherit the promises."

Had these early Christians been dutiful souls who were listening carefully and trying hard to grasp biblical concepts, and simply having difficulty doing so, the writer likely would not have been so stern with them. But this wasn't the case. He found himself reprimanding church members who should have been eagerly receiving the truth but had become apathetic. Their enthusiasm had waned. They had ceased to pay attention. As a result, they failed to understand, which prevented them from being further transformed by God's truth.

If we are not vigilant, the same could become true of us. We cannot sustain ourselves on a diet of Rice Krispies, toast, and milk. It's ok to like milk. It's ok to have it as part of our diet. But it is not ok to drink it as the sum total of our intake. That is for babies, and we are not to stay babies. We must learn to eat more nutritious food and expand our palate.

Make it your goal to continually "grow in the grace and knowledge of our Lord" (2 Peter 3:18), so that you can grapple with the implications of genuine Christian experience. Do not be someone who listens to the good news of the gospel being proclaimed and says in their mind, "Oh, I know that. I can tune out now." Do not be someone who considers Sunday morning's sermon sufficient spiritual food to last the week. Do not be someone who splashes in the shallows and never makes the effort to dive down deep into the riches of God's word. Be someone who loves the gospel and who, by God's grace, never grows tired of hearing it; and who loves God's word—loves to drink it in and chew it over, and is stirred by its truth again and again as you become more and more like its great subject, our Lord and Savior.

PSALM 119:33-48

MARCH 29

THE TRUE ISRAEL

"When Israel was a child, I loved him, and out of Egypt I called my son. The more they were called, the more they went away; they kept sacrificing to the Baals and burning offerings to idols." HOSEA 11:1-2

When Jesus was born, Mary and Joseph took Him to Egypt to protect Him from King Herod's persecution. When Matthew records that event, he includes these words from Hosea, made over seven centuries before, and explains that they were in fact a prophecy that Jesus fulfilled (Matthew 2:13-15). But Hosea's words weren't referencing an individual, but rather a nation ("they were called ... they went away... they kept sacrificing"). We may think, then, that here is a rather cavalier use of Scripture by Matthew.

But Matthew knows exactly what he's doing. He is deliberately identifying Jesus with Israel. As God had called His beloved people—His "son"—out of Egypt to worship Him in the promised land, so now, Matthew says, God was calling His one and only begotten Son, the Lord Jesus, out of Egypt and back to the promised land. Jesus, though, was different. Like the Israelites, He was tempted in the wilderness, but unlike the Israelites, He didn't sin (Matthew 4:1-11; see also Exodus 32:1-6). Jesus is the true Israel, the true Son.

At the outset of His ministry, Jesus chose twelve disciples (Matthew 10:1-4). This was significant: by choosing twelve, Jesus made a statement. He, the true Israel, was calling to Himself people to be part of a new Israel. His twelve disciples, rather than the twelve tribes of Israel, were now its foundation. In that choice, the focus of God's people was and is realigned. Since then, the true Israel is not found in what's now called the Middle East, nor does it consist only of the biological descendants of Abraham. Instead, it comprises Abraham's spiritual descendants, both Jew and Gentile. God's children are those who follow Abraham's example by placing their trust in God's promises, which are fulfilled in Jesus.

The promise, says Paul, "depends on faith" and will always "rest on grace" (Romans 4:16). It doesn't matter whether you are a Jew or a Gentile, rich or poor, male or female. It doesn't matter who you are or what you have done. The same principle always applies: "If you are Christ's, then you are Abraham's offspring, heirs according to promise" (Galatians 3:29). We are "all one in Christ" (v 28). The gospel is the same for all, for the ground is level at the foot of the cross. Religious and moral people are in need of the same salvation as someone who never attends church and has lived with no regard for any standard or creed. We have only one story to tell, but it is the only story we, or anyone, needs.

We are undeniably imperfect. We, like the first Israel, are prone to wander from our Father and to worship idols. But Jesus, the perfectly righteous one, the better and true Israel, died to bear our sins that we might come and cast ourselves upon His mercy. We have been gathered into His great company, into the framework of the true kingdom of Israel, not because of who we are or what we've done but because of who He is and what He's done. Today, through faith in Christ Jesus, you are a child of God, as beloved as He was and is (Galatians 3:26).

MATTHEW 4:1-11

Bible Through The Year: Proverbs 16–18; Titus 3

MARCH 30

ENDLESS PROFIT

"Whoever would save his life will lose it, but whoever loses his life for my sake will find it. For what will it profit a man if he gains the whole world and forfeits his soul?" MATTHEW 16:25-26

Jesus was an expert at asking questions—especially the sort of questions that made people stop in their tracks and pay attention. When we are confronted with Jesus' questions, as the disciples were here, we must be careful not to sidestep their intended effect.

At first glance, Jesus' question regarding material gain at the expense of our souls might be understood primarily as a warning of impending punishment on the selfish individual. We're tempted to read Jesus' question in a way that likens Him to a mother who says to her child, "Now, if you don't share with your sister, you know what'll happen!" But this particular question is more along the lines of an observation. Jesus is pointing out what happens when we orient our lives and decisions around our own sinful longings—around our possessions, our accomplishments, our desired identity. To live in such a way, He says, is to forfeit your very life.

The loss of life of which Jesus is speaking here is therefore both immediate and eternal. If we regard life as nothing more than what we can get out of it for ourselves, we actually miss out on its greatest joys; we end up merely existing, not actually living. Furthermore, when we place ourselves on the throne of our life, we remove Jesus from His rightful place and affirm the reality that by nature we prefer to pursue the world rather than to forsake our desires in pursuit of Christ. If we continue in this way, we will forfeit the gift of eternal life that He loves to give to His subjects.

So how are we to combat worldly desires in the here and now? First, we must recognize that, as the 17th-century mathematician and theologian Blaise Pascal put it, we have a God-shaped hole at the deepest level of our being, and nothing can fill this void save God Himself. We exist not to pursue fleeting pleasures but to enjoy relationship with the living God. Then second, we must continually reflect on the value of our souls as evidenced in the cruel scene outside Jerusalem where the sinless Christ hung on a cross—despised, rejected, pierced, scarred, and scorned—so that we might be brought into right relationship with God and freely receive eternal life. Jesus' sacrifice reveals how much the eternal destiny of our souls matters to God.

Following Jesus as your rescuer and your King and acknowledging His worth above any earthly treasure is not a momentary decision; it is a lifetime commitment that is lived out each day. If you are prepared to come to His cross daily, humbly confess who He is, and give up your life—your preferences, your comfort, your wealth—then your profit will know no end, now and for all of eternity. We could do far worse than asking ourselves the question at the start of each day that Jesus asked His disciples on the road that day: *What will it profit me if I gain the whole world and forfeit my soul?*

MATTHEW 16:13-27

MARCH 31

CRYING OUT FOR HELP

"Whenever the Israelites planted crops, the Midianites and the Amalekites and the people of the East would come up against them … Israel was brought very low because of Midian. And the people of Israel cried out for help to the Lord." JUDGES 6:3, 6

When we are helpless, we are best-placed to learn true faith.

At the beginning of Judges 6, the people of Israel once again "did what was evil in the sight of the Lord" (v 1). They had trapped themselves in a recurring cycle of rebellion and repentance, slow to learn and quick to forget that their difficult circumstances were often related to their disobedience. Ultimately, the Israelites struggled to understand that God would allow them to come to a place where their only response would be to cry out for help so that He could bring them into communion with Himself, for His glory and their good. He does this for us today, too, working out His purposes in the lives of those who know themselves to be helpless. It is those who know they are "poor in spirit," not those who think they are sufficient in themselves, to whom Jesus promises the kingdom (Matthew 5:3).

Some of us mistakenly believe that if we just follow Jesus, everything will always fall into line. Deep down, we think that God will always and immediately intervene to remove hardship. When God doesn't answer our prayers how or when we want, we wonder if we can still trust that He knows best. Perhaps you are in that place today.

Repeatedly throughout Scripture, God promises to come to our aid when we ask: "The sun shall not strike you by day, nor the moon by night. The Lord will keep you from all evil; he will keep your life. The Lord will keep your going out and your coming in from this time forth and forevermore" (Psalm 121:6-8). These are guarantees of God's word. Yet the way in which He fulfills such promises is often along rocky terrain, amid dark valleys, and in uncomfortable waiting rooms.

When God interceded with His people in Judges, He turned them back to His word, convicting them. The prophet, speaking the very words of God, reminded the Israelites of what they needed to know: "I led you up from Egypt and brought you out of the house of slavery … I said to you, 'I am the Lord your God …' But you have not obeyed my voice" (Judges 6:8, 10). But then, in a little twist of the tale, just when we anticipate God's judgment, we read instead that "the angel of the Lord appeared" with these words of mercy: "The Lord is with you" (v 12).

Where would we be if God gave to us the judgment that we deserve instead of demonstrating His mercy day by day? He did not give the people of Israel what they deserved, nor has He done so with you and me. God's mercy and grace know no end. But in His goodness, He often uses the hard things in our lives to teach us that He is all we need. The removal of a good thing causes pain but can also bring us to cry out to God and find in Him our strength and peace and hope. Cry out to Him for help, filled with the hope that the God who hears you truly knows what is best. The Lord is with you!

ROMANS 5:1-11

APRIL 1

ZEALOUS EXPECTATION

"We ourselves, who have the firstfruits of the Spirit, groan inwardly as we wait eagerly for adoption as sons, the redemption of our bodies." ROMANS 8:23

The Christian experience is both wonderful and challenging.

We have received forgiveness. We're adopted into God's family. We enjoy a fellowship with one another that runs deeper than natural affinity. We possess a sure hope of heaven, which brings about eager anticipation. We have the Spirit, God Himself, dwelling within us. We are not removed, though, from the realities of life in this fallen world. We know frustration, we know heartache, we know disappointment, and we know groaning.

While we live here on earth, we have a little taste of heaven, but we are not there yet.

Christianity does not make us immune to decay or sin. We get sick, and our bodies fail. We continue to struggle with sin and encounter opposition to our faith. Indeed, as the Westminster theologians put it back in the 17th century, the Christian is involved in "a continual and irreconcilable war" against sin.[42]

It is possible to tie ourselves in all kinds of spiritual and theological knots over our ongoing battle with sin. We may wonder, "Why is it that I still disobey?" In those moments, you and I need to remember the "three tenses" of salvation, which summarize God's work in the life of the Christian.

If we are hidden in Christ, then we *have been* saved from the penalty of sin. We have nothing to fear on the day of judgment because Jesus, by His death on the cross, bore our sins and faced punishment in our place. In the present tense, we *are being* saved from the power of sin. It's an ongoing divine ministry; none of us will ever be sinless this side of heaven, but God is at work within us, enabling us to say no to what is wrong and yes to what is right. And finally, there will be a day, when Christ returns, when we *will be* saved from sin's very presence.

Every so often we get a little taste of heaven that makes us long for what's to come. This is why Paul says that we "groan inwardly as we wait eagerly for … the redemption of our bodies." We *should* look forward to Christ's return with zealous expectation!

As Christians, we go out into the world as citizens of heaven, living for the time being as strangers and foreigners. But we're not going to have to live away from home forever. One day, Jesus will return—and when He does, He will take us to join Him, in our resurrected bodies, in His perfected kingdom. Today, do not live as though this is all there is. Lean forwards, for your best days are still to come. You are not there yet—but most assuredly you one day will be.

REVELATION 22

42 The Westminster Confession of Faith 13.2.

APRIL 2

A NEW PLACE TO DWELL

"The one who spoke with me had a measuring rod of gold to measure the city and its gates and walls. The city lies foursquare, its length the same as its width. And he measured the city with his rod, 12,000 stadia. Its length and width and height are equal." REVELATION 21:15-16

In the past, God dwelled among His people, Israel, in the temple in Jerusalem, but that was destroyed. After the temple's destruction at the hands of King Nebuchadnezzar of Babylon, God promised that He would build a new temple (Ezekiel 40 – 43). Though a second Jerusalem temple was built, it was a shadow of the first and clearly not a fulfillment of that promise (Haggai 2:2-3)—a promise that was ultimately fulfilled through the life, death, resurrection, and ascension of Jesus (John 2:19-22).

In the temple, God's presence was focused in the Most Holy Place, an inner sanctuary that was constructed as a perfect cube. Only one man was permitted to enter, and he, the high priest, could only enter once a year. Then, centuries later, and with that first temple nothing but a distant memory, the apostle John received this vision of the new city of God's eternal kingdom, and it is portrayed as a perfect cube—but now not one that would fit in a building in one Middle-Eastern city but one with an area as large as the known world of John's day.

In the new creation there will be no particular place where God's presence will be concentrated. There will be no special building to visit if we want to meet God, because there will be no distance between God and us. John "saw no temple in the city" (Revelation 21:22) because, in that day, God will be there, fully and spectacularly in a way that we cannot yet comprehend; and so *everything* will be temple space. This is a radical picture of something that is brand new—a transformation in circumstances so vast, so rich, and so wide that, as the apostle Paul puts it, we cannot imagine "what God has prepared for those who love him" (1 Corinthians 2:9).

If we are united with Christ, God's presence is with us through the Holy Spirit. Nevertheless, our knowledge of God and our intimacy with Him are still limited. Our present state is certainly not all that we might long for, nor is it all that He intends for us. That is yet to come—but come it will.

Do you live in eager expectation of this unimaginable intimacy with God? If you are sincerely anticipating this permanent dwelling place with God, it will be apparent by the purity of your life and by a passionate concern to see friends, relatives, and neighbors come to know Christ. Knowing we have this great hope, we will be purified, even as Christ is pure (1 John 3:3)—and we won't be able to help but tell others about Jesus, both by life and by lip.

REVELATION 21:9-27

APRIL 3

JESUS STANDS AMONG US

"On the evening of that day, the first day of the week, the doors being locked where the disciples were for fear of the Jews, Jesus came and stood among them and said to them, 'Peace be with you.'" JOHN 20:19

When Jesus first appeared to the disciples after His resurrection, they were cowering behind locked doors, fearing what the authorities who had crucified their leader would do next. But locked doors couldn't stop Jesus! Nothing stopped Him from entering the house and re-entering their lives, proving Himself to be their Savior and their living hope. He was able to be seen, heard, touched, known—and He approaches our lives in the same manner. No matter where we are or what we have done, Christ can enter our lives—our sadness, our darkness, our fear, our doubts—and make Himself seen and known, declaring, "Peace be with you."

Maybe you're a "doubting Thomas," quick to question matters of faith. To some degree, questions are good and healthy. Thomas was straightforward with Jesus, essentially saying, *I'm not going to believe in You unless I can actually put my finger in Your scars.* Jesus replied to Thomas, *All right, if that's what it takes for you, here you are* (John 20:24-29). Jesus can meet us in our doubts. Or maybe you're a denying Peter, quick to renounce your identity in Christ and quick to feel condemnation for how you've messed up. Jesus took Peter, who had questioned Him countless times but crumbled before the question of a servant girl, and made him the rock on which His church was built (Matthew 16:18). Jesus accepts us despite our shortcomings and uses our lives in transformative ways. Or perhaps you're a disgraced Mary Magdalene, whose past haunts you, making you feel unworthy of Jesus' love and acceptance. Yet God did not ordain Jesus' first recorded encounter after His resurrection to be with a Sunday-school teacher but with a woman who had a sordid past riddled with sin and had even suffered demon possession. It was no haphazard coincidence that the first embrace, as it were, from the resurrected Christ was with such a person. He offers this same redemptive embrace to us.

Jesus can get past locked doors; He can get through to hardened hearts. Through His death and resurrection, He was able to bridge the gap that sin had opened between rebellious humanity and a righteous God. We must receive the salvation He freely offers. It must be fresh in our minds each day.

Have you done this? Have you received Jesus unconditionally and unreservedly? Do you embrace Him daily? Do you rehearse His gospel to yourself each morning? To trust in this way means we give ourselves to God in service. We submit ourselves to His lordship as our Savior. We take God's promises to heart, and we take the salvation He freely offers. With this belief, you will see that He stands beside you, offering you an eternal, intimate peace that triumphs over and transforms your sadness, your darkness, your fear, your doubts. Hear the risen Christ say to you, "Peace be with you."

JOHN 20:24-29

APRIL 4

SEEING CHRIST IN THE SCRIPTURES

"Men of Israel, hear these words: Jesus of Nazareth..." ACTS 2:22

With each passing year, I've developed a greater tendency to wake up in the middle of the night. Worry often sweeps in when I am stirred from sleep—and, as is fitting for a pastor, one of my concerns is this: Am I seeing and teaching Christ in and from all the Scriptures?

It is possible to study the Bible without Christ as our focus. We may pride ourselves on understanding it in a very systematic fashion, but in doing so, we run the risk of becoming so enamored with our method that we fail to see Christ.

In Acts 2, when Peter addresses the crowd, he says, "Men of Israel, hear these words." (His tone seems authoritative, doesn't it?) And then notice what follows: "Jesus of Nazareth..." Peter doesn't begin by appealing to the people's felt needs or by presenting to them all the practical benefits of the gospel, nor does he embark on laying out a set of doctrines or setting forth a series of propositions. Rather, he proceeds to say who Jesus is, why Jesus came, and what Jesus did.

Peter's teaching was directed to the heart, rooted in grace, and focused on Christ. Such teaching comes at a cost—one that not everybody is prepared to pay. It is much easier to talk about the issues of the day than to truly know and share Christ. Sometimes, in churches that hold the Bible in high regard, we find it more comfortable to talk more of our favored doctrines than of the Christ who often unsettles us and challenges our lifestyles. The hard thing to do, however, is also the right thing to do. What a dreadful waste of energy, to gain insight or provide instruction about almost everything but the saving story of Jesus!

Scripture finds its focus and fulfillment in Christ. The real test of how deeply God's word is dwelling within us is not our ability to articulate a story line but to see Jesus in all the Scriptures. He is not just the start of the Christian faith but the sum total of it. Aim to go deeper into Christ, not to move beyond Him.

Perhaps this should be our prayer whenever we open the pages of our Bible:

More about Jesus would I know,
More of His grace to others show;
More of His saving fullness see,
More of His love, who died for me.

More about Jesus let me learn,
More of His holy will discern;
Spirit of God, my teacher be,
Showing the things of Christ to me.[43]

LUKE 24:13-35

43 Eliza E. Hewitt, "More about Jesus" (1887).

APRIL 5

GOD'S RULE AND BLESSING

"If you will indeed obey my voice and keep my covenant, you shall be my treasured possession among all peoples, for all the earth is mine." EXODUS 19:5

Obedience has fallen out of fashion. But it is central to the Christian life.

It's not unusual for us to hear even the best of people express a negative attitude towards authority, for we live in an anti-authoritarian age. Within the church what was once regarded as a sacred view of Scripture's authority doesn't rest happily in the minds of some. Yet in seeking to find freedom on our own terms and apart from God's authority, we also remove ourselves from His blessing.

When Adam and Eve disobeyed the rule of God in the Garden of Eden, they were separated from Him; they forfeited the blessing of His presence. Rejection of God's law has always brought about, and *will* always bring about, separation from our Maker and withdrawal of His blessings. In contrast, the restoration of God's rule always brings about the blessing of communion and fellowship that God designed for His people.

This promise of God's rule and blessing was fulfilled during Israel's history in the giving of God's law. The Israelites' obedience to the law wasn't meant to be a desperate attempt to achieve salvation; rather, it was a response to the salvation that had already been achieved for them. God first reached down and took hold of His people, redeeming them and liberating them from bondage in Egypt—and *then* the law was given to them.

In other words, God didn't give the law as a mechanism for redemption or provide it as a pathway to becoming one of His people. Instead, having redeemed the Israelites, He gave them the law as a conduit of His grace so that they might know how to live under His rule and truly enjoy His blessing. If that principle is flipped upside down, everything goes wrong. We will live our lives in the fierce grip of legalism, thinking all the time that our endeavors can put us in a right standing before God. But equally, if we forget that God saved us so that we might enjoy life under His rule, and we continue to ignore His laws whenever they do not suit our own purposes, then we will live our lives wondering why blessing seems elusive.

God's law does not save, but it is "the perfect law, the law of liberty," and the one who obeys it "will be blessed in his doing" (James 1:25). As those rescued from sin by God, we are to respond to His salvation by choosing to walk in joyful obedience.

When we walk with the Lord
In the light of His Word,
What a glory He sheds on our way!
While we do His good will,
He abides with us still,
And with all who will trust and obey.[44]

PSALM 119:49-64

44 John H. Sammis, "Trust and Obey" (1887).

APRIL 6

A PLEASING SACRIFICE

"I am well supplied, having received from Epaphroditus the gifts you sent, a fragrant offering, a sacrifice pleasing to God." PHILIPPIANS 4:18

Here is an amazing notion when you pause to consider it: you are able to bring God pleasure.

It is a mind-blowing thought: that our Creator would be pleased by our actions. Yet Scripture encourages us to see that this is a reality. As Christians, we strive to live under the smile of our heavenly Father. One of the great biblical motivators for obeying God is that the way we live can "please God … more and more" (1 Thessalonians 4:1)—and one of the ways we can do this is through our generous giving, which is "a sacrifice pleasing to God."

Paul described the giving of the Philippian church in terminology that reflected the Old Testament practice of animal sacrifice. When God's people in the Old Testament brought their burnt offerings, the burning of incense accompanied these sacrifices. Therefore, the sacrifice produced an attractive smell. In some sense, this represented the acceptability and sweetness of the offering in God's sight. In the same way, God says to His people in the first century and in the twenty-first, *When your giving comes from a heart that is in tune with Mine, it produces a beautiful aroma, and your sacrifice brings Me pleasure.*

When considering this kind of giving, we should not pass over the word "sacrifice" too quickly. Sacrificial giving is not necessarily the same as generous giving. It is quite possible for us to be generous—as, in fact, many believers are—without feeling an impact on our lives or circumstances.

In making this same point for His disciples, Jesus drew their attention to a poor widow as she was putting her tithe into the offering box in the temple. As He watched this woman deposit two copper coins, which were worth next to nothing, and compared them with the gifts of the rich people near her, He said, "This poor widow has put in more than all of them. For they all contributed out of their abundance, but she out of her poverty put in all she had to live on" (Luke 21:2-4). The wealthy were generous; the widow was sacrificial. She gave up in order to give away. And her Lord noticed and was pleased by what He saw.

We are not by nature sacrificial givers. But the whole Christian journey—in receiving and in giving, in caring and in sharing—is filled with grace from start to finish. When we give sacrificially from a heart that desires to please God, He promises to "supply every need … according to his riches in glory in Christ Jesus" (Philippians 4:19). It is reflecting on all that God has given, and all that God is giving, and all that God will give, that unlocks our hearts and enables us to give *both* sacrificially and joyfully. And when we do so, we bring God pleasure. The Philippians' actions, and their bank statements, showed that they truly believed this. To what extent do yours?

1 THESSALONIANS 4:1-12

APRIL 7

YOU SHALL BE CLEAN

"Elisha sent a messenger to him, saying, 'Go and wash in the Jordan seven times, and your flesh shall be restored, and you shall be clean.' But Naaman was angry and went away." 2 KINGS 5:10-11

Even a brief reading of history and sociology reveals humanity's inability to fix our broken world. Not so long ago, we were told that people did bad things because they were poor; if we dealt with the material need, then we would see better behavior. Now, in some of the world's most affluent countries, some sociologists explain that greed, corruption, and murder are the result of having too much. Experts and world leaders stand before these external forces in bewilderment, looking for answers in all the wrong places.

Naaman had a condition that made him unhappy and was downright ugly to deal with. He had the resources to try any cure he wanted, and he presumably was prepared to go to any length. The problem was that he was looking in the wrong places. His status, wealth, and royal connections did not produce the remedy he desired, and in going to the king of Israel for relief, his request brought dismay; the king tore his clothes because he knew he could not help (2 Kings 5:7).

The king's response was the same kind of reaction that many of our world leaders likely have as they travel the globe, seeking to do what they can in public service. Surely in the watches of the night, they must feel like tearing their clothes and saying, "How can I deal with this and make a difference? How can we bring peace? How can we bring a cure?"

What the king could not do, though, God's prophet could. But the cure sounded offensive to the leper! Naaman was looking for something grand—something that would fit his lofty status and leave him with a bolstered sense of self-importance. He thought the cure should be less simple or more impressive. He regarded Elisha's remedy as humiliating and ridiculous.

While actual leprosy has been largely eradicated, we all still live with that ugly, terminal condition called sin. Yet many are no more ready to listen to the cure than Naaman was. The message of Christ crucified as the only and sufficient remedy for our sin was "a stumbling block to Jews and folly to Gentiles" (1 Corinthians 1:23), and it is still those things to many today. Even believers are not immune to the temptation to think that when it comes to a cure for sin, we must do something.

We need daily to open our eyes to the remedy we need and to stoop down in humility, as Naaman eventually did (2 Kings 5:14). For it is the person who does that who can know that the words "You *shall* be clean" are a thing of the past, and who can rejoice that Jesus sees them and says, "You *are* clean" (John 13:10-11; 15:3). Do not look in the mirror and think that the cure is found in who you are or what you do; instead, look through the window of faith, see the cross, and know that He did it all.

2 KINGS 5:1-14

APRIL 8

GOD VINDICATES HIS PEOPLE

"If possible, so far as it depends on you, live peaceably with all. Beloved, never avenge yourselves, but leave it to the wrath of God, for it is written, 'Vengeance is mine, I will repay, says the Lord' ... Do not be overcome by evil, but overcome evil with good." ROMANS 12:18-19, 21

Imagine a child who comes home from school deeply upset by something another child said or did. On the verge of tears over a hurt looming larger than a mountain, it would be easy for her to be thinking that she would never again speak to the one who caused the harm, or to be planning out how she would get her own back one day.

Imagine, though, that her parents suggest she write a simple note, extending both forgiveness and friendship, and the next day, having done so, she is able joyfully to report back: "I did it! I took the note to school, and it worked. We hugged, and we're friends. It was fantastic!"

This is what it means to obey Paul's call here to live peaceably "so far as it depends on you." Sometimes, peace will be elusive; but never let that be because of some lack on our part. And may it never be because we are chasing or plotting revenge. Vengeance is a dish only to be served by God, and never by His people.

Quite frankly, the majority of our disputes are really just grown-up versions of what happens in childhood. Our response in the face of injustice says a lot about what we truly believe. Will we "repay evil for evil" (1 Peter 3:9), which is the way of the world, or will we respond according to the mind of Christ?

All our conflicts and hurts pale in comparison with what Jesus faced and felt. Yet when Jesus was reviled, He did not revile in return. When He suffered, He did not curse or threaten. We must not make the great mistake of accepting Jesus' salvation but ignoring His example, spending our lives trying to clear our names, defend our motives, and explain ourselves, seeking redress for every wrong and revenge for every slight. That is what comes naturally to us; and what frees us from that path is to remember that we can trust God to vindicate His people in due time. Justice will be served, and not by us. So, is there someone you need to reach out to in peace? Is there someone whom you are allowing to experience your wrath instead of your love in some way? Beloved, leave vengeance to God, and overcome evil with good. Today.

1 PETER 2:18-25

APRIL 9

NAME ABOVE ALL NAMES

"Being found in human form, he humbled himself by becoming obedient to the point of death, even death on a cross. Therefore God has highly exalted him and bestowed on him the name that is above every name." PHILIPPIANS 2:8-9

In a sense the best summary of the message of the Bible and the most fundamental truth in this universe is simply this: Jesus Christ is Lord.

Most theologians agree that "the name" that Paul refers to in verse 9 can only be "Lord" (Philippians 2:11). Here, the Greek word for "Lord" is *kyrios*, which is also used as the translation of God's divine name, *Yahweh*, over 6,000 times in the Septuagint (the Greek translation of the Old Testament)—the name that is rendered in most English Bibles today as LORD. Paul's implied use of God's divine name emphasizes Jesus' divinity, just after he has reminded us about Jesus' humiliation during His time on earth.

Comprising four consonants (YHWH), *Yahweh* is basically unpronounceable in Hebrew—and purposefully so, for Jews did not dare take this divine name of God upon their lips. Yet Yahweh, the indescribable God, came to earth as the incarnate Christ and revealed Himself to men and women. He humbly went to the cross, and then He was raised to the highest place—His rightful place—and given this name "above every name." Says one commentator, "He hath changed the ineffable name, into a name utterable by man and desirable by all the world." In the one who bears this name, God's majesty "is all arrayed in robes of mercy."[45]

Old Testament prophecy reinforces this idea again and again. In Isaiah 45, God gives a description that applies exclusively to Himself: "There is no other god besides me, a righteous God and a Savior; there is none besides me" (Isaiah 45:21). Paul, once an aggressive opponent of Christ and His followers, applies this very description to Christ, making an impressive declaration of His deity. He points out that Jesus has been publicly exalted to the position that was rightfully His even before He came to earth to suffer humiliation on our behalf. He is now seated at the Father's right hand. His majesty is there for all who know Him as Savior to see. His identity is unclouded and undoubted.

God is the only Savior—and Jesus *is* that Savior, of whom it was said, "You shall call his name Jesus, for he will save his people from their sins" (Matthew 1:21). Years after God had first revealed to Paul who Jesus is, we can still catch a sense of awed reverence and love in the apostle's words to the Philippians. Jesus Christ is LORD. He possesses the name above all names. Paul never allowed familiarity with this truth to breed complacency about it. Neither must we. Pause now and allow each word to prompt you to an awed praise of this man: *Jesus*, the Savior of His people... *Christ*, the long-promised King... *is* LORD, the indescribable, revealed God. And you get to call Him "brother" (Hebrews 2:11).

REVELATION 1:9-20

45 Jeremy Taylor, "Considerations upon the Circumcision of the Holy Childe Jesus," in *The Great Exemplar of Sanctity and Holy Life According to the Christian Institution, Described in the History of the Life and Death of the Ever Blessed Jesus Christ, the Saviour of the World* (1649), p 61.

APRIL 10

PEACE TO THE NATIONS

"Behold, your king is coming to you; righteous and having salvation is he, humble and mounted on a donkey, on a colt, the foal of a donkey. I will cut off the chariot from Ephraim and the war horse from Jerusalem; and the battle bow shall be cut off, and he shall speak peace to the nations; his rule shall be from sea to sea, and from the River to the ends of the earth." ZECHARIAH 9:9-10

The procession that led to Jesus' arrival in Jerusalem was marked by drama.

Many times in the Gospels, Jesus and the disciples had gone off on their own, away from the crowd, as quietly and secretively as possible. It would have been possible for Jesus to have entered the city inconspicuously. Instead, He purposefully determined to approach Jerusalem in a fashion that declared Him to be the Messiah-King long promised in Scripture.

The people's concept of what it meant for Him to be the King of the Jews, however, was so skewed that they misunderstood who Jesus was showing Himself to be. The people had previously tried to make Jesus a king by force, but He had slipped away from them (John 6:14-15). He knew that what they thought a king was going to do was not what He had come to do. Their heads were in the wrong place. The same was true when it was suggested that He was involved in some kind of political revolution. To this He replied, "My kingdom is not of this world" (John 18:36).

In the triumphal entry, the crowd's chants had been filled with passion, expectation, and confusion. They didn't want to live under Roman subjugation. They wanted national restoration and political revolution. They needed a political champion, and Jesus was their best hope. They were, it seems, trusting that Jesus would deliver to them something He never came to deliver. When the crowd shouted, "Hosanna!"—which means "Save us!"—they were not thinking about personal, spiritual salvation; they were thinking about the here and now.

Unless we keep the gospel at the center of our thinking, we might also fall foul of similar passionate, hopeful confusion. Even today, many of us continue to create a Jesus who can fulfill our own expectations, a "savior" of our own making who has come to bring us comfort, prosperity, or health, to bless our family and neighborhood and nation. Yet Christ did not enter Jerusalem as a conquering nationalist, riding a chariot; He came as a peace-bringing internationalist, seated humbly on a donkey. He came to fulfill the prophecy of Zechariah 9, proclaiming "peace to the nations" under His perfect, universal rule "from sea to sea." That is the message of the gospel—a message that is good for everyone, everywhere, always. It is not that our dreams and demands are too big for Him, but that they are too small.

Jesus challenges us today, as He challenged people in His day, to worship Him for who He is, not for who we think He should be. Do not tell Him to be about your business; count it a privilege for you to be about His.

ZECHARIAH 9:9-17

Bible Through The Year: Leviticus 14; Hebrews 11:1-19

APRIL 11

PUT YOUR SWORD AWAY

"Then Simon Peter, having a sword, drew it and struck the high priest's servant and cut off his right ear ... Jesus said to Peter, 'Put your sword into its sheath; shall I not drink the cup that the Father has given me?'" JOHN 18:10-11

Jesus' arrest in the Garden of Gethsemane ultimately revealed His submission to the Father. When the soldiers came for Him, Jesus had already resolved to drink the cup of suffering—His death on the cross—so that it might be for us a cup of salvation.

But which of the disciples stepped in, as if on cue? The impetuous Simon Peter, of course—wielding a sword! Peter was no stranger to impassioned acts and words. He had attempted to walk on water to Christ. He had tried to rebuke Christ. He had offered to lay down his life for Christ. And yet, soon after stepping up to Jesus' defense, he would fearfully deny even knowing Him.

Peter's reaction to seeing his Master arrested is entirely understandable but utterly mistaken. While Peter was willing to fight for Christ here, he was actually fighting against Christ. He was fighting against the very will of God, who had purposed that Jesus would be the atoning sacrifice for sins. Peter's example teaches us an important lesson; as Calvin urges, "Let us learn to moderate our zeal. And as the wantonness of our flesh ever itches to dare more than God commands, let us learn that our zeal will turn out badly whenever we dare to undertake anything beyond God's word."[46]

Knowing Peter's action needed correction, Jesus intervened with a rhetorical question: "Shall I not drink the cup the Father has given me?" He was affirming the part of God's will that He had just prayed to accept, the very action that later led Him to cry out on the cross, "My God, my God, why have you forsaken me?" (Mathew 27:46). Through His suffering, His glory was magnified, and salvation was freely offered to all who might believe. No path that Peter could have orchestrated could have been better than this one, and he was in error to resist it.

When our impatience seeks to interfere with God's plans, we must learn to put away our figurative swords. We must trust God's plan, wait on His timing, and act on His command. The more familiar we are with the Scriptures—knowing the great story, promises, and truths found within them—the more we will understand His plans. But even then, there will be times when His ways are very mysterious to us and we are tempted to fight the path He is leading us along. Perhaps you are doing that right now.

Take Christ's words to Peter to heart: "Put your sword into its sheath!" Trust God's loving hand, obey His commands, and follow His lead. He is "the author and finisher of our faith" (Hebrews 12:2, KJV), and the story He is writing is more glorious than you could imagine or direct for yourself.

PSALM 23

46 John Calvin, *The Gospel According to St John 11–21 and The First Epistle of John,* trans. T. H. L. Parker, ed. David W. Torrance and Thomas F. Torrance, Calvin's New Testament Commentaries (Eerdmans, 1994), p 156.

APRIL 12

WHAT WILL YOU DO WITH JESUS?

"My kingdom is not of this world … You say that I am a king. For this purpose I was born and for this purpose I have come into the world—to bear witness to the truth. Everyone who is of the truth listens to my voice." JOHN 18:36-37

What will you do with Jesus? On the morning of what is now known as the first Good Friday, the Jewish religious authorities took Jesus to continue His trial before Pontius Pilate, the Roman governor. We can see in the details of the Gospel accounts how God sovereignly orchestrated all of these events. The Jews' determination to secure Christ's death by crucifixion would actually fulfill God's plan from eternity. God had also planned Christ's interaction with Pilate. As they stood before one another, Pilate asked significant questions about Jesus' identity and authority. These questions formed an examination with eternal ramifications—an examination we all must make. Consider how the hymn writer puts it:

Jesus is standing in Pilate's hall—
Friendless, forsaken, betrayed by all;
Hearken! What meaneth the sudden call?
What will you do with Jesus?

Pilate believed he was holding an examination on a purely intellectual, natural level. But answering the question "Who is Jesus?" is always a spiritual, supernatural matter. Jesus wasn't a political king, but the heavenly King. He essentially told Pilate, *My kingdom doesn't find its origin in this world. The concern of My kingdom is the spiritual transformation that is brought about in the hearts of My people. The reason why I was born as a King was to testify to God's truth.* But Pilate, blind in his unbelief, had already made up his mind. Jaded and disdainful, he sought to avoid the fundamental question we all must ask: "What will I do with Jesus?" But in trying not to answer, he nevertheless gave his answer: *I shall reject His claim on me and His rule over me, and therefore His offer to rescue me.*

What will you do with Jesus?
Neutral you cannot be;
Someday your heart will be asking,
"What will He do with me?"[47]

Neutral you cannot be. You will either live under Jesus' rule or you will not. So do not close your Bible in the morning and then live as though this world and its concerns and kings are all that is or all that matters. Do not proceed as though Jesus has no place or interest in your life in this world. He stood friendless and forsaken before Pilate so that you might be welcomed as His friend into His eternal kingdom. There is no option of neutrality—but why would we want there to be?

JOHN 18:28-40

47 Albert B. Simpson, "What Will You Do with Jesus?" (1905).

APRIL 13

UNPARALLELED HUMILITY

"Jesus came out, wearing the crown of thorns and the purple robe. Pilate said to them, 'Behold the man!'" JOHN 19:5

There Christ stood—His head pierced with a crown of thorns, dressed up in another's clothes, forced to hold a reed as a scepter, all in mockery of His kingship—as the Roman governor Pilate declared to the jeering crowd, "Behold the man!" While he spoke those words with scorn in mind, they were ironically appropriate; there stood the Savior of the world, arrayed in unparalleled humility, adorned with a lavish love for the world.

We have much to learn from Christ's example. As the humble King endured royal ridicule and the "pre-death death" of brutal flogging, He did not utter a word of self-defense. And for what did they condemn Him? For healing a woman who was crippled for 18 years (Luke 13:10-13)? For bringing back to life the widow of Nain's dead son (Luke 7:11-17)? For bringing Lazarus forth from the grave (John 11:1-44)? For taking children on His knee and encouraging His disciples to understand that "to such belongs the kingdom of heaven" (Matthew 19:14)? On what basis did Christ's accusers find it in themselves to abuse Him in this way? There could be none. But they did it anyway.

When our humble Lord remained silent during His numerous trials, Pilate took offense and felt disrespected. There is great irony here, as this Roman governor attempted to pull rank on the King of the universe! And all the while, that King did nothing to assert His authority or save His own life. He humbly suffered an unjust trial, spoke truth when asked questions, and walked forward even unto death, all on our behalf.

I ask myself: Do I truly see this Man who stands before Pilate, who stands before the crowd—who stands before *me*? This is not some helpless individual who can do nothing for Himself. This is God incarnate.

Do I understand why He went down this road of humiliation? "Oh, the love that drew salvation's plan"[48]—love and salvation for you and me! Two millennia ago, there stood a sorry spectacle outside the governor's palace, in part because Jesus had our names before His gaze—names He had graven on the palms of those hands that would be pierced by the cruel nails (see Isaiah 49:16).

May we never be like the riotous crowd, mocking Christ's humility, nor like Pilate, looking for Christ to be impressed with us. Instead, behold this Man in all His humility—holding this reed, bearing this crown, wearing this costume, hanging on that cross—and see Him beckoning. Behold the Man, and know beyond all doubt that His love for you knows no end.

ISAIAH 52:13 - 53:12

48 William R. Newell, "At Calvary" (1895).

APRIL 14

COWARDLY COMPROMISE

"When the chief priests and the officers saw him, they cried out, 'Crucify him, crucify him!' Pilate said to them, 'Take him yourselves and crucify him, for I find no guilt in him.' The Jews answered him, 'We have a law, and according to that law he ought to die because he has made himself the Son of God.' When Pilate heard this statement, he was even more afraid." JOHN 19:6-8

Whose praise will you live for?

When Christ was put on trial before Pilate, the Roman governor repeatedly declared His innocence—and yet he paired his declarations with dreadful acts against Him.

Pilate said, "I find no guilt in him"—and then handed Jesus over to be brutally flogged, a beating so intense that it sometimes caused gashes and lacerations where veins, arteries, and internal organs would be exposed.

Pilate said, "I find no guilt in him"—and then let the soldiers humiliate Jesus with a mock coronation, placing a crown of thorns upon His head, dressing Him up, and scornfully "worshiping" Him.

Pilate said, "I find no guilt in him"—but did he release Jesus? No, he surrendered Jesus to a vicious execution squad to be killed.

There was never a more tormented individual that met Christ than Pilate. Here was a man of great power but who lacked the courage to stand by his convictions. Here was a man of great success but who compromised, showing himself under the trappings of his position to be a coward. Here was a governor who was governed by his own weaknesses.

We cannot be passive or indecisive regarding who Christ is to us. Is He the Savior or is He no one? To abstain from a decision about this, as Pilate sought to do, is to abstain from Christ altogether.

Pilate stands as a challenge to each of us. His conduct compels us to ask ourselves: In what situations do I, like Pilate, know the right thing to do in some way and yet fear what other people will say if I do it? Are there ways in which my words or conduct are governed more by the expectations and reaction of others, or by considerations of wealth, position, or promotion, than by the commands of Christ? Let's not compromise on our position regarding Christ. If we let the opinions of our colleagues, our neighbors, or our families concern us too much, we may find ourselves giving up forgiveness, peace, heaven, and Christ Himself in exchange for an easier life now. Instead, let's be brave.

Look again at Christ: flogged, mocked, and killed out of love for you. Then look at those who, perhaps vociferously or perhaps politely, scoff at His truth. Who would you rather offend? Whose "well done" would you rather hear? Christ is beckoning us to Him so that we might go out and live for Him. Will you come, and will you go?

JOHN 19:1-16

APRIL 15

A CHOICE TO MAKE

"Pilate also wrote an inscription and put it on the cross. It read, 'Jesus of Nazareth, the King of the Jews.'" JOHN 19:19

As Jesus was crucified upon the cross, a sign was inscribed and erected over Him, proclaiming Him to be "the King of the Jews." While this sign was meant as a taunt, it declared a truth for all to witness: Jesus was and is indeed King! Yet it also should prompt us to ask ourselves: Do I really live as though Jesus is King of *my* life?

Scripture tells us that the sign was written in three languages—Aramaic, the language of most first-century Jews in and around Jerusalem; Latin, the official language of the Roman Empire; and Greek, the popular language of commerce and culture (John 19:20). In these three languages, witnesses from all across the known world were able to read that Jesus was King. Upon reading the sign, the whole world had to make their choice about who Jesus was to them.

We see a microcosm of that world—and ours—in the range of characters throughout the story of Jesus' death. In Pilate, we see the proud, indecisive, calculating politician. In the soldiers nailing Christ to His cross, we see those focused on carrying out routine business. In those who mocked the Lord, we see people whose only interaction with the divine is to sneer at Him. In the crowd of passive onlookers, we see those who have no interest at all in eternal matters. But then, amid the darkness, on a neighboring cross we see a desperate and dying thief look to the Savior for hope—and find it. And in Jesus' nearby family and friends, we see sorrowful but faithful followers standing by Christ and His claims—and witnessing His burial in a tomb that would soon be empty.

All these people saw the sign: Jesus of Nazareth, the King of the Jews. All of them saw the man on the cross beneath it. Whether hateful or hopeful, all beheld this historic event, and all had to reconcile it and the personhood of Christ with their own lives. As the sign hung proclaiming Christ's kingship, Jesus hung proclaiming the most powerful love the world has known.

The question remains: What are we to do with this love? Each of us can find a face in the crowd with which we identify, be it one of the proud, the passive, or the faithful. All of us are confronted with the life-changing person of Jesus Christ.

How do the cross and the empty tomb affect your relationships, your work, your purpose, or your identity? If Jesus reigns over you, His death and resurrection change everything about the way you live and the meaning of your life. There is hope for eternity and purpose for today in looking at this man and agreeing with that sign. "Jesus is King"—of the Jews and the Gentiles, of the entire world, and of your life and mine.

LUKE 23:32-56

APRIL 16

NO ORDINARY DEATH

"When Jesus had received the sour wine, he said, 'It is finished,' and he bowed his head and gave up his spirit." JOHN 19:30

The events surrounding Jesus' death were largely routine motions of Roman jurisdiction. The trials, the beatings, the humiliating procession, and the painful crucifixion were all a part of business as usual for soldiers involved in executing criminals. What wasn't routine, though, was the darkness that descended over the whole event in the middle of the day (Matthew 27:45), as though God had closed His eyes on the sorrowful scene. This was both a routine execution and the greatest turning point in all eternity.

What made it so important was the identity of the man hanging on the middle cross: none other than God incarnate. Our minds should never cease to be amazed by this:

Well might the sun in darkness hide,
And shut its glories in,
When Christ, the mighty Maker, died
For man the creature's sin.[49]

Scripture does not place much emphasis on Christ's physical sufferings on the cross, because "the sufferings of his body were nothing to the sufferings of his soul; these were the soul of his sufferings."[50] Jesus fully experienced all of the pain and agony of being separated relationally from God the Father—physically, mentally, and spiritually. Whatever you face in your life, Jesus has gone through worse and therefore understands how you feel. Not only that, but the unimaginable anguish He endured was for you, so that He could triumphantly proclaim, "It is finished"—*tetelestai*: the debt is satisfied and done with.

Christ's crucifixion is often portrayed with the cross erected high above the onlooking crowd. In reality, though, once the cross was lowered into its setting, His feet were likely very close to the ground. In the same way, Christ's life, death, and resurrection do not stand high above our lives but intimately close to them. No, Jesus' death was no ordinary death, but rather a death that promises to give, through faith, true life. Everything changes when we consider all that took place on that cross and say to ourselves:

Wounded for me, wounded for me,
There on the cross He was wounded for me;
Gone my transgression, and now I am free,
All because Jesus was wounded for me.[51]

LUKE 22:7-20

49 Isaac Watts, "Alas! and Did My Savior Bleed?" (1707).

50 George Swinnock, "The Christian Man's Calling," in *The Works of George Swinnock, M.A.* (James Nichol, 1868), Vol. 1, p 194.

51 W.G. Ovens, "Wounded for Me" (1931).

APRIL 17

FROM FEAR TO FAITH

"Mary Magdalene went and announced to the disciples, 'I have seen the Lord.'"
JOHN 20:18

What turns fear to faith?

After Jesus' crucifixion, the disciples were in defeated, dejected, and huddled together in fear of persecution. One of them, Judas, was already dead by suicide. Another, Peter, had caved in under pressure and denied Jesus, their leader and teacher, whom they had witnessed being brutally killed. Their hopes and dreams had seemingly died along with Him. Yet just weeks later, this same dejected bunch were on the streets of Jerusalem boldly declaring Jesus as the resurrected Messiah. What turned these men from craven fear to courageous faith? What can make the same change in us? Only the risen Jesus.

The disciples' Jewish background led them to believe that the Messiah would appear and remain forever. This initially caused them to be crushed by Jesus' death, for it seemed to mark utter defeat rather than glorious victory. Their shift to confidently proclaiming Jesus as Messiah after His death has only one possible explanation: they must have seen the resurrected Jesus. If they had not, they would have just fondly, or perhaps bitterly, remembered Him as their beloved teacher—but nothing more. What possible forgiveness and hope can be found in a dead man? But with a risen Messiah, suddenly everything changes.

The Bible tells us in firsthand accounts that the disciples encountered the risen Christ (see for instance John 20:11 – 21:23). Some make the argument that the disciples hallucinated, only "seeing" Him because of their all-consuming faith. But remember, they didn't initially have faith in a resurrection! In fact, Scripture tells us that they sat behind locked doors in fear and disappointment (20:19). And even if they *had* imagined a risen and reigning Christ, they probably wouldn't have imagined a Jesus who cooked and ate fish on the beach, who still had scars from His brutal death, and who walked the streets and encountered them in numerous ways. Nor would they have portrayed themselves as so cowardly or included the reports of women (whose testimony was not considered valid in that culture). Rather, they would have presented themselves as the brave and prominent figures who first discovered the empty tomb. Any kind of alternative explanation for the empty tomb demands even more "faith" than trusting in what has been revealed to us in the word of God does.

The resurrection changes everything. We must consider the facts surrounding Jesus' return from the dead—but we must also consider the glorious good news that it offers us. Without the literal bodily resurrection of Jesus, Christianity is worthless; "Your faith is futile" (1 Corinthians 15:17). But since Jesus has indeed risen and is indeed reigning, then in Him is forgiveness that can be found in no other, and in Him is a future hope like no other. Have you, with the eye of faith, seen the Lord risen and reigning? Then you will, like Mary and like the disciples, see your doubt-filled fear turn to trusting faith as you boldly proclaim this hope to your own heart and to this fearful world.

JOHN 20:1-18

APRIL 18

GOD KNOWS BEST

"O Lord, my heart is not lifted up; my eyes are not raised too high; I do not occupy myself with things too great and too marvelous for me. But I have calmed and quieted my soul, like a weaned child with its mother; like a weaned child is my soul within me." PSALM 131:1-2

The process of weaning a child from his or her mother can be painful, but it's necessary for healthy development and maturity. In Western culture today, weaning occurs at a young age, before the personality really starts to show. When this psalm was written, the transition away from a mother's milk would happen much later, around the age of three.

Weaning could therefore be a confusing struggle for a child as he or she learned to go without something they had previously enjoyed. But once weaned, a child would be "calmed and quieted"; they would now understand that provision would still be made, and they would now be able to enjoy time with their mother for its own sake rather than as a means to an end. Not only that, but a weaned child would have learned that their mother knew best, even when a comfort was being withdrawn and the decision looked perplexing from their three-year-old vantage point.

As with a weaned child, it's important for us as spiritual children to recognize that we don't always know what's best for ourselves. We can trust that our Father in heaven knows best. Far too often, though, our proud hearts cause us to question God's mysterious ways. We demand to know why we are experiencing pain or trouble or loss, but without recognizing that our questions can express arrogance.

Questions are inevitable; they're part and parcel of the journey. But true contentment is found in learning how to harness our questions. Contentment says, "Even when I can't understand, still I can trust." We must be careful that in our pride we don't demand that the Potter explains why He made the pot the way He did (Isaiah 45:9). The precise will and ways of God are a mystery, but they are always good, for He is our Father.

With the Lord's help, we can train ourselves to focus on His providence and remind ourselves that our circumstances are temporary, that our Father knows what He is doing in them, and that they cannot rob us of the joy and glory that are ultimately ours in Christ. In this our souls can be still.

In the Christian life, contentment is often gained through an experience of confusion and discomfort, as we learn to say, "My Father is in charge here and is working for my good as His child. I do not need to understand, for I can trust Him. I have Him, and He is enough for me. My soul is calm, even in this storm." What a wonderful truth to be able to say today!

PSALM 34

APRIL 19

WARNINGS FOR DELIVERANCE

"Let anyone who thinks that he stands take heed lest he fall."
1 CORINTHIANS 10:12

In a biography, both the author as they write and then the readers as they read face a great temptation to gloss over the subject's faults. Scripture, on the other hand, makes no attempt to conceal or excuse the faults, failures, or sins of its heroes. And it is in the aftermath of spiritual triumph that the potential for defeat often seems to be at its peak.

In a victory of faith, Noah obediently continued, without a drop of rain falling, to build the ark. But after the flood, we read a sorry description of all that Noah allowed to happen in his drunkenness (see Genesis 9:20-27). Abram set out on the journey of faith; however, he then brought disgrace on himself and his family through his lies when he went down into Egypt (12:10-20). David triumphed over Goliath yet later found himself perpetrating adultery (and very possibly rape), murder, and chaos (2 Samuel 11 onwards).

Each of these characters are heroes who achieved great things in the cause of God, and who also failed. They stood tall, and they fell hard. The Bible gives us these examples not as excuses to hide behind but as warnings to deliver us from complacency when things are going well, and from expecting too much of others—and indeed, from expecting too much of ourselves!

The theologian A.W. Pink reminds us, "God suffers it to appear that the best of men are but men at the best. No matter how richly gifted they may be, how eminent in God's service, how greatly honoured and used of Him, let His sustaining power be withdrawn from them for a moment and it will quickly be seen that they are 'earthen vessels.' No man stands any longer than he is supported by Divine grace. The most experienced saint, if left to himself, is immediately seen to be as weak as water and as timid as a mouse."[52]

Mercifully, God does not leave us to ourselves: He provides us with righteousness, salvation, truth, and His word so that we may not only endure but stand strong amid every trial and temptation. As we recognize within ourselves the same weaknesses and defeats experienced by heroes such as Noah, Abraham, and David, we are able to rely on God's grace and power to support us through the Lord Jesus, our only true "way of escape" (1 Corinthians 10:13). Let this serve as a reminder that you are continuing in your faith, growing in holiness, or impacting the world for the kingdom not as a result of your strength or intellect or character, but because of God's grace. The person who truly knows this sees complacency as a grave danger, and sees prayer as an absolute essential, for they know that it is only the Lord who can keep them standing day by day, moment by moment. Do you?

1 CORINTHIANS 10:1-13

52 *The Life of Elijah* (Banner of Truth, 1963), p 201.

APRIL 20

SOVEREIGN LORD, GENTLE SHEPHERD

"Behold, the Lord GOD comes with might, and his arm rules for him; behold, his reward is with him, and his recompense before him. He will tend his flock like a shepherd; he will gather the lambs in his arms." ISAIAH 40:10-11

The United States of America has never been keen on sovereigns or their sovereignty. We prefer someone we can vote into a position and call upon as necessary—and vote out when we choose! And if we're honest, this is often true of our approach to God as well. We prefer to control rather than to be controlled.

God, however, cannot be managed or remade in our image. He is the sovereign Lord, whose existence perfectly contrasts with our human frailty and finite nature. We are like grass and springtime flowers, which wither and fall. It's not so with God, who has ruled and reigned over everything for all eternity. Even His word stands forever (Isaiah 40:6-8).

In His sovereignty, God has accomplished an amazing conquest: victory over sin and death. In His immense wisdom, He, the Lawgiver, came in the person of Jesus, submitted to and fulfilled the very law He had given, and then died in the place of sinners to pay our debt and give us eternal life. As Peter preached, "God raised him up ... because it was not possible for him to be held" by death's power (Acts 2:24). This is *His* victory.

While God is the sovereign Lord, though, He is also our gentle Shepherd. He doesn't come to His people like some great general onto a battlefield; instead, He carries His flock close to Him, leading them with compassion. Those who once were sad, alienated, and guilty, and living in the fear of death have now been set free. Victoriously, He declares, "I kept them in your name, which you have given me. I have guarded them, and not one of them has been lost" (John 17:12).

We can rejoice in God's sovereignty, for He is both mighty and gentle, the Shepherd seeking to bring in the lost and accomplish His mission. When He's at work, His voice speaks and the deaf hear, His light shines and the blind see. We have been gathered up to the heart of this gentle Shepherd and can live confident that this world belongs to our sovereign Father.

One challenge in the Christian life is to have a view of God that is big enough: to know Him as both "the LORD God" who "comes with might" and before whom we come with reverent awe, and as the one who "will tend his flock like a shepherd" and whom we follow in intimate friendship. The Lord Jesus is both the Lion and He is the Lamb (Revelation 5:5-6). Which do you find hardest to remember and live in light of? Remember both and you will obey Him and enjoy Him, as both your Sovereign and as your Shepherd.

EZEKIEL 34:11-24

APRIL 21

CHOSEN BY GOD

"In love he predestined us for adoption to himself as sons through Jesus Christ, according to the purpose of his will, to the praise of his glorious grace, with which he has blessed us in the Beloved." EPHESIANS 1:4-6

In William Shakespeare's *The Merchant of Venice*, the character Portia delivers a soliloquy that illustrates the playwright's regard for the principles of mercy and forgiveness:

Though justice be thy plea, consider this:
That in the course of justice none of us
Should see salvation. We do pray for mercy.[53]

When considering the doctrine of election—that God "predestined us for adoption"—we need to ask not "Why would God not choose everyone?" but rather "Why would God choose to have mercy on anyone?" The truth is, if justice alone were served, we would all face condemnation, for condemnation is what our sin deserves. Yet in His love for us, God chose that we "should not perish but have eternal life" (John 3:16). He did not choose us because of anything in us (which would be the occasion for pride in ourselves) but simply because of the love that is in Him (which should cause us to praise and worship Him).

One effect that an understanding of our election has on us as Christians is that it compels us to take our sin ever more seriously, for the purpose of Him choosing us is that "we should be holy and blameless before him" (Ephesians 1:4). In other words, while He didn't choose us because we *are* holy, we have been chosen in order that we might *become* holy. There is something dreadfully wrong when a belief in the electing love of God results in our declaring the right to live in any way we choose. In fact, individuals who consistently, continually live in sin yet claim salvation show that they have not understood God or His gospel at all.

By contrast, the evidence that we have been chosen by God, set apart for Him, and ministered to by Him through the Holy Spirit is ultimately seen as we are increasingly conformed to the image of His Son. Growth in moral purity is the ultimate indication of a deep devotion to Jesus Christ. A genuine interest in and wonder at the electing love of God produces in us a conformity to Jesus' own beauty.

What will we expect to see in the lives of people who truly understand this? Likely not bravado, self-centered talk, or empty defenses of the Christian faith. No—we will see humility coexisting with security, their conversation full of Christ instead of themselves, and lives of joy and sacrifice. That can be, and should be, what you see in yourself, imperfectly but increasingly. And that is what will grow in you to the extent that you say to yourself with a smile and a sense of awe, "It is not that *I* chose *Him*; *He* chose *me*."

EXODUS 20:1-21

53 William Shakespeare, *The Merchant of Venice,* Act 4, Scene 1.

APRIL 22

THE PATH OF UNBELIEF

"Judas, who betrayed him, was standing with them." JOHN 18:5

In the Garden of Gethsemane, as the soldiers approached to arrest the man who the Jewish leaders had decided must now die, the central figure was of course the Lord Jesus. But Judas played a key part—and teaches us a hard lesson.

Judas's betrayal of Christ reveals a deep hypocrisy rooted in a deeper denial. His treachery serves as a warning of how a heart, though seemingly close to God, hardens as it travels down the path of unbelief—a path marked by betrayed trust and corrupt company.

The Garden of Gethsemane was not just any garden. The disciples appeared to know it well. For Jesus and the Twelve it was a place of fellowship, of relaxation, and, doubtless, of many happy memories. And yet it was in this beautiful place that Judas betrayed Christ. It's quite staggering that he would choose a place of such intimacy in which to perform an act of such infamy, like an adulterer who breaks the marriage bond in their own marriage bed.

Picture Judas walking along the path and leading a group of soldiers and Jewish officials (John 18:3). He who was so dreadfully lost spiritually became a guide: the blind leading the blind. The path of unbelief is a lonely place that often begs for the false comfort of hopeless companionship.

The garden was a beautiful, tranquil place, but it nevertheless witnessed a heinous event. When we think of the places where we've been tempted to betray Christ—on a lovely vacation, in the comfort of our homes, even in places where Christ has previously met with us, blessed us, wooed us, and won us—we clearly see our heart's perversity in our willingness to join Judas in his betrayal.

Let Judas's example remind us that we must all be on guard. There is no room for complacency in the Christian life, no matter what you have done and seen and no matter what your standing in your church. After all, Judas had lived with Jesus for three years, had seen His miracles, and had heard His teaching. Yet still he betrayed Him. "Therefore let anyone who thinks that he stands take heed lest he fall" (1 Corinthians 10:12).

How do we remain followers and avoid the tragic path taken by Judas? As the word of God implores again and again, we must beware a slowly growing hard-heartedness that causes us to drift down the path of unbelief. Instead, we need to listen to the Holy Spirit as He guides us. We need to pray that we would find a tenderness in our hearts, an openness in our minds, and a prompting in our spirits telling us, "Now, go ahead and embrace this Christ!"

The hard lesson of Judas is that only by God's grace can we remain standing. So pray that you would never be found among the traitors: *Save me, Lord, from the real temptations to doubt and deny You. Show me the wonder of Your protection and provision, and renew my assurance that You will lose none of those whom the Father has given You.*

JOHN 10:11-30

APRIL 23

LIFE WILL FLOW TO ALL

"The circumference of the city shall be 18,000 cubits. And the name of the city from that time on shall be, The LORD Is There." EZEKIEL 48:35

The best is yet to come.

The Israelites had been in exile for six decades when Cyrus of Persia came to power in the 6th century BC. Soon after, the king allowed some of the Israelite captives to return to their previous home. With great hope and anticipation, Ezra and Nehemiah journeyed back and led the people in rebuilding the temple and the walls of Jerusalem.

The number of returned exiles was small, and they faced significant opposition. They were successful in their endeavors, but they were by no means triumphant. In fact, the older, wiser people wept when they laid the foundations of the temple, because they knew it would not meet the grand expectations of the prophets (Ezra 3:10-12).

The longings of those who wept reflected Ezekiel's final prophecy, which contained this great hope: a new temple would someday be built in a greater Jerusalem. It would be more magnificent than the first temple had ever been, and God would preside in the immense structure, from which a river would flow, giving eternal life to the world (see Ezekiel 40 – 48).

The Israelites knew that what they were building wasn't the temple Ezekiel had prophesied. It didn't quite fit. Nor was the homecoming from Babylon the great exodus about which the prophets had spoken. They were left looking beyond their own city and the rebuilt temple. Ultimately, Ezekiel was prophesying about the coming kingdom of God, which was beyond his comprehension.

In the book of Revelation, John describes a vision of heaven that provides a different sight: the church in the kingdom of God. God's plan was never limited only to the Israelites; it includes so much more. He is determined to completely undo the effects of sin and renew the whole world. Once again, mankind will know what it means to live continually in His presence, in the city called "The LORD Is There." God will be in our midst, and from Him life will flow to all: "I saw the holy city, new Jerusalem, coming down out of heaven from God … I saw no temple in the city, for its temple is the Lord God the Almighty and the Lamb. And the city has no need of sun or moon to shine on it, for the glory of God gives it light, and its lamp is the Lamb" (Revelation 21:2, 22-23).

Like the Israelites before us, we live looking forward. We lean towards the future in expectation of the return of the King and the completion of His salvation. We will join Jesus in His kingdom and experience the joy which comes from being with Him. Do not settle for what this life has to offer, nor grow despairing over the disappointments of the here and now. Our best days lie ahead of us, in the city of God.

EZEKIEL 47:1-12

APRIL 24

FROM SADNESS TO GLADNESS

"He showed them his hands and his side. Then the disciples were glad when they saw the Lord." JOHN 20:20

The first Easter did not look like a typical Easter celebration.

Before Jesus' resurrection was discovered, the day was marked by tears, devastation, and bewilderment—not joy, hope, and praise. The disciples were gathered out of fear, to protect one another, not to sing "Christ the Lord is risen today, Alleluia!"[54] They sat in sadness; their story had come to a grinding halt, with the next page blank.

Or so they thought.

The Bible does not attempt to deny or idealize the grief felt by Christ's followers after His crucifixion. They didn't understand what had happened, and they certainly didn't know what would happen next. Their sadness reveals humanity's limitations in knowing the bigger picture. Despite the Old Testament prophecies and Jesus' own foretelling of His death (Mark 8:31; 9:31; 10:33-34), John's Gospel tells us that they "as yet did not understand the Scripture, that he must rise from the dead" (John 20:9). They didn't understand that when Jesus said from the cross, "It is finished" (19:30), He was not expressing defeat but declaring victory.

This victory meant resurrection. And as the resurrected Savior came to the disciples in their darkness, fear, and sadness, He brought transformation. Their unbelief turned to belief and their sadness to gladness. That gladness was rooted in the fact that they understood that Jesus had risen from the dead. Their faith and their future returned and were rooted in this wonderful reality. The darkness of their despair made the light of the resurrection all the more glorious.

If you are looking for a god that will just make you glad, you shouldn't look for the God of the Bible. He *does* make us glad—more so than anyone or anything else—but He often starts by making us sad. We are saddened by this broken world, saddened by our own sin, saddened that on the cross Jesus died for our wickedness, disobedience, and disinterest. It is only through truly feeling such sorrow that we can fully understand the gladness that comes with our account being settled, our debt being paid, and our wrongs being forgiven.

We can know the gladness of a love that loves us even though we are not worthy of it—that loves us when we don't want to listen. What kind of love is this? It is the love of God for men and women, for you and me! Today, look away from yourself and look at Him. This is love, and when we know we are loved in this way, we are able to see the healing in the harm and that sadness can be the soil in which eternal gladness grows. About which part of your life—perhaps a part full of pain, or regret, or anxiety—do you need to hear this today? Remember that whatever you are walking through, it remains true that Christ the Lord is risen. Hallelujah!

JOHN 20:19-23

54 Charles Wesley, "Christ the Lord Is Risen Today" (1739).

APRIL 25

MERCY FOR THE BLIND

"When he heard that it was Jesus of Nazareth, he began to cry out and say, 'Jesus, Son of David, have mercy on me!'" MARK 10:47

Blind Bartimaeus sat in complete blackness. He could hear the crowd, the movement, the jibber-jabber of people speaking. He could hear the hullabaloo that signaled that Jesus of Nazareth was somewhere out there in the darkness, but he was unable to see Him. Recognizing that this might be his only chance to get Jesus' attention, in desperation he shouted out, "Jesus, Son of David, have mercy on me!"

The simplicity and clarity of Bartimaeus' request was a testimony to his faith; it indicated that he actually believed that Jesus was able to do what he was asking. By God's grace, blind Bartimaeus saw what countless others had missed: he saw that in Jesus he could find God's mercy. And when Jesus then addressed his need, Bartimaeus and all who observed the encounter understood that his faith was the reason for his cure. But Bartimaeus never made the mistake of thinking that all he really needed was his physical sight. That is why, as soon as he received his sight from Jesus, he "followed him on the way" (Mark 10:52).

In this encounter we see a microcosm of the whole gospel. The Bible often uses blindness as a metaphor for the predicament of men and women. For example, the apostle Paul says, "The god of this world has blinded the minds of the unbelievers, to keep them from seeing the light of the gospel of the glory of Christ," (2 Corinthians 4:4); and Jesus Himself said, "I came into this world, that those who do not see may see" (John 9:39). And earlier in Mark's Gospel, we read that even though the disciples were following Jesus, they still did not see and understand all that He was teaching them, so He asked, "Having eyes do you not see, and having ears do you not hear?" (Mark 8:18).

How, then, are the blind made to see? Just as Bartimaeus was: by going to Jesus and calling out to Him for mercy, asking for the loving forgiveness and new life that only He can provide. You will never know Jesus Christ as a reality in your life until you know Him as a necessity. That is a truth we needed to grasp in order to enjoy the first day of our new life following Him; but it is also a truth we need to remember in order to go on through our lives still following Him. In whatever way you require mercy right now, look at Him with the God-given eyes of faith and simply ask. The good news is that Jesus still hears, Jesus still cares, Jesus still stops, Jesus still listens, and Jesus still saves.

MARK 10:46-52

APRIL 26

GLORIFYING GOD IN OUR BODIES

"It is my eager expectation and hope that I will not be at all ashamed, but that with full courage now as always Christ will be honored in my body, whether by life or by death." PHILIPPIANS 1:20

Your body, and what you do with it, matters.

More than once in his writings, the apostle Paul expresses great concern about people's bodies. He asks the Corinthians, for instance, "Do you not know that your body is a temple of the Holy Spirit within you, whom you have from God?" He then goes on to say, "You are not your own, for you were bought with a price. So glorify God in your body" (1 Corinthians 6:19-20). In other words, our bodies belong to the God who created them and who sustains them. This way of thinking is at the heart of Paul's theology.

Paul found great joy in knowing that Jesus would be honored, or exalted, in his own body. It was his chief aim and prayer that in his ministry he would possess courage and faithfulness to do this. For Paul, to exalt Christ meant to make much of His great name: to give Him glory. We see this attitude expressed by John the Baptist, who said of Jesus, "He must increase, but I must decrease" (John 3:30). Similarly, you'll never find Paul drawing attention to himself. He saw himself only as a conduit leading to Christ.

It comes as no surprise, then, that when he wanted to establish his credentials as an apostle, Paul didn't say, "Let no one cause me trouble" just because he was a mighty apostle or because he was used by God to preach the gospel. No—he said, "Let no one cause me trouble, *for I bear on my body the marks of Jesus*" (Galatians 6:17, emphasis added). Through his body, his commitment was revealed. He was increasingly abused for his devotion to Christ. He finally went to his grave scarred, brutalized, and disfigured—yet through his trials, his cry remained "I will rejoice."

God was Lord over Paul's whole life: his body, his time, his totality. Only that could bring him such joy. Only that can bring us such joy.

The bottom line is that you are not your own. Nothing you have is your own. Everything is a stewardship, whether God has given you much or little. You belong to God, your Creator and your Redeemer. One day, He will raise us with glorified, imperishable bodies (1 Corinthians 15:42-44, 51-54). For the moment, in this life He calls us to serve Him in this body. In everything you do with it, then, let your body be an offering that you joyfully lay before God.

1 CORINTHIANS 6:12-20

APRIL 27

ASKING RIGHTLY

"You do not have, because you do not ask. You ask and do not receive, because you ask wrongly, to spend it on your passions." JAMES 4:2-3

Thou art coming to a King,
Large petitions with thee bring;
For His grace and pow'r are such,
None can ever ask too much.[55]

This hymn by John Newton reminds us of Jesus' words: "Whatever you ask in prayer, believe that you have received it, and it will be yours" (Mark 11:24). Jesus taught His disciples elsewhere, "If you then, who are evil, know how to give good gifts to your children, how much more will your Father who is in heaven give good things to those who ask him!" (Matthew 7:11). We can go to God and ask Him for good things. We can never ask too much of God. Yet, as James says, many of us don't receive these gifts from our Father because we don't have the courage to act on Jesus' teaching and simply *ask*. Or we do ask, but we request things not that are in line with His will but rather that we want to receive from Him in order "to spend it on [our] passions"—to use to further our priorities, and not to serve His.

When we consider what God's word teaches about prayer, we find that we are to ask—and to ask with humility, sincerity, and love, and with an understanding that God is sovereign and that His will is what we most wish to be done. When Jesus was in the Garden of Gethsemane, He prayed, "Abba, Father, all things are possible for you. Remove this cup from me. Yet not what I will, but what you will" (Mark 14:36). See the balance here. Jesus had absolute confidence in God's power, He had the courage to ask God to do something humanly impossible, and yet He also showed complete submission to the Father's will. It was only God's sovereign purpose that kept the cup from being removed as Christ prayed. It was not because Christ didn't "believe enough" to make it happen. In the same way, the boldness, childlikeness, and enthusiasm we demonstrate when asking God to do the impossible are not undermined by His sovereignty; they are mercifully controlled by it.

As God's child, you can boldly come before your Father, trusting Him to accomplish all you need and all you ask that is in accordance with His will. Following Jesus' example, you can submit your desires to your Father's loving sovereignty. As you trust God for the right thing in the right way, you can be confident that He will always give the right response. You can never ask for something that is too big for God to do. So just ask!

LUKE 18:1-8

55 John Newton, "Come, My Soul, Thy Suit Prepare" (1779).

APRIL 28

JESUS LIFTS US UP

"After crying out and convulsing him terribly, [the unclean spirit] came out, and the boy was like a corpse, so that most of them said, 'He is dead.' But Jesus took him by the hand and lifted him up, and he arose." MARK 9:26-27

There is no one whom Jesus cannot help.

In Mark 9, we read about Jesus' interaction with a child who had long been possessed by an unclean spirit. The boy's predicament had been his lot since he was young. He could neither speak nor hear. When the demon took him, it threw him down, causing him to foam at the mouth, grind his teeth, and become rigid (Mark 9:18). This young man was caught in a dreadful circumstance, essentially trapped inside his body, unable to hear any words of comfort that may have come to him from his father, family, or friends, unable to give voice to his pain and fear. His life was marred by the attempted distortion and destruction of the image of God that he bore.

In the face of such a hopeless situation, Jesus intervened, giving a divine word of rebuke to the evil spirit. Through such a powerful rebuke, Christ drew out the enemy's powerless rage, and the evil spirit, having done its worst, left the boy as though dead. And then Jesus raised him up.

This is what Jesus does. He takes people whose lives are decimated—those who are en route to destruction—and He does what only He can do: He enters that life, takes the person by the hand, lifts them up... and they stand.

Jesus is the only one who can truly say, "I am the resurrection and the life. Whoever believes in me, though he die, yet shall he live, and everyone who lives and believes in me shall never die" (John 11:25-26). He is the only one who can take someone who seems absolutely helpless and completely unable to effect change in themselves, and give them new life.

So today, Jesus comes to you and says, *Why don't you just bring your burdens to Me? You can't educate yourself out of pain and sorrows. Therapy won't give you lasting answers for all your hurt and confusion. Truly, it's good that you know you can't do this on your own. Bring your burdens to Me.*

Not only that, but He can come to others through you. There is no one you will meet today who does not need Jesus' help, and no one whom Jesus cannot help. However bright someone's life looks, there is normally regret and anxiety under the surface, and there is always the sin that is slowly dragging each of us to destruction—unless and until Jesus intervenes. When you learn to see those around you in this way, you long to share Christ with them; for there is *no one* whom Jesus cannot help.

LUKE 19:1-10

APRIL 29

RIGHTLY EXALTED

"Therefore God has highly exalted him." PHILIPPIANS 2:9

Philippians 2:5-8 is a beautiful statement concerning Christ's humanity, deity, ministry, and humiliation. Having mapped the humility of the incarnate Son of God all the way to His death on a cross, where does your mind go next? Naturally, we think of the resurrection. But Paul does not. He takes us to Christ's exaltation. There is, he says, a logical connection between Jesus' humiliation and His exaltation: "*Therefore* God has highly exalted him." What is this exaltation? It is that the Father has given His Son the throne and ordered this world so that one day "at the name of Jesus every knee should bow, in heaven and on earth and under the earth, and every tongue confess that Jesus Christ is Lord, to the glory of God the Father" (v 10-11).

But why is His exaltation fitting? Scripture gives us several answers. First, because it fulfills Old Testament prophecy and demonstrates that God keeps His word. The worldwide recognition of Jesus as Lord will occur because God promised it would. Six hundred years before Jesus arrived on the stage of human history, God prophesied through Isaiah: "My servant shall act wisely; he shall be high and lifted up, and shall be exalted" (Isaiah 52:13). And so Christ came to bear the pain and sin of the world, fulfilling the role of Suffering Servant, lifted up on a cross and then raised to be exalted on His throne. As Paul wrote elsewhere, "All the promises of God find their Yes in him" (2 Corinthians 1:20).

Second, Christ's exaltation is fitting because He is God. The Bible teaches us that the Son is one with the Father. On account of His divinity, exaltation is a necessity; there is nowhere else for God to sit! No other seat is suitable for the Son except at His Father's right hand.

Finally, Christ's exaltation is fitting because He is the dear Son of His Father. God the Father watched the Son obediently go to the cross to fulfill the covenant of redemption and heard Him cry out in pain, "My God, my God, why have you forsaken me?" (Matthew 27:46). The Father knew that the Son underwent that agony out of love for the Father and love for His people. The Father would not leave His perfect Son in that dire condition. How could the Father's love do anything other than exalt the Son from His lowly state?

Christ's humiliation for us and exaltation above us are surely enough to bring us to the point where we bow in joyful submission to Him. They show us that there is one who has the status to demand our obedience and the character to deserve our adoration. They remind us that the best thing about heaven will be the most glorious person in heaven:

I will not gaze at glory, but on my King of grace;
Not at the crown He giveth, but on His piercèd hand;
The Lamb is all the glory of Immanuel's land.[56]

ACTS 13:16-43

56 Anne R. Cousin, "The Sands of Time Are Sinking" (1857).

APRIL 30

RESPONDING TO ANOTHER'S SUCCESS

"He dreamed another dream and told it to his brothers and said, 'Behold, I have dreamed another dream. Behold, the sun, the moon, and eleven stars were bowing down to me' ... And his brothers were jealous of him." GENESIS 37:9, 11

Envy is a feeling common to humanity. It is also a monster—a giant that can eat anyone alive.

How do you struggle with envy? Who are those in your sphere of influence or your field of vision who are experiencing favor or success, and with whom in some way you wish to swap places? We must be careful. "The odious passion of envy," writes George Lawson, "torments and destroys one's self while it seeks the ruin of its object."[57] Envy tends to destroy the envier.

They did not yet know it, but Joseph's brothers were on the road to the evils of deceit, malice, and slave-trading their own sibling—to the most detestable forms of cruelty. The first step on that road was their jealousy of him. But they did not see it, and so they walked towards actions they presumably had not countenanced when Joseph first started sharing his dreams of grandeur.

We must learn to see our envy and to deal with it. So how can we handle others' success without succumbing to bitterness and jealousy?

First, we recognize that God is sovereign over the affairs of man. God determined for Joseph to have what he had and be what he was—and He determined a less significant position for Joseph's brothers. If they had been prepared to consider this, although it might have been hard, they would have been spared the self-inflicted pain of their envious hatred.

Second, we turn to God in prayer. F.B. Meyer, a great 19th-century preacher, once told of how another preacher came to minister in the same area in which he was already ministering, and suddenly there was a drift from his congregation. Jealousy began to grip his soul, and the only freedom he could find was to pray for this fellow pastor—to pray that God would bless another's ministry. Prayer loosens the grip of envy on our hearts.

God is the one who sets up and brings down. If Joseph's brothers had grasped this truth, they would have had no occasion to be envious. God is also the one who gives us every breath as a gift from Him. If they had grasped this, they would have had more desire to give thanks than to grow bitter. Today, search your own heart, recognize and repent of any jealousy that has taken root, and bow in humility and thankfulness before your sovereign God.

1 SAMUEL 2:1-10

57 George Lawson, *Lectures on the History of Joseph* (Banner of Truth, 1972), p 5.

MAY 1

THE SLEEPING SAVIOR

"But he was in the stern, asleep on the cushion. And they woke him and said to him, 'Teacher, do you not care that we are perishing?' And he awoke and rebuked the wind and said to the sea, 'Peace! Be still!'" MARK 4:38-39

Place yourself in the disciples' shoes as they sailed that stormy sea while Jesus slept in the stern of the boat. Several of them were experienced fishermen, and they understood that they were confronted with the very real possibility of drowning—yet their Master seemed to have abandoned them to it, sound asleep as He was.

The very fact that Jesus needed to sleep reveals that He had a real human body that knew the feelings of fatigue and thirst and hunger. He experienced firsthand the body's weaknesses. He even went through the trouble of finding a cushion on which to sleep, showing us that He knew discomfort. He who had made the universe could have turned the wood beneath Him into a more comfortable substance fit for a good rest, but instead the Lord of glory laid His head on a pillow, just like you and me.

If Jesus had not known the weaknesses and temptations of humanity, He would not be a sympathetic High Priest, offering us mercy and grace from the heavenly throne (Hebrews 4:14-16). But the Bible makes it clear that He did. He knew, for instance, the pain of neglect: "He came to his own, and his own people did not receive him" (John 1:11). Even some of His faithful disciples—some of the very men in this boat—eventually denied Him or deserted Him. He also knew the abuse of slander that misrepresented the wonder and beauty of His character (see for instance Luke 7:34). He wrestled for forty days and nights with the lies and temptations of the Evil One (Matthew 4:1-11). He faced utter agony and turmoil on the cross as He cried, "My God, my God, why have you forsaken me?" (27:46). There is no experience of pain or insult we might know that hasn't wrung the heart of Christ—and because He knows such struggles, He invites us to come to Him as we experience them ourselves.

Here in this little incident nestled at the beginning of Mark's Gospel is the life-changing reminder that Jesus is the living Christ, a sympathetic Savior, and a steadfast companion. There is no one better suited to deal with any predicament you or I may face than the Master whom the disciples found sound asleep on a cushion. You, like they, can cry out to Him and discover that the one who needed to sleep in that boat is also the one who could rebuke a storm—the one who reigns on high, who will never slumber nor sleep, and who will not let your foot be moved (Psalm 121:3-4).

What is on your mind today that prompts you to fear? Be assured that the Lord Jesus does understand what this life is like. Bring your fear to Him now, "casting all your anxieties on him, because he cares for you" (1 Peter 5:7).

PSALM 121

MAY 2

HE DIED TO MAKE US GOOD

"Do not be deceived: neither the sexually immoral, nor idolaters, nor adulterers, nor men who practice homosexuality, nor thieves, nor the greedy, nor drunkards, nor revilers, nor swindlers will inherit the kingdom of God. And such were some of you. But you were washed, you were sanctified, you were justified." 1 CORINTHIANS 6:9-11

The Evil One is not concerned with persuading us not to bother with many of our Christian activities—but he *is* concerned to persuade us to stop holding on to the absolute truths concerning the nature and character of God and to the absolute truths concerning the ethics of His kingdom. Recognizing this, Paul warned the Corinthian believers not to wander into the minefield of ungodly behavior. "Do not be deceived," says Paul; the unrighteous will not "inherit the kingdom of God."

Paul describes some of the areas of wickedness that had become socially acceptable in Corinth. The city was a bustling commercial center, a hodgepodge of races, creeds, and languages. As a culture, though, it was rootless and rough. In fact, the place was so badly debauched that "Corinth" became a byword for immorality itself. So what did Paul do? He ventured into this city with a strategy. He was "occupied with the word, testifying to the Jews that the Christ was Jesus" (Acts 18:5). His objective was not to enact legislation but to begin proclamation.

There is no legislative agenda that can redeem culture. Instead, there is a message sent from God to redeem men and women, and it is simply this: "Jesus Christ and him crucified" (1 Corinthians 2:2). The gospel is God's agenda for our world. He uses the power and conviction of His word to speak into people's lives and bring about radical change.

Paul didn't buy into elaborate rhetoric. He had that one message, and he kept saying it again and again. He knew that only Christ's atoning death on the cross makes it possible for men and women to be set free from their besetting sins so that they "might walk in newness of life" (Romans 6:4).

It is perilous and unnecessary to remain wicked. The gospel message sounds forth as loudly and effectively today as it did in the streets of Corinth, and it cuts through the deception of the world's relativism and of the tendency to think that laws alone can change hearts or produce faith. The great need of our lives, of our cities, and of our nations is for sinners to be saved. Do not be deceived into thinking that sin does not matter. Do not be deceived into thinking that your society most needs something other than the news of the kingdom of God. We must confess the message of the crucified Messiah:

He died that we might be forgiven,
He died to make us good,
That we might go at last to heaven,
Saved by His precious blood.[58]

ACTS 18:1-11

58 Cecil Frances Alexander, "There Is a Green Hill Far Away" (1848).

MAY 3

SECURE ON SOLID GROUND

"Light up my eyes, lest I sleep the sleep of death, lest my enemy say, 'I have prevailed over him,' lest my foes rejoice because I am shaken. I have trusted in your steadfast love; my heart shall rejoice in your salvation." PSALM 13:3-5

When you go on a camping trip, one of the most important things you can do is make sure that your tent pegs are hammered securely into solid ground. Once that step is complete, you can go about other activities with a greater peace of mind, knowing that your shelter will weather a storm—which certainly beats the alternative of coming back to a campsite and seeing that your tent has blown away!

In this verse, David is responding to feeling forgotten and disappointed in life, and being unfairly opposed by others around him. He begins by applying his mind to the situation; recalling what he already knows, David declares his trust in God's faithful love.

This trust was volitional. Though the feelings of his heart were real, David chose to bring his emotions under the jurisdiction of God's character and purposes. He staked his hope—the tent pegs of his heart—in the solid ground of God's steadfast love and unfailing mercies. Only then could he rejoice once again.

In the new heaven and new earth, life's storms will finally be stilled. In the meantime, we will pass through squalls and even deluges. We will endure with joy to the extent that we trust that our Father is wise. When He does not give us something, it's because He knows it's better for us not to have it. When He entrusts us with something hard to accept, it's because He is giving us the privilege of bearing testimony to His grace in that circumstance. When He leads us through the rain, it is because He knows it will cause us to cling closer to Him and cause our character to become more conformed to His (James 1:2-4).

When we look at the shattered remnants of our most trying experiences, it often seems as if collapse is imminent. But in those moments, we can remember that God exchanges "beauty for ashes, the oil of joy for mourning, the garment of praise for the spirit of heaviness" (Isaiah 61:3, KJV). Each trial we face is an opportunity to remind ourselves that, as with David, it is God's steadfast love that secures our souls and gives us reason to delight in His salvation.

Today, the call to each of us is to say, "Lord Jesus Christ, help me to have the tent pegs of my life staked securely in Your steadfast love, so that in life and death, in joy and sorrow, in sickness and health, I might rejoice."

HEBREWS 12:3-11

MAY 4

JESUS IS KING

"I heard every creature in heaven and on earth and under the earth and in the sea, and all that is in them, saying, 'To him who sits on the throne and to the Lamb be blessing and honor and glory and might forever and ever!'"
REVELATION 5:13

The Bible makes it very clear that history is moving purposefully towards a definite conclusion. That reality is one of the distinctive features of the biblical worldview. One way that Christianity distinguishes itself, in other words, is in the matter of how all things come to a close.

Sometimes, in looking at old photographs we may find ourselves asking, "Where am I in this picture?"—or, "Am I even *in* this picture?" When it comes to God's plan, though, every single person is included in Revelation's picture of history. No one is missing from the story. And when history comes to a close, it will end in division and separation.

Jesus spoke about this separation when He said that the sheep and goats will be divided (Matthew 25:31-46): light and darkness will be delineated, and those who believe on Jesus will be set apart from those who do not. No one will be left out, though tragically some will have chosen to be shut out. Therefore, our position in this big picture matters.

All of history's ebb and flow is to be viewed in light of the fact that there is a throne in heaven and that throne is not empty; rather, it is occupied by God, who is in control. Jesus is King, and He is seated at the right hand of the throne. Although many do not yet recognize His kingdom, it doesn't alter the reality that He reigns.

From humanity's fall to the end of time there exist, as the great fourth-century theologian Augustine of Hippo put it, two rival cities—two rival loves. By our nature, we are involved in the city of man, and only by God's grace will we ever be involved in and devoted to the city of God.

The earthly city, the city of man, is destined to pass away. But the heavenly city, God's kingdom, will go on forever and ever. Do we recognize Jesus as King? How we answer is a matter of eternal significance. And how we answer is also a matter of present consequence. If Jesus is your King, then you will live as His subject, seeking to obey Him even when His command cuts against your own preferences. If Jesus is your King, you will be loyal to Him above all others, for this world is not your home and you are just passing through. As Paul wrote, "Our citizenship is in heaven, and from it we await a Savior, the Lord Jesus Christ" (Philippians 3:20). Be sure to live as a citizen of a better country and a subject of a greater King. We will spend eternity joining with the whole of creation in bringing Him honor. May we do so in our words and conduct today, too.

PSALM 24

MAY 5

RESTORING THE TEMPLE

"Making a whip of cords, he drove them all out of the temple, with the sheep and oxen. And he poured out the coins of the money-changers and overturned their tables ... His disciples remembered that it was written, 'Zeal for your house will consume me.'" JOHN 2:15, 17

A father would understandably burn with a righteous anger if he saw drugs wreaking destruction in the life of his child. We wouldn't expect him to flippantly dismiss such devastation. No, we would expect him to do everything necessary to drive that evil out and see restoration take place.

When Jesus, the Son of God, entered His Father's house on earth—the temple in Jerusalem—and looked round at the scene, it was painful to Him. A place intended for the worship of God had become a place given over to the worship of money. A place intended to beckon the world to meet the living God had become one that kept the nations at arm's length. He found it intolerable that the name of God, the glory of God, was being besmirched and tarnished. There is no reason for us to stand back and try to mitigate Jesus' actions. The holy anger of Christ burned with zeal and purity. This was not the time for polite conversation.

Jesus knew exactly why the temple was there. It was the place of meeting God. It was meant to be the joy of the whole earth. What He found instead was completely opposed to its purpose—and in His words and actions, He made that abundantly clear.

Interestingly, when the Pharisees confronted Jesus afterwards, they didn't challenge His actions; they challenged His *authority*. Jesus responded to this challenge with a puzzling statement: "Destroy this temple, and in three days I will raise it up" (John 2:19). The temple He referred to, John explains, was Himself (v 21). One day, Jesus would come to Jerusalem not to visit the temple complex but to give His own body and blood as the full and final sacrifice for sins, and then to rise to new life and to reign forever. It was on that authority that He was making clear the difference between what God had intended the temple to be and what it had been made to become.

Here, then, we are confronted by a Jesus who is radical—who responds with zeal and protectiveness to the issue of God's glory. This Jesus is not meek and mild, always affirming and never challenging. He is the Great High Priest, who came not only to cleanse the temple precincts but also to cleanse our hearts and deal with our alienation. In Him, the true temple, God has built "a house of prayer for all peoples" (Isaiah 56:7).

So look afresh at Jesus, who brooked no compromise in pursuing the glory of God through enabling the nations to worship Him rightly. Look afresh at Jesus, who used His authority and perfections willingly to take our place and bear our punishment in His body so we could be restored. Look afresh at Jesus, of whose amazing grace you are a beneficiary. And let His zeal for God's glory also be yours.

MATTHEW 27:35-56

◇ Bible Through The Year: Numbers 20–22; Revelation 22

MAY 6

FREELY GIVEN

"It was kind of you to share my trouble. And you Philippians yourselves know that in the beginning of the gospel, when I left Macedonia, no church entered into partnership with me in giving and receiving, except you only."
PHILIPPIANS 4:14-15

To be a Christian is to be a receiver and a giver.

Many of us have been educated on the importance of having a retirement account to which we make consistent contributions. Yet while it would be wrong for us to completely dismiss the matter of making sound financial decisions, as believers we must also consider our giving and investing in light of eternity.

In his letter to the church in Philippi, the apostle Paul commended his brothers and sisters in Christ for their willingness to "share [his] trouble"—a partnership that included the sharing and giving of material gifts. The Philippians' generosity was outstanding in that it stood in direct contrast to the absence of such support for Paul from other churches. Although their church was a fledgling congregation, the Philippian believers had determined from the very outset that they would support the apostle in his gospel work.

Their support for Paul was not only outstanding but also longstanding. The Philippians' giving wasn't sporadic. Rather, it was marked by consistency and continuity as they sought to help him with his needs again and again. Although a decade had elapsed since Paul first preached the gospel to them, these men and women were still committed.

Their giving was not the result of a one-time emotional surge nor the product of external manipulation. No, this early church gave in the awareness that everything they possessed had been given freely to them. Indeed, in sending out the disciples, Jesus had reminded them that because they "received without paying," they were to "give without pay" (Matthew 10:8). In other words, the foundation of sacrificial, generous, resourceful partnership is the grace of God. That foundation is established when we understand that all we are and all we have—all our resources, our gifts, and our talents—is from Him.

We do not all have the same gifts or capacity for giving—and monetary giving is certainly not the only avenue for benevolence! Yet since we are all recipients of what God has given to us, we will all be those who look to give to others. God has purposefully put His people together in such a way that we are each to give "according to the grace given to us" (Romans 12:6). We shouldn't give simply because we've been manipulated or because we listened to a stirring song that brought us to the point of tears, nor should we give because we'll get our name on a building or a bench. No, we should give for one reason and one reason only: because God has so freely and so generously given to us.

2 CORINTHIANS 9:1-15

MAY 7

WE ALL WORSHIP SOMETHING

"I will turn the darkness before them into light, the rough places into level ground. These are the things I do, and I do not forsake them. They are turned back and utterly put to shame, who trust in carved idols, who say to metal images, 'You are our gods.'" ISAIAH 42:16-17

In the words of Bob Dylan, you gotta serve somebody.[59] It's true—we all worship something. The only question is what.

Too often in our human futility, we end up leaning on and ultimately serving crafty little creations of our own invention. Throughout history, mankind's fundamental problem has been that we keep creating false gods to whom we go seeking false salvation. These idols are simply heart-level substitutes for the real God. Rather than looking to the Lord as the object of our devotion and the source of our satisfaction, we take the good things that He created for our enjoyment and turn them into vain replacements for Him.

C.S. Lewis puts it this way: "We are half-hearted creatures, fooling about with drink and sex and ambition when infinite joy is offered us, like an ignorant child who wants to go on making mud pies in a slum because he cannot imagine what is meant by the offer of a holiday at the sea. We are far too easily pleased."[60]

Whichever heart-level substitutes we may rely on, these idols are powerless. They cannot help us. As Isaiah makes clear, they've never been able to tell us the future or even help us reflect on the past; neither can they give counsel. They meet our questions with mere silence and unfulfilled expectations (Isaiah 41:22-23, 28-29).

Only the true and living God knows everything from beginning to end. He broke through the silence, foretelling what was to come. He overwhelms darkness with His light. He replaces the "rough places" of wickedness with the "level ground" of righteousness. Although we once turned our backs on Him, He sent His Servant, Jesus, our Wonderful Counselor.

You and I are constantly confronted by idols that call out for our attention and entice us to find fulfillment in them rather than God. What are the ones that call loudest to you? Know that they are lying (though of course they don't tell you that). God's word warns us of the shame that lies in worshiping them and leads us on a better way: to find fulfillment in serving and being served by Him.

You gotta serve somebody today. Be sure to make it the living, loving God.

ROMANS 1:16-32

59 Bob Dylan, "Gotta Serve Somebody" (1979).
60 "The Weight of Glory," in *The Weight of Glory and Other Addresses* (Harper Collins, 2001), p 26.

MAY 8

THE SPIRIT'S POWER

"You will receive power when the Holy Spirit has come upon you, and you will be my witnesses in Jerusalem and in all Judea and Samaria, and to the end of the earth." ACTS 1:8

The Holy Spirit is given to us so that God's people may bring God's word to God's world.

Without the Spirit, the events of the book of Acts—which tells the story of the gospel expanding, with Jesus' disciples hitting the streets of Jerusalem proclaiming the message of the risen Christ—could not have happened. After all, a few weeks previously, these same disciples had been hiding behind closed doors, a frightened little group mourning their crucified King. What accounts for their sudden transformation?

The answer is found in Jesus' triumph over the grave and the promise He gave to His disciples—the promise of His Holy Spirit to enable and empower them. This promise was coupled with a command: Jesus' followers were to go into all the world and preach the good news.

Before the disciples went out with enthusiasm, Jesus sharpened their focus. They had not yet grasped the fact that His concern was not limited to Israel but was for all people everywhere. (And it would take them some time more to fully appreciate this truth: see Acts 10:1 – 11:18.) Jesus therefore commanded His followers to be His "witnesses in Jerusalem and in all Judea and Samaria, and *to the end of the earth.*"

Following Jesus' ascension, the Holy Spirit descended upon His followers, just as Jesus had promised—and then the great story of the spread of the church throughout the known world began. That is a story that has not yet finished, and it includes every believer as the gospel continues to be preached all around this world.

If you are in Christ, you possess this very same Spirit, and you are enabled by His power to spread the truth about Jesus throughout the world. The Spirit wasn't given so that you and I could sit around and tell other Christians about our spiritual experiences. Rather, we are to use our gifts and talents to take the gospel to the nations. For some of us, that means going overseas on mission. For others, it means crossing our street or our city, as part of that same mission.

God calls you to love and serve even those with whom you share no common earthly citizenship. He calls you to cross divides and come alongside those to whom you would naturally be indifferent, or even those who live in enmity towards you. But He does not call you to summon up the love and courage that that requires. No—we must be transformed by a power outside of ourselves, and that is what Jesus promised and what the Spirit provides. So ask God to pour out His Spirit afresh in your life today, that you may proclaim the good news with courage and zeal.

ACTS 1:1-11

MAY 9

PERFECT SYMPATHY

"He had to be made like his brothers in every respect, so that he might become a merciful and faithful high priest in the service of God, to make propitiation for the sins of the people. For because he himself has suffered when tempted, he is able to help those who are being tempted." HEBREWS 2:17-18

Many of us are discouraged by the regularity with which we face temptation. We might be embarrassed at the overwhelming allure of the temptation in our lives. It can feel all-consuming. In those moments, it is important to remember that the experience of being tempted in itself is not sin—for Christ, who was sinless, endured it. But because He didn't *yield* to temptations, as we often do, He serves as our ultimate example as we strive for righteousness.

When Christ took human nature upon Himself, He became subject to its limitations and trials. Therefore, although Jesus is the divine Son of God and our Great High Priest, not a mere mortal, we can derive encouragement from knowing that He is perfectly able to sympathize with our own struggles.

Christ's sympathy for the trials you and I face depends not upon the experience of sin but upon the experience of the *temptation* to sin, which only the one who is truly sinless can know to its fullest extent. Jesus does not demonstrate sympathy from a distance; He intimately knows the pain and challenge of enduring temptation. He walked our earthly paths.

So, when you are most aware of the temptations that face you and most aware of your weaknesses, here is where you can go. Do not lean into earthly wisdom of the "great high priests" of the 21st century, who would tell you that temptations are desires to be indulged, that guilt is an affliction to be rejected, and that shame is always unhelpful and unnecessary. Turn instead to *the* Great High Priest, who tells you that temptations are to be resisted and who provides the power to enable you to do that (1 Corinthians 10:13), and who also assures you that your guilt and shame when you give in has been borne in His body and removed at the cross.

One thing that is truly beautiful about a relationship with the Lord Jesus Christ is that you can feel confident in going before the one who died in order that you might hold firmly to the faith you profess. You can regularly, humbly, assuredly come into the presence of Almighty God Himself, who welcomes you through Christ, your perfect sympathizer. And eventually, in eternity, there will be nothing left about which you need Christ to plead on your behalf. You will simply be able to stand before God in worship, praising Him for inviting you into His perfect presence. Until then, ask the one who knows what it is to face and resist temptation to be with you as you battle your own temptations and as you strive to obey Him today.

HEBREWS 2:5-18

MAY 10

TERMS AND CONDITIONS

"If anyone would come after me, let him deny himself and take up his cross and follow me. For whoever would save his life will lose it, but whoever loses his life for my sake and the gospel's will save it." MARK 8:34-35

You can't do much online without agreeing to terms and conditions of use. And once we have checked the "I agree" box, credit cards, social media platforms, and websites will notify us from time to time that their legal policies have changed—and that in order to continue using the services they provide, we must accept the new ones.

Changes like these can be frequent and subtle. It's virtually impossible to notice or keep track of them all. Fortunately, though, the terms and conditions of being a follower of Christ have never changed, and they never will. They can't be revoked or adapted to our preferences, because God established them. In these verses, the Son of God is setting out the "terms and conditions" for becoming one of His people and being given eternal life.

We sometimes tend to act as though we have to pull ourselves up by our bootstraps in order to obey the Lord. But the truth is quite the contrary! The Bible says that just as we trust in Jesus as a response to His initiative and grace (Ephesians 2:8), so that same grace also sustains us and makes it possible for us to keep following Him (Philippians 1:6). He shapes our minds, our morals, our manners, and our means so we can be brought under the control of the one whom we've declared as Majesty.

One of the "conditions" of following Christ, then, is that our lives are no longer about us. Our individual identities and goals are not the priority. We are instead transformed to bear fruit that is visible to the outside world through our union with Christ. He calls us to radically denounce self-idolatry.

Through denying ourselves, we take up our cross and follow Him. Unfortunately, the metaphor of "taking up our cross" is often trivialized; we would be well served to remember that being crucified was actually one of the most brutal, horrible forms of execution that humanity has ever devised. By using the image of bearing a cross, Jesus is emphasizing that discipleship carries a great cost.

But Christ is not calling us to do anything that He has not already done. It was on a cross that He bought us at a price (1 Corinthians 6:20). Walking with Him in discipleship is therefore a march both towards death to one's old self and towards eternal life. It's not a stroll but a living sacrifice, because we are not our own. But take heart, for there is also beauty in that march. One day, the Son of Man will return in power and glory, and in His kingdom redeem what is broken. Until then, losing our lives on behalf of the kingdom of God is a good buy, no matter the price.

1 PETER 3:13 – 4:11

MAY 11

THIS IS THE LORD'S DOING

"Then [Naomi] arose with her daughters-in-law to return from the country of Moab, for she had heard in the fields of Moab that the Lord *had visited his people and given them food."* RUTH 1:6

Bethlehem is a prominent town in biblical history. In this town, David had looked after his sheep before being anointed to the throne. One thousand years later, when different shepherds were tending their flocks, a host of angels proclaimed the birth of Jesus Christ in the very same town.

Before both of these significant events, however, came the period of the judges, which was characterized by violence, social and political disorder, and religious chaos. During this tumultuous era, famine struck Bethlehem, making the town whose name in Hebrew means "house of bread" into a house of hunger and desperation instead.

In these desperate circumstances, a man named Elimelech chose to move his wife Naomi and their two sons to the land of Moab to find food. While Elimelech's name means "My God is King," his decision to leave God's promised land and live in the land of Israel's enemies may raise the question in our minds as to whether he really was trusting in God's provision or committed to obeying His rule.

Moab turned out to be a place of tragedy, not plenty. Elimelech and his sons died, leaving Naomi a widow. After a number of years, though, a small ray of hope broke through the darkness of Naomi's pain; news reached her that food had returned to Bethlehem. God had provided for His people in His land.

Thousands of years later, we're tempted to rush past this truth: that God provides what His people need. Perhaps you know that about your salvation—but how easy it is to forget about His daily provision! Do we have eyes to see what He is giving us and doing for us in our daily lives? At the end of each day, do we have hearts brimming with thankfulness for all He has done?

One practical example of God's continued provision is the very food we receive daily. Nobody ought to walk up and down the aisles of a grocery store with a greater sense of amazement and gratitude than a Christian! Ultimately, it is God who stocks the shelves of our stores and pantries. We can say, as we grab our eggs and our milk, "This is the Lord's doing; it is marvelous in our eyes" (Psalm 118:23).

No matter how dark and dramatic the events of life may appear to be, God still cares for His people and works out His purposes, and He often chooses to do so through unlikely people and in quiet ways. He had purposed to work great things through Naomi and her family—and it began with bread in Bethlehem. We, too, need to open our eyes to see that God's provision of food points to His provision of our greatest sustaining need—our Redeemer, Jesus Christ—and to His provision of our highest calling: "good works, which God prepared ... that we should walk in them" for His glory (Ephesians 2:10).

ACTS 17:24-31

MAY 12

THE VALLEY OF DECISION

"Ruth said, 'Do not urge me to leave you or to return from following you. For where you go I will go, and where you lodge I will lodge. Your people shall be my people, and your God my God.'" RUTH 1:16

There are moments throughout life that demand a decision. And, as pastor and author Rico Tice says, "We are the choices that we make."[61]

After being struck by the triple tragedy of burying her husband and her two sons in Moab, Naomi decided to go back to her hometown, Bethlehem. Yet instead of forcing her daughters-in-law, Ruth and Orpah, to return with her, Naomi urged them to remain in their own homeland of Moab, return to their families, remarry, and live full lives (Ruth 1:8-9). Ruth and Orpah were suddenly faced with a life-altering decision.

The lives of these three women were interwoven. They had lived with one another, experienced loss together, mourned together, and wept together. Ultimately, Orpah chose to remain behind, and Ruth decided to journey to Bethlehem with Naomi. Essentially, Orpah did what was expected and sensible. Ruth, on the other hand, abandoned the known for the unknown. She gave up the likelihood of remarriage to cling to her aged, helpless mother-in-law.

Ruth understood that her decision should not be guided by familiarity, security, or relational prospects. This moment would shape her life and her destiny. Remaining in Moab would mean remaining with the false gods of her upbringing and turning her back on everything she had presumably discovered from Naomi about the God of Abraham, Isaac, and Jacob. Naomi's God had become Ruth's God. That is why she decided to stay by Naomi's side.

Ruth's decision on the road to Bethlehem points forward to the valley of decision that Jesus calls each of us to stand in: *Do you want to be my disciples, or do you want to return to the life you've known? Who is there who will forsake his or her father and mother and everything they know—all that represents stability and security—for my sake?* (see Luke 14:26). Can we confidently say to Christ, "Where you go I will go"? Can we declare, "Though the way ahead is unfamiliar and unpopular, still I will follow"?

This is not a decision we make just at the moment of salvation. We make it every day of our lives: Will we go back to our old, sinful ways, or are we going to follow the way of truth? Will we make sacrifices and take risks in order to follow God and serve His people?

Ruth's bold, faithful response to this pivotal choice sets an example for us as we consider what degrees to earn, what careers to pursue, how we spend our time and who we spend it with, how much money we have and how we're going to steward it, or where we're going to live and serve. Such decisions, made rightly, will mark us out as different—as unreservedly committed to following Jesus Christ, the one in whom we truly find abundant life (John 10:10).

MARK 8:27-38

61 *Faithful Leaders and the Things That Matter Most* (The Good Book Company, 2021), p 83.

MAY 13

GOD OF THE ORDINARY

"So Naomi returned, and Ruth the Moabite her daughter-in-law with her, who returned from the country of Moab. And they came to Bethlehem at the beginning of barley harvest." RUTH 1:22

On any given morning as you read, watch, or listen to the news, do you ever find yourself thinking you are very small? Do you ever wonder, "Does God really know who I am or where I am? What interest would He, the Creator of everything, have in me?"

You and I are very ordinary—and we can easily believe that "ordinary" equates to "useless." Yet Ruth and Naomi's story reveals something different. In it, we discover the sovereign, providential hand of God working in and through life's routines. He knows and He cares, He sustains and He provides.

The book of Ruth's account of God's provision and care begins with a mistake. Elimelech made the ill-fated decision to leave famished Bethlehem for prospering Moab with his wife Naomi and their two sons—but he and his sons died there.

Whether Elimelech's motive was one of desperation, discontent, or distrust, Scripture illustrates through his choice that our foolishness cannot set aside God's providence. Even when we respond to circumstances with the wrong spirit—when figuratively we take ourselves up and out of the land of God's promise—He can still accomplish His purposes. When we are tempted to fear that God has overlooked our lives because of our mistakes, we can rest in His providence, which is able to work through our biggest—or smallest—missteps.

Have you seen God move in life's ordinary moments? Have you seen Him at work through your mistakes? Or are you caught in the lie that God only operates in spectacular, extraordinary ways or through our moments of greatest obedience? When we look only for the extraordinary, we miss God's glory in the ordinary—in a bowl of apples on the table, a well-prepared meal, a bird singing, a conversation with a friend, the moon shining through a cloudy night sky. When we assume God only works when we are good, we miss God's grace in working through sinners—through a conversation about Christ with a neighbor, a parent's repentance to a child after they have spoken impatiently to them, a prayer prayed for someone because anxiety has kept us from sleep. For Ruth and Naomi, the very sight of a barley field, ripe for the harvest, was in one sense a very ordinary view—but in fact it declared God's provision to them. Mistakes had been made and griefs had been borne, but the barley harvest showed that God knows, cares, sustains, and provides.

God has not changed. Although He has the whole universe to care for, He turns His gaze on you and me, and He says, *I know you. Your name is written on the palm of My hand. And as surely as I cared for Naomi and Ruth, I'm looking after you too* (see Isaiah 49:16). God is sustaining and guiding His children. Let that knowledge comfort your heart and bring you peace today—however ordinary the day may be.

PSALM 139

MAY 14

A THEOLOGY OF GRIEF

"Do not call me Naomi; call me Mara, for the Almighty has dealt very bitterly with me. I went away full, and the LORD has brought me back empty." RUTH 1:20-21

When Naomi returned to Bethlehem, leaving the graves of her husband and sons behind in Moab, we can only imagine the pain and grief she experienced as she came back to familiar places and faces. What thoughts and memories would have emerged? *Oh, that's Mrs. So-and-So, and those must be her sons. Look how they've grown! This is where I used to bring the boys. This is where Elimelech and I used to walk...*

As bitterness over her situation set in, Naomi, whose name means "pleasant," decided that a more suitable name for herself was Mara, which means "bitter." She didn't attempt to sweep life's challenges aside and convince everyone that everything was fine. To do so would have been less than honest—a betrayal of the theology underpinning her faith amid what the hymn writer William Cowper called "a frowning providence."[62]

Naomi's situation speaks to the fact that even for God's people, some pain in life will seem unbearable, some circumstances will appear unjust, and some questions will remain unanswered. Her response raises a question: what will we do when grief strikes in our own lives? The reality of suffering is a problem for the Christian, but it is no less a problem for everyone else. All people must wrestle with the problem of pain. An atheist can't do so satisfactorily, because if there is no God, we simply live in a universe of chance, where things just tumble along. But the Christian can ask—indeed, we *should* ask—"Where is God in the midst of this?"

Naomi's honest expression of emotion is matched by her theology. She doesn't attribute all that has happened to chance, but she acknowledges God's hand at work. She declares that God is right in the midst of her pain; she calls Him *Shaddai*, "Almighty," the providing, protecting God. What does *Shaddai* mean? It's the characteristic of God that means He's at His best when we are at our worst.[63] Naomi had gone through famine, loss, bereavement, doubts, and goodbyes—but because she knew God as *Shaddai*, she could leave the explanation and the responsibility for such bitter trials with Him.

Where do you turn when the waves hit, when the wheels run off the road, when everything goes haywire? It must be to your knowledge of who God is and how He deals with His people. This is a sure foundation on which to stand. Where else can we go?

When Naomi left Bethlehem, there was famine. When she returned, there was harvest. Through the clouds of grief, the light of hope began to break as the stage was set for God to provide abundantly for Naomi and Ruth. When God is at work, even hopelessness may be the doorway to fresh starts and new opportunities. He will one day dispel all darkness. God is your *Shaddai*. In which part of your life do you need to hear this today? And who around you needs you to share this with them?

RUTH 1

62 William Cowper, "God Moves in a Mysterious Way" (1774).

63 Alec Motyer, *A Scenic Route Through the Old Testament,* 2nd ed. (IVP UK, 2016), ch. 3.

MAY 15

GET UP AND GET ON

"Ruth the Moabite said to Naomi, 'Let me go to the field and glean among the ears of grain after him in whose sight I shall find favor.'" RUTH 2:2

Do you ever start your day lying in bed thinking of all that's ahead of you and around you? Do you find yourself feeling overwhelmed by the challenges of the day to come or underwhelmed by the routine of it?

As she woke up in those first few days of her new life in Bethlehem, Ruth likely had to take a moment to remind herself of where she was and all that had happened: *My husband died. I'm now living with my also-widowed mother-in-law in a foreign land. I know I made the decision to leave, but I hope I've done the right thing. What now?*

Ruth didn't sit around waiting for some miraculous intervention before she proceeded with her life. No, for her, common sense led to careful thinking, and careful thinking led to practical action. Ruth knew she and Naomi needed provision, and she realized she was capable of working. She therefore sought Naomi's advice and her approval before going out into the fields to labor and find food.

Common sense doesn't mean we rely on our own insight or abilities. We must trust God and look to Him. But we must also use the faculties He's given us to live sensible lives in accordance with His will. We must be prepared to do what we can and leave the rest in God's care. Do not mistake passivity for godliness. But, by her attitude and actions, Ruth teaches us that all that God provides—each opportunity of obtaining what we need—is an undeserved mercy and favor from the Giver of every good and perfect gift (James 1:17).

As we get up and take action, we can trust that God is not idle. He's working everything according to His will (Romans 8:28), not as a package that is let down from heaven on a string but as a scroll that unrolls day by day as we walk through life. His favor in the ordinary things of life keeps us marching for another day. Your day may not look exciting or glamorous. You may not be sure how you will overcome what confronts you. But it is the day that God has given you, and He will give you all you need to do all He calls you to.

Will you, like Ruth, get up and get on with this life you've been given, and live for God and His glory?

2 THESSALONIANS 3:7-12

MAY 16

THE TAPESTRY OF GOD'S PROVIDENCE

"She set out and went and gleaned in the field after the reapers, and she happened to come to the part of the field belonging to Boaz, who was of the clan of Elimelech. And behold, Boaz came from Bethlehem." RUTH 2:3-4

What often appears to us to be a mess of knots is just the back view of the tapestry God is weaving.

Naomi and Ruth had experienced their share of frayed threads in life. They arrived in Israel widowed and penniless—a perilous position for women in a lawless society (see Judges 21:25). In Old Testament Israelite society, the law allowed for the poor to enter the fields and pick up (glean) leftover grain as they followed the steps of the official harvesters. This law was established by God Himself and revealed His care and concern for the needy. But God's law was not always—not often—observed in this period.

Yet when Ruth resolved to go into the fields, God worked through this law to tangibly provide for her and Naomi. Ruth's seemingly mundane decision became an illustration of God's providential plan for the two women—and for all of redemptive history!

Ruth ended up gleaning on the land of Boaz, a distant relative of Naomi's deceased husband and a man of means and high standing. Ancient Israelites understood the family to be the basic unit of society, with members of the wider family having obligations to support and protect relatives who were struggling like Naomi. All of this hints at God's hand in providing generously for Ruth and Naomi, even in ways that seem unremarkable at first glance.

In fact, as we read Ruth's story, we notice that many of its details unfold as if by accident. Ruth *happened* to decide to glean that day. Naomi *happened* to encourage it. Boaz *happened* to pick that time to harvest his field. Ruth *happened* to pick his field. But when we look at the story as a whole, we see that all of these happenings were the instruments of God's providential care in unfolding His purpose of redemption. After all, out of Boaz and Ruth's lineage would come King David and, eventually, the Lord Jesus Christ Himself—a greater provider and protector who also "came from Bethlehem."

As God wove these threads into His beautiful story of provision, Ruth and Naomi surely would have thought they looked knotted, disconnected, and frayed at times. Satan often wants us to stay focused on such seemingly jumbled and discouraging circumstances, doubting God and His good provision. We so easily forget that what appears to be a mess is just the back view of the tapestry God is weaving. One day, though, when we get the chance to see His handiwork from the front, all of those strange and dark threads will prove to have been part of His glorious pattern. Today, remember that "coincidences" are no such thing, that uncertainties and difficulties are opportunities to trust in God, and that behind all of them He is working out His plans to prosper His people in faith and godliness, and to bring them home.

RUTH 2

Bible Through The Year: 1 Kings 10–11; Matthew 8:18-34

MAY 17

THE LORD BE WITH YOU!

"And behold, Boaz came from Bethlehem. And he said to the reapers, 'The Lord be with you!' And they answered, 'The Lord bless you.'" RUTH 2:4

You can learn a lot about a person from their hellos.

When Boaz entered his field (and the book of Ruth) and greeted his workers, the depth of his character and of his relationship with God became clear.

Boaz lived with the awareness of God's presence, and it showed in his daily routines. The same was true of many saints throughout the Old Testament. They saw no separation between the sacred and the secular; rather, all of life was to be lived before the face of God. When you and I live with similar devotion, we experience radical transformation and blessing in both our words and our relationships.

Notice that when Boaz showed up, he didn't simply throw the name of the Lord around casually or profanely. He intentionally and reverently used God's name in his greeting, acknowledging the place of authority and intimacy that God had in his life. Such reverence curbs superficiality in our talk and encourages us to seek God's blessing in every circumstance—when we lie down, get up, walk along the road, or converse with others (Deuteronomy 6:7).

Upon his entrance into the field, Boaz set the tone for his workers by blessing them. His example should provoke us to ask ourselves, "What tone am I setting in my workplace, in my home, at the grocery store, in my church?" If the blessing and contentment of the Lord attend your life, whether you are a CEO or an intern, whether your work involves balancing the books or changing countless diapers, you can return blessing with blessing by pointing back to Him in all you do and say.

If Christ has truly come into your life as Lord and Savior, your faith should echo throughout every moment. Don't approach "time with God" only as a fifteen-minute daily meeting, hoping that that will sustain you for the rest of the day. You'll never be able to bring others into the presence of a God in whose presence you do not live. Speak of Him in your conversation. Bring His presence and promises to mind in the small triumphs and difficulties of your day. Seek to form a habit of conversing with Him throughout your waking hours. Live with an awareness of God's presence, and it will show in your routines and reactions.

Only, O Lord, in Thy dear love
Fit us for perfect rest above;
And help us, this and every day,
To live more nearly as we pray.[64]

COLOSSIANS 4:2-6

64 John Keble, "New Every Morning Is the Love" (1822).

MAY 18

FAVOR AND PROVISION

"'Then she fell on her face, bowing to the ground, and said to him, 'Why have I found favor in your eyes, that you should take notice of me, since I am a foreigner?'" RUTH 2:10

Only a heart that knows it is unworthy of grace will be appropriately amazed by receiving it.

Ruth was a hard worker. In many ways, as she gleaned for corn behind the workers in Boaz's field, she exemplified the apostle Paul's later exhortation to the Thessalonians: "Aspire to live quietly, and to mind your own affairs, and to work with your hands ... so that you may walk properly before outsiders and be dependent on no one" (1 Thessalonians 4:11-12). So, despite being widowed in a foreign land with a widowed mother-in-law, Ruth did not sit around wallowing in self-pity and waiting for some dramatic intervention. Instead, she seized the opportunity at hand—to go into the fields to glean leftovers—in order to support herself and Naomi. She not only took responsibility to provide but also approached her task, which was filled with long hours and few breaks, with a strong, persistent work ethic (Ruth 2:7).

In all of these things, Ruth neither insisted on recognition nor felt she deserved favor. Instead of congratulating herself for her endeavors or taking credit for deciding to work in Boaz's field, she considered her labors to be nothing more than her duty. Therefore, when Boaz favored and blessed her (Ruth 2:8-9), she responded with amazement and gratitude. She knew she was not entitled to anything from him, and so received it as a gift.

Humility and thankfulness sleep in the same bed. A thankless heart pairs with pride, but a humble heart will always be thankful.

Boaz's favor and protection foreshadowed the eternal favor and protection that God offers us through Boaz's descendant, Jesus Christ. Like Ruth, we too can be humbled as we see echoes of our eternal story in her story. As Boaz offers Ruth food and water (Ruth 2:9, 14), we may see their faces transform into the faces of another man and woman—Jesus and a woman at a well in Samaria, where the Son of God offered eternal water to quench her spiritual thirst (John 4:1-45). Boaz satisfied Ruth's physical needs that day; Christ satisfies our every need eternally. He is the Living Water and the Bread of Life.

"Why have I found favor in your eyes, that you should take notice of me, since I am a foreigner?" This same question ought to be on our lips regularly: "Lord Jesus, why have I found favor in Your eyes, that You should love me, since I am a sinner?" The answer is simple: grace. No matter what we may do for our families, our churches, and our Lord, we are only and ever favored by God through sheer grace on His part. You have no other standing, and you need no other. Because of God's gracious provision, you can sing, "On Christ, the solid rock, I stand; all other ground is sinking sand."[65] Let your heart today sing with amazement at the grace you have received.

EPHESIANS 2:11-22

65 Edward Mote, "My Hope Is Built on Nothing Less" (1834).

MAY 19

WELCOME AT HIS TABLE

"At mealtime Boaz said to her, 'Come here and eat some bread and dip your morsel in the wine.' So she sat beside the reapers, and he passed to her roasted grain. And she ate until she was satisfied, and she had some left over." RUTH 2:14

You and I are called to be bridges that span the gap between the experience of isolation and a life of divine acceptance.

For Ruth, Boaz was that bridge. In the middle of a long workday, Boaz invited his workers to enjoy a meal. He also welcomed Ruth to eat among the established harvesters. It is easy to miss the significance of this. Ruth was a stranger, a foreigner, and a woman. Boaz's actions were unexpected and culturally counterintuitive. They were Christlike.

Boaz is an example of someone whose actions were the bridge between isolation and the acceptance God offers. As a Moabite, Ruth would have looked and acted differently from those in Bethlehem. Additionally, the widowed status of Ruth and Naomi would have isolated them in many social circles. But because God's love had filled his heart, Boaz disregarded any hint of prejudice he might have had and welcomed Ruth to his table.

Boaz didn't stop at making sure Ruth felt comfortable by his actions alone. No, he also made sure the other workers were treating Ruth with acceptance and kindness, and he didn't leave her to struggle as she learned the skills of her new trade (Ruth 2:15-16). He went above and beyond to provide and care for her.

Do we do the same for unbelievers, new believers, or visitors at our churches? A Christian is by definition a recipient of God's covenant love. So a Christian ought to be the first one to include the outcast—the first one to say, "You're welcome here! We're glad you're here! Please participate! Will you join me?" We are called to stand against the tide of all-too-common selfish exclusivity and the equally pernicious habit of only spending time with and extending welcome to those who are like us.

We find the bravery required to be a bridge and not a barrier when we look to our own acceptance by God in Christ. Boaz's inclusion of Ruth—despite her race, social standing, and lack of work experience—points to the eternal story of God's greatest welcome. The holy God called across the boundaries between Jew and Gentile, enslaved and free, saying to sinners, "Turn to me and be saved, all the ends of the earth!" (Isaiah 45:22). We must turn our gaze afresh to the cross, for there we learn what it means to be loved and welcomed by God. Only then will we be able to truly love and welcome others.

So, look at how God in Christ welcomes you to His table, and then ask yourself: "How is His Spirit prompting me to step over a divide? Who is He calling me to make welcome at my table?"

JAMES 2:1-13

MAY 20

INESCAPABLE GRACE

"In him we have redemption through his blood, the forgiveness of our trespasses, according to the riches of his grace, which he lavished upon us." EPHESIANS 1:7-8

The grace of God for His people knows no bounds and remains within no limits. To know the truth of this, we need look to nowhere else than the cross of Christ, by which "we have redemption through his blood."

In the book of Exodus, God instituted the Passover, which painted a picture of freedom bought at a price. He instructed the Israelites to sacrifice a family lamb and spread its blood across their doorposts to prevent a visit from the angel of death as he passed through Egypt. The residents of each of those faithful households avoided God's judgment of the death of the firstborn son only because a lamb had died in his place (Exodus 12:3-13).

The Israelites were enslaved to Pharaoh. Similarly, all of us enter this world as slaves to sin and death. The price of our forgiveness was the very blood of Christ, who accomplished redemption as the great Passover Lamb for all who might believe in Him. It is His blood that frees us from death, for life, eternally. Christ did not come to earth to tell us how to make ourselves Christians. He did not come to tell us what we have to do to save ourselves. He came to do what we could not—to save us. He acted on our behalf, offering forgiveness that is free to us but costly to God. We dare not think that God simply decided to overlook our sin; rather, Christ's death on the cross absorbed the judgment that you and I deserve. God's holiness requires sin's penalty to be paid—and His Son provided the payment.

As he considers this, Paul exclaims, "Blessed be the God and Father of our Lord Jesus Christ!" (Ephesians 1:3). Considering God's grace should always move us to praise. But notice the phrase Paul uses in verses 7-8: "the riches of his grace, which he lavished upon us." God's grace is torrential. It is overwhelming. He has poured it out over each one of His children, holding nothing back. And He will continue to do so for eternity.

Imagine you have just finished your meal in a high-end restaurant and someone picks up your check, saying, "I've got you covered—I'll pay." That's what God has said to you on the grandest scale imaginable. He isn't saying there is no payment to be made. He's saying He has already made the payment. God's grace is beyond all limits, extending further than the eye can see or the heart can grasp. So, although as you look back on the last day or week, you will know that you are sinful, you can also know this: you cannot sin as much as God can forgive, and you can be confident that He who began a good work in us will bring it to completion at the day of Jesus Christ (Philippians 1:6). You will enjoy the experience of grace upon grace upon grace for all eternity.

'Twas grace that brought me safe thus far,
And grace will lead me home.[66]

HOSEA 3

66 John Newton, "Amazing Grace" (1779).

MAY 21

ENTERING GOD'S KINGDOM

"Truly, truly, I say to you, unless one is born of water and the Spirit, he cannot enter the kingdom of God." JOHN 3:5

When we read the Gospels, we discover that a large part of Jesus' ministry involved preaching the good news of God's kingdom. He traveled through towns and villages telling people, essentially, *There is a kingdom, and I'm the King. You're not in the kingdom yet—but if you'll follow Me, you will be the King's subject and a citizen of the kingdom.*

When we pray "Your kingdom come" (Luke 11:2), therefore, our desire should be that men and women would be brought into Christ's kingdom by new birth—that they would become committed followers of Jesus. We pray for those who live in rebellion against God to be "delivered … from the domain of darkness and transferred … to the kingdom of his beloved Son" (Colossians 1:13). Jesus made it perfectly clear that the only way to enter into His kingdom is by this new birth.

Jesus' encounter with Nicodemus in John 3 underscores this truth. Nicodemus was a religious man, a man of authority and influence—and yet he was still restless, still seeking. As he engaged Jesus in conversation, Jesus pointed out the necessary prerequisite for both *seeing* and *entering* His kingdom: to be born again by the Spirit. This new birth is brought about, He said, not by nature but as a result of God's Spirit working a miracle in the human heart. No one is able to enter the kingdom without Him working in them; no one is too far away from the kingdom for Him to work in them.

When we pray for God's kingdom to come, we are asking for eyes to be opened and ears to be unstopped so that men and women may be born again. The King is coming to usher in His everlasting kingdom, and the King is at work today by His Spirit to bring men and women into that kingdom. Until the day of our King's return, may your awareness of the way people enter Christ's kingdom produce increasing wonder over your own conversion and a burning passion to pray that the Spirit would do what only He can in the hearts of the lost.

JOHN 3:1-15

MAY 22

ALIENATION CRUCIFIED

"You were dead in the trespasses and sins in which you once walked."
EPHESIANS 2:1-2

Stark though it may sound, confrontational though it may be, the Bible compares the unredeemed to the walking dead. Outside of Jesus Christ, men and women are "dead" in their trespasses and sins.

The Bible's picture of mankind ought to temper our expectations for what life can look like outside of God's kingdom. Education is vitally important. Legislation is clearly necessary. But neither one, nor both of them together, is able to deal with the basic issues of the human heart. Worldly remedies only take us so far because they cannot address the greatest problem: that our natural condition is that of being "dead in the trespasses and sins in which [we] once walked ... by nature children of wrath, like the rest of mankind" (Ephesians 2:1, 3).

The alienation that marks humanity outside of Christ is primarily vertical: an alienation from God. Yet the effects spill over in other directions. Paul goes on in his letter to the Ephesians to describe how this vertical alienation had affected horizontal relations between Jews and Gentiles (Ephesians 2:11-12). The deep-seated hostility between Jew and Gentile in the ancient world was caused by nothing less profound than human sin. Both were separated from God, as represented by the curtain that hung in the temple, and both were separated from one another by the metaphorical wall that existed between them (v 14).

The truth is that such hostilities are bound to continue apart from Christ. Though it is good to invest in our communities and to labor for real change in our society and for the good of our neighbors (and indeed, God directs His people to do so—see, for example, Jeremiah 29:7), this is not where a Christian ultimately focuses their primary energy in ministry or places their hope for renewal. In Jesus, and only in Jesus, God has created and is still creating a new society where divisive barriers are broken down by grace. God has provided in the authentic local church "the genetic blueprint" for "a broken world remade."[67] When people encounter churches where that blueprint is seen, they will experience a taste of what God is planning to do when sin and tears and sorrow are no more, when in a new heaven and in a new earth all He has purposed will be completed.

Alienation—both vertical and horizontal—is inevitable apart from Christ. But in Christ, and in the society He is building and of which He is the head, such alienation has been crucified. Taking the reality of sin seriously means that you and I will invest in whatever way we can in our local church in order to ensure that it is a place where grace has torn down barriers and the blueprint of God's future kingdom is plain to see. Until we get there, we have the opportunity to work for, and enjoy, the foretaste now.

2 JOHN 1-13

67 Christopher Ash, *Remaking a Broken World: The Heart of the Bible Story* (The Good Book Company, 2019), p 163.

MAY 23

I WANT TO SEE

"He began to cry out and say, 'Jesus, Son of David, have mercy on me!' And many rebuked him, telling him to be silent. But he cried out all the more, 'Son of David, have mercy on me!' And Jesus stopped and said, 'Call him.'"
MARK 10:47-49

All around the blind man, the Passover was approaching, and the crowd was building. There was a great sense of anticipation. For most in the crowd, there was no time for stopping—certainly not for the ever-present beggars that lay around at the city gates. They were *always* there, known well to the people on the outskirts of Jericho. Many of the crowd likely would have seen this blind man, Bartimaeus, so often that they didn't even notice him anymore.

The crowd was so consumed with Jesus that Bartimaeus was probably regarded as a dreadful inconvenience. Their reaction to his cries for mercy—to rebuke him and attempt to silence him—suggests that they thought this marginalized member of society clearly could make no useful contribution to what Jesus was doing. But in seeking to quieten him, they became a barrier to the mission of Jesus—to the very one they claimed to be following and the very cause they claimed to be pursuing.

This particular blind man didn't have merely a minor interest in Jesus, though, so he continued crying out to Him. Mark's narrative demonstrates Christ's perfect compassion with a simple phrase: "Jesus stopped"—two words of grace. Can you imagine the crowd's reaction when Jesus said to the people who had been rebuking the man, "Call him"? That surely brought a measure of deserved embarrassment!

Perhaps there are people in your life for whom you struggle to pray. Maybe there are some you just want to rebuke or ignore. Maybe you just don't want to deal with the inconvenience. It can seem like such a nuisance to invite somebody to church, sit with them, eat with them, and be involved in their lives. It is messy, and it demands time and effort. We'd rather such people heard the gospel from someone else. It is so easy to slip into this way of thinking without really noticing; but when we do, we become just like the crowd: a barrier to people meeting their Savior. Jesus says to us, *Don't rebuke them. Call them. This is precisely why I came.*

May God forgive us when we, like the crowd, are full of indignation at the interference to our plans and inconvenience to our preferences caused by those who are crying out for His mercy. Christ alone does the work of opening blind eyes, but He has entrusted us with the responsibility and privilege of proclaiming these words: "Take heart ... he is calling you."

MARK 10:35-45

MAY 24

CASTING ALL YOUR CARES

"Humble yourselves, therefore, under the mighty hand of God so that at the proper time he may exalt you, casting all your anxieties on him, because he cares for you." 1 PETER 5:6-7

Anxiety can creep up at times when we least expect it and quickly overwhelm us. Or it can take up unwelcome and apparently permanent residence in our lives. Few people do not experience it; it may take on different faces, and it may be propelled by different circumstances, but the issue itself is remarkably common.

When we face anxiety, we often try to ignore it by distracting our minds: "Let me listen to some music. Let me go for a drive. Let me run a mile. Let me do *something*... just let me run away!"

Notice, though, that in this verse, Peter does not say we are to deny, ignore, or flee from anxiety. Instead, we should be "*casting* all [our] anxieties on him." The Greek word for "cast" here is a decisive, energetic action word. It could be used to describe throwing out a bag of trash. We don't put painstaking effort into moving it; we simply grab it and hurl it into the bin. Likewise, instead of going through our days pressed down by the burden of anxiety, we are to throw it, hurl it, upon the Lord.

To do this requires us to give up our pride—our desire to control and triumph over circumstances. Being humble is what enables us to give our worries to God: humility's presence leads to anxiety's absence. When we attempt to take matters into our own hands through too much worry, we indicate an absence of humility; we're more concerned with ourselves than with our heavenly Father, or we're more determined to navigate our own course than to leave it to Him.

There will always be a circumstance that can make us anxious. Peter doesn't address any specific circumstances, though; rather, he addresses the anxiety produced by the circumstances. Our anxiety itself is what we cast upon the Lord, doing exactly what the Bible says to do: humbling ourselves under God's hand, saying, "My Father knows best. He cares for me better than I can care for myself." When worries weigh us down, we can refuse to be burdened by them by calling to mind the Lord's willingness to help.

You might be struggling through today, wondering how you're going to make it to tomorrow. Perhaps it's been a long time since you knelt beside your bed and truly cast your burden upon the only one who is able to carry it, saying, "God, I cannot live my life with this burden on my back. Take it. It's Yours."

If that's you, don't hesitate any longer. Cast your anxieties into the loving arms of your heavenly Father and experience the freedom and peace only He can provide.

LUKE 12:22-34

MAY 25

PREPARING FOR DEATH

"Martha said to Jesus, 'Lord, if you had been here, my brother would not have died. But even now I know that whatever you ask from God, God will give you.' Jesus said to her, 'Your brother will rise again.' Martha said to him, 'I know that he will rise again in the resurrection on the last day.' Jesus said to her, 'I am the resurrection and the life. Whoever believes in me, though he die, yet shall he live, and everyone who lives and believes in me shall never die. Do you believe this?'" JOHN 11:21-26

None of us know what a day will bring. Indeed, we all live with a measure of uncertainty; we cannot be prepared for every trial that comes our way. In fact, as many have pointed out, the only certainty of life is that it will end. We live in a fallen world, and we know "the wages of sin is death" (Romans 6:23). Dying, therefore, is one reality for which we must prepare.

Any consideration of death and dying that doesn't pay careful attention to Jesus' words is incomplete. A great place to start, then, is the solid instruction that Jesus provided just after His friend Lazarus died. Understandably, Lazarus's mourning sisters were deeply concerned about what had happened to their brother. In response, Jesus said that Lazarus was going to rise again. Martha, not fully understanding this declaration, said, "I know that he will rise again in the resurrection on the last day." At that point, Jesus took the conversation one step further, saying, "*I* am the resurrection and the life."

And then came the challenge for Martha: "Do you believe this?"

Your answer to that question affects both how you live and how you deal with death. Jesus has not only conquered death but also made a way for *you* to conquer death too. Even though your physical frame will fail you, when you believe Jesus is the resurrection and the life, death simply becomes a transition, a passing from one realm of life into another.

One challenge which faces believers regarding death is not simply to prepare ourselves for its imminence but also to learn how to help others face it. No matter the situation, though, Jesus' words provide the foundation for loving counsel. We are to speak both biblically and honestly, explaining the reality of eternity and the hope that is found in Him. Our words, echoing Christ's own, should not be abrupt or unfeeling but filled with wisdom and grace.

You cannot know how to live until you've settled the question of how to die. Tomorrow is not promised to any of us, but eternity is guaranteed to every follower of the one who is the resurrection and the life. You can prepare yourself—and your friends and loved ones—to meet the day of death with calm and confidence rather than with fear and uncertainty by holding these precious words close: "I am the resurrection and the life. Whoever believes in me, though he die, yet shall he live, and everyone who lives and believes in me shall never die." Yes, we believe this.

JOHN 11:1-44

◇ Bible Through The Year: 2 Kings 10–11; Matthew 13:31-58

MAY 26

GOD'S UNCHANGING WORD

"By faith Abraham, when he was tested, offered up Isaac, and he who had received the promises was in the act of offering up his only son, of whom it was said, 'Through Isaac shall your offspring be named.'" HEBREWS 11:17-18

Life can feel overwhelming. Every day brings new challenges even as old ones continue without resolution. It's easy to allow our faith to trip on the stumbling block of our own lack of understanding of our circumstances—to take the baton of faith, as it were, and toss it to the ground, saying, "I'm finished. I can't run any further." In those moments, God's word encourages us to remember that Christian faith is an enduring faith that remains resolute. It is possible to remain obedient to God's commands even when everything around us seems to contradict what He has promised.

Until the cross, perhaps nowhere in Scripture do we find a more overwhelming moment than in the life of Abraham. It was a moment that occurred entirely at the instigation of God: "[God] said, 'Take your son, your only son Isaac, whom you love, and go to the land of Moriah, and offer him there as a burnt offering on one of the mountains of which I shall tell you' ... When they came to the place of which God had told him, Abraham built the altar there and laid the wood in order and bound Isaac his son and laid him on the altar, on top of the wood. Then Abraham reached out his hand and took the knife to slaughter his son" (Genesis 22:2, 9-10). God's command to Abraham was clear—and yet it seemed to contradict God's promise that through Abraham's offspring "all the nations of the earth" would "be blessed" and that "through Isaac shall your offspring be named" (v 18; 21:12). The fulfillment of God's promises depended upon Isaac's survival. If Isaac was to die, how could the promise be fulfilled?

Yet Abraham still obeyed. Even though his circumstances could have led him to doubt and question God's word, by faith Abraham said, *God has a plan in this. His promise is that through Isaac all the nations of the earth will be blessed. Therefore, He must be going to resurrect him—to raise him up from the dead* (Hebrews 11:19). This is why earlier, as Abraham had left to perform the commanded sacrifice, he had said to his servants, "Stay here with the donkey; I *and the boy* will go over there and worship and *come again to you*" (Genesis 22:5, emphasis added). What an expression of faith! Do not miss this: when the command was given to Abraham, he obeyed it. Although it seemed to directly contradict the promises God had made, Abraham did his business, and he determined to let God do His.

We can do so too. Do not allow your circumstances, however daunting they may be, to lessen your obedience or cause you to call God's promises into question. Centuries after Abraham and Isaac climbed up, and down, this mountain, God's own Son rose from the grave on the side of that same mountain, as the ultimate testimony to the truth that God keeps His promises. So you can face whatever today brings confidently, hopefully, and prayerfully, saying, "I can keep going. I'm not finished. God will do His part, and so I can do mine."

GENESIS 22:1-19

MAY 27

COUNTERING SPIRITUAL LAZINESS

"A little sleep, a little slumber, a little folding of the hands to rest, and poverty will come upon you like a robber, and want like an armed man."
PROVERBS 24:33-34

We've all seen it. In the worlds of sports, business, and academics, less gifted individuals often go further than those with greater abilities due to one trait: diligence. Such people are willing to take seriously the challenge of laziness and do what they must to overcome its allure. You likely either *are* one of those people or *aspire* and work to be one.

But, if we're honest with ourselves, this same diligence is often lacking in our spiritual lives.

If you and I are to counter spiritual laziness, we're in need of an assessment of sorts: Do we have any indication of how we're doing? When we reflect on the past year, have we made any progress? Have we done any Bible memorization recently? Have we used "idle moments" to read or meditate on the word or to pray to our Lord? Or has laziness caused us to do what is easy rather than what is best and prevented us from storing the word of God within our hearts?

When asked to take part in Christian service, how do we respond? Maybe it's not an outright refusal, but even a hint of reluctance is a dangerous sign. What about in hearing the word of God when it's preached, when it comes home with power and impact and we know that it demands application and change? Do we take action as doers of the word and not as hearers only (James 1:22)?

Your answers to such questions can help you press on and avoid the slow drip-drip of laziness (a lie-in instead of a morning devotional here, a boxset instead of a prayer meeting or a sports match rather than a conversation about Jesus there), which leads to spiritual poverty. Do not become a master of unfinished spiritual business and unfulfilled good intentions. Often, all the started plans and kind notes, and the many words of repentance and petitions for help, die in our minds while we turn on our beds "as a door turns on its hinges" (Proverbs 26:14). Flee from this behavior and instead run to Christ, asking Him to stir your heart and make you into a man or woman of action.

Do you want to be useful to God? Do you long to make a difference: to reach people on the seas of life in all their trouble and emptiness and to be part of the means by which God builds His church? Do not neglect your souls by giving room to laziness. Without diligence in your relationship with God, you will grow no true fruit in your life. "Tomorrow" is the devil's favorite word. "*Now* is the favorable time; behold, *now* is the day of salvation" (2 Corinthians 6:2, emphasis added). Be useful to God *now*.

PROVERBS 24:27-34

MAY 28

DISCORD AND DIVISION

"You must remember, beloved, the predictions of the apostles of our Lord Jesus Christ. They said to you, 'In the last time there will be scoffers, following their own ungodly passions.' It is these who cause divisions, worldly people, devoid of the Spirit." JUDE 17-19

People seeking to cause division were not unique to the first-century church; they have been alive and well throughout the church's history. Jude's instruction here is therefore as practical for us today as it was for the believers to whom he first wrote.

Those causing division in the early church shared in a harmful combination of moral and doctrinal error. They were devoid of the Spirit, promoting sensuality and "following their own sinful desires" (Jude 16), yet they had somehow managed to creep in among God's people. Jude describes them as "hidden reefs" (v 12), which lie just far enough below the water's surface to go undetected and yet are capable of wreaking absolute havoc if any vessel runs into them. Indeed, those reefs are capable of sinking that vessel.

In response to these charlatans, Jude urged his fellow believers not to forget "the predictions of the apostles," who had warned that "in the last time"—the time between the ascension and the return of the Lord—there would be those who scoffed at the teaching of Christ and His chosen apostles and who tolerated or even promoted behavior driven by our desires. In God's providence, the early church was forewarned so as not to be caught off guard by those who in this way would cause divisions—and so, indeed, are we.

Yet God's word doesn't just call us to be on the lookout for those who create discord and division; it also directs us to deal mercifully with those struggling with genuine doubt. We are to "have mercy on those who doubt" and "save others by snatching them out of the fire" of error and sin (Jude 22-23), even as we resist the teaching and aims of false teachers. Maintaining such a balance is quite a challenge! And yet Jude does not shy away from the exhortation. Believers who are secure in their faith and doctrine are called to restore the fallen in a spirit of gentleness (see Galatians 6:1) and to intervene in the lives of those who are playing with fire.

Since God has saved and kept you, you are called to be alert to danger and pull others out of the flame, boldly but gently. And you are called to keep yourself in the love of God and to pray diligently (Jude 20), that you would be able to spot error and resist those who would divide God's church. Then you will be able to stand with your brothers and sisters and say with Jude, "To the only God, our Savior, through Jesus Christ our Lord, be glory, majesty, dominion, and authority, before all time and now and forever. Amen" (v 25).

JUDE 1-25

MAY 29

THE MEANING OF THE CROSS

"It was to show his righteousness at the present time, so that he might be just and the justifier of the one who has faith in Jesus." ROMANS 3:26

Without Christ's death on the cross, there is no gospel. It is through Jesus' sacrifice that God the Father has made it possible for sinful men and women to have fellowship with Him. If we want to know God, we must meet Him in the Lord Jesus Christ.

Only through the cross does God show both justice in punishing sin and mercy in pardoning it, paving the way for people like you and me to enter heaven without spoiling its holiness. The cross is God's answer both to sin itself *and* to His anger against sin. To those who don't believe, God's answer sounds absolutely foolish, but those who do believe understand the cross to be the very power of God (1 Corinthians 1:18).

If God were simply to overlook sin or to stop being angry at it, then He would cease to be God; for God's justice is inherent in His character, and justice demands that sin is punished. He cannot turn a blind eye to evil. This is wonderful news for us when we are sufferers at the hands of others; it is also sobering news for us because we are sinners ourselves.

The cross of Christ is the way that God can be just *and* declare innocent sinners who have placed their faith in this crucified Savior. In order to deal with sin, God in His grace sent His own Son to take the punishment that sinners deserve. Our salvation is by way of substitution. Pause to reflect on this. It is staggering, first that God would come up with this plan, and second that He would go through with it. Considering the cross should always move us to awed and humble praise.

This substitution is why all the Old Testament sacrifices point to Jesus. In Christ's death, God's anger, which is His righteous disposition towards sin, is satisfied, and His love for us is magnified. Men and women who come to trust in Jesus no longer need to face His wrath; we're invited instead to rejoice at the love displayed at the cross. Indeed, all of the gospel's blessings and benefits become ours as a result of what Jesus has accomplished in His life, death, and resurrection.

Jesus came to bear all of God's condemnation of sin. When Christ took our place, He brought the judgment that we deserve and are due to face on the last day to the cross, so that we might stand before God's throne and say, "I'm with Him. He lived the life I could not live. He died in my place."

In his first letter, John writes of how at times "our heart condemns us" (1 John 3:20). This is an experience common to all humanity. But the Christian does not need to sear their conscience in order to still the condemnatory voice, nor must they be crushed by that voice. We can be very honest about the depth of our sinfulness because God's love is deeper still. "There is … now no condemnation for those who are in Christ Jesus" (Romans 8:1). Jesus came to meet us at the cross. Forgiven sinner, will you meet Him and marvel at Him there?

LUKE 15:11-32

MAY 30

PROMISED PROVISION

"Jesus said to them, 'Children, do you have any fish?' They answered him, 'No.' He said to them, 'Cast the net on the right side of the boat, and you will find some.' So they cast it, and now they were not able to haul it in, because of the quantity of fish." JOHN 21:5-6

What do we bring to Jesus? Only our need.

The post-resurrection fishing scene in John 21 echoes an earlier fishing scene for the disciples on the Sea of Galilee, recorded in Luke 5. In both stories, despite their professional fishing experience, the disciples toiled and toiled but caught nothing. In both instances, Jesus appeared and had them bring in a tremendous load of fish. The first encounter was to teach them to be fishers of men; the second was to remind them to continue in their work of adding to God's kingdom. Both miracles illustrated the point that the disciples could only succeed through God's power. Jesus was as much in control of the Sea of Galilee when the disciples caught nothing as He was when they caught everything. He was just as sovereign over their emptiness as He was over their fullness. Christ desires that we see our poverty in order that we might bow in wonder at His provision. When you and I are all too aware of our own emptiness, we can trust that God is in control of that too. He invites us to seek that every void in life be filled with His goodness and strength.

When Jesus called out to the disciples to ask if they had caught any fish, He forced them to face their needy condition and answer honestly. Christ has questions for us in our emptiness today, too. He's not looking for excuses, dialogues, or debates. He wants our honest recognition of our need. The disciples' condition mirrors our own: we cannot even do what we are good at without the Lord's help. We can neither speak nor listen, sing nor write, work nor play without God's enabling grace. As Jesus had said earlier in the Gospel of John, "Apart from me you can do nothing" (John 15:5).

Jesus did not leave the disciples in their poverty, nor did He provide just enough for them to get by; He *abundantly* supplied a large haul. Such provision reflects how, by promising eternal life to all who believe in Him, Jesus continues to give immeasurably more than we could ask or imagine. When Christ intervenes in our lives by His Spirit, He doesn't merely run a trickle of water through them to tease us; He promises that out of our hearts will flow rivers of living water (John 7:38). Just as Jesus went on to invite the disciples onto shore to eat breakfast with Him (21:9-10), so He invites you to His table to fill your hunger. And as He invites you to join Him, He also comes to you on the way, offering more than enough strength for the journey.

Jesus said, "Blessed are those who hunger and thirst for righteousness, for they shall be satisfied" (Matthew 5:6). Bring your need to Him today. Be honest about your own lack. And then trust Him to give you far more than you need in order to walk towards your heavenly home, serving His glorious purposes as you do.

JOHN 21:1-14

MAY 31

WE NEVER MOVE ON

"You, who once were alienated and hostile in mind, doing evil deeds, he has now reconciled in his body of flesh by his death, in order to present you holy and blameless and above reproach before him, if indeed you continue in the faith, stable and steadfast, not shifting from the hope of the gospel that you heard, which has been proclaimed in all creation under heaven." COLOSSIANS 1:21-23

Most 21st-century Western people would say that human beings are, overall, good. One day's worth of news, however, will quickly call such a notion into question. And one day in our own company should also undermine the claim. For, if we're completely honest, we must admit that our own hearts are unruly and out of control—and popular solutions to this problem, such as greater education or changes to social circumstances, never seem to fix things. Humanity continues to be a mess.

When we turn to the Bible, we discover an ugly truth about ourselves: the reason we feel alienated from the people around us—the reason *I* sometimes feel alienated from *myself*—is because we're alienated from *God*. Our horizontal alienation is indicative of a far more serious vertical alienation. God made us so that we might have a relationship with Him, yet our minds are turned away from Him. We don't think of Him. We don't love Him. We don't even look for Him.

There is, however, good news. As followers of Christ, while we were once wasting away, we've now been renewed. We were alienated, but now we've been reconciled. We lived in a dark place, and now we've been brought into the light. We were trapped, and now we've been set free. We were dead, and now we've been made alive with Christ. That's the experience of those who know God as He has revealed Himself through His word.

This transformation isn't simply the result of a decision to revamp life. At some point, most of us have thought, "I'm turning over a new leaf and making a change. I'm going to be more thankful this year than I was last year." And good! There's nothing wrong with that at all. Our friends and family would probably be thrilled to hear it. That alone is not the end goal for a Christian though. Rather, change in the Christian's life is motivated and initiated by the saving grace of God. We go on as we began: by grace.

The good news of the gospel is the fact that Jesus of Nazareth came on our behalf to bring an end to our alienation. He, and He alone, has done what we most need but could not do for ourselves. So the call to us is very simple: to "continue in the faith … not shifting from … the gospel." We never need to move on from the simple gospel of Christ crucified, risen, and reigning; in fact, we dare not. And yet how easy it is for us to grow cold to these truths; for familiarity to breed if not contempt, then complacency. So consider your heart honestly. Acknowledge your sin. And come back to the gospel once more, in awe "that thou, my God, shouldst die for me."[68]

PSALM 32

68 Charles Wesley, "And Can It Be?" (1738).

JUNE 1

THE PROPHET'S BURDEN

"The oracle that Habakkuk the prophet saw." HABAKKUK 1:1

The significance of true prophets was never found in who they were but in the message they proclaimed. It should be the same for us, too.

Take Habakkuk, for example. Biographical content about him is virtually nonexistent. All that we know of him is derived from the book of prophecy that bears his name, and that tells us very little; you can't find him anywhere else in the Old Testament. However, this silence is significant. Habakkuk's credentials were to be found entirely in his call.

We encounter this same perspective throughout biblical prophecy. We know more about some prophets than others—but even the things we know are not profound or compelling. Amos, for example, was simply "a herdsman and a dresser of sycamore figs" before God laid His hand upon him (Amos 7:14). Similarly, when John the Baptist was pressed for information about who he was, he testified, *I'm a voice crying in the wilderness. I'm a light that is shining for a little while, but Jesus is the Light of the World. I am a finger pointing to Christ; He must increase, and I must decrease* (see John 1:23; 5:35; 3:30).

In this opening verse of Habakkuk, the word for "oracle" is sometimes translated "burden." What was the burden? It was the burden the prophet felt in seeing things according to the insight God had given, of looking at circumstances that others had seen but didn't understand, and of bringing God's wisdom and designs to bear upon those who listened.

Despite our modern preoccupations with personalities and credentials, in gospel preaching, teaching, and sharing it is the *message* that should always be the main focus. Every sermon preached and lesson taught and gospel conversation held eventually withers like grass. Its only worth is found insofar as the unerring truth and reliability of God's word anchors itself in the listener's soul. As David Wells writes, preaching—and any form of communication of God's truth, based on God's word, for that matter—"is not a conversation, a chat about some interesting ideas … No! This is *God* speaking! He speaks through the stammering lips of the preacher where that preacher's mind is on the text of Scripture and his heart is in the presence of God."[69]

Whether we are called to preach, teach, or share God's word with a neighbor, there is an important lesson here: in our very core, there should be a genuine humility that comes from understanding the compelling nature of God's call upon our lives. There should also be an excitement about it, though, for what would we rather give our lives to than this message that is so much bigger than ourselves, whose effects in the lives of others will last for eternity? Today, do not be too concerned with the messenger's aptitudes and abilities; rather, make your concern the sharing of the message, however and with whomever you have been called to do it.

ROMANS 10:11-17

69 *The Courage to Be Protestant: Truth-Lovers, Marketers and Emergents in the Postmodern World* (IVP, 2008), p 230.

JUNE 2

WILL HE FIND FRUIT?

"Seeing in the distance a fig tree in leaf, he went to see if he could find anything on it. When he came to it, he found nothing but leaves, for it was not the season for figs. And he said to it, 'May no one ever eat fruit from you again.' And his disciples heard it." MARK 11:13-14

Here is a narrative which "bristles with difficulties."[70]

What's staggering about Jesus cursing a fig tree here is that this is a miracle of destruction. Everything else that we see Jesus doing up to this point in Mark's Gospel has been a miracle of transformation or of restoration. Since this is a complete aberration in contrast with Jesus' other actions, we need to dig deeper into its significance.

In the Old Testament, both the vine and the fig tree are routinely used as metaphors to describe the Israelites' status before God. When good fruit is growing from the vine or the tree, all is well; when bad fruit or no fruit is growing, God's people have gone astray. As Jesus observed the utter emptiness that was represented in the religious activities at that time, these words of the prophet Micah may have come to His mind: "Woe is me! For I have become as when the summer fruit has been gathered, as when the grapes have been gleaned: there is no cluster to eat, no first-ripe fig that my soul desires" (Micah 7:1).

Jesus' cursing of a fig tree, then, was far from arbitrary. This scene was an acted parable of prophetic symbolism. He used the fig tree to demonstrate the judgment that was about to fall on Jerusalem. Jesus had come to the center of religious life looking for prayerfulness and fruitfulness and had discovered neither. The barren fig tree was emblematic of a ceremonial, religious legalism that claimed to satisfy the hungry heart and to please God, but proved unable truly to satisfy those who committed themselves to it—and this act of the divine Son shows that God was far from pleased.

Does this prophetic warning hold any significance for us, who live so far away from fig trees and temples? Yes! The challenge to bear good fruit is for us as well. Yet we must also beware confusing religious observances or rule-keeping self-righteousness with true fruit. God's people are always in danger of an empty legalism replacing a vibrant relationship. What is the way to heed the warning of the withered fig tree? Elsewhere, Jesus tells us, "Every branch in me that does not bear fruit [the Father] takes away … I am the vine; you are the branches. Whoever abides in me and I in him, he it is that bears much fruit, for apart from me you can do nothing" (John 15:2, 5). In other words, we must look not to do better but to know Jesus more.

Is any aspect of what this fig tree represents true of your life? When Jesus comes and searches us, will He find fruit on our branches? Will He find faith? Remain humbly connected to Jesus, our Vine, and His Spirit will grow in you the very fruit for which He is looking.

JOHN 15:1-11

70 C. E. B. Cranfield, *The Gospel According to Mark,* Cambridge Greek Testament Commentary, ed. C.F.D. Moule (1959; reprinted Cambridge University Press, 2000), p 354.

JUNE 3

LEAVING A LEGACY

"Always be sober-minded, endure suffering, do the work of an evangelist, fulfill your ministry." 2 TIMOTHY 4:5

Each of us is leaving a legacy. Every day we are adding something to the portrait of our lives, and eventually what we leave behind—our decisions, our contributions, our priorities—will remain, at least for a time, for others to reflect upon and consider.

At the end of Paul's second letter to Timothy, we find the words of an older man whose life was coming to an end: "I am already being poured out as a drink offering," he says, "and the time of my departure has come" (2 Timothy 4:6). In this context, he exhorts Timothy to take his responsibilities seriously, to consider his legacy, and to contemplate both the helpful and harmful legacies left behind by many that Paul encountered.

In the opening chapter, Paul had reminded Timothy that "all who are in Asia turned away from me, among whom are Phygelus and Hermogenes" (2 Timothy 1:15). These individuals receive one mention in the Bible, and it is to record the fact that they deserted a man in need. Paul also warns Timothy to be on his guard concerning people like Hymenaeus and Philetus, whose "talk ... spread like gangrene" and who "swerved from the truth," or like Alexander the coppersmith, who, Paul says, "did me great harm" (2:17-18; 4:14). When we look at the portraits these individuals left behind, we see a legacy of desertion, false teaching, and opposition to the gospel.

But Paul's letter is also replete with mention of those who left helpful, beneficial legacies. For example, Lois and Eunice demonstrated sincere faith, which Paul is certain now dwells in the young pastor Timothy (2 Timothy 1:5). Likewise, Paul exhorts his protégé to remember Onesiphorus, who "often refreshed me and was not ashamed of my chains, but when he arrived in Rome he searched for me earnestly and found me" (v 16-17). Onesiphorus left behind a legacy of faith, courage, and conviction. If he said he'd be somewhere, he was there. He was a man on whom Paul could fully rely.

We are all leaving a legacy. When we walk out of a room, either we leave behind the aroma of Christ that spreads the knowledge of Him everywhere (2 Corinthians 2:15-16), or we are leaving the less pleasant smell of self-promotion or the vacuum of saying and being nothing much at all. A legacy of faithfulness, godliness, kindness, gentleness, honesty, integrity, love, and peace is a legacy that will be remembered with affection. But most importantly, it will point people to the one whose life matters most—the Lord Jesus.

A legacy is the accretion of daily decisions to make a difference for Christ: to love Him and love our neighbor, to pursue peace and speak of Him. Today, you will build a small—or perhaps major—part of your own legacy. So do the work God has prepared for you to do and make a difference for Him. After all, we never know when we've just made our final deposit in the legacy we're leaving.

TITUS 2:2-14

JUNE 4

MEANT TO SHINE

"Do all things without grumbling or disputing, that you may be blameless and innocent, children of God without blemish in the midst of a crooked and twisted generation, among whom you shine as lights in the world." PHILIPPIANS 2:14-15

As people who have been set free by the blood of Christ, we are meant to shine. There should be a glory about those who know Jesus. But grumbling will always obscure that glory. Although it's a children's song, these lyrics should resonate with us:

Come leave your house on Grumble Street
And move to Sunshine Square,
For that's the place where Jesus lives,
And all is sunshine there.

It is vital for Christians to have a solid grasp of the reality that because of Jesus, we have been cleansed from the guilt and stain of sin. We have remarkable freedom in Christ, and through the Spirit's indwelling we experience both that freedom and the hope it provides amid life's chaos and in a world that rejects Christ. The gospel is not just a starting point for our faith; it is the *whole* point. And the Lord kindly provides constant reminders of the truth that we are His children so that we can progress in our walk with Him.

Our standing in Christ is unalterable. Once we've been adopted into His family, God will never loosen His grip on our souls. During our best week, we are no closer to God than during our worst week, because our standing with the Father is built upon Christ's righteousness, not ours. We are put right with God not on account of something done *by* us or from *within* us but *for* us.

As Martin Luther said, in one way, the gospel is all outside of us.[71] If we constantly look within to see how well we're doing, we'll feel as if we have no standing before God. But when we realize that God's eternal purpose is to conform us to the image of His Son, *and* that the ongoing process of obeying Christ enables that very thing, we will begin to experience the Spirit-empowered joy that God so graciously provides. When that happens, we will find ourselves with far less cause to complain!

We must work out our own salvation with fear and trembling, because it's God's good work in us that allows us to live for His pleasure and, in doing so, for our joy and contentment (Philippians 2:12-13). As we do so, we learn to truly shine—and others will then see Christ through us. So, what do you find yourself grumbling about? Has the glory of being a child of God grown cold to you? Today, when you realize you are about to grumble, whether in your own heart or to someone else, instead turn those words into ones of gratitude for all that the Lord has done, and is doing, for you. Then you will shine.

MATTHEW 5:1-16

71 "Two Kinds of Righteousness."

JUNE 5

WORSHIPING THROUGH TRIAL AND TOIL

"The Lord caused all that he did to succeed in his hands." GENESIS 39:2-3

If all that Joseph had was his famous brightly colored coat, he would have been ruined when his brothers took it from him and sold him into slavery. But there was character inside the man who wore that coat—and when Joseph lost his coat, he didn't lose his character. Rather, he continued to be formed and framed as a slave in Potiphar's household. In this crucible of affliction, God poured out blessing and favor on Joseph's life.

It would have been understandable if, finding himself a slave in an Egyptian household, Joseph had retreated into a cocoon of isolation, refusing to become involved in the world around him, protesting Egypt's paganism, and resenting Potiphar's authority. This approach, though, would not have afforded him an opportunity for witness or testimony. Instead of shutting down, Joseph seemingly determined that he would be the best servant that Potiphar ever had, because he knew he ultimately served God.

While Joseph prospered on account of God's goodness, he remained a slave. His day-to-day life was filled with drudgery—something most of us can relate to! But if you and I want to flourish in the worst or most mundane of circumstances, we must learn how to take life's routine experiences and see God's hand of blessing in them.

Because Joseph was able to trust God through his trials, Potiphar, we're told, saw that the Lord was with Joseph and caused all his success. Joseph didn't have to tell Potiphar that there was special favor on his life. When God's blessing is on a life, it will be apparent—and sometimes, as we see with Potiphar, even unbelievers can't help but notice.

We need to learn to live with the awareness that every matter we deal with, every moment we spend, and every move we make is an opportunity to bring glory and praise to God. Wherever we find ourselves, we can (as Paul wrote to those who found themselves, like Joseph, both God's people and enslaved) "work heartily, as for the Lord and not for men, knowing that from the Lord [we] will receive the inheritance as [our] reward [because we] are serving the Lord Christ" (Colossians 3:23-24). Only when we understand that we were created for His glory can we turn life's trials and toils into acts of worship. Our responsibilities, says the Bible, are opportunities to reveal our dependence on God and evidences of His blessing. Whether we find ourselves as CEOs or street-sweepers, trading shares or building houses or changing diapers, we will be both humbled and lifted up as we pray:

Teach me, my God and King,
In all things thee to see,
And what I do in any thing,
To do it as for thee.[72]

GENESIS 39

72 George Herbert, "The Elixir," *The English Poems of George Herbert,* ed. Helen Wilcox (Cambridge University Press, 2007), p 640.

JUNE 6

BE HONEST WITH YOURSELF

"Blessed is the man against whom the L*ORD counts no iniquity, and in whose spirit there is no deceit."* PSALM 32:2

In Dostoevsky's *The Brothers Karamazov*, one of the characters advises another, "Above all, do not lie to yourself. A man who lies to himself and listens to his own lie comes to a point where he does not discern any truth either in himself or anywhere around him, and thus falls into disrespect towards himself and others."[73] Nearly three millennia before, David also described the potential effects of self-deceit about what we're really like.

Honesty is vital to the discovery of happiness. Joyful, contented people do not lie to themselves or to anybody else. We cannot deceive ourselves and enjoy genuine happiness; deceit and happiness don't sleep in the same bed.

The Bible calls us to be as honest about ourselves as it is honest. It turns a searchlight onto our hearts and minds, revealing the truth of the human predicament. We are told that we live in iniquity, which results in an internal bias towards wrongdoing and a nature corrupted by sin. We're transgressors, going where we shouldn't go. We're sinners, failing to live up to our own standards, let alone the standard God has set.

The surprise of this verse is that David starts off with the word "blessed" or "happy," but then immediately introduces such hard realities as our iniquity and our capacity for lying to ourselves and God about it. But the reason he can do that is because the predicament he faces is more than matched by the cure God offers.

Notice that David doesn't say, *Happy is the individual whose iniquity the Lord does not count.* He says, "Happy is the man against whom the LORD counts no iniquity." Because God is holy, He *must* count sin—but He counts it against someone else. He counts it against His Son, our Lord Jesus Christ. We find in David's words the amazing doctrine of justification by faith, which we first see in God's relationship with Abraham, who "believed the LORD, and he counted it to him as righteousness" (Genesis 15:6). The moment we truly believe that our sins have been counted against our Savior, we will be blessed; we will be happier than ever before.

So the path to blessing starts with honesty. We are not good people who make the odd mistake. We are not wonderful individuals with a few flaws that can be blamed on our upbringing, our environment, or our lack of sleep last night. We are sinners with deceitful hearts, who fall short of God's glorious standards and by nature stand to inherit only wrath (Jeremiah 17:9; Romans 3:23; Ephesians 2:1-3). Be honest about who you are. Be specific about how you have sinned against the Lord. Then you will be ready to embrace the most joyful news in the world: that each day, though "our sins they are many, His mercy is more."[74]

PSALM 38

73 Fyodor Dostoevsky, *The Brothers Karamazov: A Novel in Four Parts with Epilogue*, trans. Richard Pevear and Larissa Volokhonsky (1990; reprinted Farrar, Straus, and Giroux, 2002), p 44.

74 Matt Papa and Matt Boswell, "His Mercy Is More" (2016).

JUNE 7

VENGEANCE IS THE LORD'S

"You have heard that it was said, 'An eye for an eye and a tooth for a tooth.' But I say to you, Do not resist the one who is evil. But if anyone slaps you on the right cheek, turn to him the other also." MATTHEW 5:38-39

When Jesus uttered these familiar words, to whom was He speaking? Who was Jesus telling to endure evil and resist retaliation?

It may seem simple, but this question gets at an important distinction that was in the mind of the apostle Paul as he penned his letter to the Romans. In chapter 12, he exhorts his readers to "repay no one evil for evil" (Romans 12:17) and to "overcome evil with good" (v 21), echoing the Lord's teaching: that we should turn the other cheek. And yet, just a few verses later in Romans 13, he says that God has established civil authorities as His servants for the purpose of approving what is good and punishing what is evil (13:1-4). Sometimes, then, evil is repaid, and at other times it is not—at least not immediately.

Both Paul and Jesus recognized an important distinction that we must remember between the way individual Christians ought to respond to evil done to them (dealt with in Romans 12) and the execution of the rule of law (dealt with in Romans 13).

Christians are not to take justice into their own hands. Rather, we are to entrust the repayment of evil to the authorities God has put in place. Civil authorities are one example. When they fulfill their roles rightly, they serve as a terror to bad conduct but not to good. They are there to faithfully execute the rule of law and to punish those who violate it.

Understanding that God is perfectly just will free us to obey Jesus' command to turn the other cheek. This is not a call to pretend that the evil done to us is not evil or to embrace a despairing outlook that says there is no justice. Nor is it a call to accept, when we are victims, that we must not make recourse to the civil authorities. No, Christians are called to and can endure evil because vengeance belongs to the Lord (Romans 12:19). On occasion, He permits that vengeance to be carried out in this life as He authorizes human governments to "bear the sword" (13:4). But on the day of the Lord, He will be the one directly carrying out justice, and every evil done in His world will be repaid in full.

You and I, then, are free to seek justice from the authorities that God has instituted to protect people and punish wrongdoing. Equally, we are free to turn the other cheek, resisting the all-too-natural urge to take matters into our own hands and enact our own vengeance. Justice will come, and not from our hands.

MATTHEW 5:38-48

JUNE 8

GIDEON'S QUESTION

"The angel of the LORD appeared to [Gideon] and said to him, 'The LORD is with you, O mighty man of valor.' And Gideon said to him, 'Please, my lord, if the LORD is with us, why then has all this happened to us?'" JUDGES 6:12-13

The moment in Judges 6 when Gideon meets an angel is both dramatic and incongruous. The angel calls him a "mighty man of valor" while he is hiding out in a winepress in an attempt to thresh wheat without being seen by the occupying Midianites (Judges 6:11). There is not much might or valor about him!

It's as if God focused the camera on Gideon as a microcosm of His people. Perhaps in that moment, Gideon looked over his shoulder, wondering if the greeting was really meant for him. After all, the Lord had allowed His people to be reduced to hiding out in caves. So he asked, "If the LORD is with us, why then has all of this happened to us?"

It's a sensible question: if God is who He claims to be, then why does He allow troubling circumstances in our lives? We can surely relate. All of our lives are full of ifs, buts, and whys. We should be encouraged, though, to know that if God could answer Gideon's question or the cries of Israel, He can surely handle our difficult questions—even if His answer is not always what we expect.

When the Israelites cried out for God's help in Judges 6:7, He responded not by sending a warrior to deliver them but a prophet to teach them (v 8). God knew that they needed to hear His word in the midst of their trials. Ultimately, they needed to turn back to Him and trust in His promises. The prophet told them in outline what the angel would tell Gideon: "The LORD is with you." The presence of God and the existence of trials can co-exist.

The questions we raise are finally answered not in some list of "five easy steps" but in God's disclosure of Himself through His word. In Gideon's case, God's response seemed to be no answer at all. There was no dialogue concerning Israel's circumstances or any explanation about their enemies. Instead, the Lord turned to Gideon and said, "Go in this might of yours and save Israel from the hand of Midian; do not I send you?" (Judges 6:14).

Gideon felt inadequate: "How can I save Israel? Behold, my clan is the weakest in Manasseh, and I am the least in my father's house" (Judges 6:15). Often, though, it's exactly when we admit our inadequacy that God begins to work in us. Until we reach the point where we can see our weakness, we will not be inclined to pray, to walk steadfast through trials, or to stop trusting in ourselves. Only when we know our own shortcomings and listen to God's promise to be with us and to work in and through us will we commit to serving Him with all that we have, weak though we feel and are. For in His word God promises that our weakness plus God's strength is sufficient for any task He calls us to (Philippians 4:13).

JUDGES 6:11-24

JUNE 9

PUTTING THE PIECES TOGETHER

"You search the Scriptures because you think that in them you have eternal life; and it is they that bear witness about me, yet you refuse to come to me that you may have life." JOHN 5:39-40

One Christmas, our family decided that we were going to become a jigsaw family. We set up a table, sourced the most enormous jigsaw puzzle that we could find, and laid out all its pieces. Unfortunately, our enthusiasm soon proved unequal to the task. From time to time, one of us would walk up to the table, pick up a few pieces, fail to put them together—and then give up and walk away.

It is entirely possible for you and me to study the Bible as if we are picking up bits and pieces of a jigsaw puzzle, failing to put them together, and never seeing the magnificent picture in front of us. In other words, as the book of Hebrews puts it, we can study the Bible and find that it's "of no value" to us because we "did not combine it with faith" (Hebrews 4:2, NIV1984). We might be meticulous in our Bible study and disciplined in our Bible memorization and yet all the time refuse truly to accept the Messiah about whom we are reading. To such people, Jesus offers challenging words: "You do not have [God's] word abiding in you, for you do not believe the one whom he has sent" (John 5:38).

It's sobering to think that even when men and women put themselves in a position to consider God's word, they might still refuse to come to Jesus, the Giver and Sustainer of life. By nature, we have our fingers in our ears to silence God's voice. By nature, Scripture tells us, "no one seeks for God" (Romans 3:11).

As one author writes, though, while "there is no life in the Scriptures themselves … if we follow where they lead, they will bring us to Him, and so we find life, not in the Scriptures, but in Him through them."[75] The word of God in Scripture and the Word of God incarnate are interwoven, with the Spirit bringing God's word to people so that they might meet and discover Christ.

Are you carrying around pieces of the Bible in your mind without putting them together and then standing back to see the beautiful picture of Jesus, arms outstretched, ready to save those who will come to Him in repentance and faith? Will you combine your knowledge of God's word with true belief so that you avoid the pitfall of knowing a lot about the word without ever knowing the Word? Will you come to God's word each day expecting to encounter Jesus as His Spirit works through His word? Let us be those who echo the prophet Samuel as we open God's word: "Speak, for your servant is listening" (1 Samuel 3:10, NIV).

2 TIMOTHY 3:1-17

75 G. Campbell Morgan, *The Gospel According to John* (Marshall, Morgan, and Scott, 1933), p 94.

JUNE 10

JUSTICE, KINDNESS, AND HUMILITY

"He has told you, O man, what is good; and what does the LORD require of you but to do justice, and to love kindness, and to walk humbly with your God?" MICAH 6:8

When John Newton, the eighteenth-century hymn writer and pastor, preached on this verse, he entitled his sermon "No Access to God but by the Gospel of Christ." Why would he use a title that seems to lack any connection to the verse?! Newton commented, "There is hardly any one passage in the Bible more generally misunderstood."[76] His sermon title, it seems, was aimed at correcting the common misunderstandings.

Newton's title alerts us to the danger of reading the virtues described here and then attempting to live them out *without* the gospel, or proclaiming them *in place of* the gospel, as a means of access to God. Neither of these does justice to what the prophet—and the Lord—intended. The best way to understand Micah 6:8 is not as a list of things that *contribute* to our justification but as *evidences of* our justification. When we view it this way, with the proper motivation and goals established, we can understand what the Lord was calling Israel, and is calling us, to do.

The Lord, through Micah, tells us first to "do justice." This means a commitment to act in accord with God's will and purpose. For example, in Deuteronomy, Moses says that God "executes justice for the fatherless and the widow, and loves the sojourner, giving him food and clothing" (Deuteronomy 10:18). We want to care about the things God cares about, which means taking such priorities seriously, seeking to "do good to everyone, and especially to those who are of the household of faith" (Galatians 6:10).

Second, the Lord tells us to "love kindness." If doing justice is the action, then loving kindness is the heart attitude that fuels it. It's warm-hearted compassion, ensuring that we pursue justice not as a performance of some duty but as a glad action of benevolence.

Third, we are to "walk humbly." In other words, we are to walk in submission to God's will, embracing our utter dependence on Him every step of the way. Why does Micah end this verse with humility? First, because humility is what is required to acknowledge that we do not perfectly obey the call to love kindness and do justice—and so we need the Lord's forgiveness and not just His commands. And second, because even as we do obey Him in the way Micah 6:8 calls us to, the fruitfulness of our labors is ultimately not up to us.

You and I cannot fix the world; we must instead entrust the solution to the world's King and Judge. Doing so both motivates and sustains us, with God's help, to live out the gospel that has saved us, through expressions of justice, kindness, and humility, for the good of our neighbors, for the witness of the church, and for the glory of Christ. Across the centuries, Micah calls you today to reflect humbly on your need for the gospel, to look to your heart and ask the Spirit to grow it in Christlike kindness, and then to look to your world and actively pursue fairness and justice.

MICAH 6:1-8

76 *The Works of the Rev. John Newton* (1808), Vol. 2, p 543.

JUNE 11

AN EAR OPEN, A WILL READY

"The Lord said to him, 'Rise and go to the street called Straight, and at the house of Judas look for a man of Tarsus named Saul, for behold, he is praying.'"
ACTS 9:11

In the Bible, there is no mention of Ananias before his appearance in Acts 9, and there is only one brief mention of him after that (Acts 22:12). By all accounts, he was not a tremendous man who had done great things by the world's standards. Even so, God saw a faithful heart within him and chose to use him in a tremendous way in the conversion of Saul (who subsequently became known as Paul).

Like Ananias, you may not have done tremendous things in your life, gone to amazing places, or gained any sort of great popularity. But God is in the business of setting His hand upon certain individuals and using them to accomplish His will. Our part is simply to be like Ananias, with ears open and wills ready to hear and obey our God.

The emphasis in this verse is not on the way in which God spoke to Ananias but on the way in which Ananias responded: "Here I am, Lord." His ear was tuned to hear God. What about yours? Do you hear God speak through His word? Is the posture of your heart such that whatever it is He is calling you to do, that you will say, "Here I am, Lord"?

Ananias' response to God is remarkable when we consider what God was calling him to do, and for whom. He had "heard from many about this man [Saul], how much evil he has done to your saints at Jerusalem," and he knew that in Damascus Saul had "authority ... to bind all who call on your name" (Acts 9:13-14). Yet he willingly chose to obey God's call despite any fear or resentment he had of Saul and his reputation. He heard, and he acted. How often do we make excuses for our own inaction in response to God's call? How often do we hide behind our fear or live with excessive caution, forgetting that "God gave us a spirit not of fear but of power and love and self-control" (2 Timothy 1:7)? Ananias displayed this powerful spirit through his obedience.

Our culture values big names, big accomplishments, and big ratings. God does not have the same preoccupations. Ananias had no great name or huge fanfare; he simply had an ear open to God's voice and a will obedient to His command. This resulted in a life sacrificed for usefulness in God's service. And on this day, it meant that he was the first to tangibly extend God's love and grace to Saul as he reached out and called him "brother" (Acts 9:17). And so, though he may be a small character in the Bible, there is much you and I can learn from him. You may receive little to no recognition for your faithfulness to Christ in this life. You may take risks and make sacrifices in service to Him and feel that not much changes and no one notices. But far better than anything this world can give, you can look forward to hearing God's "Well done, good and faithful servant" (Matthew 25:21) as you enter the kingdom of heaven. No good work done in His service is ever wasted. He weaves it all into the great story of salvation.

ISAIAH 6:1-13

JUNE 12

THE FATHER'S WILL

"Then I said, 'Behold, I have come to do your will, O God, as it is written of me in the scroll of the book.'" HEBREWS 10:7

When parents and grandparents coo over a newborn member of their family, they often share hopes and plans for what this little girl will accomplish or who this little boy might become. It would be quite remarkable, however, if young children were to declare their own intentions and purposes in life. Yet this is one more way in which Christ is unique: He *did* enter the world declaring, "I have come to do your will, O God."

When he was twelve, Jesus' parents found Him conversing in the temple with the religious leaders and teachers. They had been looking for Him for three days without thinking to look there, and were baffled; but He replied, "Did you not know that I must be in my Father's house?" (Luke 2:49). He understood His express purpose from His earliest days.

What was the will of the Father that Christ came to accomplish? The Bible tells us that in sending Jesus, God gave His people the one who would satisfy all the law's demands through full submission and who would then suffer the penalty of sin to set men and women free from its bondage. The coming of the Savior had been planned from all of eternity and promised through all of the Old Testament, the "scroll of the book." Jesus—who entered the world as a baby in a manger—is the very fulfillment of our salvation.

Every moment of His life, whether He was being tempted by Satan or experiencing agony in the Garden of Gethsemane, Jesus knew and remembered His purpose. He understood that He was there according to the Father's will. Though He pleaded for His cup of suffering to pass, He submitted to the Father in perfect obedience. As any human would have been, He was tempted to shrink from the Father's will, yet still He prayed, "Nevertheless, not as I will, but as you will" (Matthew 26:39-46).

Jesus was not vague concerning the reason for His arrival—and because He lived according to the Father's will, we will join Him in eternity, rejoicing in all He accomplished on our behalf.

Not the labor of my hands
Can fulfill Thy law's demands;
Could my zeal no respite know,
Could my tears forever flow,
All for sin could not atone;
Thou must save, and Thou alone.[77]

Today, you and I can live to do God's will, not in fear of punishment if we do not obey but with faith that we are already blessed in Christ. Because He always obeyed, we are forgiven for our failures to do likewise and freed joyfully to pursue our Father's will—not because we must but because we desire to.

ROMANS 5:12-21

77 Augustus Toplady, "Rock of Ages" (1776).

JUNE 13

MY TIMES ARE IN YOUR HAND

"But I trust in you, O Lord; I say 'You are my God.' My times are in your hand; rescue me from the hand of my enemies and from my persecutors! Make your face shine on your servant; save me in your steadfast love!" PSALM 31:14-16

Most of us are a mixture of emotions and experiences. The good, the bad, and the ugly wash over us regularly. The key issue is what we do with these feelings and experiences. How does being a believer shape the way in which we view our world? "My times are in your hand" is a six-word affirmation to remind Christians that despite disasters and difficulties, we are under the care of Almighty God.

In the opening verses of Psalm 31, it is apparent that David is in anguish. As we read on, we seem to find him in a position of assurance just a few verses later, only for him to return immediately to a state of distress. This cycle of pain and joy is not an unusual experience for the Christian pilgrim. In fact, the recurrence of disappointment and discomfort is fairly common along the path of faith.

In her book *The Hiding Place*, Corrie ten Boom tells the story of looking forward to her first railway journey. Although her trip was not for many weeks, she would regularly go to her father and ask him if he had the tickets. He would tell her over and over that he did. She realized that her problem was a lack of trust in her dad; she did not believe he would take care of everything. She was worrying that he would lose her ticket and that somehow she would be without it on the day she was to travel. In that lesson, she learned that God gives us the ticket on the day we make the journey and not before.[78] He, of course, is much better at keeping it safe than we are.

In our own pilgrimages through heartache, disappointment, the loss of loved ones, and personal failures, we can learn that this is indeed true. Therefore, we must trust Him. On the day we make the journey from time to eternity, if we know Christ, we know He will give us the ticket. If that day is today, then the ticket is on the way. If not, then what is the use in lying awake and letting our emotions control us and our worries crowd in on us?

We are not at the mercy of arbitrary, impersonal forces; we are in the hand of our loving God. He says to us, *Come to Me, all who are weary and heavy laden. Come to Me with all your burdens, fears, panics, anxieties, and heartaches. Take My yoke upon you. Live underneath My loving rule, because My yoke is easy and My burden is light, and you will find rest for your souls, forever* (see Matthew 11:28-30).

This is your security. Your times—short or long, rich or poor, sad or happy—are in His hand. He will give you good works to do each day, and then on your last day, He will bring you safely through to the place where your days are infinitely long, unimaginably rich, and unutterably happy.

PSALM 31

78 *The Hiding Place* (1971), ch. 2.

JUNE 14

THE REALITY OF GRIEF

"When Jesus saw her weeping, and the Jews who had come with her also weeping, he was deeply moved in his spirit and greatly troubled. And he said, 'Where have you laid him?' They said to him, 'Lord, come and see.' Jesus wept."

JOHN 11:33-35

Grief is "a life-shaking sorrow over loss. Grief tears life to shreds; it shakes one from top to bottom. It pulls him loose; he comes apart at the seams. Grief is truly nothing less than a life-shattering loss."[79] You may know this experience all too well. I remember its first intrusion into my life when I was a teenager and my mother died. Nothing could ever be quite as it had been before.

You do not have to live long as a believer to discover that faith does not insulate us from grief and the fear of it. Paul wrote about the near-death experience of his friend Epaphroditus: "Indeed he was ill, near to death. But God had mercy on him, and not only on him but on me also, lest I should have sorrow upon sorrow" (Philippians 2:27). The thought of losing Epaphroditus broke Paul's heart. He understood that death was not the end, but he also recognized that in experiencing loss, or even in the prospect of that, there is true sorrow.

Grief is hard because something has been lost, and certain joys are now irretrievably gone. But we also know that grief is a reality to which Scripture plainly speaks—a reality that will one day be redeemed by a far greater joy. And we know that grief is a reality with which our Savior is personally acquainted. As Jesus stood at the grave of His friend Lazarus, He—the second Person of the Trinity—grieved with those who had gathered there. Though He was about to raise Lazarus from the dead, He still wept because He was sincerely sad. The mystery in this scene is that Jesus so identified with our humanity that He shed genuine tears at the loss of His beloved friend.

Although the Bible introduces us to the reality of Christ's victory over death and the grave, it doesn't call us to some kind of glossy, heartless triumphalism. Rather, as Alec Motyer writes, "tears are proper for believers—indeed they should be all the more copious, for Christians are more sensitively aware of every emotion, whether of joy or sorrow, than those who have known nothing of the softening and enlivening grace of God."[80]

The fact that our loved ones who died in Christ are now with Him lightens but does not remove the anguish of loss and loneliness. We continue to long for the day when such pain will have ceased. Until that day comes, we can find comfort in knowing that Jesus was "a man of sorrows and acquainted with grief" (Isaiah 53:3) as we look to Him as our example, as we see that He is "the resurrection and the life" (John 11:25), and as we look to Him for our eternity. Knowing this is what enables grief and hope to coexist in our hearts.

JOHN 14:1-7

79 Jay E. Adams, *Shepherding God's Flock: A Handbook on Pastoral Ministry, Counseling, and Leadership* (Zondervan, 1975), p 136.

80 J. Alec Motyer, *The Message of Philippians,* The Bible Speaks Today (IVP Academic, 1984), p 90.

JUNE 15

THE CITY OF MAN

"Come out of her, my people, lest you take part in her sins, lest you share in her plagues; for her sins are heaped high as heaven, and God has remembered her iniquities." REVELATION 18:4-5

We shouldn't be surprised or alarmed when Christians face opposition. Humanity's natural disposition is one of proud defiance towards God and therefore against His people. Man, on the unstable foundation of his pride, "builds a city" (to use the picture language of Revelation) and constructs a lifestyle that is set against God's ways.

Humanity has been doing this since the fall. The first godless building project was on the plain of Shinar, at Babel (Genesis 11:1-9)—the place that later bore the name Babylon, and to which God's people were exiled. Revelation 18 therefore refers to the city of man, constructed in defiance of God, as Babylon; and Babylon is then personified as a prostitute, enticing people to commit spiritual adultery. Alluring and seductive, the city of man is effective at turning many away from God. It is "the great city that has dominion over the kings of the earth" (17:18), and its influence is significant and destructive.

How, then, are citizens of the city of God to respond to this worldly rival? We are to be in the world but not of the world. We are to be salt, which has a distinctive taste and a preservative quality; and we are to be light, which exposes what darkness covers but also guides others along the way to safety (Matthew 5:13-16). We are to live in the tension of being members of this world but not belonging here: residing here but also being separate from those whose hearts and minds are set against God. The sins of the city of man must not characterize us, John says, lest we "share in her plagues." If we yield to Babylon's seduction, we prove our identity was never truly that of a citizen of God's kingdom.

Those who follow Christ must be committed to the Bible's truth. Christianity is more than a moral code. It's more than a framework for living or a method to improve one's life. Where is the cross in that? Christianity is distinct from all other religions in that we hold fast to Jesus' death on the cross as our means of reconciliation to God. We were once dead in our sins, deserving of God's wrath and judgment—but He redeemed us through Christ's perfect life, atoning death, and victorious resurrection.

For now, the world goes on as it always did. But one day Christ will return and silence every false prophet, every citizen of Babylon, and even the devil himself. We may see the church hard-pressed, mocked, legislated against, and persecuted. The world will see it as weak, on the wrong side of history, and not worthy of respect or acceptance. But we take hope in this triumphant affirmation: neither the gates of Babylon nor the gates of hell will prevail because Christ will build and keep His church (Matthew 16:18). So for now, as you live in Babylon, what of its sins do you find most alluring? In what ways are you most tempted to live as though this city is all there is? And what opportunities have you been given to be salt and light to those around you? Be sure both to resist the city of man and to beckon others to the city of God.

REVELATION 18:1 – 19:10

JUNE 16

A CALL TO COMMITMENT

"I appeal to you therefore, brothers, by the mercies of God, to present your bodies as a living sacrifice, holy and acceptable to God, which is your spiritual worship." ROMANS 12:1

When asked to explain the impact of his life, William Booth, who founded the Salvation Army, replied in one striking phrase: "Jesus Christ has all of me."

There was nothing presumptuous or proud in that response. It was simply the only way Booth could explain why it was that he, an ordinary man of insubstantial means, had been used in such a remarkable way and had had such a remarkable impact at that particular point in history.

What would it mean for Jesus Christ to have all of you?

At the beginning of Romans 12, after eleven glorious chapters celebrating the salvation from sin that God wrought at the cross and His sovereign mercy in electing a people for Himself, Paul issues the call to those who are trusting Christ to commit 100 percent of themselves—body, mind, and spirit—to the Lord Jesus Christ. The word he uses for "spiritual" here comes from the Greek *logikos,* which gives us our word "logical." In other words, his exhortation is not based on emotion or manipulation. Rather, Paul is making a rational, urgent entreaty to his readers, all on the strength of God's mercy.

There is no dimension of our humanity that is not affected by our willful rebellion against God. Yet by His mercy, God doesn't count His people's sins against them, and He has withheld the condemnation we deserve. Instead, He has taken our sins and counted them against His only beloved Son.

If we ignore the "by the mercies of God" part out of this appeal, we immediately go wrong. This is a call to people who have received God's enabling grace to offer up their lives—not so they might be accepted but on account of the fact that they *are* already accepted. This plea is for those of us who have already been set free by grace to become all that God intends for us to be, wholly devoted to Him.

God doesn't ask us to offer our money or possessions. He wants us to offer not less than these, but more: our very selves. All that we are, all that we think, all that we feel, all that we do, and all that we know—offering this to the God who has given His Son for us is the only logical response to His mercy. When we give all of ourselves to God, all our capacities, as limited as they are, can be used for His glory and purposes. The Christian life comes with no option for half measures or holding back. It is an all-in life.

There is something glorious about the kind of commitment that says, "I'm putting the whole thing in." If you will go all in, then there's no limit to what will happen in and through you. Will you be the kind of person who can say, "Jesus Christ has all of me"?

PHILIPPIANS 1:19-30

JUNE 17

RENEWED MINDS

"Do not be conformed to this world, but be transformed by the renewal of your mind, that by testing you may discern what is the will of God, what is good and acceptable and perfect." ROMANS 12:2

Airport control towers are fascinating places. For such small rooms, they contain tremendous capacity and power. The instructions given from these towers prevent chaos and ensure safety. If anything goes wrong in them, the impact is felt beyond their walls and often constitutes great peril.

Similarly, we could say that our minds are the control towers of our bodies. What we do with our bodies is directly related to what is happening in our minds. In our minds we have the capacity to consider possibilities, make decisions, judge our feelings, and shape our affections. It's no wonder, then, that Paul says that if we are to "present [our] bodies as a living sacrifice" in response to God's mercy to us in Christ (Romans 12:1), our minds are crucial.

Being a Christian involves taking on a radically altered mindset that results in increasingly pure thoughts and holy behavior, which are not seen in a life without Christ. As Paul writes earlier in Romans, "Those who live according to the flesh set their minds on the things of the flesh, but those who live according to the Spirit set their minds on the things of the Spirit" (Romans 8:5). This change in perspective comes by the power of the Holy Spirit as He instructs us in the truth of God's word.

Such a change is a process. Each day, we are being conformed to the image of Jesus Christ. Our minds—indeed, our entire lives—are being renewed. We're neither all we ought to be nor all we're going to be—but we're also not what we once were. And when our minds are under the jurisdiction of God's Spirit and God's word, the rest will inevitably follow as He intends. We realize that God's way is best and are delighted to walk in it. We think before we act. We refuse to be shaped by the molds of this world, learning to see where we are being sold a mindset that is based on a lie rather than the truth of God's word.

So trust that the power of God's word will renew your mind, and ask the Spirit to work it in you. Look for ways in which the world is calling you to conform, and see those as opportunities to allow your mind to be transformed by godly wisdom instead. And do so not because you ought to but because it is your joy to, for you know that "blessed is the one who finds wisdom, and the one who gets understanding, for the gain from her is better than gain from silver and her profit better than gold … Her ways are ways of pleasantness, and all her paths are peace" (Proverbs 3:13-14, 17).

PROVERBS 3:1-18

JUNE 18

VIEWING OURSELVES RIGHTLY

"By the grace given to me I say to everyone among you not to think of himself more highly than he ought to think, but to think with sober judgment, each according to the measure of faith that God has assigned." ROMANS 12:3

No one is immune to the sin of self-exaltation. To find evidence of this, simply enter any kindergarten classroom. In this little group of children, soon enough somebody will be singing their own praises about building the tallest block tower or drawing the best family portrait—in other words, thinking of themselves more highly than they ought.

Constantly comparing ourselves with other people is a worldly way to think. An exaggerated view of ourselves is a dreadful problem—one that puts others down and ignores our place before God. The answer, though, is not found in self-denigration, which is the opposite and equal error to self-exaltation. This self-disparagement is also the product of pride because it still surfaces from comparison. It is still self-focused.

The Christian's view of self should be grounded in a mind renewed by God (Romans 12:2). With this perspective, we find our value in God's mercy and grace. Our significance, identity, worth, and role all find their foundation in who God is and what He has done for us, not on account of who we are or what we've done for Him.

We are reminded of this proper perspective of self when we sing the lines "When I survey the wondrous cross, on which the Prince of glory died."[81] To survey the cross is to focus on the gospel—the truth that another has died in our place and borne our punishment. In doing this, we realize that "my richest gain I count but loss, and pour contempt on all my pride." The cross raises us and lowers us at the same time, and this frees us from needing to push ourselves forward in life and enables us to acknowledge ways in which God has gifted us. This is thinking of ourselves with "sober judgment."

The church, then, is to be noticeably different from the world in the way we view ourselves and each other. When we come together, united by the gospel, all else that relates to our identity, though not irrelevant, loses its primary significance, and we use our gifts not to please ourselves but to serve others.

Look at the cross, where your Savior bled and died for your sins because He loves you. There is no room for you to feel proud. There is no need for you to compare yourself to others. Instead, you can use all that He has given you in selfless, joyful service of others.

1 CORINTHIANS 4:1-7

81 Isaac Watts, "When I Survey the Wondrous Cross" (1707).

JUNE 19

TOGETHER IS WHERE WE BELONG

"As in one body we have many members, and the members do not all have the same function, so we, though many, are one body in Christ, and individually members one of another." ROMANS 12:4-5

Every so often, someone may ask you, "Do you belong here?" It's usually asked in relation to a country club, a gym, or something similar. They're wondering, "Is this a place that identifies you as being on its lists? Do people here know you and accept you, and would they miss you if you were absent?"

Paul often uses the illustration of the body to describe the church. We don't have to stretch our imagination to make sense of it. We all have a body that is made up of a variety of parts, and each part has a unique function. Not all parts are seen, but all of them are important. If one part is not working or is missing, it makes a difference to all the rest. The effectiveness of someone's entire body depends on its control by the head. This holds true as well in the body of Christ, each local church: the spiritual body functions properly only when it works together under Jesus' headship. When that happens, we function with...

- *unity,* because we're not living in isolation from each other.
- *plurality,* because we're made up of different bits and pieces.
- *diversity,* because the functions of the body are necessarily varied.
- *harmony,* which we enjoy when things are working in cohesion.
- *identity,* showing that each of us cannot truly be ourselves when we are by ourselves.

In other words, when as an individual you understand the nature of the body of Christ, you better understand who you are and where you fit. As a member of the body of Christ, you do belong somewhere. When God's grace has transformed us, we should find that it matters increasingly to us that we have been called into relationship with one another—into community. We're diverse in the gifts that have been given; none of us can make up the body individually but only together. Each of us belongs to one another. We gather as church, then, in order to give of ourselves both to each other and, ultimately, to our Lord. We contribute to the body by our presence, our songs, our prayers, and our fellowship. As Isaac Watts wrote:

My tongue repeats her vows,
"Peace to this sacred house!"
For there my friends and kindred dwell.[82]

Church is not a place for you merely to show up at and attend. It is a body. It is your kin, your family. You need your church; and your church needs you. The more committed to your church you are, the more blessed by it you will be; for few things in life are better than when God puts His people together, because together is exactly where we belong.

1 CORINTHIANS 12:12-27

82 Isaac Watts, "How Pleased and Blest Was I" (1719).

JUNE 20

GIFTS FROM ABOVE

"We, though many, are one body in Christ, and individually members one of another. Having gifts that differ according to the grace given to us, let us use them." ROMANS 12:5-6

Spiritual gifts are tools, not toys. They are not to be played with or used to attract people to ourselves but employed by God, through us, for His purposes and for His glory.

Whatever our gifts may be—be they abilities to do with speaking or with serving—they are given for the well-being of the church. God gives these gifts in order that, as we use them as He intends, the body of Christ as a whole might be strengthened. They're not given as an opportunity to advance an individual's cause or for displays of greatness but in order that the unity, harmony, and progress of all God's people might be strengthened. That is why we have gifts that differ: so that we would learn to serve each other and depend on each other.

Yet God's gifts are only able to promote harmony and well-being when they are exercised in a spirit of genuine humility. The body of each local church grows only to the extent that "each part is working properly" (Ephesians 4:16). Before encouraging his readers to use their gifts, Paul had already prefaced his discourse on spiritual gifts by mentioning humility, urging everyone "not to think of himself more highly than he ought to think, but to think with sober judgment" (Romans 12:3). Without humility, spiritual gifts can lead to chaos. We would not give power tools to teenagers without proper instruction and oversight, nor would we give them chain saws to run around with—unless we wanted absolute havoc! Similarly, spiritual gifts must be used for their proper function and in the right manner so that mayhem does not ensue. So Paul tells the Corinthian church—a church full of gifts but not full of wisdom about how to use them—that while it is good to desire and celebrate spiritual gifts, the "more excellent way" to put them to use is to do so patiently, kindly, and humbly—that is, with love (1 Corinthians 12:31 – 13:7).

We must remember that gifts are *gifts*. Their source is God; therefore, boasting as if they are our own is foolish, and using them for our own benefit is inexcusable. If, however, we practice humility as we use them and learn to live in harmony with one another, then we will see the fruit of God's work in and through us. In what ways has God gifted you? Rejoice in that. In what ways is He calling you to use those gifts for the good of your church and for the glory of His Son? Go do that.

EPHESIANS 4:1-16

JUNE 21

GENUINE CHRISTIAN LOVE

"Let love be genuine." ROMANS 12:9

Film can capture magnificently the dissonance that can occur between what a character says and what's actually going on inside their mind. It's usually seen in a close-up on the eyes: "Well, how wonderful to see you again, Mr. Jenkins!" says her mouth, and yet from the expression, the audience realizes she doesn't really mean it. What she really means is "I would have avoided bumping into you if I could have avoided it, Mr. Jenkins—but now I'm stuck here with you."

What the mouth says is not necessarily what the truth is. Too many hearts have been broken and lives ruined by someone who said, "I love you" without really meaning it. True Christian love, according to Scripture, is *always* genuine. Paul confronts the danger of superficiality and deception by encouraging the believer to love with sincerity—that is, with a heart that matches our words. We are set free from the tyranny of acting as if we like everyone or thinking we have to be liked by everyone; and in Christ we are then also supernaturally enabled to love even those we previously wouldn't have wanted to be near.

Indeed, Christian love, says W.E. Vine, "does not always run with the natural inclinations, nor does it spend itself only upon those for whom some affinity is discovered."[83] In other words, it isn't natural. What is natural is to love only those whom we deem lovable—those who are like us, fit within our framework, and meet our expectations. But genuine love isn't conventional. It transcends the boundaries of race, intellect, and social status. It transcends all the boundaries put in place by man.

This is the love of Romans 5:8: "God shows his love for us in that while we were still sinners, Christ died for us." Sincere love can only come as a product of God's grace. It's a reflection of Jesus' sacrifice for us. When God's love shapes a believer's life, our words and deeds will overflow with that love.

Paul's hope was that when people saw the early church in Rome, they would say, "There's something different about the way these people love one another." God's call to you in your relationships with other Christians today is the same. Do not settle for a superficial, weak, or fake love. Do not let your heart be cold even while you are saying all the right things. Let your love be genuine—by gazing at the one who loved you unto death, sinner that you are. Let your prayer be that your love would be different, and deeper, so that you can point to the one from whom all true love flows.

JOHN 15:12-17

83 *Vine's Expository Dictionary of Old and New Testament Words* (Thomas Nelson, 1997), s.v. "love."

JUNE 22

NO NEUTRALITY

"Abhor what is evil; hold fast to what is good." ROMANS 12:9

Any patient who has undergone a bone marrow transplant knows the importance of being isolated from any possibility of infection. Because their immune system is so depleted, they are far more susceptible to disease than the average person. If a visitor arrives coughing and spluttering, excusing it as "no big deal" would be abhorrent to the patient and to their doctors. Any sickness is to be resisted like a plague because its consequences are potentially fatal.

Christian love should reflect this kind of radical mentality when it comes to evil. We cannot say that we genuinely love others if we cherish, or even only tolerate, evil in our hearts and distance ourselves from good. We cannot toy with wickedness, seeking to establish some laissez-faire approach to particular sins. "Abhor" is as strong a word as it is possible for Paul to use. He has no notion of neutrality when it comes to purity.

At the start of this verse, Paul has already instructed his readers to "let love be genuine." Isn't it interesting, then, that Paul immediately follows "love" with a word that essentially means "hate"? We often think that if we love, we shouldn't hate anything or anyone—but that's just sentimentality. Paul makes it clear that love "does not rejoice at wrongdoing" (1 Corinthians 13:6). If you love your spouse with a passionate purity, you hate everything which would rob you of that relationship; otherwise, your love is not love. The same applies to our love for the things of God. We cannot love holiness without hating its opposite.

As Paul continues, he turns from the negative to the positive, using the same phrase, "hold fast," that Jesus uses to describe a husband and wife's relationship (see Matthew 19:5). Paul doesn't use this phrase arbitrarily. Marriage is the closest human union possible—psychologically, intellectually, and spiritually. So Paul is saying here that Christian love should have a "superglue" commitment to goodness.

We must be careful not to fall into the world's trap of calling "evil good and good evil" or being those "who put darkness for light and light for darkness" (Isaiah 5:20). God's people understand that there is a time for love and a time for hate (Ecclesiastes 3:8). So how would you describe your attitude to evil—especially those sins that are most attractive to you or most celebrated by those who live around you? What would change if you abhorred them? Today, rely on God's Spirit to enable you to love properly by hating what God does, echoing the prayer of John Baillie: "O God, give me the power to follow after that which is good. Now as I pray, let there be no secret purpose of evil formed in our minds, that waits for an opportunity of fulfillment."[84]

MARK 9:42-50

84 "Sixth Day, Evening," in *A Diary of Private Prayer* (Fireside, 1996), p 31.

JUNE 23

BROTHERLY LOVE

"Love one another with brotherly affection. Outdo one another in showing honor." ROMANS 12:10

Young siblings are inclined to elbow and nudge each other and to complain about each other. If we are honest, sometimes our idea of "brotherly affection" in the church is marked more by that kind of thinking and conduct than it is by love and gratitude. When we look around at one another, instead of singing that we're glad we're part of the family of God,[85] we can often think deep down, "I'm surprised *you're* part of the family of God."

Paul calls us to a better way.

In this verse, love is described using family words. *Philostorgoi*, translated here as "love," comes from the Greek word *storge*, which refers to the devoted love of parent for child. *Philadelphia*, translated here as "with brotherly affection," is the word used for the love between siblings (as in the name of the city of Philadelphia, the "City of Brotherly Love"). Back in Romans 8, Paul has already reminded his readers that they're together as members of one family by God's grace (Romans 8:12-17). Now, because they have each been brought into the family on the same basis—namely, in Jesus—they have every reason to be devoted to one another.

This kind of love requires not only genuine affection but also humility. The NIV translates the second sentence in this verse as "Honor one another above yourselves." This resembles what we see in Philippians 2, where Paul writes, "In humility count others more significant than yourselves" (Philippians 2:3). Scripture calls us to put others first. We are to learn to play second fiddle without complaining or perversely seeking to be commended for doing so. The only competitive element among a church family should be that of seeing who can raise up and do good to others the most.

Thinking of this kind of loving brotherly affection brings us back to Jesus, who loves to call us His brothers and sisters (Hebrews 2:11-15). For Jesus, "though he was in the form of God, did not count equality with God a thing to be grasped, but emptied himself, by taking the form of a servant" (Philippians 2:6-7). It is Jesus who shows what true brotherly affection is; it is Jesus who loves His family perfectly in this way, outdoing all others in showing honor; it is Jesus whom we are called to be like, and whom we are living like each time we choose to love with Christlike brotherly affection. Today, then, love like Him.

1 SAMUEL 20

85 Gloria Gaither and William J. Gaither, "The Family of God" (1970).

JUNE 24

DIVINE ENTHUSIASM

"Do not be slothful in zeal, be fervent in spirit, serve the Lord." ROMANS 12:11

Picture a kitchen in an old British farmhouse, in which sits a pan on the stove, full of water bubbling away. That is the image Paul provides here regarding spiritual commitment. He essentially says that in Christ we are to keep the spiritual pot boiling. We're not to go hot and then cold—we're not to be enthusiastic at one moment and lose steam the next.

Once God's grace has laid hold of us and we have been transformed by Christ and received His righteousness by faith, we must apply that righteousness to our living. Part of this applied righteousness is to do the work of Jesus with a certain divinely inspired, divinely commanded enthusiasm.

It is easy, though, to be prone to laziness and to lapse into a spiritual half-heartedness. The book of Proverbs has much to say, often with a tinge of humor, about the dangers and the results of a lazy life. One proverb describes a man who is so lazy that having put his spoon into the bowl from which he's eating, he can't bring himself to lift it back out (Proverbs 19:24; 26:15). Another describes laziness in a man burying himself under his blankets and staying there: "As a door turns on its hinges, so does a sluggard on his bed" (v 14).

By contrast, the ultimate goal of Spirit-empowered zeal is to serve the Lord. How important it is for us to keep that goal in mind! When we do so, we recognize how even the most trivial activity—greeting a client, cleaning up a mess at home, loading or unloading the dishwasher, teaching each other, taking notes, giving an injection, speaking to our children, anything—can become a spiritual act of worship. Even the most routine part of our day can reflect our divine enthusiasm.

What brings your spiritual zeal to the boiling point these days? Serving Christ in worship? Sharing your faith with a colleague or stranger? Caring for your aging parents? Supporting the work of Christ across the world? Whatever it is, don't let up on your zeal. Keep the water boiling by serving the Lord in every moment of every day in response to the grace that He pours out on you every moment of the day. Come to Him each morning and ask Him to ensure that you will not grow weary. Then in all things His name will be proclaimed, and He will be glorified.

GALATIANS 6:1-10

JUNE 25

REJOICING WITH OTHERS

"Rejoice with those who rejoice, weep with those who weep." ROMANS 12:15

Shared joy is a great expression of sympathy. We typically use the word sympathy to describe a shared grief—but it applies to joy too.

We understand sympathy when we use it in a sentence, but the word itself can be difficult to define. So consider its opposite: apathy. If apathy is akin to saying, "I couldn't care less," sympathy is akin to saying, "I couldn't care more." Sympathy is an identification with the experience of another person.

Many of us find it natural to "weep with those who weep." It is instinctive for us to enter into the disappointment and pain of those we love and to cry at the sight or thought of their sadness. This is a good thing, for to "bear one another's burdens" is to "fulfill the law of Christ" (Galatians 6:2). To enter into the joy and success of others, however, is often the greater challenge because it requires us to work against the grain of the fallenness of our human nature, which is prone to resentment and bitterness. Instead of someone's success serving as an occasion for us to bless God and thank Him, it so easily becomes an occasion for envy.

Most of us know how to avoid expressing envy. But there is a massive difference between not *expressing* envy and not *feeling* envy. We can modify our behavior enough to keep from showing it, but it requires spiritual transformation to get us to the point of not feeling it. This transformation begins with a right understanding of our identity as members of Christ's body. Paul says that "we, though many, are one body in Christ, and individually members one of another" (Romans 12:5). To be in Christ means we are members of Him and of one another.

To put this another way: if we are in Christ, we are all on the same team. When we grasp this, it will be as natural for us to enter into another's joy as it is for a soccer player to rejoice at their teammate's game-winning goal in just the same way as if they had scored it themselves. As God's people, we win and lose—we enjoy and we grieve—*together*.

God's word calls you to "let love be genuine" (Romans 12:9)—and genuine, Christ-like love conforms your feelings so that jealousy gives way to joy and apathy to true sympathy. Is there anyone who you are standing aloof from in some way, either in their joy or their sadness? Have you considered whom you could encourage today? There is almost certainly someone who needs you to reach out and let them know that you are with them, praying for them and there for them as they walk a deep valley. Likewise, there will be someone whose joy you can share, and you can simply let them know that you praise God for His favor on their life. Be someone of whom it can increasingly be said, "They couldn't care more." Ask the God of all compassion and comfort to work in you by His Spirit to mold you into that person today.

2 CORINTHIANS 1:2-7

JUNE 26

LIVE IN HARMONY

"Live in harmony with one another." ROMANS 12:16

It requires skill and godliness to disagree graciously. It's easy to get along with people with whom we share everything in common, where there is no concern about disagreement. But to live in harmony with people who look different and live differently than we do—that is a true sign of Christian maturity. So the expectation of the apostle Paul is that as Christians we will make the effort to do just that.

Paul's call toward harmony is not a call toward a type of uniformity, where we all dress the same, act the same, vote the same, and talk the same. Indeed, the church in Rome was most certainly a varied group of people, diverse in background and in gifting. Paul emphasized that these differences were not to become a source of division or shame.

As the King James Version renders this verse, Paul wanted the Roman church to "be of the same mind one toward another." In just the same way, he appealed to the Corinthians, "by the name of our Lord Jesus Christ, that all of you agree, and that there be no divisions among you, but that you be united in the same mind and the same judgment" (1 Corinthians 1:10).

The gospel does not erase our distinctions or our disagreements. In fact, the unity that God's people share in the main things—the gospel of Christ and the truth of His word—frees us to acknowledge our distinctions and disagreements on secondary matters. Christian unity does not lie ultimately in our politics, our social status, or what color we think the carpet should be, but in the one whom we know to be "the way, and the truth, and the life" (John 14:6).

Sadly, churches can be distracted by their disagreements, and Christians can elevate their personal concerns and preferences too highly. Some of us make every issue into one to divide over, and so we become legalists, splitting hairs and never happy until we are in a church of one. Some of us find it hard to make any issue one we will stand on and not compromise over, and so we become theological liberals, letting central gospel truths become negotiable. The harmony Paul calls us to contend for is gospel harmony. We need to know ourselves well enough to discern whether we are prone to be legalists or liberals. We need to ask God to grant us clarity of mind and charity of heart toward our brothers and sisters in Christ. And then we need to take a moment to examine our hearts to see if there is anyone with whom we are not in accord and take steps to promote, and not corrode, the gospel harmony that Christ died to bring us into.

PSALM 133

JUNE 27

AT HOME IN CHRIST

"Do not be haughty, but associate with the lowly." ROMANS 12:16

A home can be a wonderful thing. For many of us, home is where we can be honest, where we're with our family, and where all things—even the flaws—feel familiar. Perhaps most importantly, though, a true home is where we can be ourselves, in genuine humility. Such ought to be our experience in the fellowship of God's people.

Paul's call for Christians to "not be haughty, but associate with the lowly" is a way of calling us to treat one another like family in the household of God. Another way to translate the command "Associate with the lowly" is to say "Be willing to do menial work." Both translations are helpful; we shouldn't be so proud that there are either people with whom we won't associate or jobs we refuse to do.

In the secular world, respectability is measured by status, significance, influence, wealth, intellect, and so on. This must not be the case among Christian men and women. Indeed, one of the distinguishing features of God's people should be that characteristics such as materialism, pride, and slander, which mark the wider community, are no longer prevalent.

How could we dare give in to the broader culture's influence when our Lord described Himself as having "nowhere to lay his head" and as being "gentle and lowly in heart" (Matthew 8:20; 11:29)? He came not to save those who are well but those who are sick (Mark 2:17). He continues to call the weak of the world to shame the strong (1 Corinthians 1:27). Even the apostle Paul, that eminently qualified teacher of the law, deemed his entire resumé rubbish in order to gain Christ (Philippians 3:8).

Jesus is building a church, and the church He's building is the family of God. Our Father is in heaven, our elder Brother is reigning, and our brothers and sisters are worshiping with us. Next time you're with your church family, take a step out of your comfort zone and get to know a member of the family you don't normally interact with. Next time you're asked to do a job or take on a role that you would not naturally be drawn to, ask yourself if this is an opportunity to be humble and not haughty. After all, our elder Brother did not consider a cross beneath Him, and He died there to raise up lowly sinners like you and me. The ground is level beneath His cross. And so His family is to be marked by humble love.

MARK 1:40 – 2:17

JUNE 28

PEACE THAT IS POSSIBLE

"If possible, so far as it depends on you, live peaceably with all."
ROMANS 12:18-19

The Bible is a wonderfully practical book. Its wisdom is both rich and realistic, and the longer we live, the more meaningfully we hear it speaking to our every situation. As we age, many of us realize that our parents were often correct in their warnings and wisdom; and as we walk by the light of God's word, so it will be proven right in time, every time.

Paul displays this timeless, realistic wisdom here. On one hand, this sounds simplistic: *just try to be at peace with everyone*. It's not difficult to understand. But that is not all he's saying. The instruction is preceded by two qualifications: "if possible" and "so far as it depends on you." The implication is that it may not always be possible!

Paul is not providing a loophole here. He's not telling us to be at peace so long as we can control our temper or emotions, but otherwise we're free to harbor bitterness. His call to us is to ensure that any ongoing conflict in our lives is in spite of us, not because of us. The responsibility for ongoing animosity must never be traceable to reluctance for reconciliation on our part.

But even if we've done our part, there are two situations in which peace may not be possible. One is when the other party is unwilling to be at peace with us. We may be dealing with someone intent on harming us and with no interest in resolving the conflict. In that situation, it may not be possible to change that person or prevent their cruelty—but it *will* be possible for us not to fight back. When we ensure that we are not contributing to the conflict, we are pursuing peace "so far as it depends on" us.

The other obstacle arises when the terms of peace are incompatible with principles of holiness, truth, and righteousness. The writer of Hebrews had such a situation in mind when he instructed his readers, "Strive for peace with everyone, and for the holiness without which no one will see the Lord" (Hebrews 12:14). These are not two disjointed instructions; our striving for peace and for holiness must not take us in separate directions. The pursuit of peace is not to become the pursuit of peace at any price. Some of us need to take care that our distaste for conflict and confrontation does not lead us to pursue peace at the cost of righteousness.

You cannot change a heart; that is the Lord's business. You must not compromise your integrity; that is the Lord's chief concern. But God is giving you an imperative, as much as it is up to you, that you pursue peace. Do you need to be prompted by this command to temper your words, change your behavior, or make the first step toward repairing a conflict, today?

DANIEL 6

JUNE 29

LOVE IN ACTION

"Beloved, never avenge yourselves, but leave it to the wrath of God, for it is written, 'Vengeance is mine, I will repay, says the Lord.' To the contrary, 'if your enemy is hungry, feed him; if he is thirsty, give him something to drink; for by so doing you will heap burning coals on his head.'" ROMANS 12:19-20

The "burning coals" in this passage are not a metaphor for revenge or pain. Rather, they signify the shame and remorse that individuals feel when, instead of giving them the retribution we think they deserve, we show them kindness and generosity. It is the effect caused when Christians treat those who have wronged them in a way that is entirely without malice or vengefulness, and is therefore foundationally supernatural. When that happens, John Calvin observes, the mind of the enemy may well be "torn in one of two ways. Either our enemy will be softened by kindness, or ... he will be stung and tormented by the testimony of his conscience."[86]

These coals, therefore, are not to ultimately bring hurt but healing. Our generous actions are to encourage reconciliation, drawing the individual *to* us, not pushing them *from* us. It's just like the mercy we received from God when we were still His enemies (Romans 2:4; 5:8).

If we are honest, though, those are not really the kind of coals we are looking for when we are wronged and hurt. Many of us would be quite happy to find out that coals actually *would* land on our enemies' heads, burning and scarring them. After all, it's nothing less than they deserve! But this reflects our fallenness and not our faith. This doesn't look or sound like Jesus. That is what makes these verses so incredibly challenging.

Notice that God's word calls us not merely not to react in vengefulness but to be proactive in blessing. When we manage not to retaliate, we have not yet fully obeyed. As disciples of Jesus, we're not only to refrain from doing our enemies evil; we're actually to *do them good*. It is easy to convince ourselves that ignoring our foes will take care of the problem or is the most we can realistically be expected to do; but here we discover that we're actually supposed to show them hospitality! Our role is to respond to wrongdoing with a spirit of generosity, trusting that God will always judge justly and therefore we do not need to judge, and indeed must not do so (1 Peter 2:23).

Even as members of Christ's body, many of us still seek to justify our disobedient, retributive actions or thoughts. Yet while our enemies' minds may be able to cope with our arguments and their spirits will be strong enough to stand against our threats, love in action might bring them to repentance. So how does your heart need to be transformed or your actions affected by these verses? Do not duck the challenge of them. Part of growing in Christlikeness is to look for ways to do good to your enemies, acting out of the overflow of God's radical kindness and generosity.

LUKE 22:47-53

86 *The Epistles of Paul the Apostle to the Romans and to the Thessalonians,* Calvin's Commentaries, ed. David F. Torrance and Thomas F. Torrance, trans. Ross Mackenzie (Eerdmans, 1995), p 279.

JUNE 30

OVERCOMING EVIL

"Do not be overcome by evil, but overcome evil with good." ROMANS 12:21

While studying at Cambridge University in the 1940s, a young woman became the Secretary of the Communist Party. The winter of 1946-47 was phenomenally severe, causing water pipes to partially freeze and therefore resulting in a water shortage. The female students were limited to one bath each week, and as they waited in the long line, there was a lot of grumbling and jockeying for position—including on the part of the Communist Party Secretary.

One of the girls who had the most direct access to the bathroom was a Christian. The Communist student noticed over time that this girl never asserted her rights and responded gently to the selfishness of others. The Christian was practicing and living what the young Communist claimed to believe but did not do. That observation led to a conversation, a conversion—and, eventually, a new missionary in the Far East.

Whenever we try to defeat evil by our own evil words and deeds, we are consumed. Evil cannot be overcome by a similarly evil force. Evil is doubled rather than negated. If we lose control of our ourselves as we engage with an enemy, then we have been defeated not by that person but by the Evil One. We are the ones who have been overcome and have lost the opportunity to do what is right in God's eyes.

Overcoming evil is a popular notion in our culture. We hear it in songs and motivational slogans. Often the idea is that if we can just "stand together," we will succeed in defeating the ills that plague us. It's a noble idea, but it lacks the necessary power. We *can't* overcome evil on our own; it simply won't work. We are "more than conquerors" *only* "through him who loved us" (Romans 8:37). The power of God by His Spirit and His word gives us both the impetus and the strength we need to triumph.

This is the path that Jesus took. He did not take vengeance into His own hands but entrusted Himself to the hands of the Father. Christ went to the cross, where love triumphed over evil. As we choose to be gentle, do good, and walk the way of the cross, we will experience God's power at work in us to overcome evil with the goodness of His love.

The hymn writer Charles Tindley reminded us of this truth when he wrote:

With God's Word a sword of mine,
I'll overcome some day …
If Jesus will my leader be,
I'll overcome some day.[87]

By His grace, you will overcome all the challenges and injustices of this world someday. And as you meet wrong with right, slights with kindness, and negativity with blessing, by His grace you will overcome evil with good today.

1 PETER 3:8-14a

87 Charles Albert Tindley, "I'll Overcome Some Day" (1900).

JULY 1

ON OUR BEHALF

"Alas, this people has sinned a great sin. They have made for themselves gods of gold. But now, if you will forgive their sin—but if not, please blot me out of your book that you have written." EXODUS 32:31-32

When the Israelites were redeemed from bondage, God instructed them to ask their former Egyptian landlords and owners for gold, silver, and clothes to take with them as they crossed over into the promised land. This would provide the material for the construction of the tabernacle-tent in which God would dwell among His people.

The Israelites hadn't gone far when Moses was called up Mount Sinai to meet with God. When Moses was gone longer than expected, though, the people grew impatient and demanded of his brother, Aaron, "Make us gods who shall go before us" (Exodus 32:1). So Aaron told them to "take off the rings of gold ... and bring them to me," and he used that gold to make a golden calf: "and they said, 'These are your gods, O Israel'" (v 2, 4). God had provided them with all they needed for the work He would call them to, and instead they abused His gifts to chase after their own ambitions and to worship a false god of their own making. We might not make a golden calf, but we are not immune from doing the same thing with what God has graciously given us.

When Moses returned, he was dismayed at all he observed. Bowing low to the ground before God, he interceded on behalf of the people, essentially saying, *You're the God who has made a covenant with Your people. Please, keep Your covenant! Even though we've taken what You have provided for us and have wasted it in the construction of false gods, don't leave us alone. Please don't abandon the work of Your hands* (Exodus 32:11-13).

It is remarkable that Moses, who was entirely blameless, should so identify himself with the people. It is still more remarkable that he should be more willing to be blotted out of the Lord's "book" of His people than he was to see the people cast off by God.

In Moses' intercession, we see glimpses of what ultimately would be fulfilled in the New Testament. God is never the author of unfinished business when it comes to His children. Christ intercedes on our behalf, and "all the promises of God find their Yes in him" (2 Corinthians 1:20). In other words, God's promises—that He will keep His people and complete the good work He has begun in them—are utterly fulfilled in Jesus Himself.

We are "prone to wander" and "prone to leave the God [we] love."[88] We are those who use what God gives to pursue our idols. We need an intercessor—and we have one! The Lord Jesus was blotted out in order that we might be forgiven our sin. When we confess our sin to Jesus, we are coming to the one who has already intervened on our behalf. Let His remarkable love for you win your heart back from wandering after idols, and come back to using all you have to serve the God who gave you all you need.

JAMES 4:4-10

88 Robert Robinson, "Come, Thou Fount of Every Blessing" (1758).

JULY 2

LEGACIES OF FAITH

"Faith is the assurance of things hoped for, the conviction of things not seen. For by it the people of old received their commendation." HEBREWS 11:1-2

What does faith look like? In chapter 11 of his letter, the author of Hebrews tackles this question by presenting us with a portrait gallery, as it were, of the saints of old—men and women who were commended on account of their faith. This biblical record of commendation is not meant to elevate these individuals to some superhuman status. Instead, we are to view Noah, Moses, and the rest as ordinary people from whom we can derive strength and encouragement as we reflect on how God helped them and honored their faith.

If we want to follow their example of a living, lived-out faith, we need first to see what the faith of these individuals was *not*. It was not a warm, fuzzy feeling deriving from emotion or circumstances, nor was it a vague notion that everything would just work out in the end. No, for these men and women, faith in practice meant believing what God had said, taking Him at His word, and then regulating their lives accordingly. In other words, as these verses tell us, their faith was an assured conviction that what God had promised would indeed come to fruition.

Furthermore, these saints of old regarded their future reality as if it were present and that which was invisible as if it were actually visible. Even if they didn't see God's promises fulfilled in their lifetime, they trusted His faithfulness to His word in light of eternity. Their faith was a deep-seated trust not in their circumstances in the present but in the one who had made promises about their future.

By living out their faith in such a visible way, these saints made a radical impact on their day—and so can we in ours. Whenever an individual, a couple, a family, or a church is prepared to take God at His word and do what He says, lives will be transformed. If we do so, we will better understand who God is and what He has done, and we will be better placed to make a difference in this world and for eternity.

Of all that was true of the saints presented in Hebrews 11, the one unifying characteristic which brought them to this portrait gallery was their faith in the living God—an assurance that God's promises were able to bear the weight of their hopes and a steady conviction that what God had said was as real as what they could see. Is that your faith? Meditate on all the promises that are yours from God in Christ. Reflect on all the promises God has already kept through history and supremely in the death and resurrection of His Son. Then you will be able, with joy and determination, to set your priorities and make your decisions based on His promises, not on your circumstances.

HEBREWS 11

JULY 3

SON OF ENCOURAGEMENT

"When [Paul] had come to Jerusalem, he attempted to join the disciples. And they were all afraid of him ... But Barnabas took him and brought him to the apostles and declared to them how on the road he had seen the Lord." ACTS 9:26-27

One evening in the 1960s, an unkempt hippie arrived at a very large and proper church near the coast in San Francisco. When he walked in, none of the ushers greeted him. The church was packed, and as he looked along the rows, nobody moved—and so he continued to walk. Eventually, having walked all the way to the front without finding a seat, he sat down right in the middle of the aisle, cross-legged on the floor. At just that point, the senior deacon—a small man in a three-piece suit, with a pin in his tie—started to walk forward from the back. He walked right up to the young man—and he sat down on the floor beside him!

That deacon was a "Barnabas." One Barnabas out of a group of 500 made all the difference in the life of a brand-new convert.

As a new convert to Christianity himself, Paul had no place to go. The believers in Jerusalem were fearful and doubted whether he'd experienced a radical life change. Paul needed somebody at this juncture in his life to encourage him, to lead him, and to introduce him to the church. For this task, God chose an ordinary man whom He had been forming all along. This man was a foreigner from Cyprus with a great religious background who had been given a new name by those who knew him: Barnabas, which means "son of encouragement" (Acts 4:36). It was this characteristic of Barnabas—his encouraging nature—which made him influential in Paul's life. Scripture doesn't tell us that Barnabas directed Paul anywhere, drew him a map, or suggested someone he might talk to. No, it simply gives us four wonderful words: "But Barnabas took him." When you take somebody where they need to go, it involves time, effort, and a rearrangement of plans. Where many wouldn't bother, Barnabas stepped up.

Barnabas would become Paul's companion on his first great missionary journey (Acts 13:1-3). Not just the start of Paul's Christian life but the start of his witness to the Gentiles owed much to this largely unsung hero. Only in heaven will it become apparent just how much of Paul's ministry successes were a result of the way God initially and continually placed Barnabas by his side.

We need people with the spirit of Barnabas in our churches—people who exude this kind of compassion, who will give time and effort and rearrange their plans in order to reach out to and welcome in those who are new or who are struggling. Indeed, in many congregations, they're already there; the church is sustained every single week as a result of men and women who recognize that there are no inconsequential moments in their days. There are no chance encounters. There are no irrelevant people. There are no insignificant tasks. Every church needs such people, who are willing to do what is necessary to "take" someone as Barnabas took Paul. Will that be you?

ACTS 4:32-37

JULY 4

A YOKE OF FREEDOM

"Come to me ... For my yoke is easy, and my burden is light." MATTHEW 11:28, 30

A yoke is a wooden frame placed across the back of oxen or other strong animals, joining them together in order to haul a heavy load. The yoke's purpose is to evenly distribute the weight on both sides, making it possible for the animals to walk while bearing it.

Jesus uses this illustration to offer those who might follow Him the chance to find unparalleled freedom under His yoke. With His invitation to take His "easy" and "light" yoke, Jesus distinguishes Himself from mere religion, with its heavy burden of rules and regulations. The Pharisees of Jesus' time were consumed with doing what was right—not only seeking to abide by God's law but adding a great number of their own rules as well. Such man-made obligations and expectations create crushing burdens. Repeatedly saying, "Come on now, try harder; come on now, do this," will figuratively wear down anyone's neck.

But Jesus' yoke is different.

To be under the yoke—the authority—of Jesus is not a burden; it is a delight. How can this be? There is a freedom found in Christ—not a freedom to do what we want but a freedom to do what we *ought*. Since by nature we cannot do what we ought, we are yoked to our own desires. That path promises much but delivers little. We need somebody—Jesus—to set us free from our bondage to sin so that we might live in freedom and obedience to God's will: to become the people we were designed to be. So it is that Christ's commands are "the perfect law that gives freedom," and so it is that those who obey them "will be blessed in what they do" (James 1:25, NIV).

This is why we declare with joy, "Jesus is my Lord." This is His identity—and because of His lordship, when we respond to His invitation and receive His yoke upon our shoulders, we accept a newfound obligation to live freely under His perfect will. The issues of morality, sexuality, business, family—all these things and more are gathered under the yoke of the Lord Jesus Christ.

For those who still feel yoked to a burdensome weight, be it impossible rules or sinful desires, Jesus extends the invitation to come and let Him lift these burdens. You need to hear this today. Where are you struggling with sin? How are you seeing the commands of the Lord as burdensome? In what ways might you be struggling against His ways? Hear Him again: *Come to Me. I'm humble. I'm gentle. Your burden is so severe that I had to die on the cross for you, and I did so willingly. Come and be yoked to Me. My burden is light.*

ROMANS 6:15-23

JULY 5

A CALL TO BE DIFFERENT

"Beloved, I urge you as sojourners and exiles to abstain from the passions of the flesh, which wage war against your soul. Keep your conduct among the Gentiles honorable, so that when they speak against you as evildoers, they may see your good deeds and glorify God on the day of visitation." 1 PETER 2:11-12

How are Jesus' followers supposed to act? It's a vital question. The answer is both simple and challenging: we are called to be *different*—different from those who don't follow Jesus.

Throughout all of eternity, God has purposed to have a people of His own. God's people are called to be a holy people, set apart both from sin and to God, who is in Himself "holy, holy, holy" (Isaiah 6:3; Revelation 4:8). We find this principle of a people set apart recorded for us throughout Scripture. In Leviticus, for example, the Lord commands His people, the Israelites, not to imitate the Egyptians and the Canaanites in their pagan practices. Rather, they are called to obey God's laws and decrees (Leviticus 18:1-5).

But God's laws were not introduced so that His people could simply give the appearance of obedience. No, true obedience to God's decrees is an expression of a transformed heart—a heart that rejoices at holiness. In other words, God says, *You're My people. You belong to Me. Therefore, I want you to delight in being set apart.* Our external actions will only endure and will only please God when an internal change has already taken place.

So it is that in the New Testament we find Peter exhorting believers to remember that they are "a chosen race, a royal priesthood, a holy nation, a people for his own possession" (1 Peter 2:9). As God's people today, we are still called to live differently: to keep our conduct honorable, and to make choices about our entertainment, finances, relationships—indeed, every facet of our lives—that are in step with God's exhortation to be holy as He is holy (1:16).

The great challenge for us as believers is to identify with the world in its need but not in its sin. The people of our world do not need us to make them feel comfortable about their immoral behavior and rejection of their Creator. Instead, as Peter explains, we are to live in such a way that we will "proclaim the excellencies of him who called you out of darkness into his marvelous light" so that others might see our good deeds and give God all the glory (1 Peter 2:9). So Peter's words should provoke us each to ask: Do I expect to be different? Am I willing to be different, even if it leads to others speaking against me? Will I love this world enough to be quite unlike this world, that I might point the people of this world towards a better one?

DEUTERONOMY 4:1-8

JULY 6

TRAIN WITH DISCIPLINE

"Every athlete exercises self-control in all things. They do it to receive a perishable wreath, but we an imperishable. So I do not run aimlessly; I do not box as one beating the air. But I discipline my body and keep it under control."
1 CORINTHIANS 9:25-27

Corinth was host to the Isthmian Games, in size and significance second only to the Olympics. Athletics consumed the culture. Its citizens knew that for an athlete, the effort expended during a race is only a small fraction of the effort demanded throughout life. So when Paul wrote to the church in Corinth, he didn't speak only of running and competing. He spoke also of training.

In Corinth, children as young as seven were put through rigorous exercises to prepare for competition. Contestants were expected to show they'd undergone strict training. Nobody could run a race if they hadn't practiced for months leading up to the event. Similarly, the Christian life should be marked by a discipline that reveals an eternal commitment to run God's race. To express resolve to live the Christian life without following up with disciplined action is nonsense. It's like expressing the need to wake up earlier or lose weight and resolving to do so, but then never actually setting the alarm, exercising, or eating well. The resolution is made worthless by the failure to take action.

The discipline Paul refers to is not a feeling within; rather, it is a willed, conscious decision about how we use our time, on what we set our affections, and the way we approach all of life. As the nineteenth-century English bishop J.C. Ryle wrote, "True holiness ... does not consist merely of inward sensations and impressions .... It is something of 'the image of Christ,' which can be seen and observed by others in our private life, and habits, and character, and doings."[89]

During ancient times, when the triumphant athlete returned to his city, he didn't just come through the gate out of which he had departed; he had a section of the wall broken down in his honor. He entered through a brand-new gate, and the city population gathered and welcomed him with great acclaim. Training within the Christian life does not earn salvation. That is won by Christ alone. It does, however, win us an abundant entry into heaven. When we reach His kingdom, to hear the Lord's greeting of "Well done, good and faithful servant" (Matthew 25:21) will be a moment of honor and joy greater than any newly made gate!

That's the picture of the entry into heaven which God's word says is possible for those who will run the race, who will endure the training, who will run to win. So ask yourself: Where am I expressing resolve but not taking action? In what area of Christian growth do I need to put disciplined practices in place so that I will become more like my Lord? And then look forward to the moment you finish your race and enter into glory, for that will motivate all the training that you require.

ROMANS 13:8-14

89 *Holiness* (Reformed Church Publications, 2009), p 8.

JULY 7

JOSEPH'S TEMPTATION

"Now Joseph was handsome in form and appearance. And after a time his master's wife cast her eyes on Joseph and said, 'Lie with me.' But he refused."

GENESIS 39:6-8

Temptation is an enticement to evil or to sin. Everyone has faced it—even the Lord Jesus Himself. In and of itself, therefore, temptation is not sin; it is our response to it which leads us either in the paths of righteousness or down into the quicksands of disobedience.

The actions of Potiphar's wife demonstrate how temptation expresses itself. Her approach was first subtle. She began in her mind to look at Joseph differently. The eyes are a gateway into our souls and the path through which many temptations come. A lustful heart begins with lingering eyes.

Her eyes having ensnared her soul, she lost any notion of modesty. How could she proceed to such a barefaced invitation to adultery? The answer is that she was clearly feeding lust at the level of her imagination, which is bound to increase the chances that we actually do what we've been thinking about. Sin is always ready to break forth in an instant, driven by blind, furious, and nearly (though never totally) irrepressible desires. There comes a point where we have gone so far down the road in our minds that all we need is the occasion—and so when the occasion arises, so does the outward sin.

You and I can learn from the misdeeds of Potiphar's wife. Be sure that what you allow your eyes to look at and your mind to dwell on will sooner or later affect how you act. Temptations, and the desires they awaken, will be fed or they will be fought. Are we prepared to "take every thought captive to obey Christ" (2 Corinthians 10:5) instead of feeding lust or other sins? Are we willing "to enter the kingdom of God with one eye" (Mark 9:47), or is eternal life not worthy of such a price?

What temptations do your eyes and your mind face today? While each is a dangerous invitation to sin, it also provides an opportunity to choose obedience. Pray for wisdom and boldness to recognize those moments, and respond to those temptations in a manner that leads you in paths of righteousness.

GENESIS 4:1-16

JULY 8

COME HUMBLY, SEEK HONESTLY

"The Pharisees came and began to argue with him, seeking from him a sign from heaven to test him. And he sighed deeply in his spirit and said, 'Why does this generation seek a sign? Truly, I say to you, no sign will be given to this generation.'" MARK 8:11-12

School teachers and college professors often experience two types of questioners: those who ask humbly with genuine interest and those who aim to challenge in an adversarial manner. The former clearly seek to understand. The latter are more interested in advancing an agenda, reinforcing their opinions, or simply looking smart.

Unlike the crowds of people who witnessed and marveled over Christ's miracles, the Pharisees often challenged Jesus' teaching and public ministry in order to test Him and to undermine Him. They weren't there to see His wonderful works and consider whether He was actually the person He claimed to be. They were there to trip Him up and trap Him.

Jesus responded to the crowds that followed Him with compassion. He had divine kindness for those who came to Him in humility of heart, recognizing their need. He turned away no one who came genuinely seeking truth. But He met the antagonistic religious leaders with righteous frustration—divine impatience for those who came seeking to prove their own position and to challenge His claims.

There are two ways to ask a question: humbly or arrogantly. And the Teacher always knows the difference.

Some people who say they are religious still get nothing out of the Bible's teaching. They listen to sermons Sunday after Sunday, looking for reasons not to rest wholly on Christ's completed work. They ask questions aimed at holding the Lord at arm's length, and then wonder why they never find satisfactory answers. That is not the way of the child of God. With meekness and curiosity, we should seek to learn from our Teacher and, when our hearts are troubled, come to Him humbly, asking for help to be open to the answer and without demanding that Jesus follow our agenda or expectations.

If you have a big brain, the Bible is able to satisfy your intellect. If you have a big head, you'll find pride distorts your ability to see the clarity and truth of God's word. Christ is more than willing to cater to intellectual integrity, but He is entirely unwilling to pander to arrogance.

We all have questions for Jesus about this world, about our life, about the way we should go. Jesus will never turn away those who come to Him, and He welcomes His brothers' and sisters' requests. But in addition to considering your questions, consider your heart. Ask your questions, but first think through how you are asking: are you motivated by faith seeking understanding or by pride seeking to be right?

MARK 10:2-22

JULY 9

A WORD TO FATHERS

"Fathers, do not provoke your children to anger, but bring them up in the discipline and instruction of the Lord." EPHESIANS 6:4

In Roman society, a father's power was all-prevailing. As William Barclay wrote, "A Roman father had absolute power over his family ... He could bind or beat his son; he could sell him into slavery; and he even had the right to execute him ... If ever a people knew what parental discipline was, the Romans did."[90]

Notice, then, that here Paul is not simply calling for the exercise of parental authority. Rather, he is both assuming its rightfulness and tempering it. His instruction is first negative: "Do not provoke your children to anger." He urges fathers to exercise restraint in disciplining their children, lest they do more harm than good by exasperating them or causing them to become discouraged, resentful, or angry.

How might we provoke our children to anger? Through selfishness, severity, inconsistency, unreasonableness, favoritism, nagging, fault-finding, failure to appreciate progress... Yet such a daunting list shouldn't discourage us; instead, it should remind us that this responsibility is entirely beyond us apart from God's grace.

And yet Paul's instruction is not only negative but also positive. The verb "bring them up" can also mean "nourish." There is something horticultural about it—a reminder not only that we are to rear our children tenderly but also that doing so is no momentary task; rather, it's a journey over many years. At the same time, this nourishment involves "discipline"—namely, the discipline of Scripture, by which the father himself is conformed to the image of Christ—and "instruction," which involves gently bringing God's word to bear upon our children's minds so that their character is actually transformed.

If you are a parent, how can you accomplish such a task? It takes grace. It also takes patience. In stock-market terms, parenthood is not day trading; it's long-term investing. It's amazing how a monstrous four-year-old who is constantly treated with godly love and discipline can become a thoughtful and loving young adult by her late teens. So if you are not a parent, pray for those who are. They need it! And if you are a parent, consider your own approach. How are you establishing parental authority in the home? In what ways are you most in danger of provoking your children as you do so? How will you instruct your children in God's word, and how can you see your own character being formed into Christlikeness through the experience of parenthood? In all this, remember that parenting is an act of grace. We are to discharge our responsibilities faithfully. But you will be crushed if you do not remember that grace is sufficient to overcome any and every mistake—a truth to build you up and keep you on your knees!

DEUTERONOMY 6:1-15

90 *The Letter to the Hebrews,* The New Daily Study Bible (Westminster John Knox, 2002), p 208.

JULY 10

DEATH'S STING IS DRAWN

"'O death, where is your victory? O death, where is your sting?' The sting of death is sin, and the power of sin is the law. But thanks be to God, who gives us the victory through our Lord Jesus Christ." 1 CORINTHIANS 15:55-57

Most recent generations have exhibited a widespread unwillingness to face the reality of death, and perhaps none more so than ours. People constantly attempt to cover it up or to ignore its existence in the hope that perhaps it will just go away. But of all people, Christians ought to be prepared to do what many will not: look death full in the face and acknowledge that there is no way to deny it and there is no way to escape it—but that there is also no need to, for it has been defeated.

Indeed, Christianity changes the way we view everything. The Bible confronts us with the reality that life is brief, death is certain, and judgment awaits. But we also have within the Scriptures clear, wonderful, and guiding statements concerning how to think of a believer's death.

For the Christian, death's sting is drawn. Consider it in this way: if you've ever gone outside with a little one and an angry wasp comes around, you will purposely put yourself between the child and the wasp to take or "draw" the sting. Once that's done, the child has nothing to fear. So Jesus, through His work on the cross, has dealt with the penalty of our sin. He has broken the bondage of sin's power in our lives. He has drawn the sting of sin and death. Christ's victory is our victory; death has been defeated. We shall still experience death, but we shall pass through it. It shall not claim us.

Scripture uses the picture of sleep to describe a Christian who has died, for sleep is a temporary, not a permanent, state. And it uses it in relationship to our bodies, not our souls. In one of his letters to the Thessalonians, Paul says, "Since we believe that Jesus died and rose again, even so, through Jesus, God will bring with him those who have fallen asleep" (1 Thessalonians 4:14). In other words, we may say to Jesus what many young children say to their moms or dads at bedtime: "Will you stay with me while I fall asleep?" And Jesus says, *Yes, I will. But even better than that, I will be with you in that sleep*. To fall asleep—to die—in Christ means we are ushered immediately into His presence, into the enjoyment of the Lord in glory.

Jesus is alive, and every new day can remind us of His resurrection. Every morning, we awaken to a new sunrise as a reminder of that glorious day when the trumpet will sound, the dead in Christ will rise first, and all who are alive and remain on earth will be caught up together with them. As believers, we have been born again with the living hope that because Jesus Christ was victorious over the grave, we will forever be with Him. That is how we look at death: we look *through* it. And once we are able to die without fear, we are able to live without it too.

REVELATION 3:7-13

JULY 11

CHRISTIAN MATURITY

"Not that I have already obtained this or am already perfect, but I press on to make it my own, because Christ Jesus has made me his own … I press on toward the goal for the prize of the upward call of God in Christ Jesus. Let those of us who are mature think this way, and if in anything you think otherwise, God will reveal that also to you." PHILIPPIANS 3:12, 14-15

There are few things quite so endearing as youngsters who go into great flights of fancy and make unrealistic claims, either about their parents—"My dad can do this" or "My mom is great at that"—or about themselves. It is not so endearing when it comes from someone aged 25 or 50! At that point, someone needs to say, "Act your age, for goodness' sake!"

Just as we expect to see maturity in those who have been doing life for a while, and just as we know there are certain marks of maturity in the physical, emotional, and mental realms, so we should expect to see maturity within the realm of spiritual living. And if we are truly growing in maturity, Paul explains, certain characteristics will mark our life and our walk with God.

Most of our society is constantly urging us to be aware of what we are, what we have achieved, or how far we have come. In contrast, Christian maturity has as its beginning an awareness of *what we are not.* Where immaturity leads us to think of ourselves more highly than we ought (see Romans 12:3), maturity rejects exaggerated claims. It's marked instead by a sane estimate of our spiritual progress. It's not exemplified by lofty talk but in a life of humble, steady consistency.

In the old fable "The Tortoise and the Hare," the hare goes flying off at the start of the race while the tortoise simply plods along. The hare is so convinced that he's won the race that he decides he'll sit down and rest, relax, and fall asleep. And as the fellow who started so dramatically falls asleep, the wee tortoise comes along—at the same pace, slowly, slowly, slowly—till eventually he is the winner and the hare is nowhere to be found.

It can be quite a challenge to be surrounded by spiritual hares, always leaping and bounding about, announcing their great aspirations and saying where they're going, what they're doing, and what they're achieving. How dispiriting I find that as I simply try to keep on in the Christian life!

As a wise pastor, Paul doesn't try to be the hare. Instead, he encourages us by saying, *I want you to know that I'm a pilgrim. I want you to know that I'm still in process, still on the journey—that I still have plenty of ground to cover.* Paul is pressing on toward the finish line, and he is urging us to do the same. Rather than a boast about a flashy start or impressive pace, his words are a call to resolute, repeated commitment to the basics.

Humility and consistency: these two are marks of the mature Christian life, which knows that by grace it has reached this far, and by grace it will press on to reach home. How will these grow as marks of maturity in your life?

1 PETER 1:22 – 2:6

JULY 12

A CALL TO THANKSGIVING

"Make a joyful noise to the LORD, all the earth! ... Enter his gates with thanksgiving, and his courts with praise!" PSALM 100:1, 4

The one hundredth psalm, with its call to worship, is one of the most well known in the Psalter. This familiarity can make it difficult for it to impact our hearts, though. In many ways, it's easier to study passages that are less familiar because then we aren't complacent in our study. We don't assume that we already know them.

We should never feel so comfortable with the invitation to thanksgiving that we brush over it, as if it were only rhetoric. This psalm urges us into action! As God's people, we are called to joyful worship and to thankful praise.

"Make a joyful noise" is an invitation to exuberant, vocal adoration. Such praise should not be treated as a forced obligation, as if we've swallowed something distinctly unpalatable. Instead, it should be a response to God's activity in our lives, which leads us, to borrow a phrase from C.S. Lewis, to be "surprised by joy." The opportunity for worship lifts the spirits of the genuine believer—and nobody is left out of the exhortation. God has made "all the earth" for the praise of His glorious grace.

The invitation also beckons us to "enter ... his courts with praise." Consider the experience of the commoner outside Buckingham Palace in London, where the best you can do is poke your nose through the railings and hope for a fleeting glimpse of royalty from afar. The gate is purposefully closed to protect the sovereign. But that is not our experience with the Father. Jesus' death tore the temple curtain in two (Matthew 27:51) and opened a new way of living for us. Through Jesus we have gained access to the Father, and the gates are thrown wide open in welcome.

Our expressions of gratitude in joyful worship and thankful praise are not to be tied to our circumstances or feelings. The real foundation for thanksgiving is in knowing that the Lord is God and that He has invited us into His courts, to surround His throne as His subjects but also as His children. To recognize this is to have firm ground underfoot so that each of us can say with the psalmist:

"He drew me up from the pit of destruction,
  out of the miry bog,
and set my feet upon a rock,
  making my steps secure.
He put a new song in my mouth,
  a song of praise to our God." (Psalm 40:2-3)

One day you will stand there, in His courts. Until then, each Sunday you can stand with others in your local church—an embassy of that heavenly throne room—and anticipate that future day by singing with joy to the Lord.

PSALM 100

JULY 13

OUR DEBT HAS BEEN PAID

"God made [us] alive together with him, having forgiven us all our trespasses, by canceling the record of debt that stood against us with its legal demands. This he set aside, nailing it to the cross." COLOSSIANS 2:13-14

Why did Jesus Christ come to earth, die on the cross, and rise from the dead? To provide eternal redemption and divine adoption for those who believe. It's a reality that no other religion can claim: God Himself paid the debt of human sin so that we might be called His children. The hymn writer expresses the wonder of that payment:

O perfect redemption, the purchase of blood!
To ev'ry believer the promise of God;
The vilest offender who truly believes,
That moment from Jesus a pardon receives.[91]

Our encounter with Christ's redemption is like the story of "Old Betty," an elderly woman who lived in poverty because of substantial financial debt. One day, a Christian minister and his congregation graciously decided to intervene in Betty's life and pay off her balance. The minister sought Betty out at her home—but, fearful of being arrested, she avoided the first several knocks at the door. Once he was finally able to tell her the good news, she looked at him and said, "Just think: I locked and barred the door against you. I was afraid to let you in, and here you were, bringing such a generous gift."

At some point in life, we have all been like Old Betty. Once, we knew ourselves to be indebted to sin. We were weighed down with regret, fearful that people would come knocking, ready to reveal our problems to others. Most of all, we were afraid of God, for the knock of His hand on the door of our lives could surely only mean judgment. But then we discovered that in Christ God knocks on the door to offer not what our debts deserve but what His love has won: a fresh start, a blank slate, a new story. Our debt was canceled, and we joyfully opened the door of our lives and welcomed Him as our Savior, Friend, and Lord.

To be a Christian is to live in the awareness of this paid debt. We are no longer slaves to sin and its penalty; instead, we've been set free and adopted as children of God. And now, our adoption as sons and daughters is why we have the great privilege of calling God our heavenly Father and knowing Him so intimately. We no longer hide behind our doors, clutching our debts, because we have tasted the freedom that came knocking and have let it into our lives.

What rest is found in knowing our debt is canceled! What joy is found in knowing that our status before the living God has been transformed from anxious debtors to adopted sons and daughters. Now the question is this: How will you allow these truths to change how you see yourself and how you see the tasks that lie before you today?

GALATIANS 4:21 – 5:1

91 Fanny Crosby, "To God Be the Glory" (1875).

JULY 14

THE SOUL'S ONLY CURE

"Naaman, commander of the army of the king of Syria, was a great man with his master and in high favor, because by him the LORD had given victory to Syria. He was a mighty man of valor, but he was a leper." 2 KINGS 5:1

From any angle, it appeared that Naaman had made it.

Naaman was a man of the great Syrian city of Damascus. Two rivers that began in the mountains of Lebanon flowed with pristine beauty into a fertile oasis where this city had been built. It was a place of wealth and leisure, and provided the cultural attractions of art, music, and recreation. As the successful commander of the Syrian army, Naaman had an enviable position of power and prestige, and he was highly regarded, including by his king. And, no doubt, with his power and prestige came great possessions. In other words, here was a man who had everything going his way. Except for one thing.

There was one dimension to Naaman's existence which cast long shadows over everything else that he enjoyed. His many proud achievements were dimmed and dominated by this one clause: "But he was a leper." All that he enjoyed—his many opportunities and his possessions—could not come close to tackling his problem. There wasn't anything that he was able to do… and the leprosy was spoiling his life.

The physical condition that plagued Naaman is a picture of the spiritual condition from which each one of us suffers. His leprosy was a scarring, contagious, ugly condition. It is a classic biblical picture of humanity's nature, which is tainted by sin.

When we describe ourselves and our context to others, we might list who we know, the places we've been to, and all that we've achieved. Yet at the end of all of that, without Christ, we're inevitably heading for that same little word as Naaman: *but…*

Leprosy had no regard for Naaman's status, and sin has no regard for ours. "All have sinned and fall short of the glory of God" (Romans 3:23), and "all" truly means "all." There is not a man or woman who is omitted from the scope of that all-inclusive statement. There is no wealth that can buy us out of sin and no goodness that can cover it over.

We all suffer from the leprosy of our souls, for which there is no cure apart from Christ. Only when we admit that our status and possessions cannot deal with our greatest issue can we then turn to Jesus, our Great Physician, who took on our condition so that we might be healed. Just as He was willing to reach out and touch a leper, rendering Himself unclean but healing the man entirely, so on the cross He became sin so that we might become righteous in God's sight (2 Corinthians 5:21).

Today, you are surrounded by Naamans: people who enjoy prestige, power, and possessions—people who have made it but who are nonetheless spoiled by sin and facing judgment. Here is a truth that undermines our envy of others and arouses compassion instead. As Naaman required a cure for his leprosy, every man and woman requires a solution for sin—and you know the cure.

LUKE 5:12-32

JULY 15

THE MYSTERY OF GOD'S WILL

"[He is] making known to us the mystery of his will, according to his purpose, which he set forth in Christ as a plan for the fullness of time, to unite all things in him, things in heaven and things on earth." EPHESIANS 1:9-10

When you watch new construction on a building from the outside, everything that is going on under all the scaffolding and house wrap can seem like a mystery. Something is obviously taking shape, but for anyone other than the architect it can be difficult to fully imagine the end result.

In the unfolding drama of the Old Testament, the mystery of God's will resembles scaffolding and wrap, shrouding certain parts of the biblical story until, as Paul puts it, "the fullness of time had come" (Galatians 4:4). Even as the prophets themselves prophesied concerning the one who was to come, they could only guess at the full meaning behind all the hints and clues laced throughout their writings (1 Peter 1:10-11).

In biblical language, a "mystery" isn't a puzzle waiting to be solved by human ingenuity. Rather, it is a secret that is waiting to be revealed by God. Through the work of His Spirit in our hearts and minds, many of God's mysteries become comprehensible to us. Apart from His work, we cannot understand them.

After His resurrection, when Jesus had the opportunity to address the unhappy travelers on the road to Emmaus, He responded to them in a loving yet strategic way (Luke 24:18-27). At first, they hadn't recognized Him, asking, "Are you the only visitor to Jerusalem who does not know the things that have happened there in these days?" (How ironic!) Jesus simply responded, "What things?" He wanted to draw them out. Then, after they had shared the story of His crucifixion and resurrection, He said to them, "O foolish ones, and slow of heart to believe all that the prophets have spoken!" They hadn't yet understood the mystery—and so, Luke tells us, the Lord clarified it: "'Was it not necessary that the Christ should suffer these things and enter into his glory?' And beginning with Moses and all the Prophets, he interpreted to them in all the Scriptures the things concerning himself."

"The mystery of his will" has been—indeed, is being—made known to God's people so that He might "unite all things in him." One day, when all the seasons which the Father has fixed by His own authority have run their course, all of this unity will come to fruition. Finally, the scaffolding, tarps, and wrapping will be stripped away, and we will see the building in its completion. Until that day, we can be grateful that the Lord has revealed the mystery of salvation to us, and we can walk in service and praise of Him, confident that while we may not understand the plans or the progress toward completion, the divine Architect is working out all things for the good of His people and the glory of His Son.

REVELATION 5:1-14

JULY 16

CALLED TO SERVE

"[Jesus] said to them, 'Follow me, and I will make you fishers of men.' Immediately they left their nets and followed him." MATTHEW 4:19-20

Have you ever been somewhere—maybe in a restaurant, a doctor's office, or a department store—and asked a worker why they do what they do? Perhaps they're trying to support a family. Maybe they've had a keen interest in the field since they were young. Among a variety of answers, you'll occasionally hear someone say, "This is my calling." In a very real sense, they express accurately the New Testament's perspective on ministry.

Those who are in Christ are all called to a life of service. It's not that we are all called to Christ but only some go on to serve; service is an integral part of Christian discipleship. When Jesus called His disciples to become "fishers of men," He was saying to them, *I have a job for you to do. I want you to be involved in My ministry.*

Whether a Christian is called to serve as a preacher or teacher of God's word, as a Bible-study leader for youth, as a volunteer in the church nursery, as a witness in their factory or office, as a parent raising children in the home or a child caring for an elderly parent, or in some other role, God's call to service equally applies. Any distinction between "full-time servants" and "lay servants" is a distinction not of value but only of function. The service itself is what's most important.

In the Bible's terms, service is not a pathway to greatness; service is greatness. "Even the Son of Man came not to be served but to serve, and to give his life as a ransom for many" (Mark 10:45). We don't serve sacrificially in hopes that we'll be "promoted," as in the workplace or in academic circles, nor do we serve so that one day we'll serve no more. Jesus says, "If anyone would be first, he must be last of all and servant of all" (9:35). When our actions demonstrate our understanding of this paradox, all glory will go to God.

Christian service is ultimately nothing less than the ministry of the risen Lord Jesus among and through His people. The apostle Paul understood this clearly when he wrote, "It is no longer I who live, but Christ who lives in me. And the life I now live in the flesh I live by faith in the Son of God, who loved me and gave himself for me" (Galatians 2:20). Jesus gave His life for us in order that He might take our lives from us and live His life through us. If you understand that, you will truly be able to serve as Jesus served—and your life will count for far more than if you had used it to serve yourself. Let us be about our calling today.

MARK 9:30-37

JULY 17

GUARDING AGAINST UNBELIEF

"As the Holy Spirit says, 'Today, if you hear his voice, do not harden your hearts as in the rebellion, on the day of testing in the wilderness, where your fathers put me to the test and saw my works for forty years.'" HEBREWS 3:7-9

Before the Israelites entered the promised land, God had them send twelve spies into Canaan on a reconnaissance mission. Two of those spies, Joshua and Caleb, are famous for their "minority report," which concluded that the land was ripe for the taking. The people, though, would not listen to them, demonstrating their distrust of God. Despite all the evidence they had had of God's reliability, the Israelites quickly reverted to trusting their own judgment.

In a moment of unbelief, the people feared they would die if, as Caleb and Joshua were urging them to, they chose to rely on God's power to overcome a great enemy (Numbers 13:25 – 14:4). God responded with judgment: instead of enjoying the promised land, an entire generation spent the remainder of their lives in the wilderness, never experiencing the joy God had offered them (14:21-23).

Like the Israelites, you and I have a propensity for unbelief. The writer of Hebrews warns us, "Take care, brothers, lest there be in any of you an evil, unbelieving heart, leading you to fall away from the living God" (Hebrews 3:12). Such an exhortation wouldn't be necessary if it weren't possible for us to have sinful, unbelieving hearts! We *do* want to sin. We *do* want to go our own way. We *do not* wish to trust.

Unbelief hardens us so that when the Bible is preached, instead of God's word coming into our hearts and minds like seeds sown in the ready earth, our hearts and minds become like a corrugated tin roof. The more the Bible is taught, the more its effect on us becomes like rain hitting against that which it cannot permeate.

So be on guard, lest your heart become impervious to the truth of Scripture. Be wary that you don't become someone who defends the Bible, tells other people about it, and quotes from it, but all the while hardening your heart against what God is saying to you in it.

How do we protect ourselves against such unbelief? Exhort others to remember what God has done in and through Christ, and ask them to do the same for you (Colossians 3:16). And ask the same Spirit who authored Scripture to work in your heart as you hear His voice. As you are reminded of God's power and care and as the Spirit goes to work in you, your heart will be softened to receive the seeds of His word.

LUKE 13:18-35

JULY 18

GOD'S KING

"And God said to [Jacob], 'I am God Almighty: be fruitful and multiply. A nation and a company of nations shall come from you, and kings shall come from your own body.'" GENESIS 35:11

The book of Judges tells the story of the Israelites in the promised land after the death of their leader, Joshua. It's a depressing story because the people very quickly rebelled, beginning a cycle that repeats itself throughout the book. First, the people sinned; second, God allowed them to be defeated and oppressed; third, they cried for help; and, fourth, God intervened by raising up a judge, or leader, to defeat Israel's enemies and restore peace to the land. But peace never lasted for long before the sequence was repeated.

Throughout the period of the judges, Israel was collapsing—religiously, socially, morally, and economically. In response, the people started to think that life would be a lot better if only a king were appointed, as God had declared to Jacob one would be. Yet, seeking to be like the nations around them, they rejected God's kingship—the very thing that made them unique. They wanted a monarchy instead of a theocracy. And, rather than looking for a king who would govern under God and lead them in obedience to His rule, they were looking for a king who would rule *instead* of Him.

Remarkably, despite the sinfulness of the Israelites' motivations, God fulfilled their request. Many kings of Israel followed, but never the king they truly needed. There was still someone greater to come.

In a way that only He could orchestrate, God used the people's shortsighted demand for a king like those of other nations to fulfill His ultimate purpose for a King who would one day rule those nations. Eventually, Israel's royal line would culminate in Jesus, the coming King whom God had promised—one whose "scepter shall not depart from Judah, nor the ruler's staff from between his feet, until tribute comes to him; and to him shall be the obedience of the peoples" (Genesis 49:10). The true kingdom would be established by the Messiah, who would rule under God's authority and would be His supreme gift to an unworthy people.

See how immense God is, that He is able to sweep into His purposes even foolish requests and bad motivations! God is bigger than our choices and even our mistakes. He is sovereign over every misstep. Though we, like Israel, may fail at times, we can surely trust God to overcome our failings as He accomplishes His purposes. And we can gladly obey His King in our lives today, rather than seeking to serve anyone or anything in His stead.

2 SAMUEL 7

JULY 19

IRREVOCABLY INTERWOVEN

"If there is any encouragement in Christ, any comfort from love, any participation in the Spirit, any affection and sympathy, complete my joy by being of the same mind, having the same love, being in full accord and of one mind." PHILIPPIANS 2:1-2

Becoming a Christian is a bit like getting married. In marriage, two single individuals come together, and their lives become irrevocably interwoven. Likewise, when we embrace Christ in all of His love and accept the salvation He won for us at the cross, we are united with Him—and we are never the same again.

Just as the Philippians were reminded by the apostle Paul, we today can recognize the encouragement that exists as a result of our union with the Lord Jesus Christ. Our relationship with Him is a gift of God's grace to us, and we can find security in the knowledge that through the power of His Spirit, He is with us everywhere we go. If you are united with Christ by faith, He is closer to you than you are to your own hands and feet. Your life is permanently interwoven with the Lord.

One of the prevailing difficulties of 21st-century life is that so many of us feel at times forlorn, bereft of companionship, and alone, even when we're in the midst of a crowd. We may try to disguise our feelings of isolation with superficial conversation or the thin veneer of a smile, but at times we walk away from companies of people feeling desperately lost. Truly, though, Christians need not feel that despair, because we know and experience the reassurance of our union with Christ. He both knows us completely and loves us infinitely. There is great comfort in knowing this! The "comfort" Paul speaks of here isn't just a simple, cozy feeling; the word describes something with power and attractiveness to it. It is a *doing* word: comfort flows out into our relationships with each other, for the Spirit unites us not only to Himself but also to one another even on this side of heaven. The more we enjoy the benefits of our union with Christ—the most precious of which is Christ Himself—the more we will grow closer to, and more deeply loving of, our brothers and sisters in faith.

Yet while such comfort blesses us, it also obligates us. Our knowledge of Christ's mercy and compassion ought to compel us to show affection and sympathy to one another as we grow in our union with Him. It is possible for us to be hardened by life's bumps and bruises, possible for us to lack the grace which reveals itself in tenderness, possible for us to be so taken up with ourselves that we fail to love others. How do you need encouragement or comfort today? Reflect on your union with Christ, and find them in Him. Then ask the Spirit to show you anyone who needs encouragement or comfort today, and be the means by which Christ's comfort is brought to them.

COLOSSIANS 3:1-11

JULY 20

THE TRUE TABERNACLE AND TEMPLE

"The Jews said to him, 'What sign do you show us for doing these things?' Jesus answered them, 'Destroy this temple, and in three days I will raise it up.'"

JOHN 2:18-19

Some understand the Bible to be little more than a mixture of philosophical information and spiritual tidbits. Nothing could be further from the truth, for the Bible contains the unfolding drama of God's intervention in our world. The theme of God's kingdom provides us with one useful way of entering and following the thread of its story. And in every kingdom, there is a dwelling place for the king.

Throughout much of the Old Testament, the tabernacle was the place where God dwelled with Israel. While the tabernacle was among God's people, though, it was not open to them. Even Moses himself could not enter when the cloud of God's glory settled upon it (Exodus 40:34-35). Then, once Jerusalem had become the capital of the land, the tabernacle tent was replaced by a permanent building—the temple. Here was God, the King of His people, dwelling in the capital city of His people and their land. But still the way to Him was barred by the curtain that separated the Most Holy Place from the rest of the temple complex (26:31-34).

And then "the Word became flesh" and literally "tabernacled among us" (John 1:14).

In reading the New Testament, we discover that just as the people of old looked to the tabernacle for an encounter with God, now we look to a person—God Himself, who pitched Himself in human flesh and lived among us. John's language specifically communicates that God, in Jesus, dwelled among His people physically and now dwells in His people by His Spirit (John 14:16-18). He is here among us. Jesus, in other words, is the true tabernacle.

This is what He was seeking to explain when, after He had cleansed the temple by driving out the merchants and money-changers who had set up shop there, He was challenged about His authority to do such an audacious thing (John 2:13-16) and He answered, "Destroy this temple, and in three days I will raise it up." John explains that after Jesus was crucified, was buried, and rose from the dead, His disciples understood that "he was speaking about the temple of his body" (v 21).

When Jesus died, the curtain in the temple tore, signifying that through Christ we now have unfettered access to God; but also showing that the temple building was now obsolete, for its fulfillment had come. A few decades later, the temple in Jerusalem would ultimately be destroyed.

If we want to meet with God, we must go to Jesus. We no longer need a specific building or special icons or shrines. God meets with His people—when we are gathered and when we are scattered—not in places but in the person of His Son, the true temple. Whatever day today is, and whatever you are up to, there is nothing and no one standing between you and a living encounter with the holy God. The King dwells in you today.

JOHN 2:13-22

JULY 21

FROM MILK TO FOOD

"For though by this time you ought to be teachers, you need someone to teach you again the basic principles of the oracles of God." HEBREWS 5:12

If you keep lots of exercise equipment in your basement but never pick up the weights to train your muscles or strengthen your cardiovascular health, it will be useless. Muscles grow through consistent use. A personal trainer may be helpful, but we must also make a commitment to train ourselves. When Paul wrote to Timothy, "Train yourself for godliness" (1 Timothy 4:7), he was emphasizing that no role model, leader, or friend could do the hard work for him.

As we grow in our Christian walk, we learn elementary truths, slowly putting them into practice and growing in spiritual discernment. This process helps us transition from milk to solid food (Hebrews 5:12-14), from spiritual infancy to spiritual maturity, so that we can eventually begin to teach others. It is a God-designed life cycle meant to expand His kingdom.

To change the metaphor, Christianity's fundamental truths are vital; everything else we learn about Christ is built upon them. But it isn't productive to camp on them forever. We must be diligent in making progress in the Christian life, constantly striving to grow in holiness, asking the Spirit to build us up as we go deeper into His inspired word.

God does not conform His children to the image of His Son in isolation from life or the instruction of His word. As you are trained in the Scriptures and lay hold of them, so you make progress. Does your Bible show signs of daily, disciplined use? Do you seek intentionally to learn from those who are further on in their walk than you, and do you wrestle with difficult doctrines rather than leaving them for "the experts"? And do you read and wrestle and meditate with a view to growing in your love for Christ and your ability to serve others in your church and in your community, rather than with a view only to knowing more? Never let it be said of you that you could have grown more and done more to help God's people. Seek to grow. That will require God's help—but as we seek Him, He will surely honor our efforts!

HEBREWS 5:7 – 6:3

JULY 22

A REMINDER TO PRAY

"When he had entered the house, his disciples asked him privately, 'Why could we not cast it out?' And he said to them, 'This kind cannot be driven out by anything but prayer.'" MARK 9:28-29

In Mark 6, Jesus had sent the disciples out two by two to proclaim the need for repentance. He had given them not only specific instructions but also "authority over the unclean spirits" (Mark 6:7). Because of this, they had developed a great track record: "They cast out many demons and anointed with oil many who were sick and healed them" (v 13).

Considering their previous success in the ministry that Jesus had given them, it's easy to see why the disciples were surprised and confused when their efforts to help a boy with an evil spirit proved futile, until Jesus arrived and stepped in to restore him (Mark 9:14-27). Perhaps in asking, "Why could we not cast it out?" the disciples expected Jesus to give them some sort of secret knowledge. Sometimes that is what we too believe, misunderstanding Jesus' reply as saying that a very special ability or ministry is needed. But that is not the case. Jesus is simply reminding His disciples, and us, of this: *You didn't succeed because you forgot to do something very important: you didn't pray.*

In their success, the disciples had gotten comfortable. They had lost track of the fact that it was only because of God's immense mercy and power that they could do anything. They were still in Christ's company, yet they were already forgetting. They needed a reminder.

Sometimes we need to be reminded as well. To imagine that God's power is simply at our disposal and under our control is tantamount to unbelief; it's trusting in ourselves rather than trusting in God. Prayer, by contrast, is ultimately aligning our will with God's. It acknowledges that God must work wonders because we ourselves can't. And until we rely on God's grace, we're unable to intervene in anyone's circumstances and make an eternal difference.

There are many reasons why we don't pray. We don't think we have to. We don't want to. We overestimate our own abilities. Each is an absolute presumption on our part. When we try to do things on our own, we will often find ourselves failing miserably. So the next time you're tempted to figure something out yourself, or to assume that God's power will bring you through because it did last time (and that "next time" is likely to be today!), consider what the disciples had forgotten and what Jesus reminded them of: pray to the one who has all the power, showers us with mercy, and deserves all the glory. For when you pray and watch what God does, you discover that He does far more than you had even dared ask or thought to imagine (Ephesians 3:20).

MARK 9:14-29

JULY 23

GOD WILL MEET OUR NEEDS

"We were not idle when we were with you, nor did we eat anyone's bread without paying for it, but with toil and labor we worked night and day, that we might not be a burden to any of you." 2 THESSALONIANS 3:7-8

Depending on God does not conflict with working to earn our daily bread. Indeed, work and the ability to do it are part of God's provision. If we doubt that, we should consider the fact that Jesus Himself worked. Even though He came from heaven and all things belong to Him, He labored as a carpenter for years, confirming the pattern that was laid out for humanity in Genesis (Genesis 2:15).

Similarly, the apostles, living by faith and wholeheartedly pursuing the growth of the church, worked diligently "night and day." They refused to be lazy or to eat anyone's food without paying. As ministers of the gospel, they did have the right to ask for help with provisions (1 Timothy 5:17-18); however, they took responsibility for themselves and practiced the trades they knew, serving as "an example to imitate" (2 Thessalonians 3:9).

In the midst of our own labors, we must recognize that we can abuse work in at least two ways: through either laziness or overactivity. The warning of Proverbs applies to us: "The sluggard does not plow in the autumn; he will seek at harvest and have nothing" (Proverbs 20:4). Or, as Paul puts it, we must not be idle. But we must pay equally careful attention to the psalmist's words when he says, "It is in vain that you rise up early and go late to rest, eating the bread of anxious toil" (Psalm 127:2). Yes, we are to labor with our hands. If we aren't working for God's glory, though, we are left toiling at a feverish pace, yet in vain.

Nowhere is this more apparent than when we ignore the Sabbath principle. Nothing so reveals our unwillingness to take God at His word and to trust Him for daily provision as when we abuse the command to work six days and rest for one (Deuteronomy 5:12-15). Why do we think we need to work all day, every day? The answer is, quite frankly, because we struggle to trust that God will meet our needs. We must find our security not in our work but in the God who provides both the work and the means to carry it out.

In our materialistic culture, it is not easy to work faithfully while learning to be satisfied with our God-given lot. Take a moment to reflect on your own work, be it in the home, the field, the factory, or the office. In what ways are you tempted towards laziness? And in what ways towards overactivity? What will it look like for you to work hard and trust God? In a world ensnared by materialism, your contentment—in your work and in God's provision—will be a compelling testimony to the divine love that alone provides true satisfaction.

DEUTERONOMY 5:1-3, 12-15

JULY 24

UNRIGHTEOUS ANGER

"As soon as his master heard the words that his wife spoke to him, 'This is the way your servant treated me,' his anger was kindled. And Joseph's master took him and put him into the prison, the place where the king's prisoners were confined, and he was there in prison." GENESIS 39:19-20

Potiphar was a shrewd judge of character. As an officer of Pharaoh and captain of the guard, he'd had many people under his control for most of his life. His experience enabled him to see that Joseph had something distinct about him.

Joseph was like no other servant; he was the *best* of servants. All of Potiphar's affairs prospered under Joseph's jurisdiction, and Potiphar gave everything into his care—everything, that is, except his wife.

It's hardly surprising, then, that Potiphar reacted in anger and rage when his wife accused Joseph of attempting to assault her. Any husband worth his salt would react in this way. There is a rightness about that sort of protection, and we should expect Potiphar to have displayed it.

Potiphar's mistake was not his initial response but the speed with which he pronounced judgment against Joseph. There's no mention of Potiphar processing the information he was given, nor do we see him stepping back and setting his wife's accusation against the backdrop of Joseph's record of faithful integrity. Instead, Potiphar allowed his anger to run away with his judgement. Rage blinded Potiphar to both truth and reason.

Potiphar also permitted himself to be unduly influenced by his wife. Of course, all of us are swayed by our closest companions, and mercifully so on many occasions. But none of us are to be unduly influenced by any one person, save God. When we allow such sway to take hold, especially in moments of decision-making, we put not only ourselves but everybody around us in peril. Instead, we must seek safety and victory in an "abundance of counselors" (Proverbs 11:14; 24:6) who will point us to the wisdom of God's word in every circumstance. The greater the magnitude and the consequences of a decision, the more counsel we should seek and the more time we should spend on our knees.

Potiphar allowed himself to make a decision while he was angry—and his decision was an unjust one. Unchecked anger blinds the mind. Once kindled, it is easier to let anger blaze than to stamp it out. But even in circumstances in which anger is the correct response to injustice or sin (and we follow a Lord who Himself responded with anger when appropriate—see Mark 11:15-18), we cannot give rage permission to direct our emotions and dictate our decisions. Be quick to ask God to reveal any source of ongoing anger in your life so that you might repent where necessary, forgive when called to, and move forward in wisdom and faith.

GALATIANS 5:16-24

JULY 25

GRACE, MERCY, AND PEACE

"To Timothy, my beloved child: Grace, mercy, and peace from God the Father and Christ Jesus our Lord." 2 TIMOTHY 1:2

The way in which Paul refers to Timothy throughout his letters is striking. He doesn't keep this younger man at arm's length; instead, Paul addresses Timothy as his "beloved child," his "child in the Lord," and a "fellow worker" in proclaiming the gospel (2 Timothy 1:2; 1 Corinthians 4:17; Romans 16:21).

Initially, we might not think that Timothy was an obvious choice to be the recipient of Paul's words or letters, at least not from a human perspective. He wasn't strong or mature but relatively young, physically frail, and naturally timid—a rather diffident chap who must have looked too inexperienced for what he was doing. When he got anxious, it went to his stomach (1 Timothy 5:23). He was not a high-caliber candidate. Really, though, this isn't unusual. This is most believers. This is me and you.

And yet Timothy was God's man.

He was God's man because God had chosen him. God delights to pick up men and women—including those who are comparatively young, naturally weak, physically frail, or obviously reserved—and say, *This is what I have lined up for you. You're My chosen servant for the task to which I have appointed you.*

The 18th-century evangelist George Whitefield was used by God to bring tens of thousands of people to saving faith. Yet he was often overwhelmed at the prospect of his own ministry. Once, on his way to preach in the chapel of the Tower of London, Whitefield records, "As I went up the stairs almost all seemed to sneer at me on account of my youth; but they soon grew serious and exceedingly attentive."[92] Why did the reaction of his listeners change? The answer is simply that Whitefield, like Timothy, was God's chosen man.

How Timothy must have drunk in Paul's greeting, which reminded him of his resources! God had redeemed and commissioned Timothy, and God would supply grace for the trials, mercy for the failures, and peace in the face of dangers and doubts.

What do you and I need today? Exactly what Timothy needed: grace, mercy, and peace. All that was available to Timothy is available to us too. So you can lean on God and the provisions He's made for you in Christ. His resources are sufficient to meet your every need and to accomplish every task He calls you to.

2 TIMOTHY 1:1-14

92 *George Whitefield's Journals (1737-1741),* ed. William V. Davis (Scholars' Facsimiles and Reprints, 1969), p 57.

JULY 26

GOD-CENTERED FOCUS

"I am the vine; you are the branches. Whoever abides in me and I in him, he it is that bears much fruit, for apart from me you can do nothing." JOHN 15:5

Amateur photographers often don't know what they're focusing on. They know what they *think* they're focusing on—but then the pictures end up containing blurry faces and buildings askew. Then they may look at their work and respond, "This isn't what I was pointing at!" But the fact of the matter is, the photos reveal exactly where and how the lens was positioned.

In life's highs and lows—and every moment in between—the way you and I react to circumstances reveals the angle of our camera lens, the focus of our hearts and minds. The challenge for believers, then, is to live with a focus that is centered on God.

Jesus made it very clear that in order for us to embrace a God-centered focus, we must first understand who we are without Him. In fact, Jesus explained to His disciples that apart from Him they could do nothing; after all, "in him all things hold together" (Colossians 1:17). Our need for Jesus is not partial; it is total. None of us can even breathe without God's enabling. How can we think of taking credit for any work that He's done through us? We are absolutely impoverished without divine help.

This principle runs throughout the entire Bible. Moses, chosen by God to lead the Israelite people out of bondage and slavery, was adamant that he couldn't do the job unless God was with him—and he was right (Exodus 3:11-12). Amos was a keeper of fig trees and a shepherd; he had nothing to contribute to the ministry when God appointed him as a prophet (Amos 7:14-15). Daniel, likewise, with his amazing ability to interpret dreams, was quick to give every bit of credit to God (Daniel 2:26-28). Each of these men recognized his utter dependency on God. In fact, no one in Scripture who achieved great things for God did so without relying wholly on God. For their ability to do the work they were called to do, they looked up rather than looking in.

As Christians called to live with a God-centered focus, we must not ascribe too much attention to ourselves or our abilities, for in doing so, we may very well obscure God's grace and power in our lives. In Christ, we ought not to boast in our abilities or seek any opportunity to draw attention to ourselves. Instead, we should merely wish to be known as servants of the living God, to be useful in His service as He works in us according to His good purpose, and to point away from ourselves and to Him in all we do and say.

Where will your focus be today? And when success or praise come your way, to whom will you point?

LUKE 17:7-19

JULY 27

CONSIDER HIM

"Consider him who endured from sinners such hostility against himself, so that you may not grow weary or fainthearted." HEBREWS 12:3

Have you ever been tempted to give up on your faith? Maybe during a tough week, you've considered your circumstances and thought, "None of this is working to my benefit. It's time to forget about Christianity and live as others live." In those moments, it's easy to look around and see our unbelieving friends, family, and coworkers living differently and more easily and seemingly having a great time. Envious glances allow doubt and disillusionment to creep in and steal our resolve to stay on the straight and narrow path.

This was the experience of the psalmist Asaph. He "had almost stumbled" because he "was envious of the arrogant when [he] saw the prosperity of the wicked" who were "always at ease" (Psalm 73:2-3, 12). This, it appears, was also the experience of the Christians to whom the writer of Hebrews addressed himself. They had "not yet" had to shed blood in order to stand firm in the faith (Hebrews 12:4), but it was clear that the struggle against sin within and the struggle to withstand opposition from without were taking their toll.

What should they do? *Consider Jesus.* The biblical antidote to faintheartedness and weariness is to fix our eyes on Him who endured hostility—who endured the cross—in order to obtain the joy set before Him (Hebrews 12:2).

At some point in our lives, all of us will face unjust suffering in words, deeds, or circumstances—and we can admit that we don't want to take the dig in the ribs and the spikes in the shins. All of us will face the reality that we have not yet defeated the sins that we have struggled with for years and years. All of us will face days when we don't want to be in the race, when we are tempted to give up and drop out. What should you do on those days? Hear God's word saying, *Consider Him. Consider the life of Christ: what it was like and where it led.* He opened the door to glory; now we walk the path behind Him. Look at Jesus, who ran this race and is now "seated at the right hand of the throne of God" (Hebrews 12:2). Day by day, no matter whether the course runs uphill or the wind feels full against us, we consider Him and "run with endurance the race that is set before us" (v 1).

PHILIPPIANS 3:3b-16

JULY 28

BE A DOER

"Be doers of the word, and not hearers only, deceiving yourselves." JAMES 1:22

As believers, our lives can and should be marked by minds that are trained in and subjected to the truth of God's word, and we should surround our circumstances with prayer (Philippians 4:6-8). But still, if we are to know and enjoy God's power at work within us, we must take what we hear in the Scriptures and put it into practice. We should be diligent in our attention to the Scriptures each day, and in our attendance when the word of God is being expounded, but we should never fall into the trap of thinking that attending, paying attention, and listening carefully are enough. We must be "doers ... and not hearers only."

In John 13, on the night before Jesus' death and after He has been teaching the disciples for a while, He says to them regarding His lessons, "If you know these things, blessed are you if you do them" (John 13:17). If you wonder why you're not experiencing God's blessing, it may be because you aren't putting His words into practice. The Lord has given us rich instruction and He has given us the Spirit to be our Helper. Now we are responsible for drilling our minds in the truth of God's word and then *doing* what we have learned, received, and heard.

What a great sadness it is when churches become like dusty old libraries, filled with so many lives that are like volumes of truth just sitting there, never used. The temptation as we become increasingly aware of the truth is just to sit and think about it without ever taking action. James puts that kind of life in stark terms: it is to deceive yourself. No—a church is to be a gallery of living experience. There ought to be a vibrancy about believers, so that when we face the world's many problems—problems we ourselves are not immune to—we can see them for what they are and respond by holding out the truth of God's word as we ourselves live it out.

Determine today not to be a hearer only, and so deceive yourself into thinking you are a growing Christian when in fact you are a shriveling one. Resolve to be a doer of the word. Look honestly over your life now and identify any areas about which you have heard how to live for Christ but have never actually obeyed. That will be the part of your life about which the Spirit is saying to you right now, *Do not be a hearer only. Be a doer—for that way blessing lies.*

JAMES 1:19-27

JULY 29

EMBRACING INTERFERENCE

"As he was walking in the temple, the chief priests and the scribes and the elders came to him, and they said to him, 'By what authority are you doing these things, or who gave you this authority to do them?'" MARK 11:27-28

None of us like someone else interfering in our business.

When someone insists on our attention or demands our obedience, we instinctively respond negatively. Generally speaking, we don't want people telling us what to do, least of all in spiritual matters. It is always tempting to buy into the notion, particularly popular in our day, that our spirituality is no one else's business—a personal matter to be known only to us.

In reading the Gospels, then, we may become distinctly unsettled as it becomes clear that Jesus interferes in our lives. Yes, it's for our good—but nevertheless, He interferes. Indeed, in his autobiography, C.S. Lewis refers to Jesus as the "transcendental Interferer."

From the beginning of Jesus' ministry, people recognized that He spoke with authority (see Mark 1:22, 27). He said things in such a way that they couldn't be sidestepped or simply dismissed. But they could be resisted and rejected. His authoritative teaching became a thorn in the religious teachers' side, and they began to oppose Jesus, soon plotting to kill Him so that they would not have to open up their spiritual lives to Him (3:6).

Like the religious leaders, we often prefer a personal spirituality that is molded by our agenda and lifestyle: "This is what I believe. This is what I hold to. This is what we've always done. This is our tradition." Jesus comes crashing into those notions, turning everything upside down, taking man-made values and upending them. In fact, at the end of Jesus' earthly ministry, He declared that all authority had been given to Him (Matthew 28:18-19). He doesn't share that authority with anyone. Our spiritual lives are, in fact, His business. We bow down before His authority and embrace Him as Lord and Savior now, or one day we will bow before Him and meet Him solely as our Judge.

Adding Jesus to a little corner of our existence is easy and nonintrusive; it's another thing entirely to allow the "transcendental Interferer" to take over every aspect of our lives and command from us complete obedience. His perfect authority is an issue we must consider in every decision we make. So we are faced by the unsettling question: Am I living according to my natural desires and the rules I have fashioned? Or am I seeking to joyfully submit to my Savior on every day and in every way? It is only when we choose to bow down before Jesus' authority, acknowledging His lordship over our time, our talents, our money—our everything—that we can truly begin to embrace Him as Lord and Savior and enjoy knowing Him as a friend and a guide. Are you keeping Him at arm's length in any way? That is precisely the place where He calls you to let Him interfere; it's the place where you have the opportunity truly to treat Him as the one who has all authority. He will certainly disrupt your life—but He alone has the right to, and He alone can set you free.

DANIEL 7:9-14

JULY 30

HIS POWER IN OUR WEAKNESS

"The LORD said to Gideon, 'The people with you are too many for me to give the Midianites into their hand, lest Israel boast over me, saying, "My own hand has saved me." Now therefore proclaim in the ears of the people, saying, "Whoever is fearful and trembling, let him return home and hurry away from Mount Gilead."' Then 22,000 of the people returned, and 10,000 remained." JUDGES 7:2-3

God's purpose for His people in every age is that we might depend upon Him entirely.

When God called him to save the Israelites, Gideon was faced with an overwhelming task: his army had to face the Midianites. Their army was said to be as overwhelming as locusts, and "their camels were without number, as the sand that is on the seashore in abundance" (Judges 7:12). Gideon's army of 32,000 paled in comparison. And then the Lord said to him, "The people with you are too many for me to give the Midianites into their hand." And so 22,000 left the army. No doubt Gideon was doing the math and wondering how he could strategically match strength for strength with even fewer soldiers. What he didn't know was that he was about to learn the necessity of weakness.

God is always at work in our circumstances to bring us to a greater dependence on Him and a deeper praise for His rescue. In Gideon's life, as in our own lives today, God left no doubt that He alone is God. His glory won't be shared with or stolen by anyone else. God is wholly adequate; we are not. Both then and now, He helps us see the necessity of humbly acknowledging our weakness in order to magnify His greatness. The truth is, our pride is at its ugliest when it emerges as spiritual pride—when we begin to boast in our experiences with God or our successes for God. That was the tendency of the "super-apostles" of whom Paul spoke in 2 Corinthians 12:11; they seemed so powerful, full of stories of being filled with the Spirit's power. But Paul simply answered, "If I should wish to boast, I would not be a fool, for I would be speaking the truth; but I refrain from it, so that no one may think more of me than he sees in me or hears from me" (v 6). He understood that humility, weakness, and inadequacy are all key to usefulness in God's kingdom.

That is why God further reduced Gideon's army to a mere 300 (Judges 7:7). He was going to achieve His plan with so few people that when the victory came, everyone would know the source of the victory. And in God's kindness, He still does this for us today. He reminds us that those who are most useful to His plan and purpose are those who, in the world's eyes, are not up to the task—because then it is clear that it is His work and not theirs. This is bad news for you if you would like to hold on to your pride and self-dependence. It is bad news for you if you would like to receive praise. It is, however, amazing news for you if you know you are inadequate for the tasks that God sets before you. What among the things you are facing do you feel wholly ill-equipped to handle? Depend on Him and walk forward in obedience, and you will discover that His power is displayed in your weakness (2 Corinthians 12:9-10)—and you will praise Him all the more.

JUDGES 7:1-23

JULY 31

STEPPING OUT IN FAITH

"By faith Abraham obeyed when he was called to go out to a place that he was to receive as an inheritance. And he went out, not knowing where he was going."
HEBREWS 11:8

If we seek to understand better what it means to put faith into action and to take God at His word, then we need look no further than the life of Abraham. He's described in the book of Romans as the father of all who have faith (Romans 4:16). He was "fully convinced that God was able to do what he had promised" (v 21), and this was the conviction that spurred him on to obedience and action.

God's call to Abraham was costly and radical: "The LORD said to Abram, 'Go from your country and your kindred and your father's house to the land that I will show you'" (Genesis 12:1). Abraham was asked to leave his country, his friends, and his extended family—essentially, all that he knew and held dear. God did not stop at the command, though. He promised to bless Abraham in the new land, to make him "a great nation" and to make his name great (v 2).

And Abraham obeyed and went.

Why would anybody ever do that? Abraham had nothing to go on save the command of God and the accompanying promises. But that was enough for him! That is faith in action. That is faith in every day and in every generation: taking God at His word and stepping out in obedience.

"The callings of God," I remember once hearing the Scottish minister Graham Scroggie say, "seldom leave a man or a woman where the calling finds them. Indeed, if we fail to go forward when God says 'Go,' we cannot remain stationary." Refusing to step out and act in faith results in backward movement even as we never take a step.

Abraham, though, walked forward. He departed in obedience, "not knowing where he was going." It was sufficient for him that God had told him to go, and so he did not need to be told where he would end up. And by stepping out in faith, Abraham stepped into the heart of God's plan to save His people and bring blessing to His world. Abraham would discover that the only place to be is where God wants you, and the only purpose that you should ever seek to fulfill is that which God has made known to you.

Has God been speaking to you through His word about stepping out in faith and obedience to His leading? Then "today, if you hear his voice, do not harden your hearts" (Hebrews 3:15). God's command may run absolutely contrary to everything you have been planning and thinking about, and it may require you to leave behind everything that represents security to you—but if He is calling, you must go.

ROMANS 4

AUGUST 1

TRUE WEALTH

"It is easier for a camel to go through the eye of a needle than for a rich person to enter the kingdom of God." MARK 10:25

It is generally true that things are easier for the wealthy. Money opens doors. In most areas of life—education, health care, travel, leisure—we find that the mechanisms are oiled by access to a great amount of cash. No wonder that money is often regarded as the universal passport!

But there is one important door that wealth will not automatically open. The rich young ruler discovered that in seeking eternal life, his wealth proved to be not a benefit but a barrier to his entry into the kingdom of God. His way to salvation was blocked by his unwillingness to surrender his possessions and follow Jesus, so he left his conversation with the Messiah sad, with his wealth intact but his soul in peril (Mark 10:22).

This man's sadness was more than matched by that of Jesus. He recognized how easy it was to rely on possessions and lose sight of what really matters. And the way Jesus viewed the rich young ruler was consistent with His teachings elsewhere in the Gospels. On one occasion, for example, He told the story of a farmer who tore down his barns to build bigger ones (Luke 12:13-21). This was a legitimate choice, but the man foolishly relied on his wealth to determine his spiritual condition, saying, "Soul, you have ample goods laid up for many years; relax, eat, drink, be merry" (v 19)—and Jesus said he was therefore a fool, for he was not ready for death and could not buy his way through it (v 20). After all, "What will it profit a man if he gains the whole world and forfeits his soul?" (Matthew 16:26).

Too often, we too are guilty of finding our security in "stuff." We may do so through acquiring assets for ourselves or even through philanthropic giving for the sake of our reputations. Either way, though, in our pursuits we so easily (to paraphrase the song "Mr. Businessman") place value on the worthless while disregarding what is actually priceless.[93]

Nothing you or I have or do is sufficient to pay our way through death and into eternal life. "With man it is impossible," the Lord Jesus told His followers after the rich man left, "but not with God. For all things are possible with God" (Mark 10:27). The danger of wealth is that it makes us proud and self-reliant, and we forget that God and God alone is the one who saves.

Would you be willing to give up your wealth (whatever level you enjoy) if Jesus asked you to do so in His cause? Or would you hold back because the demand was too big and the cost too great? Repent of any way that you have been relying on your possessions, and rejoice in the salvation that comes because of God's mercy. It is no secret what God can do. Whoever comes to Him, He will never turn away.

LUKE 12:13-21

93 Ray Stevens, "Mr. Businessman" (1968).

AUGUST 2

LIVING IN THE SPIRIT'S FULLNESS

"Do not get drunk with wine, for that is debauchery, but be filled with the Spirit, addressing one another in psalms and hymns and spiritual songs, singing and making melody to the Lord with your heart." EPHESIANS 5:18-19

At certain times in life, such as the birth of a new child or a cross-country move, a lot seems to happen all at once. The beginning of a new life in Christ is perhaps the greatest example. When we believe in Jesus, a number of changes occur simultaneously: we are justified by faith, we are adopted into God's family, we're given a new status as His sons and daughters, and—as this verse highlights—we're indwelt by the Holy Spirit.

When someone believes in Jesus, the Holy Spirit begins residing in them, providing them with the desire and the power to do what God desires. This fullness of the Spirit is fundamental to the reality of Christian experience. And yet the truth is that even as believers we do not always live in the fullness of God's Spirit. It remains possible to grieve the Spirit who lives in us by our disobedience (Ephesians 4:30). It remains possible for us to be more influenced by something other than Him—which is why, here, Paul underlines that we cannot be under the influence *both* of alcohol *and* of the Spirit.

We must understand that if we are God's children, we can never remove ourselves from the fatherhood of God; however, living in disobedience can remove us from the sense of His fatherly blessing, presence, and enjoyment of us. A child who flat-out disobeys his parents may still sit at the breakfast table, knowing that they are still his parents and he is still their son, but the enjoyment of the relationship will be diminished. So it is with us: we cannot live in disobedience—we cannot allow some other consideration, priority, or substance to guide us—and simultaneously live in the fullness of the Spirit.

This is not a problem we can remedy ourselves. We do not fill ourselves with the Holy Spirit. We not only receive the Spirit's fullness from God; our very enjoyment of His fullness is because of God. We cannot fill ourselves, but we can and must open ourselves to being filled. The expectation for every Christian life is that this evidence of being filled—what Paul calls "the fruit of the Spirit" (Galatians 5:22)—will gradually become more and more apparent.

The great need of your life, and of every church, is to be filled with the Spirit—to be directed by Him rather than by anything else. That is what brings true transformation, and joy and peace and love. That is what overflows into songs which praise Christ in our hearts as well as with our lips when we gather together. So, pray for Him to fill you anew:

Spirit of God, descend upon my heart;
Wean it from earth; through all its pulses move;
Stoop to my weakness, mighty as Thou art,
And make me love Thee as I ought to love.[94]

EZEKIEL 11:14-20

94 George Croly, "Spirit of God, Descend upon My Heart" (1854).

AUGUST 3

THE PERFECTED KINGDOM

"He who was seated on the throne said, 'Behold, I am making all things new!'"
REVELATION 21:5

Everybody always wants to know how the story ends. The book of Revelation gives us the opportunity to flick forward to the final page, in order that we might walk towards the end of history with greater faith, confidence, and joy.

Scripture is very clear that all of history is moving towards a final goal. This is a matter of extreme significance; God has created men and women to know that something exists beyond death. Indeed, He has set eternity in our very hearts (Ecclesiastes 3:11).

Every religion and worldview attempts to make sense out of history. Hinduism, for example, teaches that the reality in which we find ourselves is not moving towards a destination but is actually going round in circles—that history is cyclical. Atheistic naturalism argues that there is no pattern to history and no purpose or end goal; history is simply the tale of atoms rearranging themselves (and so are each of us). Christians, however, recognize that the Bible shows history to be linear: there was a point of beginning, there will be a point of ending, and there is purpose to its direction. Christ's life, death, resurrection, and return are the central theme of all of history. All of humankind's story must therefore be viewed within that framework. Jesus will return; He will complete God's eternal plan of salvation, and He will usher in God's perfected kingdom. He will make all things new and perfect.

What is the perfected kingdom that Jesus brings in? It's a kingdom that centers on His cross. It's a kingdom that changes hearts and lives, and its citizens bow before Jesus as King. It's a kingdom of love and justice, of compassion and peace. This kingdom is growing and reaching out to the ends of the earth—and at the appointed time, which is unknown to us, God the Father is going to give His Son the nations as His inheritance (Psalm 2:8).

Even now, God is working out His sovereign plan and the mystery of His will. When John writes concerning the end times, he reminds us that "salvation belongs to our God" (Revelation 7:10). If salvation belonged to another or if it were left to chance, God's plan might not be fulfilled. But He is the author of history and the ruler of the future. He has purposed to save His people, and He will. One day we shall hear Him say, "It is done" (21:6).

God has begun the work of our salvation through Jesus' death and resurrection, and one day He will bring all things under one Head, Jesus. Therefore, if we are united with Christ, "we are more than conquerors" (Romans 8:37), enabled to reign forever with the Son. How do we respond? With faith, confidence, and joy! For while we do not know how our lives will go, we do know how the story ends—and how our eternity begins. So we pray with eager anticipation, "Our Father in heaven … Your kingdom come" (Matthew 6:9-10).

ISAIAH 60

◇ Bible Through The Year: Psalms 63–65; Acts 23:1-15

AUGUST 4

NO IDEAL PLACE

"I intend to pass through Macedonia, and perhaps I will stay with you or even spend the winter, so that you may help me on my journey, wherever I go ... But I will stay in Ephesus until Pentecost, for a wide door for effective work has opened to me, and there are many adversaries." 1 CORINTHIANS 16:5-6, 8-9

There are many reasons to admire the apostle Paul, but here is one that is little mentioned: he was always planning ahead. He was static about nothing. He was like a general poring over a map in the battle headquarters, saying, "Now, where can we advance next? Where can we send the next group of troops? Where can we go find the enemy?" Because of his righteous ambition, he didn't remain comfortable anywhere for very long.

Here is what we can learn from Paul: there's no ideal place in which to serve God, but we can always serve God where we are. He writes in his letters about ministering in such widely dispersed places as Ephesus, Macedonia, and Corinth—but irrespective of geography, he realized that all he was supposed to be doing was evangelizing unbelievers and encouraging Christians. When his service was complete in one location, he knew he was called to move onward.

Paul was not concerned about comfort or convenience. He didn't aspire to take up residence in a little cottage on the Adriatic Sea in a snug retirement. Even when he could say that "a wide door for effective work has opened to me," still there were "many adversaries." He accepted the challenges as they came and considered opposition a great privilege rather than a hindrance.

So many of us are conditioned to believe that if we're in communion with God and if we're really in the place we should be, life will go smoothly. This may be a prevalent notion, but it's also an unbiblical one. Do we really think we can stand against Satan and not face his fiery darts? Do we think we can invade enemy territory and not meet opposition? We are not called to be people who live complacently in cozy, comfortable Christian communities that know no resistance. It is possible to dampen our witness so much that we're ineffective for Christ, but that doesn't have to be the case, nor should it be.

The same conditions that Paul faced surround us today: idolatry, sexual immorality, racism, religious bigotry, and a host of other evils. You have an opportunity in the midst of opposition, no matter where God plants you, to serve His kingdom. As my dear friend Eric Alexander once told me, "There is no ideal place to serve God—except where He has set you down!"

ROMANS 15:17-33

AUGUST 5

RUINED AND RESTORED

"What is this that you have done?" GENESIS 3:13

The Highlands of Scotland are full of castles which are no longer inhabited. In the evening sunlight, it's not difficult to recognize that at one time these must have been magnificent places. Although they no longer have windows or tapestries, much less residents, the splendor of these ancient structures speaks to their former glory, even in their now-ruined condition.

This world is full of ruined glory, for this world is full of people. Adam and Eve were the apex of God's creative handiwork, and He was absolutely satisfied with them. They were created with an inclination to do good. But in lusting after a throne they could never inhabit—God's throne—they found themselves degraded, losing the place and the privileges they were created to enjoy.

In tempting Eve, the serpent's first strategy was to cast doubt on what God had said, subtly challenging the truthfulness of His word—and she succumbed. She believed the lie that God could not be trusted to do good. Having sown the seed of doubt, the serpent then watered it with ambition. Once a hint of uncertainty began to fill Eve's mind, pride's appeal was more than she could withstand.

Eating the fruit was wrong simply because God had said not to eat it. Yet the opportunity for immediate gratification seemed to anesthetize Adam and Eve from the painful consequences of their future actions and the ruin that would come upon the splendor they knew. Then, as if the disobedience itself weren't bad enough, amid deception and disobedience, they sought to deny responsibility.

Like Adam and Eve, we, too, are prone to assume that we, and not God, are the final judges of truth. Once we have decided to seek to remove the Creator God, who speaks an authoritative and true word, we deny Him the right to command our obedience. But when we reject God's rule, we don't become our own masters; we simply put ourselves under the rule of a whole host of lesser masters: deceit, darkness, despair, and death.

"What is this that you have done?" We have all believed the lie that our way is better than God's. But He has gone to the extent of sending His Son in order that the hardness of our rebellion might be overwhelmed by His kindness, which "is better than life" (Psalm 63:3). He has shone His word right into our hearts, that we might see His splendor now and forevermore, and that we might be remade in His image and restored to the glory God always intended His image-bearing creatures to have. Seeing His goodness and coming under His rule are what liberates us from the mastery of deceit, darkness, despair, and, yes, even death.

GENESIS 3

AUGUST 6

THE GREAT DIVIDE

"Do you think that I have come to give peace on earth? No, I tell you, but rather division." LUKE 12:51

Did Jesus come to bring peace on earth, as the angels sang at the first Christmas (Luke 2:14)? Or did He come to bring division, as He Himself announces here?

Yes.

Let us first acknowledge the apparent contradiction. The way Jesus answers His own question here—"Do you think that I have come to give peace on earth? No..."—seems mutually incompatible with both the angels' declaration and with Jesus' instruction to His followers to be peacemakers (Matthew 5:9). Indeed, it seems that Jesus is refuting the emphasis of His whole earthly ministry by associating Himself with division and discord. How, then, are we to reconcile Jesus' claims that He would bring both peace and division?

What Jesus meant when He spoke about bringing division is directly tied to the work that He accomplished in effecting peace. In other words, when we come to understand the good news—that "for our sake [God] made him to be sin who knew no sin, so that in him we might become the righteousness of God" (2 Corinthians 5:21)—we can never be the same again. It is too magnificent a work to result in apathy.

When we are renewed at our core, everything about us changes—our values, our focus, our purpose, our dreams. We are now at peace with our Creator, and we are able to live at peace with ourselves. But sooner or later, this transformation will prove divisive. In sharing, speaking about, and living out the miracle of our reconciliation with God, we will be met with disdain, hostility, and judgment, sometimes even from those within our own homes, as Jesus went on to warn (Luke 12:52-53).

Jesus' coming to bring peace laid bare the division and conflict between the Creator and His image-bearing creatures that had existed since Adam and Eve first rebelled. Your words and actions, directed as they are by the commands of heaven and not by the ways of this world, will lay bare that same division. For many of us, the division caused as a result of trusting in Christ is a trying and painful reality of life.

Yet there is a great hope for all of us: Jesus' ultimate objective is not division but harmony. The Bible is absolutely clear that the Prince of Peace will one day reign eternally. In the meantime, do not be under any illusions: following Jesus has a cost—a cost that you can, by the power of His Spirit, joyfully pay as you risk division in order to hold out the divine offer of peace.

ACTS 17:1-15

AUGUST 7

WE NEED A MIRACLE

"You have been born again, not of perishable seed but of imperishable, through the living and abiding word of God; for 'All flesh is like grass and all its glory like the flower of grass. The grass withers, and the flower falls, but the word of the Lord remains forever.'" 1 PETER 1:23-25

The gospel is not an exhortation to well-meaning people, inviting us to add a little religion to our lives. God's word comes to the rebel heart and commands obedience. It is a word that brings the dead to life.

How is this work accomplished? Only by God's Spirit. It is the Spirit's work to achieve what cannot be done in any other way, by any other means: to bring about new life.

By nature, we are all rebels against God. No one seeks after Him (Romans 3:11). Even if I call myself an agnostic or a seeker or open-minded, in reality I am rebelling. And God "commands all people everywhere to repent" (Acts 17:30). God calls every one of us to do an about-turn—to turn decisively from sin and rebellion and to come under His rule.

Apart from a miracle, we cannot do this. Left to ourselves, we are dead and without hope for eternity. Thankfully, it is the very task of God's Spirit to perform that miracle *for* us. New life is something God achieves, not something we engender. The Spirit convicts us of sin and convinces us that Jesus, by His death on the cross, has dealt with it.

Scripture is absolutely clear on this: when we were dead in our sins, we were made alive in Christ (Ephesians 2:1-5). The Spirit brings us to understand what by ourselves we are unprepared to face—namely, that we have a deep, endemic problem we cannot fix. We need a miracle. And that's what God does. He brings about new life. He saves us by His grace.

Everything about us fades; like the grass, Peter reminds us, all of us will one day fall. But there is a seed which produces that which is imperishable, which is planted in us by the Spirit and which will bloom and thrive for all eternity: the life that has been born anew through the gospel. The word of God remains forever, and so does the one who has been brought to new life as the Spirit works through it.

Once that has happened to us, we no longer see the Bible merely as some history book or inspiring story. By the work of the Spirit, it becomes a light, illuminating true life, and our eyes are opened to understand who God is. This is why we study the Bible: to better see and know the one who has saved us and with whom we will spend eternity.

So, may the love of Jesus draw you to Him. May the joy of Jesus enable you to serve Him. May the peace and contentment that comes in knowing Jesus grant to you stability and clarity as you reflect on where you've been, consider where you are, and meditate upon where you are headed. Your earthly flesh will fall; but you will remain forever.

PSALM 119:65-80

◇ Bible Through The Year: Psalms 72–73; Acts 26

AUGUST 8

REMEMBERING GOD'S MERCY

"Now the word of the LORD came to Jonah the son of Amittai, saying, 'Arise, go to Nineveh, that great city, and call out against it, for their evil has come up before me.' But Jonah rose to flee to Tarshish from the presence of the LORD."
JONAH 1:1-3

God delights to save people.

When God commanded His servant Jonah to go to Nineveh and preach against it because of its wickedness, the reluctant prophet recognized that the people might repent of their evil ways and that God would respond in mercy (see Jonah 4:2). He knew that God is "a God merciful and gracious, slow to anger, and abounding in steadfast love and faithfulness, keeping steadfast love for thousands, forgiving iniquity and transgression and sin, but who will by no means clear the guilty" (Exodus 34:6-7). He knew the truth that God would one day speak through the prophet Jeremiah: "If at any time I declare concerning a nation or a kingdom, that I will pluck up and break down and destroy it, and if that nation, concerning which I have spoken, turns from its evil, I will relent of the disaster that I intended to do to it" (Jeremiah 18:7-8).

Jonah knew that God's heart is a heart of mercy—so Jonah refused to obey God's command. Why?! Apparently, he simply didn't like the people of Nineveh, and understandably so, for the Ninevites were aggressive, vicious, and violent pagans and were feared enemies of Israel. Jonah did not want the Lord to spare them—so later, when the people of Nineveh turned from their wickedness, "it displeased Jonah exceedingly, and he was angry" (Jonah 4:1). Jonah felt they were deserving of God's judgment. And he was right! But thankfully, God's ways of dealing with nations and cities and individuals are not our ways. God's desire is to show mercy, and not to bring judgment.

God's compassion on Nineveh is a reminder to us that He does not wish that any should perish and that He delights in saving people, especially those who appear least deserving (2 Peter 3:9). Jonah wanted to preach only where *he* wanted to preach and to whom he wanted to preach. But the gospel message is for everyone, everywhere. Today the good news of Jesus is not limited to "nice" people, to people who look and act and think like us. Indeed, Jesus commanded His followers, "Go … and make disciples of *all* nations" (Matthew 28:19, emphasis added).

What immense mercy! God is passionate in His pursuit of the proud, the stubborn, and the defiant—people just like me, people just like you. He calls us to be zealous to "rescue the perishing, care for the dying," to "tell them of Jesus, the mighty to save."[95] The triune God desires to save sinful people—He desires their salvation enough to come and die for them. Do you share His heart? If you do, you will desire the salvation of those around you—whoever they are and whatever they have done—enough to go and share Christ with them.

1 CORINTHIANS 9:19-23

95 Fanny Crosby, "Rescue the Perishing" (1869).

AUGUST 9

DISOBEDIENCE AND RELUCTANCE

"Jonah rose to flee to Tarshish from the presence of the LORD. He went down to Joppa and found a ship going to Tarshish. So he paid the fare and went down into it, to go with them to Tarshish, away from the presence of the LORD."

JONAH 1:3

The course of disobedience is always a downward trajectory—that is, until God intervenes.

In Jonah's haste to flee from the Lord's command to preach a message of repentance to the Ninevites, he went "*down* to Joppa," "*down* into" the ship, and "*down* to the land whose bars closed upon" him in the belly of the great fish (Jonah 2:6, emphasis added).

When Jonah was fast asleep below the ship's deck, trying to flee from God, "the LORD hurled a great wind upon the sea ... so that the ship threatened to break up" (1:4). Yet in the midst of a raging tempest and the feverish activity of sailors who were shouting, crying, praying, and hurling things into the water, Jonah slept on.

How could Jonah possibly have been so exhausted? Surely he was physically and spiritually worn out by his decision to run away from God. While disobedience may be exhilarating in the moment—while it may provide a momentary buzz—it is always exhausting in the end. It is hard to kick against the goads (Acts 26:14). There can hardly be found a more miserable or disconsolate sleep than that which follows our rebellion against a word from God and the ensuing desire to hide from anyone and everyone by retreating to the privacy of our bed.

Jonah wanted God to leave him alone. God, however, was too merciful to do so. So He sent a storm, and the storm sent the captain of the ship to find Jonah and rouse him. The captain used the same word God had previously spoken to call Jonah to preach: "*Arise*, call out to your god!" (Jonah 1:6, emphasis added; compare 1:2).

Here, then, is a picture of great reluctance—not only Jonah's reluctance to do what he's told but *God's* reluctance to leave His servant in the dejection and misery of his sin. The three days Jonah would soon spend in the belly of the great fish further testify to this truth about God. Although Jonah's rebellion merited punishment, God would soon rescue Jonah from perishing at sea and restore him in order that he would preach judgment and mercy to the people of Nineveh.

God comes to us again and again in our disobedience, unwilling to let us wallow in our sin. Even if we put our fingers in our ears and pretend not to hear Him, and even if we flat-out refuse to obey, God pursues His wandering children. He loves us so much that He doesn't want to leave us to our own devices. In our sin, we cannot outrun the mercy of God, the one who will never leave us or forsake us.

JONAH 1

AUGUST 10

LORD OF ALL CREATION

"Jonah rose to flee to Tarshish from the presence of the LORD. He went down to Joppa and found a ship going to Tarshish. So he paid the fare and went down into it, to go with them to Tarshish, away from the presence of the LORD. But the LORD hurled a great wind upon the sea, and there was a mighty tempest on the sea, so that the ship threatened to break up." JONAH 1:3-4

We are not in control of creation. But God is—and He is therefore worthy of all our praise and adoration.

Divine control over the oceans—indeed, over all creation—was a reason for constant praise in the psalmists' work. When we read the Psalms, we discover again and again that God's people delight in praising His sovereign power over the created order: His control over the seas, even over the ebb and flow of their tides. We see in Psalm 33, for instance, that "he gathers the waters of the sea into jars; he puts the deep into storehouses" (v 7, NIV). It's a dramatic picture—and it is part of God's excellence and glory. In the same way that we may move and pour a gallon of lemonade, God Almighty is able to simply gather up the oceans of the world and put them in jars. How right and fitting, then, that we worship our Creator God in awe and reverence!

Likewise, God's authority over creation encourages us to trust in His providential care. Later in Jonah's story, we discover that the Lord "appointed a plant," He "appointed a worm," and He "appointed a scorching east wind" to fulfill His plans for Jonah and for the people of Nineveh (Jonah 4:6-8). How different this is from the pagan mindset both in Jonah's day and in our own. The crewmen on Jonah's ship regarded the sea as an uncontrollable primeval force at whose mercy they were all captive. In the same way, we are confronted today by the notion that "Mother Nature" is an untamable and merciless force. But the truth is that all things, including the entire created order, are God's servants (Psalm 119:91). We are not left to be cast about on the sea of chance or buffeted by blind, impersonal forces. No, God "determines the number of the stars; he gives to all of them their names" (Psalm 147:4).

Only the sovereign Creator Lord can gather the seas in heaps and command all of creation to do His bidding. Not only that, but He chooses to direct His commands for the good of His people. The great wind that God hurled upon the sea as Jonah's boat sailed toward Tarshish was not intended to be a curse upon him but rather a call to him to return to faithful obedience to his God. What God sent upon Jonah, God also saved Jonah from. How remarkable: God summoned up the immense power of a storm simply to bring one errant child back home.

Truly, all things are arranged for the glory of God and the good of His people—including you. It is this God we praise, this God we trust, and this God to whom we commit our lives. Let this truth be on your lips today: "Great is the LORD, and greatly to be praised, and his greatness is unsearchable" (Psalm 145:3).

PSALM 145

AUGUST 11

DRY LAND AWAITS

"Then Jonah prayed to the LORD his God from the belly of the fish, saying, 'I called out to the LORD, out of my distress, and he answered me.'" JONAH 2:1-2

Here is a word for the struggling believer, to the backslidden believer, to those of us who find ourselves in the depths because of our disobedience.

The emphasis of the book of Jonah is not on Jonah's predicaments so much as it is on God's provision. God used extraordinary measures to save Jonah from his sin and disobedience. The prophet acknowledges that it was God who "cast [him] into the deep, into the heart of the seas" (Jonah 2:3). Yes, it was the sailors who had tossed Jonah overboard, but Jonah recognized that what took place was under God's sovereign hand, and that the sailors acted as His instruments. God had pursued him and had him thrown into the raging waters in order that he would come to a place where he could say, "I called out to the LORD, out of my distress, and he answered me."

Furthermore, in the belly of the great fish, the prophet felt the sting of being separated from God, of being "driven away from [His] sight" (Jonah 2:4). For Jonah, the physical terror of almost drowning in the ocean and being swallowed by a fish paled in comparison to being forever estranged from his heavenly Father. Jonah knew God's love; he knew what it was to be in God's presence. He was able to understand what it would mean to be separated from God, even though—and this is the perversity of sin—he himself had chosen to separate himself from God.

What a word for us! It is God who, when we are wandering away from Him, comes to us in the storms and valleys, who alters our circumstances to catch our attention, who allows us to feel isolated and separated all in order that we might say, "This is not where I belong. This is not what God wants for me. I cannot get myself out of this predicament. But He is able."

Today, you might be dealing with a deep sense of failure and regret. You have been running. You have disobeyed the clear voice of God and attempted to hide. But your story doesn't have to end there. In His grace and kindness, God is determined to save you and to complete the work in your life which He has begun (Philippians 1:6). In the Christian life, there is always a need to repent but never any reason to despair.

When Jonah ended up on dry land, it was not because he deserved to. It was because of God's grace. Likewise, it is God alone who comes to us in our sin and disobedience in order that He might cleanse, save, and restore us to His purposes. Can you see the dry land today?

JONAH 2

AUGUST 12

MERCY PROCLAIMED

"Then the word of the LORD came to Jonah the second time, saying, 'Arise, go to Nineveh, that great city, and call out against it the message that I tell you.' So Jonah arose and went to Nineveh, according to the word of the LORD."

JONAH 3:1-3

God is the God of second chances.

Jonah had responded to God's call to warn Nineveh of His coming judgment by running off to hide. But when the call came again, he did not drag his feet the second time. Aware of his failure and of God's grace toward him, he seemed eager to preach to them at the first opportunity. When we finally read of Jonah calling the people to repentance, we can imagine the weight of his own experience as he spoke firsthand about the divine consequences for disobedience. He brought a warning, and with it surely a personal testimony of the fact that God is both willing and able to save sinful people from even the most extreme circumstances. Though he would later prove not to have fully embraced the magnitude and scope of God's grace (Jonah 4:1-3), the mercy that God had shown Jonah surely pervaded his message to the Ninevites. The one who had been given a second chance through the divine provision of a fish now held out a second chance to a city of men and women who had determinedly turned from the Lord.

Have you grasped that God is the God of second (and third and fourth) chances? Have you grasped that you cannot outrun God's mercy or plumb the depths of His grace? If you have, then you surely will hold out the gospel message to others. And the way that you do so will reflect the mercy you have received. If Christians sound brittle, heartless, and legalistic as they talk about the faith, their hearts have not yet been softened enough by God's mercy, grace, and love. If, however, there is a sense of the winning, wooing wonder of God's mercy in a Christian's words and deeds, it's safe to assume that he or she has known such mercy. Charles Wesley, won over by God's mercy, readily proclaimed:

Depth of mercy! Can there be mercy still reserved for me?
Can my God His wrath forbear? Me, the chief of sinners, spare?
I have long withstood His grace: long provoked Him to His face;
Would not hearken to His calls; grieved Him by a thousand falls...
There for me the Savior stands, shows His wounds and spreads His hands:
God is love! I know, I feel; Jesus weeps, but loves me still.[96]

Reflect on God's mercy to you now—in bringing you to faith and then in His ongoing patience with you and forgiveness of you. Let the sense of wonder at His dealings with you permeate the way in which you tell the story of His redeeming love to others. And if there is someone you know whom you have failed to show God's mercy or to share it with them when you had the opportunity, pray now for a second chance—and then seize it.

PSALM 30

96 Charles Wesley, "Depth of Mercy" (1740).

AUGUST 13

A REMINDER ABOUT REPENTANCE

"The people of Nineveh believed God. They called for a fast and put on sackcloth, from the greatest of them to the least of them. The word reached the king of Nineveh, and he arose from his throne, removed his robe, covered himself with sackcloth, and sat in ashes." JONAH 3:5-6

Can you imagine your president or prime minister making a national broadcast in which they call for the nation to give up their violent deeds, turn away from the evil they have embraced, and seek God's mercy so that He might come and save them from His judgment? This is essentially what happened in Nineveh, before Jonah's very eyes.

It's quite remarkable that the Ninevites believed God as quickly and as completely as they did. As they listened to Jonah's warning of coming judgment, their reaction was widespread and heartfelt, as evidenced by their garments of penitence. And this public response was more than matched by the royal response. The king changed his garments, replacing his royal robes with sackcloth; he changed his place, exchanging his throne for a seat in the dust; and he changed his tune, issuing a proclamation of repentance.

This stands in contrast to many people of Jesus' day, and perhaps our own. As Jesus Himself taught, the Ninevites "repented at the preaching of Jonah," whereas countless people He spoke to refused to recognize that "something greater than Jonah"—namely, Christ—was now proclaimed (Luke 11:32). They rejected what the Ninevite king had grasped when he said, "Let everyone turn from his evil way … Who knows? God may turn and relent and turn from his fierce anger, so that we may not perish" (Jonah 3:8-9). He recognized that the Ninevites' repentance did not necessarily mean that God would be forbearing in His reaction. He was still uncertain about whether their turning would be accompanied by a divine turning.

It's a reminder to us of this: even the repentant have no case to argue for God's acceptance. They remain solely dependent on God's grace. Repentance is necessary for forgiveness, but it does not earn it. Like the Prodigal Son, the person with a genuinely repentant heart says, "Father, I have sinned against heaven and before you. I am no longer worthy to be called your son" (Luke 15:18-19). Repentance begins with acknowledging that we are truly deserving of God's judgment and with declaring our desperate need for His mercy.

Because "something greater than Jonah" is now here, we can know and declare that repentance will always be met by forgiveness, for "everyone who calls on the name of the Lord will be saved" (Romans 10:13). But we should learn from this pagan king that we do not manipulate God's hand by our repentance or obedience, and that true repentance is not skin deep but heartfelt, always involving a change of attitude and of behavior. This is a lesson we must heed every day of our Christian lives—for, as Martin Luther said, "When our Lord and Master Jesus Christ said, 'Repent,' he intended that the entire life of believers should be repentance."[97]

LUKE 11:29-32

97 The Ninety-Five Theses, First Thesis

AUGUST 14

OUR UNCHANGING GOD

"When God saw what they did, how they turned from their evil way, God relented of the disaster that he had said he would do to them, and he did not do it."
JONAH 3:10

The Bible makes clear that God is unchanging. At the same time, the book of Jonah affirms that He can and does change His attitude towards people and His way of dealing with them. How are we to make sense of this apparent contradiction?

We see this tension elsewhere in Scripture. In His dealings with King Saul, for instance, God said, "I regret that I have made Saul king, for he has turned back from following me and has not performed my commandments" (1 Samuel 15:11). But a few verses later we're told, "The Glory of Israel will not lie or have regret, for he is not a man, that he should have regret" (v 29). It seems that God regrets His decision, but then we are told that He doesn't have regret.

Yet there is no ultimate inconsistency between these two modes of expression. When God is said to have regret or change His mind, the descriptive language is an accommodation to our finite human perspective. It appears that there has been a change in God, but what has actually changed is our human conduct. Simply put, Saul was no longer the man he had once been. He had become persistently disobedient, and God responded to that changed circumstance in a way that was entirely consistent with His character. Similarly, in response to Jonah's preaching, the Ninevites changed their conduct—this time, in the opposite direction: they turned away from evil. God is consistently against sin and favorable towards repentance and faith; His character does not change. His warnings are intended to alert the wayward and bring them to repentance—and if repentance occurs, then God responds accordingly.

Only because God responds in this way can the sinner who believes in Jesus come to know His acceptance. Because "Jesus Christ is the same yesterday and today and forever" (Hebrews 13:8), we can know that when we come in penitence and childlike faith, God receives us with compassion and mercy. That is His nature, and He will not change. From our perspective, it may look as if He has changed His mind—but God always remains true to every word He has ever spoken. In a world that is always changing and where even the best of us cannot always keep our word, here is great ground for your confidence and joy today.

JONAH 3

AUGUST 15

IN HARMONY WITH GOD'S PLAN

"When God saw what they did, how they turned from their evil way, God relented of the disaster that he had said he would do to them, and he did not do it. But it displeased Jonah exceedingly, and he was angry." JONAH 3:10 - 4:1

Even prophets sometimes have a lot to learn.

After his time in the belly of the fish, Jonah was no longer disobedient, but he was perplexed in his obedience, wrestling still with God's sovereign grace. Although, having initially sought to run away from God's purposes for him, Jonah had gone where he'd been told to go and had said what he'd been told to say, he was by no means in harmony with God's gracious plan for Nineveh. Revival had broken out in a city that had been completely hardened to the God of Israel—and the prophet of God responded in anger towards his God!

Yet even though Jonah was churlish and narrow-minded and responded wrongly to God's kindness, God didn't write him off. He had already provided a large fish to save Jonah from disobedience; He could justifiably have provided a large lion to eat him too! But He didn't, because He is gracious and compassionate. He treated Jonah with patience and kindness to bring him to the realization that what was wrong, more than any other thing, was his attitude.

Jonah's reaction to the Ninevites' repentance was strange for a preacher. We may have expected him to be grateful that God chose not to cast him off but to give him the privilege of being used in His service. Instead the city's repentance "displeased Jonah exceedingly." A literal translation of this verse takes it a step further: "It was evil to Jonah, a great evil." The absence of the calamity that he expected—a judgment which he thought and hoped would come upon Nineveh—proved to be a calamity in his own heart and mind.

Unpalatable though it sounds, we may see our attitudes and reactions reflected in Jonah's. We may go where we're told to go, we may say what we're told to say, we may externally conform to all that God has called us to do… and yet, at the very core of our lives, we may not really be in harmony with how His plan is unfolding. We may long for judgment to fall rather than mercy to be extended. We may chafe against God blessing others in ways that He has not blessed us or blessing others without them showing the commitment to His mission that we think we have displayed. We may find ourselves telling God how He ought to arrange things in His world.

What will bring us into line with His compassion and send us joyfully on His mission? Simply this: to understand that we are no better than anyone else—no less deserving of His wrath and no more deserving of His kindness. As it demonstrates the mercy of God, the cross humbles our hearts and fills them with the same compassion and grace that took His Son to Calvary. Are you struggling to live with such compassion toward others? Gaze at the cross and ask the Lord to teach you what Jonah also needed to learn.

COLOSSIANS 1:21-29

◇ Bible Through The Year: Psalms 91–93; 1 Peter 5

AUGUST 16

UNDESERVING SERVANTS

"And [Jonah] prayed to the LORD and said, 'O LORD, is not this what I said when I was yet in my country? That is why I made haste to flee to Tarshish; for I knew that you are a gracious God and merciful, slow to anger and abounding in steadfast love, and relenting from disaster…' And the LORD said, 'Do you do well to be angry?'" JONAH 4:2, 4

When children do something wrong, they often seek their parents' forgiveness, receive it, and then say, "I know I was wrong, but… there was a perfectly good reason that I was doing what I was doing." We see something similar with the prophet Jonah. God had forgiven him, picked him up, and put him back on track, and still he tried to justify his previous disobedience. He was simultaneously feeling angry, arguing, and praying—which is not an easy feat!

In Jonah's arguing, notice how many times the personal pronoun "I" pops out. There was a bit too much "Jonah" in his speech—and therefore in his heart—as he presented his case as a matter of his word against the Lord's. He foolishly supposed that his way was better than God's.

Jonah's complaint was also rooted in a double standard. Though he had recently been the recipient of God's compassion and mercy, he found fault with God for displaying that very same mercy to those who Jonah felt should be beyond redemption.

The big issue for Jonah was God's sovereign grace. He was angry at God for acting in a way that he did not understand or approve of. But the Lord had long ago declared, "I will be gracious to whom I will be gracious, and will show mercy on whom I will show mercy" (Exodus 33:19). Divine grace towards sinners can never be explained. It does not have a reason; it simply reflects who God is.

In response to Jonah's reaction, the Lord did not ask him if he was angry but whether he had a right to be angry. That was the core matter: did Jonah—a representative of a people whom God had favored even when they'd gone astray, and who in his disobedience had personally known the saving hand of God—have any valid grounds to object to God's compassion toward others? The answer is clear: no. Neither do we have any right to challenge God on how and to whom He extends His mercy or how He directs all things in order to save His people and glorify His Son.

If we find ourselves angry with God and complaining about the way He has chosen to go about fulfilling His purposes, it is because we have forgotten just how undeserving we are of receiving God's grace. Here is the danger: that we become so tolerant of our own disobedience that we think we are entitled to God's favor and blessing. But all is of grace, every day. Only when we have been gripped by grace will we be able to rejoice in the abundance of God's mercy that is lavished upon His undeserving saints.

JONAH 4

AUGUST 17

MYSTERIOUS PROVIDENCE

"The LORD God appointed a plant and made it come up over Jonah, that it might be a shade over his head, to save him from his discomfort. So Jonah was exceedingly glad because of the plant. But when dawn came up the next day, God appointed a worm that attacked the plant, so that it withered."

JONAH 4:6-7

When Jonah left Nineveh, the city had been saved, but the prophet was sulking. *I knew You'd forgive them despite all the evil they've done*, he said to the Lord. *Now I'd rather be dead than have to see my enemies forgiven* (Jonah 4:2-3).

Jonah made a little shelter for himself (v 5), presumably out of stones or mud bricks; the heat of the sun would have made it very uncomfortable for him to sit out in the open air. Picture him as he sat in his little hut, wishing that he were dead, and then realizing that a wonderful plant was growing around him. Suddenly the heat of the day was eased by this plant's shadow—and Jonah was very, very happy.

But his gladness was short-lived. The same God who provided the plant to make Jonah happy also provided the worm that brought about its destruction. The plant shriveled up not in some unnatural way but as a result of normal processes taking place under God's divine control.

God the Creator is sovereign over all that He has made. In His mysterious providence, He was continuing to work with His servant according to the purpose of His will. There is a recurring phrase in the book of Jonah: "God appointed." He appointed a great fish, a plant, a worm, and a scorching east wind, all as an expression of His love and concern for His servant (Jonah 1:17; 4:8). Whether through a gigantic fish or a small worm, God was at work—as He still is—directing everything to its appointed end.

We see this doctrine of providence addressed in Question 27 of the Heidelberg Catechism: "What do you understand by the providence of God?" The answer comes: "God's providence is His almighty and ever present power, whereby, as with His hand, He still upholds heaven and earth and all creatures, and so governs them that leaf and blade, rain and drought, fruitful and barren years, food and drink, health and sickness, riches and poverty, indeed, all things, come not by chance but by His fatherly hand."[98]

Throughout life's journey, as you encounter both "plants" that make you comfortable and happy and "worms" that remove comfort or company from your life, you can find encouragement in knowing that you're not held in the grip of some blind, fatalistic force. Rather, your heavenly Father, who holds you with a loving embrace, is ordering everything that He might achieve His ultimate purpose in your life: to make you more like His Son and bring you home to His side. So consider your life. Where are the plants? Where are the worms? And will you seek to give thanks for both, secure in the knowledge that both are given by a loving Father for your eternal good?

JAMES 1:9-18

98 Heidelberg Catechism, Q. 27.

AUGUST 18

A MATTER OF CONCERN

"You pity the plant, for which you did not labor, nor did you make it grow, which came into being in a night and perished in a night. And should not I pity Nineveh, that great city, in which there are more than 120,000 persons who do not know their right hand from their left, and also much cattle?" JONAH 4:10-11

Jonah considered himself a victim. He was convinced that he was right in believing that Nineveh should receive judgment and that God was wrong to have rescued the city. He was also convinced that God was wrong in allowing the shade-bearing plant to shrivel, leaving him to suffer in the heat.

In response, God did not engage with the prophet according to his sorrowful objection but instead raised an important question: "Do you do well to be angry for the plant?" (Jonah 4:9). God was arguing from the lesser to the greater: if Jonah could be so phenomenally concerned about a plant that had come and gone in the space of 24 hours, didn't He, the living God, have a right to be concerned about the people of Nineveh? God was calling Jonah to review his scale of priorities.

God's question to Jonah is a question for us as well. Is there anything in our lives that we are more concerned about than seeing unbelieving people become committed followers of Jesus Christ? If we're alert to our own hearts, we may realize that in regard to our time, finances, gifts, and freedoms, "Is there anything?" quickly becomes "How many things?" Those who observe us may think we're far more concerned about matters of our own comfort than we are about the many souls who have never heard the gospel.

What was Jonah's response to God's question? We don't know. The book of Jonah finishes with this divine question. But the most important question is not about how Jonah responded. The emphasis of the entire book is upon the compassion of God Himself. The most important question is this: How do we, the readers of the book, perceive God's grace? Will His example establish in us a pattern of concern for others that longs for them to turn from sin and trust in Him? Will our hearts be more like Jonah's or like the Lord's?

It is time to stop setting any worldly concerns ahead of reaching the lost souls in our communities for Christ. We have the joy of knowing God's compassion in our lives through Jesus. And the only fitting response to this great privilege is to give of ourselves so that others would come to know Him as well. *What do you most care about?* asks God. *Your home? Your possessions? Your tech gadgets? Or the people in your street who do not know Jesus?*

MATTHEW 28:16-20

AUGUST 19

THE TRUE KING

"This cup that is poured out for you is the new covenant in my blood."
LUKE 22:20

Jesus fulfills God's promises and dispenses His every blessing. He has ushered in the new covenant and assumed His long-anticipated role as the true King. From Jesus, every blessing flows. Through Him, every promise is kept. To Him, all the glory is given.

Christians acknowledge these truths at the Communion table when we take the cup and remember that Jesus poured out His blood, the blood of the new covenant, for the forgiveness of our sins. On the cross, Jesus died to take the penalty that we deserve so that sinners, who do not deserve His mercy and grace, may enjoy the blessings of forgiveness.

This means that when we place our faith in Jesus, we may be sure that He has taken our sin and its judgment and given all His righteousness to us in exchange. Jesus died the death we deserve. He lived the perfect life we could not live. God has wrapped us up in the blanket of His forgiveness through the provision of His Son. We should never fail to be amazed that these things are true, by faith, of *us*.

The Old Testament prophets were clear: there was going to come a King who would be a descendant of David, and He would fulfill God's promises. He would establish God's rule, introduce a new age, and deal with the effects of evil. Jesus may not have looked much like a king as He hung on the cross, but it was His moment of greatest victory. And when Jesus strode out from the tomb, His resurrection declared that He was not simply the son of David but also the Son of God, able to conquer even the grave.

All authority rests with Him, and through Him flows an unending stream of grace and mercy. Only the one who is the source of such power can transform a heart and prove worthy of our souls' affections.

Jesus right now rules and reigns at the right hand of the Father, but He also reigns in the hearts of those who trust Him. There is no better day than today for the lost to give up their arms of rebellion, humbly bow before this worthy King, admit that He is the very Savior they so desperately need, and ask Him to reign on the throne of their lives. Is Christ your King? Then as His subject, worship and praise Him, and as His ambassador, go and let others know about this hope you have found.

1 CORINTHIANS 15:12-28

AUGUST 20

THE MOMENT OF CHOICE

"By faith Moses, when he was grown up, refused to be called the son of Pharaoh's daughter, choosing rather to be mistreated with the people of God than to enjoy the fleeting pleasures of sin." HEBREWS 11:24-25

We cannot be friends with the world and friends with God at the same time (James 4:4). Those who attempt to walk that middle course discover sooner or later how empty and futile it really is: that it makes us, in the words of Kris Kristofferson, "a walking contradiction."[99]

As the adopted son of Pharaoh's daughter, Moses enjoyed social status, physical comfort, and material wealth. As an Israelite, outside the precincts of Pharaoh's establishment there was for him only obscurity, impoverishment, and slavery. Moses knew that remaining in Pharaoh's courts would make his life far better in every single worldly way. He could have reasoned that it would also enable him to exercise an influence on behalf of God's people that would never be possible if he went and joined himself to them.

But Moses didn't stay in Pharaoh's family. Instead, he renounced the privileges of Egyptian citizenship and identified with a lowly, despised, oppressed group of people who had no political rights. Why? Why would someone give up so much to embrace so little?

The answer is that Moses realized he couldn't identify himself with God's people and the Egyptians simultaneously. He realized that he was either a slave with his people or a compromiser in Pharaoh's court. He couldn't say that he was an Israelite who believed in the God of his ancestors and also live as an Egyptian.

Moses chose ill treatment and disgrace, we're told, "for the sake of Christ" (Hebrews 11:26, NIV)—for the sake of the one from Eve's offspring and Abraham's family who would fulfill all God's promises to them (Genesis 3:16; 12:1-3). His calculation was the same as was made over a millennium later by the apostle Paul, who had exactly the "right" kind of background—the education, the sophistication, the heritage—yet said, "I count everything as loss because of the surpassing worth of knowing Christ Jesus my Lord" (Philippians 3:8).

Moses made a radical decision—the kind of radical decision that some of us may need to make. Perhaps your background is relatively similar to that of Moses; you grew up with all your material needs being met and with great prospects in the world. Whoever we are and wherever we have come from, though, we all face the moment of choice that Moses did. Will we live as friends of the world or of God? There is no middle way. Today, are you going to live by the world's standards, laugh at the world's jokes, employ the world's methodologies, and adopt the world's priorities? Or are you going to take your stand with Jesus Christ, go absolutely against the flow, nail your colors to the mast, and confess by word and by deed that He is Lord? Perhaps today is the day when for the first time, or for the first time in a long time, you need to live "by faith" and make that radical decision.

LUKE 18:18-30

99 "The Pilgrim, Chapter 33" (1971).

AUGUST 21

NOW AND THEN

"To me to live is Christ, and to die is gain. If I am to live in the flesh, that means fruitful labor for me. Yet which I shall choose I cannot tell. I am hard pressed between the two. My desire is to depart and be with Christ, for that is far better. But to remain in the flesh is more necessary on your account."
PHILIPPIANS 1:21-24

Do you remember visiting family when you were a child? Perhaps some visits were met with dread because the person you were visiting wasn't someone you felt close to or warmed to. But then there were the special visits with those you really loved. Maybe you were greeted at their door with a hug or the smell of freshly baked cookies. You couldn't wait to see them! They were precious to you, and you looked forward to being in their presence.

For the apostle Paul, Jesus was such a person. Paul was joyful, even while imprisoned, because of what Christ meant to him. He looked forward to the prospect of being ushered into His presence. Jesus was his all in all.

Can you and I say the same about Jesus? Or is our joy earthly, fixed on temporal matters like our marriages, children, livelihoods, or influence? If all that thrills your soul and all that forms your identity is wrapped up in worldly matters, then being with Jesus loses its allure. So we would be wise to remember that our identity is found in Him, because one day everything else will be left behind.

You may have heard of someone being so heavenly-minded that they're no earthly use. Well, we can also be so earthly-minded that we're no heavenly use. Sometimes, we are tempted to want things like perfect health, an end to sorrow, and life without any uncertainty *right now*. The reality is that we are going to lose loved ones, receive dreadful hospital reports, or face disappointment and disaster. But that is all part of the *now*. Paul's dilemma in this letter was balancing the *now* with the *next*. Although he desired to depart, it was not so that he could escape his current circumstances. He certainly endured many difficult trials, but for him, heaven was not simply relief from earthly suffering. He was not shuffling off life to embrace death; he longed to be with Jesus because he knew it would be fantastic.

Living faithfully in the present while anticipating the reality of being with Jesus is something we all have to work out. Paul recognized that while he still drew breath, he was to continue steadfastly in his earthly ministry until Christ called him home to heaven. So spend some moments considering Christ in all His loving perfections. Then spend some time enjoying the great truth that one day you will see Him as He welcomes you into His glory. Then reflect on the truth that the doorway to that moment is death. This is your future. One day, it will be your present. And until then, you can do what Paul did and live all in for Christ, knowing that death will be only gain.

2 TIMOTHY 4:6-18

AUGUST 22

FINDING GOD AT ROCK BOTTOM

"Joseph's master took him and put him into the prison ... But the Lord was with Joseph and showed him steadfast love and gave him favor in the sight of the keeper of the prison." GENESIS 39:20-21

After Potiphar's wife falsely accused him, Joseph hit rock bottom... again. Once more he found himself condemned—not to a pit this time but to a dungeon. The bottom had dropped out of his world.

And yet, as a man of God—as a man of principle—Joseph displayed enduring patience. He had fled the seductive temptation from Potiphar's wife on the strength of his convictions, making his decision on the basis of purity and rightness. Clearly, Joseph feared God more than he feared a dungeon. He would not sleep with Potiphar's wife because to do so would have been to sin against God. For Joseph, that was the end of any internal discussion, and it was sufficient basis for his decision.

Such a view will keep us, too, on the narrow way. True faithfulness comes not from pragmatism but from principle. It is the forming of decisions in the quiet place, without all of life's fanfare distracting us. It is obeying despite the consequences. It is being so resolved to be a man or woman of God that when the pressure to sin is greatest or when everything comes crashing down on us, we know how to respond.

As Joseph endured wrongful suffering, God demonstrated His love by granting him favor with his jailer. There is nothing in the narrative to suggest that Joseph tried to manipulate the circumstances to his own end—and even if Joseph *had* been looking around for a friend or ally, he never would have anticipated that the prison warder would fill that role! But God had other ideas. The Lord's presence remains with His people even in the most extreme circumstances.

From time to time, we all feel as if we are in the dungeon—a new low in our lives—and are confined by chilling isolation. Maybe that's you today. Maybe you, like Joseph, have been the victim of false accusations or are counting the cost of your determination to obey your Lord, or maybe something entirely different is weighing down your weary soul. No matter what, the Lord knows. He has never been taken by surprise, and He loves you with an everlasting love. His love is steadfast and is not changed by circumstances. He loves you enough to have walked through the dungeon of death and the terror of hell in order that you need never do so. Take comfort in knowing that, as the prophet Zechariah declared, "he who touches you touches the apple of [God's] eye" (Zechariah 2:8).

LUKE 8:22-39

AUGUST 23

GOD IS BIG ENOUGH

"Paul, standing in the midst of the Areopagus, said: 'Men of Athens ... [what] you worship as unknown, this I proclaim to you.'" ACTS 17:22-23

We cannot declare the gospel of Jesus without understanding the doctrine of God. As J.B. Phillips writes in his book *Your God Is Too Small*, "Many men and women today are living, often with an inner dissatisfaction, without any faith in God at all ... They have not found with their adult minds a God big enough to 'account for' life."[100] We must spare no fitting word, then, when we speak of God's character, of His grandeur, and of His glory made known.

When Paul shared the gospel, he went to the religious, the commoners, and the intelligentsia alike, because he recognized that the good news of God was all-encompassing and sufficient for all their concerns (Acts 17:24-31). We can learn from his approach, which was one that introduced listeners to God by identifying five key aspects of His nature:

- *God is the Creator.* He made the world, while He Himself is uncreated, standing distinct from His creation and outside of time. He is not a force—not even the greatest force of all—nor can He be contained or manipulated into a form of our own design.
- *God is the Sustainer.* He is the one who gives life and breath. The Sustainer of life is not served by human hands, nor does He have need of sustenance.
- *God is the Ruler.* He commands the nations. History, geography, governments—the whole universe!—are under His control. No event takes our God by surprise; He sweeps into His purposes even the sinful acts of man. Furthermore, as Ruler, He has put everybody in a certain place, in a moment in history, that we might seek Him, find Him, and praise His holy name.
- *God is the Father.* People are His "offspring" (Acts 17:28) and, in the sense that He has given life to each human, starting with Adam, He is every human's Father (Luke 3:38). He has created each of us in His image. We are moral beings, made with a sense of right and wrong, and we are able truly to flourish only in relationship with Him.
- *God is the Judge.* He has authority over all the earth. There will be a judgment day that is fair and final, when every injustice will be dealt with and all wrongs be put right. Indeed, God has already intervened in His Son Jesus, and in Jesus' resurrection He has declared Jesus' divine appointment as Judge. It is God's kindness and forbearance that announces judgment so that before then we might repent and and be forgiven.

God is big enough for—indeed, far bigger than—anyone's interest in mere religion. He's big enough for you and me, for all our cares and our sorrows. He's big enough to satisfy every intellectual quest and big enough to deal with every emotional longing—and ultimately, big enough to live for. To the extent that you know God as He truly is, so will you live in glad obedience to Him and speak with joyful confidence about Him.

ISAIAH 44:6-8

100 *Your God Is Too Small: A Guide for Believers and Skeptics Alike* (Touchstone, 2004), p 8.

AUGUST 24

RECOGNITION AND RESPONSE

"He said to them, 'Cast the net on the right side of the boat, and you will find some.' So they cast it, and now they were not able to haul it in, because of the quantity of fish. That disciple whom Jesus loved therefore said to Peter, 'It is the Lord!' When Simon Peter heard that it was the Lord, he put on his outer garment, for he was stripped for work, and threw himself into the sea." JOHN 21:6-8

When the figure standing on the shore told the fishermen to cast their net on the other side of the boat—and when those fishermen saw that, having caught nothing all night, their nets were now bulging—they began to recognize who it was who had called out to them. Perhaps until now they had been supernaturally kept from identifying Him, like the men on the Emmaus road (Luke 24:16). Or perhaps the early morning mist or the distance from land to the boat was what kept them from fully recognizing their Savior.

Whichever was the case, it was not long before John, "that disciple whom Jesus loved," realized who had spoken to them—and as soon as he shared his dawning insight with Peter, Peter launched into action. John's *recognition* and Peter's *reaction* make up a partnership that beautifully displays God's intent for complementary diversity. God takes the Johns and the Peters of this world, and He puts them together so that they may be what they cannot be on their own. Throughout John's Gospel, we see John display a contemplative, steady faith. When he and Peter visited the empty tomb, he considered the meaning of graveclothes lying empty where a body should have been, and he believed (John 20:8). His declaration from the boat likewise reveals a man who did not consider his circumstances hastily but rather pondered them and then confidently believed. When John realized it was Jesus before him, he made that known to Peter. Peter responded to John's recognition as he often did: by taking faith-filled, impassioned, immediate action. You can just imagine him jumping into the water and then thrashing about, half swimming, half walking, straining desperately to get to his Savior on the shore. He showed no hesitation in getting out of the boat. His only thought was to reach his Lord.

Without the contemplative, insightful nature of Johns, the Peters of this world would burn out in feverish activity. Without the boldness of Peters, the Johns of this world would waste away in introspection. We all need partners to serve Christ well. Whether you are a Peter or a John, or whatever your particular temperament, God made you as you are to serve a purpose in His kingdom. Many of us spend too much time wishing we were more like others. Others of us have no problem recognizing our personality type or particular strengths, but we do have a problem with humbly using them in the service of others or with being patient with the ways of others who are different from us. What would change in how you see yourself and your purpose if you realized that every aspect of your temperament is God-given, and that God intends for you to use it not for your own ends but in obedience to Him, in the company of His people, for the glory of His Son?

1 CORINTHIANS 12:12-27

AUGUST 25

RENOUNCING RETALIATION

"Beloved, never avenge yourselves, but leave it to the wrath of God."
ROMANS 12:19

Revenge is one of our most natural instincts. It is the way the world works, for we live in a "dog eat dog" world, where if you get in my way I will get you out of the way. It is a natural response to being wronged, then—but it is not a Christian one. Therefore, we should guard against it continuously. Even if we avoided it yesterday, that's no guarantee we will do so again today.

Perhaps the sports field is the place where we see most how easily revenge becomes the motivator for our plans and actions. If an opposing player fouls you and it is not picked up on and punished by the referee or umpire, what do you do? Our instinct is to find a way to get them back. So we plot and plan and pick our moment and "make it even." And as it goes on the sports field, so it goes in life—at least in our imaginations if not in our behavior.

But then the Scripture cuts across that natural instinct with the words "Never avenge yourselves."

Paul did not only outline the principle; he demonstrated it. He was ministering in an environment that gave him every reason for retaliation: he himself was defamed, beaten, mocked, and imprisoned; and he was most likely still alive when Emperor Nero and his government were turning Christians into torches in the palace backyard. They tied faithful followers of Jesus to stakes, drove those stakes into the ground, covered them in wax, and set them on fire—and still the command was "Never avenge yourselves."

We often fail to distinguish between the application of divine law, which is God's prerogative; the application of criminal law, which is the state's God-ordained responsibility (Romans 13:1-4); and the practice of personal revenge, for which the Bible gives us no mandate. We are permitted to pursue criminal justice from the state, always remembering that it will not be perfect and was not designed to be final; but most of all, though, we are called to entrust ourselves to God's divine justice, just as His Son did (1 Peter 2:23). We must live remembering that today is probably not the day of final judgment, and that you and I are certainly not the judge.

We have a calling as citizens of an eternal kingdom rather than any earthly kingdom. Unbelievers will not be drawn to Christ if they see His followers proclaiming that He is the just Judge and then acting as though they are the ones who have the right to mete out judgment. Our actions will affect those around us who are struggling with sin. Let it be that they are won to Christ by our love and never driven away from considering Christ by our retaliation.

ROMANS 12:9-21

AUGUST 26

THE PATIENT SAVIOR

"They woke him and said to him, 'Teacher, do you not care that we are perishing?' And he awoke and rebuked the wind and said to the sea, 'Peace! Be still!' And the wind ceased, and there was a great calm. He said to them, 'Why are you so afraid? Have you still no faith?'" MARK 4:38-40

When the storm raged and the disciples feared, Jesus displayed not only peace but also patience in His response to them.

They had accused Him of not caring that they were perishing. Yet His rebuke wasn't for them but for the wind and the waves. That is remarkable! No teacher ever had such slow learners as Jesus had in these characters—yet no other students have ever had such a patient and forgiving teacher, either.

While Jesus' patience was showcased by this episode, it was by no means exclusive to it; throughout His ministry, He consistently displayed patience in response to His disciples' feelings and failings. In Mark 6, after Jesus had fed 5,000 people from five loaves of bread and two fish, the disciples doubted Him when they saw Him walking on water, yet He lovingly replied, "Take heart; it is I. Do not be afraid" (6:50). Later on, Jesus repeatedly instructed them as to the necessity and purpose of His death, despite their lack of humility and understanding (8:31-33; 9:30-32; 10:32-34). Once He had risen, He did not even rebuke the disciples for being surprised by the resurrection He had foretold. Instead, He joyfully and calmly asked them thought-provoking questions and revealed His true identity to them.

We see our own frail faith reflected in the disciples. If we had been with them, we too probably would have been scrambling around in fear and voicing our doubts and accusations to Jesus. Yet still today, Christ shows us patience through our fears and doubts. He does not reject us for a moment of unbelief. He does not dismiss us for cowardice. There is no teacher like Him. Therefore, as recipients of Christ's long-suffering patience, let us return such patience to others. If you are a parent, coach, manager, ministry leader, teacher, or simply a friend, remember Jesus' example. If we want God to tolerate our faltering faith, then we should also aim to demonstrate His patience to others, and to ourselves.

Most of all, though, we are not called to follow Jesus' example but to enjoy His perfections. His patience will not fail. He never neglects or deserts those in His care. Your sins and your struggles cannot push Him beyond the limits of His forbearance. He will be patient with you today. He is your Savior, your Redeemer, your ever-patient Teacher—your Jesus.

EXODUS 33:18 – 34:8

AUGUST 27

FINDING FAVOR

"But Noah found favor in the eyes of the LORD." GENESIS 6:8

The Noah of popular imagination is a spiritual giant, a hero of the faith. In truth, though, he was just an ordinary man. He was like everybody else as he went about his daily tasks, earned a living, and raised his kids.

Before Noah's story unfolds, we're told that "the LORD saw that the wickedness of man was great in the earth, and that every intention of the thoughts of his heart was only evil continually. And the LORD regretted that he had made man on the earth, and it grieved him to his heart" (Genesis 6:5-6). No distinctions are made here. Without exception, the whole human race was involved in wickedness—including Noah.

The point is clear: All had sinned. All were alienated from God. All must face judgment.

"But Noah..." By God's grace, the reality of sin and judgment is always tempered by a divine "but." God's grace, unexplained and unmerited, was extended to Noah. This was the only thing that eventually distinguished him from the rest of humanity. God chose Noah and his family to be the recipients of His grace, establishing a relationship with him that had not existed before. Because of this grace, Noah became "a righteous man" who "walked with God" (Genesis 6:9).

Noah could make no claim on God. Without any virtue on his part, and against all the odds, God simply intervened in Noah's life.

Many people are under the impression that grace isn't found in the Old Testament—that in the early days, it was all fire and brimstone, law and judgment, and it's not until Jesus arrives that grace comes. The reality, though, is that grace not only precedes creation but also unfolds in the midst of judgments throughout history and on every page of the Bible.

And throughout the Bible, grace works itself out. Noah built a boat in obedience to the word of God when the word of God was all he had to go on. When we experience grace in all its fullness, it diminishes us and exalts God. It makes us realize that life is all about Him and His kindness to us. It moves us to trust His word and obey His commands.

The only thing that distinguishes you from the culture around you is the same thing that marked Noah out from the people of his day: the unmerited, outreaching favor of God. So be on guard against spiritual pride as much as worldly compromise. None of us are smart enough to grasp the idea of salvation or good enough to merit the joy of salvation. You and I are not deserving—but nevertheless, God has intervened. Only when the grace of God grips our hearts will we, like Noah, walk in the way of our Creator rather than the way of our world and live in obedient humility and confident hope. Only grace has that effect.

GENESIS 6

◇ Bible Through The Year: Psalms 120–122; 2 Corinthians 6

AUGUST 28

A JOURNEY OF REPENTANCE

"I am writing these things to you so that you may not sin. But if anyone does sin, we have an advocate with the Father, Jesus Christ the righteous." 1 JOHN 2:1

Christianity hinges on the message of forgiveness. Other religions may offer moralism. They may offer methods that will help us tidy up our lives or make us feel that we are good people. Christianity, however, is for the unworthy, the lost, the beleaguered, and the sinful. It's for people who need to hear that they can be forgiven. In other words, it's for everyone.

From first to last, the gospel is about what God does, not about what we must do. It is God, by His mercy, who gives us the desire to even want to be forgiven—and it is only when we put our faith in Jesus that we are fully pardoned. When we turn to Him in repentance and faith, we are able to look back and say we have been saved from sin's penalty. All that was against us, all that kept us from knowing God, all that kept us from discovering His love and His goodness—all of the penalty that we deserve—has been eradicated, erased through the saving work of God's Son on the cross.

As believers, then, we can—we should—rejoice in the fact that sin no longer rules over us. Yet the reality is that in our earthly lives, we still sin. We still miss the mark; we still fail to reach God's standard. And when we do, the Evil One loves to whisper, "Are you really saved? Will God really forgive you this time?" To which we must answer, "Yes, I am; and yes, He will, for the one who died for me is at this moment advocating for me."

Knowing forgiveness is not a license to sin; indeed, John wrote with the purpose "that you may not sin." When we sin, the joy we have found in God begins to fade. While He remains our heavenly Father, it should be no surprise that if we harbor sin, we will fail to enjoy all the blessings He intends for us.

And so we seek to live in obedience to our Lord, and yet, since we will not do so perfectly, we also must live in repentance to our Lord. Jesus underscored the need for and importance of daily repentance in John 13 when, while He was in the midst of washing His disciples' feet, Peter protested and said, "You shall never wash my feet." Jesus responded, "If I do not wash you, you have no share with me" (13:8). Forgiveness is not ours until we are washed by Jesus, and then He continues to wash us through our daily repentance and faith.

One day, you will be taken to heaven and saved from sin's presence. But until that great day, your Christian life is to be a journey of repentance. You *have been* saved. You *will be* saved. But for now, day by day, you are mercifully *being* saved as you repent and turn back to Jesus.

ROMANS 7:7 – 8:2

AUGUST 29

A NAME LIKE NO OTHER

"Let them praise the name of the Lord, for his name alone is exalted; his majesty is above earth and heaven." PSALM 148:13

God has made Himself known to us by making His name known to us. When we think of God's name, we ought to think of His nature—His essence, His character, and His attributes. His name sets Him apart from everyone and everything else, representing all of who He is.

God's encounter with Moses at the burning bush, recorded for us in Exodus 3, underscores the relationship between God's name and His character. As Moses approached the bush, God instructed him to take off the shoes from his feet, as he was standing on holy ground. In the ensuing dialogue, after being commanded to go to Pharaoh and demand the Israelites' release, Moses understandably asked, "If I come to the people of Israel and say to them, 'The God of your fathers has sent me to you,' and they ask me, 'What is his name?' what shall I say to them?" God's answer? "I AM WHO I AM" (Exodus 3:13-14).

God uses the verb *to be*—"I AM" to convey His name. By using this verb, He distinguishes between Himself and all false gods, which ought to call themselves "I'm not." Idols are made by human hands—or, in our day, often within our hearts. Craftsmen fashion them out of wood, stone, or ivory and fasten them on pedestals. Nevertheless, they inevitably topple over and need to be righted again. An idol demands our service, but it cannot save. It never delivers what it has promised.

But for the Creator of the ends of the earth, it is justifiable and right that He should be known as I AM, for He is like no one else. He was not created. He is completely self-existent. He is completely self-fulfilled. He is in need of no one and nothing. That which He has always possessed, He still possesses. He knows neither beginning nor end. He fulfills all of His promises. He is the God of limitless life and power.

We are to exalt His name, and His name alone, for this is what we were made for. All of us struggle not to bow down before idols—those created things that we worship and make sacrifices for because we think they will bring us life. But if we would worship Him as we ought to, our idols must fall before Him. He is the only Creator, the only I AM—the only one who rules earth and heaven.

ISAIAH 46:3-11

AUGUST 30

A TIMELY PRAYER

"'And now, Lord, look upon their threats and grant to your servants to continue to speak your word with all boldness' ... And when they had prayed, the place in which they were gathered together was shaken, and they were all filled with the Holy Spirit and continued to speak the word of God with boldness." ACTS 4:29, 31

When we feel that our culture is more determinedly turning its back on the gospel and opposing more fiercely the claims of the Scriptures, the natural question is: What do we do? Our answer should not be based on what feels comfortable but on what the Bible says.

The early church was no stranger to social upheaval. Knowing that hope and salvation could be found in Christ's death and resurrection, Peter fearlessly preached at Pentecost, just a few weeks after he had denied knowing Jesus and being His follower (Acts 2:1-41). The bold preaching of Peter and the other apostles led to the rapid growth of the church—but it also led to tumult and persecution for the believers (v 1-22).

It's no surprise, then, when we read that they lifted their voices to God. They knew the opposition they faced, and they prayed—knowledgeably, biblically, and boldly.

"And now, Lord..." If we were asked to finish that prayer, we'd probably ask God to remove the threats, stifle the opposition, or keep us from persecution. That was not the prayer of the early believers, though. Instead, they prayed that they would declare the gospel "with all boldness."

Theirs remains a timely prayer. Surely the great need of the hour in the church today is simply this: for Spirit-filled, Christ-centered courage. We live in a culture shaped by an incoherent mix of opinions and tensions. In that context, God calls us to go out and say, "I am not ashamed of the gospel, for it is the power of God for salvation to everyone who believes" (Romans 1:16). As we do so, we would do well to remember that at the very heart of the gospel is the cross. If we are going to speak the word with boldness, then we will declare, in the words of Isaiah, that on the cross Jesus "was pierced for our transgressions; he was crushed for our iniquities; upon him was the chastisement that brought us peace, and with his wounds we are healed" (Isaiah 53:5). As Rico Tice points out, this will require us to be brave enough to press through the pain barrier and risk the hostility of those who disagree in order to find hunger among those in whom the Lord is already at work.[101]

The whole gospel has been given to the whole church to reach the whole world. Whether you're a musician, engineer, farmer, or pharmacist, it doesn't matter; the charge of God to each of us is to speak His word, the mystery of the gospel.

So are you willing to be bold enough to pray for boldness? Not for an easy or comfortable or healthy or admired life but for a life of witness? Will you daily make the prayer of the early church your own, asking that by God's Spirit you would be filled and emboldened to share His gospel, whatever the cost, with a world that is desperate for truth?

ACTS 4:1-22

101 *Honest Evangelism* (The Good Book Company, 2015), p 15.

AUGUST 31

HOW ARE WE JUSTIFIED?

"Whatever gain I had, I counted as loss for the sake of Christ ... For his sake I have suffered the loss of all things and count them as rubbish, in order that I may gain Christ and be found in him." PHILIPPIANS 3:7-9

Life is so often about what we must do in order to gain entry or acceptance. "What do I have to do to get into that school? To gain acceptance by that social circle? To reach executive status?" By nature, humans therefore wonder the same thing about spiritual realities: "What must *I* do to inherit eternal life?" (Luke 18:18, emphasis added).

We often rely on our activities—attendance at church, prayer, Bible reading. We feel confident when we do them and condemned when we don't. We see God's law as a ladder up which we climb to His acceptance of us.

In the passage leading up to this verse, Paul has just rehearsed all the earthly "gain" in his life, both inherited and achieved, from his privileged birth to his elite education. The purity of his pedigree was never in question from the day of his birth. Paul essentially says, *If these factors achieve acceptance with God, you can see I had them all. Did I dot all the spiritual i's and cross all the religious t's? Absolutely.*

Paul had once thought he was a spiritual millionaire. He had thought he was advancing in holiness. Then one day it all changed. In one journey from Jerusalem to Damascus, Paul came to realize he was spiritually bankrupt—that he wasn't even on the path of holiness.

What gave Paul hope? On that same journey, he met the risen, crucified Jesus (Acts 9:1-19), and he grasped the doctrine of justification: that God declares the sinner to be righteous on the basis of His Son's finished work.

Far from being a ladder, God's law is more like a mirror that shows us we're in the wrong and we can't put ourselves in the right. Like Paul, every advantage we previously considered a gain is now seen to be a loss, a failure.

How can you know that Christ accepts you? Not because you come to Him with a righteousness of your own; rather, because your sin has been transferred to the account of Christ, who knew no sin but became sin for you so that you might receive His perfect righteousness (2 Corinthians 5:21). You cannot add anything to being justified with God. You cannot subtract anything from being justified with God. Justification is full because God gives believers Christ's righteousness, and it is final because it depends solely on God's gift of His Son.

Once you know you cannot lose your entry into eternal life, you are ready to give up everything else for the sake of the one who has gained you entry: reputation, wealth, prominence, status, possessions. Whatever you once thought gain, you can joyfully now count loss. You are willing to lose your life for Christ for you know that through Christ you have gained true life. What do you struggle to give up for Jesus? Let your justification be the engine of your wholehearted obedience.

ACTS 26:1-29

SEPTEMBER 1

OVERFLOWING WITH GENEROSITY

"Moses said to all the congregation of the people of Israel, 'This is the thing that the LORD has commanded. Take from among you a contribution to the LORD. Whoever is of a generous heart, let him bring the LORD's contribution.'"

EXODUS 35:4-5

God's people give thankfully in response to His grace.

Or at least, we should do. But often our reasons for giving are very different ones. Many see giving as something they must do or ought to do, perhaps because of their social position or the perceptions of others. Some give in response to a measure of guilt, attempting to make amends for their bad deeds. Others give out of fear, thinking, "I'd better give, or God won't want to bless me."

But the principle of giving which runs throughout the Bible is very different.

In the wilderness, as the Israelites prepared to construct the tabernacle for the Lord, Moses began a collection for the work. His request wasn't heavy-handed or manipulative; he simply told the people that the Lord was willing to receive from all who were willing to give, and every generous heart brought an offering. They not only gave from what they had, but they also gave on the basis of who they were and the abilities that God had given them, from building and cloth-making to craftsmanship and artistry.

Many gave, and they gave overwhelmingly. As a result, Moses had to issue a second directive, sending word throughout the camp: "Let no man or woman do anything more for the contribution for the sanctuary" (Exodus 36:6). They knew that God had given them everything they had. Fueled by the immensity of God's goodness, they overflowed in generosity—to the extent that Moses had to tell them to stop!

The Lord needs nothing, yet He is willing to receive from those who, by His grace, are the beneficiaries of His many gifts. God doesn't administer His grace in percentages; He lavishes it—and out of the abundance of His heart, in Jesus, He has given to His people one blessing after another. When we, the recipients of His grace, give of our time, money, talents, or anything else abundantly and thankfully, God is glorified.

God's desire for generous hearts never wanes. He has a plan for saving people through the work of His Son, and He yearns for followers who are willing to join in gospel work through giving. It is grace, and grace alone, that moves a person to give both sacrificially *and* cheerfully. If your giving—of your time, your talents, or your money—is limited or grudging, reflect on the grace of God in lavishing so much upon you, not least in the Lord Jesus. Be stirred by His grace, and you'll find you abound with thankfulness that overflows in generosity, bringing glory and praise to God.

JOHN 12:1-8

SEPTEMBER 2

REVERENCE FOR CHRIST

"... Submitting to one another out of reverence for Christ."
EPHESIANS 5:20-21

People submit to one another for many reasons—on the basis of politics or social structures, or even on the basis of pragmatism. Sometimes it's much easier (and certainly nicer!) just to submit to people than it is to take the risk of seeming rude or confrontational.

None of these reasons, however, are the motivating factors for Christian submission. Instead, the distinguishing feature of our submission to one another should be that it is done "out of reverence for Christ." Bowing our knees to Jesus keeps us from being preoccupied with ourselves. Reverence for Christ doesn't only pull us away from ourselves; it pulls us toward Jesus. In Him we see how to heed the call of submission, for it was Jesus Himself who taught, "Whoever would be great among you must be your servant ... even as the Son of Man came not to be served but to serve, and to give his life as a ransom for many" (Matthew 20:26, 28). He not only said those words but lived them. Consider, for example, Jesus' washing of the disciples' feet in John 13. As John records, "Jesus, knowing that the Father had given all things into his hands, and that he had come from God and was going back to God, rose from supper. He laid aside his outer garments, and taking a towel, tied it around his waist. Then he poured water into a basin and began to wash the disciples' feet" (John 13:3-5). What was happening here? Nothing less than the submission of God the Son to God the Father. He who came from God and is God was making Himself nothing by "taking the form of a servant" (Philippians 2:7).

Jesus came to do not His own will but His Father's (John 6:38). As a result, He accepted hardship. He was isolated and ill-treated. He endured malice, misunderstanding, and death. Jesus was broken in order that our broken lives may be repaired and transformed. It was He who came to die on a cross, submitting Himself to the will of the Father, in order that He might provide a ransom for all who are humble enough to bow down and say, "*That* is the very Savior I need."

When we consider Christ as He truly is, we cannot but be moved to revere Him. Who else would we respect and love more than the divine second Person of the Trinity, who was willing to submit Himself even to death in obedience to His Father and for the good of His people? And when we revere Christ, we are ready to have the same attitude as Christ: one that does not grasp for prominence or strive for authority or stand on our rights, but one that obeys God by submitting our own interests to those of our brothers and sisters.

There are many reasons why we may choose to submit to another (and many more reasons why we may choose not to do so). But let this be true of you: that you submit yourself to others in your church out of reverence for Christ, who submitted to His Father and, in doing so, became your Savior.

PHILIPPIANS 2:17-30

SEPTEMBER 3

A WORD TO WIVES

"Wives, submit to your own husbands, as to the Lord." EPHESIANS 5:22

The word submission tends to trigger all kinds of negative responses. This is due in part to the reality that, as John Stott wrote over 40 years ago, "submission to authority is out of fashion today. It is totally at variance with contemporary attitudes of permissiveness and freedom."[102] The intervening four decades have only increased submission's negative reputation, and nowhere more so than within marriage.

Yet the fact remains that, properly understood and rightly applied, submission lies at the heart of relationships as God established them. Children are to submit to their parents (Ephesians 6:1), church members are to submit to their church leaders (Hebrews 13:17), and, here, wives are to submit to their husbands "as to the Lord." Submission to others, depending on the roles to which we are called in life, is part and parcel of our relationships with each other.

A wife's submission to her husband reflects God's divine ordering for marriage, then. But how, specifically, are we to understand this teaching? First of all, the directive for a wife to submit to her husband in no way implies her inferiority. The Bible is *very* clear that men and women are equal in dignity, as both are made in God's image (Genesis 1:27). As believers, we are also equal in redemption—and that equality is seen in the fact that we are heirs together of God's grace (1 Peter 3:7). Our standing as men and women before God is entirely equal. A difference in role does not mean a difference in value.

Second, women are to submit to *their own husbands*, not all men in general. Paul isn't giving a blanket instruction about the place of women in society; he is giving a specific directive concerning the wife's role in the family. Within that context, a woman's desire to submit to the Lord is revealed in part by her submission to her husband.

Third, this submission isn't the same as unconditional obedience. Husbands are not to coerce their wives, nor are they to call them to submit, and certainly not to that which the Lord has not ordained. A wife is not in the hands of one who has the authority to command what he pleases. Rather, a husband is to "love his wife as himself," to give himself up for her, and to lead her in holiness (Ephesians 5:33). If you are a husband, then it needs underlining that if at any point you seek to lead your wife away from obedience to Christ rather than deeper into it, your wife is under no biblical obligation to follow your lead.

If you are a wife, the Bible does not call you to slavish, unthinking obedience. Rather, your submission is to be a joyful loyalty to and commitment to following the lead of your husband as part of a mutual partnership which pursues God's glory in all things. Wholehearted and without reluctance, this kind of submission is only possible by God's enabling so that you might do your husband "good, and not harm, all the days of [your] life" (Proverbs 31:12). This biblical submission is certainly not fashionable. It is often not easy. But, in the sight of God and of His people, it is beautiful.

PROVERBS 31:10-31

102 *The Message of Ephesians:*, The Bible Speaks Today (IVP Academic, 1979), p 215.

SEPTEMBER 4

GOD'S DESIGN FOR MARRIAGE

"A man shall leave his father and his mother and hold fast to his wife, and they shall become one flesh. And the man and his wife were both naked and were not ashamed." GENESIS 2:24-25

Marriage is a God-given gift that we have tarnished by our sin. These verses describe a perfectly trusting, perfectly shame-free, perfectly united partnership of love. Sadly, one tangible effect of our living in a fallen world is that outside of the movies no marriage is only and ever like that. The tragedy of human sin is that it is in our very nature to corrupt what God has created for our good and His glory, causing the beauty and enjoyment of marriage as He intended to be lost. But there is hope! For believers, God's Spirit enables us to consider marriage according to His design.

We must first acknowledge that outside of Christ, men and women are in flat-out rebellion against God's purposes. It's not that we are simply confused about the nature of marriage; it's that our sinful desires are completely opposed even to what we do understand. Marriage as it is given to us in the Bible is often perceived as a cage, a restriction, or a human contrivance put together long ago—a kind of useless vestige left over from previous generations. If we see God's design for marriage in this light, it's because we are predisposed to say, "I don't like God's plans. I'll do this my own way."

When we are united with Christ, however, God enables us to view marriage according to His design. No matter what any government legislates, Scripture is absolutely clear that any relationship other than a monogamous, heterosexual relationship cannot be and is not a marriage before God, because that is what He decided marriage should be in the very beginning. Jesus' affirmation of the Genesis 2 depiction of marriage demonstrates that nothing between the beginning and now has changed God's design (Matthew 19:4-6). We must not tamper with or readjust the Bible to accommodate social trends which would define marriage differently. Though God's pattern for biblical marriage may be looked down upon by our fallen world, if we believe the Bible to be the very word of God, then we will uphold its teaching—in how we choose to order our own lives and in how we speak of and pray for other people's relationships.

As believers, we must recognize that God's concern for marriages in all cultures and at all times is that they would reflect Christ's love for and commitment to His people (Ephesians 5:22-25). And we must remember that all that is distorted as a result of the fall, the Lord Jesus came to renew and repair. Only in and through Christ is it possible to view marriage according to God's pattern and plan. Instead of us living according to our own way, He has graciously invited us to bow our hearts under His design, which is like no other. For some, it will call for great personal sacrifice to obey God's commands in this area. For all of us living in the 21st century, it will call for courage to stand up for God's ways in the face of man's. In your particular context and circumstances, what will it mean for you to think, speak, and act in a way that reflects God's design for His great gift of marriage?

GENESIS 2

SEPTEMBER 5

A WORD TO HUSBANDS

"Husbands, love your wives, as Christ loved the church and gave himself up for her, that he might sanctify her." EPHESIANS 5:25-26

By God's grace, every Christian marriage is about more than marriage.

The purpose of human marriage is to point away from itself to the ultimate marriage made in heaven: that of Christ, the Bridegroom, and the church, His bride. Marriage, in other words, is about God's ultimate purpose "to unite all things in [Christ], things in heaven and things on earth" (Ephesians 1:10). This is why Paul offers specific instructions for husbands: so that their marriages might display the union God intends.

In marriage, the husband's primary objective is not to make sure his wife is physically and emotionally sustained. That is part of it, of course—but his *ultimate* objective should be that his wife will be prepared to meet Jesus. To that end, the word that Paul uses for "love" here, *agape*, is important: it expresses self-sacrifice and self-abasement. It's about what we give, not what we get. It's about what we owe, not what we're due. It's not about seeking what's good for you; it's about giving yourself up for what's truly good for your wife, so that she might be "holy and without blemish" (Ephesians 5:27). This was the purpose for which Christ gave His life for His church; and, as a picture of this, it is what a husband is to give himself up for and pursue for his wife.

But if you are a husband, how do you love in this way in the day-to-day reality of life? One practical step is to look for the absence of "NAG-ing". That is, you must renounce *neglect*, physically, emotionally, and spiritually—and, if career, club, or church responsibilities interfere, you may need to re-evaluate your commitments. You also need to renounce *abuse*, which, while including more egregious sins, also encompasses belittling your wife, talking down to her, treating her with disregard, or acting as if she's really fortunate to be married to you. And finally, you need to ensure you never take your marriage for *granted*, which can become so easy as time goes by.

Yet as helpful as such practical reminders are, the ultimate yardstick for, and motivation to, love is the cross-shaped love of Christ for His bride. Without a clear view of how Jesus loves His church, our best intentions will flounder, and our failures will crush us. So we must look to Christ, who, although He needed no one and nothing, came and gave Himself up in order that we, in our need, rebellion, and emptiness, may be caught up in His embrace, welcomed into His heart, brought into His family, and considered a part of His bride.

Do you find yourself saying, "Why would He ever love me like that?" If so, you see what a high calling it is for husbands to "love your wives, *as Christ loved the church.*" So if you are a husband, or hope to be one day, it must start with prayer: prayer that the Holy Spirit will enable you to think biblically, live obediently, and truly love selflessly. And if you are a wife, or hope to be one day, this should likewise be your prayer for your husband, for the sake of your joy and his, but most of all for God's glory.

EPHESIANS 5:22-32

SEPTEMBER 6

THE CONSEQUENCES OF JEALOUSY

"A tranquil heart gives life to the flesh, but envy makes the bones rot."
PROVERBS 14:30

Envy is a spiritual cancer, destroying a person from the inside out.

The consequences of jealousy are grave. King Solomon does not mince words as he warns us of this diagnosis with graphic imagery and directs us instead towards a life of health and peace.

Envy harms us. Even if it does nothing to anyone else, it will still destroy the one who envies. It influences our perception of others. It breeds a destructively critical spirit, leading us to view our neighbors with unwarranted suspicion and anger. It leaves us incapable of being happy for others, and it undermines any chance of contentment, for there is always someone else with more for us to feel resentful of. Envy makes the bones rot.

Jealousy can invade swiftly and subtly. Take the apostle Peter, for example. Prior to the crucifixion, he had made a mess of things by denying Christ three times. John records that after His resurrection, Jesus made breakfast for Peter and some other disciples on the beach, and Jesus spoke with Peter, restoring their relationship, reminding him of His call to Peter to follow Him, and tasking him to shepherd and feed His people. If you had asked Peter the day before what his heart most longed for, it would have been this. But when Jesus added that one day Peter would be called to give his life for his Lord, how did Peter respond? By looking at John and saying, "What about this man?"

Jesus, though, fully aware of the dangers of jealousy, replied, "If it is my will that he remain until I come, what is that to you? You follow me!" (John 21:22).

How easy it is, even in moments of great advance, for jealousy to infect us and cause us to forget all that Jesus has done for us and given us! How, then, do we find any kind of cure for this spiritual rottenness?

The last thing that we want to do is the first thing that we need to do: recognize envy for what it is—sin—and bring it into the light of God's presence through confession. Then, we must prayerfully reject jealousy, moment by moment, asking the Spirit to enable us to reflect on all we have in Christ, until we are gripped not by jealousy but by joy. Those who count their blessings are more able to praise God for the blessings He bestows on others. And a tranquil heart gives life.

Do not let your envy eat away at you unchecked. In what way does it have a hold on you? Confess it, pray about it, and fight it with gospel truth.

JOHN 21:15-23

SEPTEMBER 7

THE PEOPLE OF GOD

"No one is a Jew who is merely one outwardly, nor is circumcision outward and physical. But a Jew is one inwardly, and circumcision is a matter of the heart, by the Spirit, not by the letter." ROMANS 2:28-29

Every kingdom has citizens, and the kingdom of God is no different. Who, then, are citizens in God's kingdom? Who are God's people?

The people of God comprise all who have placed their faith in Jesus Christ. These people are not a part of God's kingdom because of their intellect, power, or any other external factor, but simply and only because God has chosen to love them and so has given them the gift of faith in His Son. Jesus rebuked the Pharisees for assuming that they were members of God's family because of their lineage: "If you were Abraham's children," He said, "you would be doing the works Abraham did" (John 8:39). And what did Abraham do? He trusted in the promises of God; he "believed God, and it was counted to him as righteousness" (Galatians 3:6).

We are full members of God's family, then, not because of something we do but by the work of God's Spirit in convicting our hearts, causing us to believe, and leading us to repentance. We don't need to undergo the ritual requirements of Jewish law or be physical descendants of Abraham to be included among God's people. In Romans 2:29, Paul essentially asks, *Who are the children of Abraham?* The answer is: anyone who undergoes "circumcision ... of the heart, by the Spirit."

As we consider these truths, we may wonder whether Paul thought there was any benefit in being a Jew. Paul explained that there was actually a phenomenal advantage, because the Jews were the first to receive God's promises, giving them a unique opportunity to understand the signs that pointed forward to fulfillment in Christ (Romans 3:1-2). But that understanding itself does not make anyone a citizen of God's kingdom. That is open to, and reserved for, those who become subjects of its King. Whether we are Jews or Gentiles—whatever our background, wherever we were born, and however we were raised—God offers salvation to all who come to faith in Christ. Our citizenship in God's kingdom is not tied to ethnicity or externals but to humble, childlike faith in the Messiah.

The world is full of people struggling to find where they fit or striving to maintain their position in a company, society, friendship circle, or even their own family. God does not ask you to struggle or to strive but simply to enjoy. If you belong to God's people by faith in Jesus, then you have been rescued by His name, you have been freed from shame, and you are part of His people. It is here that you fit, here that you find your home.

EPHESIANS 2:11-22

SEPTEMBER 8

REJOICING ALWAYS

"Rejoice in the Lord always; again I will say, rejoice." PHILIPPIANS 4:4

How are we supposed to rejoice always? Is it even possible to achieve this? Or are we supposed to understand Paul's exhortation to "rejoice in the Lord always" as a kind of hyperbolic statement which Paul never intended us to actually experience in our Christian life?

No, we are not! Paul meant what he said. As believers, we really are to rejoice *always*.

One of the reasons why we experience such difficulty with this appeal is because we tend to think of joy in the same incorrect way as we view love—namely, as a product of our emotions rather than a servant of our wills. When seen like that, joy is a product of our circumstances and our feelings; and with that view it is only possible to rejoice when we're feeling good, when the sun is shining, and when everything seems to be going our way.

But the Bible means what it says when it tells us to rejoice always, including when life is not what we wished, the clouds are gathering, and we feel low. Therefore, we must seek to understand joy.

In Habakkuk 3, we read that the prophet trembled over the day of trouble to come (3:16). Everything in the realm of feelings pointed Habakkuk toward panic. But instead of succumbing to anxiety, he made his feelings yield to what he knew of his Provider. On the strength of right thinking, Habakkuk concluded, "Though the fig tree should not blossom, nor fruit be on the vines, the produce of the olive fail and the fields yield no food, the flock be cut off from the fold and there be no herd in the stalls, *yet I will rejoice in the Lord*" (v 17-18, emphasis added). He demonstrates that it is possible to rejoice always—even in the midst of deep trial and deep pain—when our joy does not depend on external factors but on God alone.

God has purposed that our thinking is to be informed and shaped by His revelation—what He has made known of Himself through His word and creation. To borrow the words of the 16th-century scientist Johannes Kepler, we are to "think God's thoughts after him." As we learn to *think* correctly, we will increasingly be able to bring our emotions into line with our right thinking.

When your joy is rooted in God's unchanging character, you are delivered from joy being held captive by yourself and your circumstances. Yes, your joy might be challenged by the difficulties and disappointments of your day, but it will not be overturned. In the moments today when your joy is challenged, take these words to your lips:

'Tis what I know of Thee, my Lord and God,
That fills my soul with peace, my lips with song:
Thou art my health, my joy, my staff, my rod;
Leaning on Thee, in weakness I am strong.[103]

PSALM 20

103 Horatius Bonar, "Not What I Am, O Lord, but What Thou Art" (1861).

SEPTEMBER 9

THE HUMBLE SERVANT

"You call me Teacher and Lord, and you are right, for so I am. If I then, your Lord and Teacher, have washed your feet, you also ought to wash one another's feet." JOHN 13:13-14

Andrew Martinez was one of the greatest caddies in the history of golf, caddying for greats like Johnny Miller, John Cook, and Tom Lehman. He was also a talented athlete in his own right. Part of what made him extraordinary as a caddie was his devotion to his boss, which started as soon as he stepped into the caddie shack and put on the white overalls. In his role, he lost himself. He was still Martinez, but the name on his back read differently; he existed solely to serve someone else, despite his own giftedness and capabilities.

The night before He died, in what is one of the most memorable scenes from His earthly life, Jesus washed His disciples' feet. One of the reasons He did so was to model humble service, for the work of foot-washing was the role of a slave, not of a king. We can all benefit from following His example: the Creator washed the feet of His creatures and, in so doing, He served both His feuding disciples and His betrayer, Judas. Such an action was above and beyond the typical hospitality this ritual entailed.

Jesus' actions were an example for us to follow ("you also ought"), but they were not merely an example—and if all we latch on to in this account is the call to copy Jesus' humble behavior, we risk getting lost in moralism and missing Christ's full and glorious intention. As He washed His disciples' feet, Jesus knew what the immediate future held. He was acutely aware that a time of great sorrow—His coming crucifixion—was imminent. His action showed that the future is always in the Father's loving hands. The cleansing of His followers' feet symbolized the future cleansing of their souls—a cleansing not by the water in His bowl but by His blood on the cross. In His humility, the Son of God offers to wash us clean of the stain of our sin, and we must meet His humility with ours by accepting our desperate need and asking to be so washed.

Only once we appreciate how we have been served by our Savior will we serve others in the same way. Peter, who at the time was confused by what Jesus was doing (John 13:6-8), would one day grasp his Lord's message. Years later, he would encourage his fellow believers to "humble yourselves … under the mighty hand of God so that at the proper time he may exalt you" (1 Peter 5:6). He knew that Christ's example was meant to do far more than modify our behavior; it was meant to humble us and then to assure us of our forgiveness.

In what way are you called to wash the feet of others today? How can you sacrifice your own time or comforts to serve those around you in ways that can be motivated only by humble love? And most importantly, how can you serve others in ways that point them to the greatest act of service—the cleansing that Christ's blood, shed on the cross, provides?

JOHN 13:1-17

SEPTEMBER 10

THE PRIEST WE NEED

"Since then we have a great high priest who has passed through the heavens, Jesus, the Son of God, let us hold fast our confession ... Let us then with confidence draw near to the throne of grace, that we may receive mercy and find grace to help in time of need." HEBREWS 4:14-16

The Old Testament underlines again and again the weight of responsibility on high priests in Israel (see, for example, Exodus 29 and Leviticus 16). Being the high priest was not to be taken lightly. Only he could enter the Most Holy Place, the inner chamber of the Jewish temple. Only he could offer a blood sacrifice "for the unintentional sins of the people" (Hebrews 9:7). Although he was not without sin, he served as an advocate for his community before God.

But, as the writer of Hebrews shows us, there has been one Great High Priest—namely, Jesus—who did what no other priest could do and shouldered a responsibility the weight of which no other human could bear.

Jesus did not go through a curtain into the Most Holy Place in the Jerusalem temple. Instead, as God's Son, He passed through the heavens, so that He now appears on our behalf before the Father's throne. We need not lament His physical absence on earth, not only because He is present with us through the Holy Spirit but also because His absence means that even now He is directly speaking to God the Father on our behalf (Hebrews 7:25).

That is why in the New Testament, ministry is not set apart for an order of priests who make blood sacrifices. Those who are called by God and given both the privilege and responsibility of leading and teaching God's people do not have to advocate before God for His people in the way Old Testament priests did. Because our Great High Priest has offered up *the* one great sacrifice for sins, there is no need for any other advocate. Indeed, His priesthood leaves room for no other offerings for sin, either in heaven or on earth. He alone could die for us and speak for us, and He alone has done it.

The very greatness of Christ's priesthood lies in the fact that He has offered Himself for our sins once and for all. We need nothing more than to recognize that "he holds his priesthood permanently, because he continues forever" (Hebrews 7:24). Jesus alone is able to save those of us who come to God on the basis of His merits. He always lives to intercede for His people. He is doing so, right at this very moment, for you. So you can live confident of access to the heavenly throne room whenever you pray, and access for your soul on the day you die. Today, all you need to do is hold fast to your confession of faith in the Great High Priest, who has done all that is needed.

HEBREWS 7:23-28

SEPTEMBER 11

STORIES OF GOD'S PROVISION

"As for you, you meant evil against me, but God meant it for good, to bring it about that many people should be kept alive, as they are today." GENESIS 50:20

Children who love their grandpas tend to love their grandpas' stories. As Joseph's grandfather, Isaac would surely have had occasion to sit down with him and relay story after story of God's provision—to speak truth into his grandson's life. You and I can only imagine how Joseph must have cherished Isaac's stories and instruction. But the goodness of God to his family in generations past appears to have sustained Joseph even in his most painful moments, for a remarkable truth about this man is that he was always aware that God was in control. Surely Joseph was learning to say, as the psalmist would later sing, "I believe that I shall look upon the goodness of the LORD in the land of the living!" (Psalm 27:13).

Indeed, Joseph was given one opportunity after another to witness God's providential care. As a 17-year-old boy, he saw God at work even in the midst of his brothers' hatred. Reuben's suggestion that they put him in the pit ultimately spared his life, but it was God's intervention that gave Reuben the idea and enabled Joseph's brothers to go along with his plan.

Shortly afterward, an Ishmaelite caravan arrived at just the right time, as if by divine appointment (which it was!) They were doing their business as usual; they could have taken a look at Joseph and said, *Forget it. We don't need him.* Yet God's providence determined that they would buy Joseph.

In each case, God used the selfish interests and desires of others as instruments in saving Joseph's life, and eventually the lives of many.

The truth of Genesis 50:20 is the foundation of Joseph's life: although his brothers intended evil, God intended good—and God's intentions always win out. Joseph's earthly father may have been back in Canaan, but his heavenly Father went with him into Egypt. His path may have been rerouted by the envy of his brothers, the lust of Potiphar's wife, the anger of Potiphar, and the selfishness of the cupbearer, but supremely it was directed by his God, for the good of His people.

Do we treasure this truth about God, as Joseph did? God will accomplish His purposes, even when we have no idea where we are headed or what He is doing. This is our hope in every circumstance. When trials come, then, we must not shun them, since we know they come from the hand of a kind Father and that they somehow further His plans to save and sustain His people. We see the goodness of God in the lives of our spiritual family in generations past—in Scripture and throughout the history of the church. You can be certain that in all your days and doubts, in all your fears and failures, in all your fractured relationships and broken dreams, you remain under His fatherly care.

GENESIS 49:28 – 50:21

SEPTEMBER 12

HE BROUGHT US FORTH

"Of his own will he brought us forth by the word of truth." JAMES 1:18

Johnny Carson, the legendary television host, once described an interaction between a disgruntled teenager and a disappointed father as they warred with one another. The teenager, about to slam the door and storm off, shouted, "I didn't ask to be born!" In response, the father shouted back, "And if you had, I would have said no!"

None of us asked to be born. And in fact, none of us asked to be born again. James points out the humbling truth that our spiritual birth was not something we prompted God to do. In God's goodness, our new birth in Christ was *His* choice, unpressured by our helplessness and unaided by our supposed goodness. He acted solely in accordance with His free, sovereign will. As Jesus put it, "The wind blows where it wishes, and you hear its sound, but you do not know where it comes from or where it goes. So it is with everyone who is born of the Spirit" (John 3:8).

Apart from the work of the Spirit in showing us Christ, our foolish hearts remain darkened, and sin has a deadening effect on our sense of morality. By nature we are lost to sin's grip, desperately needing to know the solution to our predicament but unable even to see what the nature of our predicament is. But even having each become a member of God's family by grace, through faith, we are still sometimes inclined to believe that our salvation is the result of what we did—that we chose, and must continue to choose, to turn away from sin and turn to God in childlike trust. The truth is that it was "of his own will" that God "brought us forth" as we heard and were enabled by Him to respond to "the word of truth." When we put the pieces together, we discover that our choice of Him was and is made possible only by His choice of us.

As the Alec Motyer put it, "It is no more possible for us to be agents or contributors to our new birth than it was for us to be so in our natural birth. All the work, from initial choice to completed deed, is his ... And until his will changes, his word alters or his truth is proved false, my salvation cannot be threatened or forfeited."[104]

What security, peace, and comfort are found in knowing that the goodness of God through Jesus Christ not only *brought* you to repentance and faith but will also *keep* you in the faith! If your faith and salvation depended on you, they would never be secure, and you would always be anxious. But it depends on Him, "with whom there is no variation of shadow due to change" (James 1:17). You did not ask to be born; He willed it. Therefore you can be sure that you are His child—now, tomorrow, each day, and forever.

EZEKIEL 36

104 *The Message of Ecclesiastes,* The Bible Speaks Today (IVP Academic, 1985), p 60.

SEPTEMBER 13

HOW LONG? WHY?

"O Lord, how long shall I cry for help, and you will not hear? Or cry to you 'Violence!' and you will not save? Why do you make me see iniquity, and why do you idly look at wrong?" HABAKKUK 1:2-3

It is tempting to assume we are far removed from the circumstances described in the Old Testament. But as we read Habakkuk's complaint in these verses we can recognize that although we're distanced chronologically and geographically, we are not so far from the situation in which he found himself.

Habakkuk described problems with people *within* God's people. They had strayed from what God had designed for them, and there was no end in sight. Worse, God apparently wasn't intervening. The issue as Habakkuk viewed it was twofold: God's timing (*How long will You tolerate wrong?*) and God's tolerance (*Why do You tolerate it?*). These questions can also be found on the lips of many thoughtful believers today as they look at the church: "How long will *this* go on? Why is it that the good, moral, all-powerful God whom we serve tolerates spiritual and moral dry rot among those who profess to be His followers?"

Have you ever wrestled with these questions? You are not alone; this is not a new issue. God's faithful people have wrestled with it throughout history. Here are two observations that will be beneficial to us as we confront the "How longs" of our lives.

First, we can be thankful that God is not so *un*kind as to answer our prayers in our timeframe. God's delays are always purposeful. His perspective is far more comprehensive than we could ever imagine. He may delay so that He can deal with our selfishness or an area of disobedience in our lives, to teach us how to trust Him or to save us from ourselves. This is one reason why the Bible frequently calls us to wait upon the Lord. Our disappointments, failures, and confusions can be brought under the security of God's eternal purpose.

Second, we can follow the prophet's example in calling on God for help. Habakkuk took his complaint to the only place where we ought to take ours: to the Lord. He recognized what the psalmist says: "My help comes from the Lord, who made heaven and earth" (Psalm 121:2). The Psalms are full of godly believers bringing their confusion and questions to God. This gives us permission to do the same. He understands when we cry out "How long?" and "Why?" His ultimate answer is given to us in Jesus and His triumph. He loves to bring the glimmers of dawn after the darkest of nights. So, as you look at your own heart or life, or at the church, and are moved to ask, "O Lord, how long shall I cry?" you can find solace in words such as these:

God is still on the throne,
And He will remember His own;
Tho' trials may press us and burdens distress us,
He never will leave us alone.[105]

PSALM 121

105 Kittie L. Suffield, "God Is Still on the Throne" (1929).

SEPTEMBER 14

SHARING IN SERVICE

"Concerning our brother Apollos, I strongly urged him to visit you with the other brothers." 1 CORINTHIANS 16:12

The body of Christ is no place for one-man bands, at least when it comes to the work of ministry. The Christian life is a team game, not a competition. The apostle Paul reminds us of this time and time again in his letters to the early church.

Even in the infancy of the Corinthian church, Paul knew turf wars were a threat and that some people favored Apollos's care over his own (1 Corinthians 3:3-7). If Paul himself had been looking out for his own interests and to bolster his own reputation and this church's reliance on him, he could have made certain that Apollos never returned to Corinth. But we read that he didn't do that. Quite the opposite, in fact. All he wanted was for God's people to be ministered to. He knew that ministry was designed to be a shared effort.

God chose to put the early-church ministry team together in wonderful ways. Take Timothy, for example. Paul told the Corinthians, "When Timothy comes, see that you put him at ease among you, for he is doing the work of the Lord, as I am. So let no one despise him. Help him on his way in peace, that he may return to me, for I am expecting him with the brothers" (1 Corinthians 16:10-11). To many, Timothy would have appeared inadequate for service: he was naturally timid (which is likely why Paul reminded the church to treat him kindly), physically frail (he was known to take a little wine for the sake of his stomach), and younger than most (1 Timothy 4:12; 5:23). But Paul knew that God had assigned a task to Timothy, and he meant to help him fulfill it.

A host of others—men and women such as Phoebe, Prisca, Aquila, Fortunatus, and Achaicus—rallied round in ministry with Paul too. None of them looked or acted the same. They weren't gifted in the same ways. But they were still all vital in the work of ministry. The same is true of the church body today: we are all entrusted with different tasks by the Lord. It is therefore crucial that we resist the urge to serve only with those to whom we are most similar or with whom we are most impressed. We shouldn't say, "Well, I only like the way he preaches," "I can listen only to her voice," or "I just don't get on with him." Instead, we should be grateful for all of God's servants.

Most of us will live our lives without anybody knowing about us beyond our immediate circle of influence. But it can be enough for our epitaphs to read, "Here lies So-and-So: a great help to those she knew." Do you believe that "there's a work for Jesus none but you can do"?[106] When God puts His hand on you and assigns you a task, do you take it seriously, even if it seems inconsequential? We are meant to serve Him together in community, as a unified team on behalf of His kingdom. There will be joy and satisfaction in playing your part, and in encouraging others as they play theirs, today.

1 CORINTHIANS 3:1-23

106 Elsie Duncan Yale, "There's a Work for Jesus" (1912).

SEPTEMBER 15

THE ADVANTAGE OF WEAKNESS

"We are powerless against this great horde that is coming against us. We do not know what to do, but our eyes are on you." 2 CHRONICLES 20:12

It doesn't take much for us to see our inadequacies—especially in living for and serving God. When life's circumstances press in on us, we become painfully aware of the challenge set before us and can quickly sense ourselves recoiling from it. We grow weary of people telling us what we can do when we know that we can't; but at the same time we are unwilling to face up to our weakness in a world that calls us to be strong and confident.

If you find yourself in that predicament, take courage. You're not alone.

King Jehoshaphat of Judah was a phenomenon who implemented changes that helped God's people rediscover God's law (2 Chronicles 19). He reminded them of the importance of understanding and obeying God's word so that they could serve God faithfully, wholeheartedly, and courageously.

Nevertheless, Jehoshaphat was not immune to fear. When Judah's enemies threatened his nation, he was acutely aware of their superiority and of the inadequacy of his own people. Yet he also knew that the proper response to inadequacy was to depend entirely upon God. As he confronted the reality of his powerlessness and uncertainty, he kept his gaze firmly fixed above, praying, "We do not know what to do, but our eyes are on you."

When the enemy whispers to us that we are a disaster or completely useless, we can set his lies against the truth of God's word and say, "I am sure of this, that he who began a good work in you will bring it to completion at the day of Jesus Christ" (Philippians 1:6). When we feel that we are powerless in our battle against temptation, we can rest on the truth of God's word and say to ourselves, "God is faithful, and he will not let you be tempted beyond your ability, but with the temptation he will also provide the way of escape, that you may be able to endure it" (1 Corinthians 10:13). When we wonder if we have been left alone, we can be assured that "he has said, 'I will never leave you nor forsake you'" (Hebrews 13:5).

When we admit our weakness, our mighty Savior will use it for our good and His glory. When we do not know what to do, we can keep our eyes on Him and ask Him to guide us and deliver us, just as He did Jehoshaphat and the whole of Judah (2 Chronicles 20:14-17, 22-25).

As with the men and women who served the Lord throughout the Bible, God still chooses to use unlikely, timid, and hesitant people. What set those individuals apart was not their strength or ability or self-confidence but that they were not consumed by their weaknesses; instead, they embraced them and relied on God's power to overcome.

Will you do the same?

2 CHRONICLES 20

Bible Through The Year: Lamentations 1–2; John 6:22-51

SEPTEMBER 16

ETERNAL DIVIDENDS

"Not that I seek the gift, but I seek the fruit that increases to your credit. I have received full payment, and more. I am well supplied, having received from Epaphroditus the gifts you sent, a fragrant offering, a sacrifice pleasing to God."
PHILIPPIANS 4:17-18

Paul's version of "Thank you for your financial support" as he writes to the Philippian church is novel, to say the least: he says that their generosity made him glad not because of what their gifts meant to *him* but because of what their gifts would mean to *them*. He tells them that their giving will be of more benefit to them than to him, the recipient!

Paul's excitement over their generosity flowed from the assurance that they would benefit from it for all of eternity. His confidence was grounded in Jesus' teaching. In Luke's Gospel, for example, Peter had said to Jesus, "See, we have left our homes and followed you" (Luke 18:28). We don't exactly know what Peter's motivation was for this remark, but we do have Jesus' response: He said, "There is no one who has left house or wife or brothers or parents or children, for the sake of the kingdom of God, who will not receive many times more in this time, and in the age to come eternal life" (v 29-30). Jesus was saying that Peter and the other disciples had not given things up so much as invested in their future.

The Bible is absolutely clear concerning both the present day and the nearness of eternity. We find it easy to live in such a way that eternity has no bearing on how we give, think, and live now, but the fact is that eternity could be one breath away for every one of us and that it lasts far longer than this fleeting life. It is therefore fitting to give in anticipation of the rich dividends that will pay out in eternal life.

Our ability to give with open hands and in light of eternity is rooted in the generosity of God Himself, who is *the* great Giver. Perhaps the greatest way we can err in giving is by not giving at all. We might be tempted to think that we can't afford to give—but the truth is, we can't afford *not* to give! As Jesus so lovingly promises us, "Give, and it will be given to you. Good measure, pressed down, shaken together, running over, will be put into your lap. For with the measure you use it will be measured back to you" (Luke 6:38).

So, consider your investments—not in retirement plans, or in the stock market, or in a college fund, but the kind of payment that "increases to your credit" in eternity. There is great gain in gospel giving. Let the life to come determine your spending in your life today, and you will find yourself giving both generously and cheerfully.

2 CORINTHIANS 8:1-15

SEPTEMBER 17

THERE IS NO OTHER

"Turn to me and be saved, all the ends of the earth! For I am God, and there is no other." ISAIAH 45:22

Every day, as dawn approaches, swelling crowds make their way to the banks of the Ganges in India to worship the river and the rising sun. Many scatter the ashes of loved ones on the water in the hope of securing their eternal bliss. Representative of the millions of Hindus in India, these men and women believe that "god" is in everything.

While the sights and sounds of such worship may seem far removed from many of us, in another sense, we are much closer to this than we're prepared to acknowledge.

Look around at our own culture and you'll notice that idolatry and its subtleties are just as prevalent as ever. It is found in the notion that what you believe does not matter, since the great religions of the world "agree on the essentials." Corrupted and diluted varieties of Christianity are abundant, for we are very good at worshiping a "God" we have made up, who just happens to fit with our desires and agree with our choices. And superficial forms of panentheism can be discovered in upscale spas and yoga classes, for we are likewise very good at treating ourselves and our bodies as gods.

In fact, we have hundreds of substitute gods—idols that promise us freedom but, in reality, demean and enslave. Worship sex and it will corrode your ability to love or be loved. Worship alcohol and it will ensnare you. Worship money and it will consume you. Worship your family and you (or they) will collapse under the burden of unfulfilled expectations. Worship any substitute god and you will find that it cannot satisfy.

If we become increasingly entangled with idols, it often accompanies a growing loss of confidence in the Bible as the unerring word of God. When this happens, there's no longer any place for a straightforward declaration of the exclusive claims of Jesus of Nazareth as the second Person of the Trinity, Creator of the universe, resurrected Lord, ascended King, and—someday—returning Christ. So it is an act of grace—albeit an unsettling one—that in His word God says, *I'm commanding you, all people everywhere, to repent, to turn from your little idols, and to worship Me, the Creator, the Sustainer, the Ruler, the Father, the Judge* (see Acts 17:30).

What is the antidote to your heart's continual desire to worship idols, which offend the Lord and cannot save? Simply this: "Turn to me and be saved, all the ends of the earth! For I am God, and there is no other." Identify the idols you are prone to worship and set them alongside the Creator and Sustainer of all things. He is God, and they are not. He can save, and they cannot. Turn once more from them, and to Him.

ISAIAH 45:18-25

SEPTEMBER 18

NOW AND FOREVERMORE

"Then I saw a new heaven and a new earth, for the first heaven and the first earth had passed away, and the sea was no more." REVELATION 21:1

What do we know about Jesus Christ's return? The Bible tells us certain facts that are straightforward. We know that Jesus is going to return personally, physically, visibly, and gloriously. We also know that the timing of His reappearance will be secret, it will be sudden, and it will bring separation between those who are waiting for Him and those who are rejecting Him.

Further, what was declared to the suffering saints in the first century in the book of Revelation is still being declared to us: no one should be alarmed at our world's troubles because Jesus is in control. Christ's reigning power will be established when His kingdom comes in all its permanent fullness, and His return will usher in a new heaven and a new earth.

This idea that heaven can come to earth—that one day the "new Jerusalem" will come "down out of heaven from God" (Revelation 21:2)—is one echoed imperfectly in so many other modern views of the world, especially in the West. Our culture is by nature confident, and so it attempts to restore our world with a little more education, a little more social welfare, and a little more consideration for everyone. No man-made agenda can ever truly accomplish the restoration that our world needs, though. Human effort can improve things, but it cannot perfect things. Heaven will not come to earth until Christ does. Creation is presently held in sin's grip, and only God, at the end of all things, can and will fix it, as His people bow down before the Lamb and declare His praises.

For the time being, you and I live as exiles in a foreign land. We live in a world that's hostile to Christ, hostile to His word, and hostile to a life lived in obedience to Him. The temptation for us, as believers, is to run away and hide, to gather into a little holy huddle and not to concern ourselves with the world. But, as Jeremiah told the exiles in Babylon to seek the welfare of the city they were in (Jeremiah 29:7), so we are to seek the welfare of the world we are in. That requires us to be in this world though not of it, living lives and speaking words that point to a different place.

Rejoicing in the triumphant story of Christ crucified, risen, reigning, and one day returning is what gives us the confidence to point beyond this world. Hope for His return and eternal life in His presence is the perfect motivation for a life of both sustained holiness and zealous evangelism in His name. Look forward now with the eye of faith to His return—and then go and live for the welfare of those around you today.

1 CORINTHIANS 15:50-58

SEPTEMBER 19

A SACRIFICE FROM THE HEART

"By faith Abel offered to God a more acceptable sacrifice than Cain, through which he was commended as righteous, God commending him by accepting his gifts." HEBREWS 11:4

What makes our actions commendable to God?

Genesis 4 recounts the story of the first two children born in this world—Cain and Abel: "In the course of time Cain brought to the LORD an offering of the fruit of the ground, and Abel also brought of the firstborn of his flock and their fat portions. And the LORD had regard for Abel and his offering, but for Cain and his offering he had no regard" (Genesis 4:3-5). It is this sacrifice to which the author of Hebrews refers when he tells us about Abel and his faith.

First of all, he tells us that it was "by faith" that Abel offered a better sacrifice than his brother. It was through this sacrifice that Abel was "commended as righteous." It would be easy to get lost in speculative theories as to why God accepted Abel's actions but not Cain's. But we need to stay focused on the facts that are given—and, at the heart of what we're told, this fact is unequivocal: the actions which God accepts are satisfactory not because of their material content but because they are an outward expression of a devoted and obedient heart.

The reason why Abel's sacrifice was acceptable was not because he offered a beast as opposed to a vegetable. The distinction wasn't between the sacrifices offered but between the sacrificers themselves. John Calvin, commenting on this, notes that Abel's sacrifice was preferred to his brother's for no other reason than "that it was sanctified by faith."[107]

This distinction concurs with what God communicates through the prophets. In Isaiah, for example, God says, "Bring no more vain offerings; incense is an abomination to me. New moon and Sabbath and the calling of convocations—I cannot endure iniquity and solemn assembly" (Isaiah 1:13). It's as if God is saying, *I'm not interested in all the bleating of the calves and the goats and the lambs. I yearn for obedience more than sacrifice* (see 1 Samuel 15:22). *If you want to rely on these works as a means of making yourself acceptable to Me, I want you to know it will never happen.*

"Without faith it is impossible to please God" (Hebrews 11:6, NIV). Our good works are a result of our acceptance by God, not a means *to* acceptance. They are our response to His love, not a means of securing it. If your actions, like Abel's, are ever to bring God glory and pleasure, it will be because they are an outward expression of your love for, devotion to, and personal faith in Him. So today, do not obey Him in order to be accepted by Him or to remain accepted by Him. It is faith that secures that. Equally, do not complacently fall short of obeying Him because you are already accepted by faith. Instead, enjoy your place in His affections and let His pleasure be the motivation for your obedience.

ISAIAH 1:10-20

107 *Commentaries on the Epistle of Paul the Apostle to the Hebrews,* trans. John Owen (Calvin Translation Society, 1853), p 267.

SEPTEMBER 20

ADMITTING WE ARE POOR

"He lifted up his eyes on his disciples, and said: 'Blessed are you who are poor, for yours is the kingdom of God.'" LUKE 6:20

Jesus exalts what the world despises and rejects what it admires.

That is the great challenge of the Beatitudes, and nowhere more so than in Jesus' teaching here on wealth. We live in a world that cries for us to make much of ourselves, particularly in the realm of finances and material wealth. Comfort is king in our consumer culture, and that culture is the water in which we all swim.

So it confronts us that Jesus begins His teaching in this sermon by saying, "Blessed are you who are poor." What is He doing? Is He suggesting that material poverty is somehow the key to salvation? Absolutely not! Rather, He is explaining that those who truly become aware of their *spiritual* poverty will enter the kingdom of God.

There are, of course, those who claim Jesus was teaching that if you're poor, you ought to be really glad because you're automatically a part of the kingdom of heaven. But that kind of poverty is not the key to entry into God's kingdom, nor are riches themselves the main reason for someone's exclusion. Indeed, poor and rich alike are welcomed into the kingdom upon realizing their need for forgiveness and coming to trust in Jesus as their Savior. If this were not the case, then a woman named Lydia, who lived in Philippi as a prosperous merchant, would never have had her eyes and heart opened to the truth of the gospel (Acts 16:11-15). No, it is an awareness of our spiritual poverty apart from Christ that is needed.

It is important to notice, however, that financial poverty may well be a means of spiritual blessing. Such poverty often leads men and women to discover their utter dependence upon God not only for physical and material needs but also for spiritual blessings. For this reason, poverty tends to yield a far greater response to the gospel than affluence. Enjoying plenty materially can so easily blind us to our deepest need: to be brought into the kingdom of God. Wealth is often the ground in which pride blooms, so that our hearts forget that for the rich just as much as for the poor "like a flower of the grass" we "will pass away" (James 1:10).

As John Calvin explained, "He only who is reduced to nothing in himself, and relies on the mercy of God, *is poor in spirit*."[108] Poverty brings its trials; but have you ever realized that wealth does too, in its temptations to pride, self-reliance, and spiritual complacency?

So are we willing to admit our spiritual poverty? Or are we too self-assured and satisfied with our earthly riches? Here is one way to know the true answer to those questions: can your heart echo the prayer of Agur in the Proverbs: "Give me neither poverty nor riches" (Proverbs 30:8)?

LUKE 6:20-36

108 *Commentary on a Harmony of the Evangelists, Matthew, Mark, and Luke,* trans. William Pringle (The Calvin Translation Society, 1845), Vol. 1, p 261 (emphasis added).

SEPTEMBER 21

THE BLESSING OF PERSECUTION

"Blessed are you when people hate you and when they exclude you and revile you and spurn your name as evil, on account of the Son of Man! Rejoice in that day, and leap for joy, for behold, your reward is great in heaven; for so their fathers did to the prophets." LUKE 6:22-23

It is a truth self-evident to almost all of us that it is immensely important for people to like us. So it comes as a shock to learn that Jesus taught emphatically about the blessing we will come to know when others hate us, exclude us, and insult us "on account of the Son of Man."

It's because of our relationship with Jesus that such condemnation comes. In fact, Jesus described something that will be true of every believer: when we stand with Christ, we will be rejected by the world. Jesus develops this truth elsewhere in Scripture. For example, the night before He died, He reminded His followers that the world hated Him before it hated them and that, as His servants, they (and we) must expect the same persecution that our Lord experienced (John 15:18-20).

You may have experienced such persecution at school; maybe you took a stand for the Bible, and then you suddenly found yourself isolated from your peer group. You may have tasted the pain of being ostracized by a friendship group, or passed over for promotion at work, because you had explained to someone who Jesus is, why He died, and what that means. You may even know the pain of being spurned by members of your own family because of your faith. If you stand up and stand out for Christ, then ever so subtly and yet so very clearly the hatred begins to spill out, and the sense of scorn is nearly overwhelming.

There is nothing easy or enjoyable about being maligned or left out when we live in obedience to God. Indeed, there is great heartache that accompanies rejection. How, then, are we to find blessing and comfort in its midst?

We must cling to the truth Jesus speaks of here: that when we find ourselves on the receiving end of the world's hatred as a response to our faithfulness to the Son of Man, nothing has gone wrong: we are, in fact, in a place to know blessing. In other words, this sort of mistreatment is tangible evidence of our genuine faith and relationship with the Lord. Furthermore, Jesus promises that if we acknowledge Him before men, He will also acknowledge us before His Father in heaven (Matthew 10:32).

The man or woman who leads a holy life—who is prepared to speak and obey God's word with boldness and who refuses to seek the nonexistent middle way between an obedient life and a popular one—will eventually collide with the ungodly and incur the enmity of the world. How are you being called to risk rejection in order to speak of Christ or live for Christ? Do not lose heart! Instead, respond to slander against you or dislike of you on account of the gospel by rejoicing, "for behold, your reward is great in heaven." The world has nothing to offer that comes close to comparing with that.

DANIEL 3

SEPTEMBER 22

THE LAW OF LOVE

"I say to you who hear, Love your enemies, do good to those who hate you."
LUKE 6:27

When you read the Bible and it describes Christianity, and then you look at yourself, do you ever wonder whether you're a Christian at all? I know I do.

Neither our assurance as believers nor God's love for us hinges on our ability to live out certain Christian principles; rather, both depend on what Christ has achieved for us on the cross. Even so, the Bible teaches us to look for evidences of our salvation in the present. If we truly are the Father's children, we are bound to display a love for others that resembles Jesus' love for us.

Jesus calls for us to love people in a way that is not related to their attractiveness, merit, or lovability. We know that this is exactly how God loves us—His love is not based on us cleaning up our act, deserving His attention, or demonstrating that we're predisposed towards or useful to Him. None of these things contribute to God's love for us. No—"God shows his love for us in that *while we were still sinners*, Christ died for us" (Romans 5:8, emphasis added).

The greatest measure of our faith, then, is love—love that reflects the love that we have received in such abundance. We engage in *agape* love—unconditional, sacrificial love—because it is an expression of the character of God and all He's done for us. We don't exercise this kind of love for our enemies because we are blind to who they really are but because we have gazed at God's love for us. Jesus says that when we see others as they are—in all of their ugliness and spitefulness, all of their cursing, all of their hatred, and all of their unwillingness to pay us what they owe us—we are to be realistic about all of it, and then love them. *Seeing all of that enmity,* says Jesus, *I want you to love your enemies.*

By nature, we are incapable of displaying such love. But consider the kind of difference we would make to our culture if we were prepared to live out, in both everyday and extraordinary ways, a Christlike love which seeks to do what's best for those who have acted in enmity towards us. That would be revolutionary—without any question at all.

ACTS 9:10-28

SEPTEMBER 23

IMITATING THE FATHER'S MERCY

"Love your enemies, and do good, and lend, expecting nothing in return, and your reward will be great, and you will be sons of the Most High, for he is kind to the ungrateful and the evil. Be merciful, even as your Father is merciful."
LUKE 6:35-36

"Be merciful, even as your Father is merciful" is a summary statement of Jesus' famous teaching in the Beatitudes (Luke 6:20-23) and indeed would be a good motto for every believer's life. These words underscore all that Jesus has previously said concerning how we are to treat others—especially those who hate us on account of our faithfulness to Him (v 22).

This should, however, prompt us to ask: what does being merciful actually look like? As our wise and tender Shepherd, Jesus does not leave us to figure out this principle for ourselves. Rather, He gives us specific instructions on what it means to imitate our merciful heavenly Father.

God "is kind to the ungrateful and the evil." As His children, we must realize that we are called to demonstrate this same kindness by loving our enemies, returning good for evil, and giving to others without expecting anything in return. Notice Jesus lists no exemptions or get-out clauses here.

Having called us to be vessels of God's kindness, Jesus then immediately says that we are not to judge others (Luke 6:37). He is not asking us to suspend our critical faculties in our relationships; we have to use our minds to discern between truth and error or good and evil. Likewise Jesus is not teaching that we are to turn a blind eye to sin or refuse to point out errors. Rather, when Jesus commands us not to judge, He is condemning a spirit of self-righteous, self-exalting, hypocritical, harsh judgmentalism—an approach which seeks to highlight the faults of others and always brings with it the flavor of bitterness.

An unkind spirit completely violates Jesus' exhortation to overflow with mercy towards both friend and enemy. Each of us needs to identify any spirit of judgment we may be harboring, to root it out, and to replace cruelty with kindness and harshness with understanding.

This is how we show to others the kind of mercy that God has shown to us. A (possibly apocryphal) story is told of how, when Queen Elizabeth II was a girl, she and her sister, Margaret, would be told by their mother before they went to a party, "Remember: royal children, royal manners." Their behavior would not make them members of the royal family, but it would demonstrate their membership in that family.

Christian, you and I are members of the royal family of the universe, with the King of creation as our Father. Be sure that your manners reflect who you are and whose you are. Be merciful, even as your Father is merciful.

EPHESIANS 4:25 – 5:2

SEPTEMBER 24

SPEAK LIFE, NOT CONDEMNATION

"Judge not, and you will not be judged; condemn not, and you will not be condemned." LUKE 6:37

The reason we sometimes assume we have the right to condemn another is that it appeals to our sinful nature. If we're honest, the minute we acquire any position of leadership or authority, big or small, it's shocking how quickly we are faced with the temptation to condemn rather than to show mercy.

We must remember that we are not qualified to condemn. Why? Because we cannot read another person's heart. We are unable to assess someone else's motives accurately. God alone can say, "I am he who searches mind and heart, and I will give to each of you according to your works" (Revelation 2:23). Since you and I are not God, we are not to condemn.

One of the ways we easily and often ignore Jesus' command here is with our tongues; we pronounce condemnation by saying things that harm someone's reputation. In Christian circles, we may even have clever ways to make our slander sound like a prayer request or a concern—but in truth, half the time we're delighted to say it: "Did you hear about *her*? Do you know about *him*? Do you know why they did *that*?" The spirit of the Pharisee—of condemning others in order to show ourselves in a better light by comparison—is alive and well among believers.

Therefore, we must be exceptionally wary of how we use our words. Rather than using our mouths to condemn, we must ask the Holy Spirit to enable us to speak words of life. Before we open our mouths, we ought to heed the advice of the missionary Amy Carmichael and ask: Is what I'm about to say kind? Is it true? Is it necessary? Scripture is absolutely clear on this point. Indeed, the book of Proverbs teaches us that "a fool's mouth is his ruin, and his lips are a snare to his soul," but "he who is trustworthy in spirit keeps a thing covered" (Proverbs 18:7; 11:13).

We have in Jesus a Savior whose blood cleanses us from the sin of every careless word and every condemning comment—a Savior who forgives us from the sinful tendency that rises in our hearts to try to play a role which is His alone. In light of that, we need to repent daily of the sins of our lips and ask the Spirit for a renewed desire to make both the words of our mouths and the meditations of our hearts acceptable in our Father's sight (Psalm 19:14).

LUKE 6:37-45

SEPTEMBER 25

THE IMMENSITY OF FORGIVENESS

"Forgive, and you will be forgiven; give, and it will be given to you."
LUKE 6:37-38

Nothing will corrupt our hearts and our thinking faster than an unforgiving heart. But the reverse is also true: nothing grants freedom, joy, and peace of heart and mind more quickly than the genuine experience of offering forgiveness. Indeed, our readiness to forgive is a litmus test of our spiritual status; when we forgive from the heart, we provide evidence that we actually are sons and daughters of the Most High (Luke 6:35).

Jesus often places our being forgiven and our willingness to forgive next to each other (see Luke 11:4). So when we think about practicing forgiveness, we first have to ask where we can find it. The answer is that the source of all true forgiveness is found in God alone. Indeed, out of the abundance of God's mercy comes forgiveness.

That forgiveness is as indispensable to the life and health of our souls as food is to our physical bodies. Scripture is filled with reminders that point to God as one who forgives. The psalmist says, "If you, O LORD, should mark iniquities, O Lord, who could stand? But with you there is forgiveness" (Psalm 130:3-4). Similarly, the prophet Daniel says, "To the Lord our God belong mercy and forgiveness" (Daniel 9:9). The divine Son of God, as He was spat upon and mocked, stripped of His clothes, beaten, nailed to a cross between two criminals, and abandoned in agony declared, "Father, forgive them" (Luke 23:34). God's spirit of forgiveness knows no rival.

As God's children by faith in Christ, we are to imitate our Father and our Lord by practicing forgiveness. It is so integral to the life of the true Christian that Jesus goes as far as to say that if we are not willing to forgive, then we should ask ourselves very seriously whether we are truly forgiven: that is, whether we have really grasped the gospel in our hearts (see Matthew 6:14-15). If you are harboring unforgiveness in your heart, do not excuse or belittle it. Instead, bring the gospel to it. Reflect on the immensity of what you have been forgiven through Christ. Reflect on the forgiving nature of your Father, whom you are called to reflect in your life. Recognize the corrupting, life-draining burden of unforgiveness. Specify what you need to do, and for whom. That is the path to enjoying the peace and freedom of forgiving just as you have been forgiven.

LUKE 7:36-50

SEPTEMBER 26

THE SPECK AND THE LOG

"How can you say to your brother, 'Brother, let me take out the speck that is in your eye,' when you yourself do not see the log that is in your own eye? You hypocrite, first take the log out of your own eye, and then you will see clearly to take out the speck that is in your brother's eye." LUKE 6:42

I recall a time when, sitting at a desk in an exam, I turned the paper over and immediately began to look around to see if everybody else felt as bad about the first question as I did. Then I was startled by the teacher's exhortation: "Never mind looking at others. Just concentrate on yourself!"

Jesus makes a similar point in these verses, using a striking metaphor to instruct His listeners to deal with their own sin before they attempt to point out the sins of others. The word Jesus uses for "speck" often describes very small bits and pieces of straw or wood. In contrast, the word for "log" refers to a load-bearing beam in a house or structure. If I have a log in my eye, it clearly requires my attention more than a speck in someone else's does.

As fallen creatures, we're prone to think it's our responsibility to deal with everybody else's spiritual condition before dealing with our own. Yet Christ hasn't called us to be preoccupied primarily and initially with the specks of others. No, He says we must be diligent in examining *ourselves* in light of Scripture and the standard that He has set.

Jesus' instruction poses a great challenge. Sometimes we may point out the faults of others under the guise of caring about their spiritual condition. But if we have not first been honest about and ruthless with our own sins, that is hypocrisy! We often fall prey to the mistaken notion that if I can find your flaw and deal with you, then I won't have to deal with my own issues. It's far more pleasant to tell someone else about their dreadful condition than it is to face our own.

If we truly want to help others, then we must first be prepared to face the dreadfulness of our own hearts—to acknowledge with Robert Murray M'Cheyne that "the seeds of all sins are in my heart."[109] When we understand and believe that, then when we go to approach others we will stand on the low ground of genuine love and humility rather than the high ground of presumption. Between those two perspectives there's all the difference in the world.

JUDE 20-25

109 Quoted in Andrew Bonar, *Memoir and Remains of Robert Murray M'Cheyne* (Banner of Truth, 1995), p 153.

SEPTEMBER 27

KNOWN BY THEIR FRUIT

"No good tree bears bad fruit, nor again does a bad tree bear good fruit, for each tree is known by its own fruit." LUKE 6:43-44

Students will always reflect the instruction of their teachers. No matter how far a student may excel beyond his or her teacher's abilities, they will always be indebted to the guidance that was given.

When Jesus spoke of trees and their fruit, it was with an eye to the spiritual leaders of His day. In making His point, He gave us a warning: namely, not to choose the wrong teacher. And how are we to discern between good and bad teachers? Jesus says it's by their fruit—the results that follow their teachings and actions.

We must think of fruit in relation to the teacher's character—and character can't be tested by measuring eloquence or giftedness. Rather, when Jesus gave instruction concerning the vine and the branches, He implied that fruitfulness equals Christlikeness (John 15:1-8). Each tree is recognized by its own fruit; therefore, the fruit of the Spirit—love, joy, peace, patience, gentleness, kindness, goodness, faithfulness, and self-control (Galatians 5:22-23)—will be evident in a good teacher's life.

We must also examine the content of the teacher's instruction. Paul addressed this issue when he wrote to his pastoral protégé Timothy, telling him to "keep a close watch on yourself"—that is, his character—"and on the teaching" (1 Timothy 4:16). Not everybody who shows up with a Bible has the listener's best interests at heart. Not everybody who names the name of Christ is a true teacher of God's word. False prophets abound. It is imperative, then, that as believers, we learn from the Bible not only to grow in holiness but also to be able to recognize sound doctrine, which is a mark of a godly teacher. Furthermore, we can take comfort from the indwelling of the Holy Spirit, who teaches us about everything and enables us to distinguish between truth and falsehood (see 1 John 2:27).

There is a direct correlation between the character of a teacher and the content of his teaching, and the impact he makes upon those who are taught. So choose your spiritual teachers and mentors wisely. Look not at their speaking gifts or their cultural connectedness or their confidence or their humor but at character and content. Without question, you will show the world the fruit of the teaching you receive. When people come around you, what will they discover? Will they see judgmentalism or bitterness or haughtiness or self-righteousness? Will they sense passivity and a lack of conviction? Or will they taste the sweet fruit of joy, peace, love, and righteousness?

2 TIMOTHY 2:15-26

SEPTEMBER 28

EVIDENCE OF GENUINE FAITH

"Why do you call me 'Lord, Lord,' and not do what I tell you? Everyone who comes to me and hears my words and does them, I will show you what he is like: he is like a man building a house, who dug deep and laid the foundation on the rock." LUKE 6:46-48

Jesus wants to see our lips and our lives align. Hence he ends His Sermon on the Plain with this most searching of rhetorical questions: "Why do you call me, 'Lord, Lord,' and not do what I tell you?" He saw a contrast between what people were saying and how they were behaving, and He wanted to call them to perform a serious spiritual self-examination. He wanted them, just as He wants us, to see that a verbal profession of faith in Him must be accompanied by moral obedience to Him.

Jesus did not teach that entry into the kingdom of heaven is through the good works of obedience. Salvation is by grace alone, through faith alone, plus nothing (see Ephesians 2:8). All that we bring to Christ is the sin from which we need to be forgiven. What, then, is He teaching? Simply this: that only those who obey Him—those who express their faith *by* their works—have truly heard and have been transformed by the gospel. As the Reformers observed, it is faith alone that saves, but the faith that saves is not alone. The apostle John, picking up on Jesus' words, says in his first letter, "If we say we have fellowship with him while we walk in darkness, we lie and do not practice the truth" (1 John 1:6). Scripture makes it clear that the manner in which we hear and obey Jesus' words has significance for all of eternity because it reveals the true state and reality of our faith.

No accumulation of visible religious works and no number of religious words will be able to disguise our private behavior from God. The real test of those who name the name of the Lord, says Paul—and let's not evade for one instant the chilling demand of this—is that they "depart from iniquity" (2 Timothy 2:19). Therein lies the evidence of genuine faith.

While none of us will live a perfect life, we are all called to live changed lives. We live under the lordship of Christ; His Spirit is now within us. Will we have complete success? No. But we will be different, and our lives will increasingly demonstrate that we have "turned to God from idols to serve the living and true God" (1 Thessalonians 1:9). So consider your own life. Do you call Jesus Lord? Good! But, crucially, can you point to evidence in your life—in what you do not do and in what you do, in the temptations you fight and the virtues you strive for and the forgiveness you repentantly ask for—that He is truly *your* Lord?

JAMES 2:14-26

SEPTEMBER 29

OUR COMPASSIONATE SHEPHERD

"When the Lord saw her, he had compassion on her and said to her, 'Do not weep.' Then he came up and touched the bier, and the bearers stood still. And he said, 'Young man, I say to you, arise.'" LUKE 7:13-14

The coming of the kingdom of God was not heralded by spectacular and dramatic victories over the powers and authorities of the world but through something much more transformative: the great compassion of its King.

Throughout their accounts of Jesus, the Gospel writers present us with encounter after encounter demonstrating Christ's unparalleled compassion. In these incidents, Christ's power is revealed as His compassion is extended. In chapter 7 of his Gospel, for instance, Luke highlights Jesus' compassionate response to a sorrowful widow—a response which clears any doubts about His greatness.

The woman in this part of Luke's narrative was in true need. Her husband was already gone, and now her son had just died. In an ancient Middle-Eastern society, this meant that she had no means of protection or provision. She faced a life of sadness, loneliness, and precariousness—and then the end of the family line.

But then Jesus entered into the extremity of this woman's life, and "when the Lord saw her, he had compassion on her and said to her, 'Do not weep.'"

All it took to arouse the compassion of our tender Shepherd was seeing this grieving woman. Literally, that word "compassion" means "His bowels moved"—our equivalent would be "His stomach churned." When Jesus, through whom and for whom all things were created, sees sadness and grief in this broken world, He *feels* it. Here is a King who cares deeply.

Even more beautiful is that Jesus had the power to meet this widow's need, and so He chose to do something only He could do: to bring the dead back to life. He didn't just restore a deceased son alive again to a mourning mother and thereby meet her need and obliterate her grief, though. More importantly, Jesus revealed Himself to the crowd (and to us!) in all of His power, kindness, and authority—even authority over death.

Scenes such as this show us that Jesus doesn't simply comment on or cry over sickness and death, those great enemies of mankind. He overcomes them. He hears the cries of the sorrowful, and He comforts them, not only in an earthly, temporal sense but also in a final, perfect, and eternal way, by offering Himself as the means of salvation to all who believe.

Your King is not merely infinitely powerful; He is infinitely compassionate. And the combination of those two qualities in Him is sufficient to bring you through every sadness and grief of this world, until you stand in His presence and He wipes every tear from your eye.

LUKE 7:1-17

SEPTEMBER 30

ONE MIND, ONE PURPOSE, ONE SPIRIT

"Complete my joy by being of the same mind, having the same love, being in full accord and of one mind. Do nothing from selfish ambition or conceit, but in humility count others more significant than yourselves." PHILIPPIANS 2:2-3

While it is of course beneficial for church members to take initiative in ministry, a healthy body of believers will not be driven by individual ideas and agendas. Our minds must first be united in the gospel if the church is truly going to be under Christ's headship. Without that unity, we will instead be driven by our own selfish and competing desires and agendas.

The Bible has so much to say about our minds because as we think, so we are. When we train our minds to think correctly, we will then learn to love properly and serve together in one spirit and purpose. Part of our mental battle is rooted in our old, selfish, human nature. One of our greatest stumbling blocks is not so much hate as self-love: we are inclined toward an attitude of conceit, which runs completely counter to the character of our Lord, and our lack of humility becomes an obstacle that prevents us from experiencing harmony with those around us. Even our good deeds often have tainted motives.

If we are to be unified in Christ, we cannot insist on our own way. Instead, we need to "count others more significant than ourselves." This means that we remind ourselves of the best in others before thinking of ourselves, that we are quicker to ask what would be best for others than what would be most convenient for ourselves, and that we are willing to enter into the lives and struggles of others rather than standing aloof. Genuine humility doesn't take the front seat or begin with "me" all the time. It is instead "the nothingness that makes room for God to prove his power."[110] It is a trait, Paul tells us, that Jesus Himself exhibited: "Let each of us please his neighbor for his good, to build him up. For Christ did not please himself" (Romans 15:2-3).

When we think of ourselves first, it is difficult—impossible, in fact—to put God's word into action. But when we learn to put others first, we will be far more ready to care for their concerns before our own. In so doing, we can truly be unified within the body of Christ. You likely know people who exhibit this kind of godly humility. Praise God for them now, and pray that you will see how you can follow their example—and, supremely, follow the example of Christ Himself. He counted what you needed as of greater significance than His own comfort—even than His own life. Paul's challenge to each of us is this: "Have the same mindset as Christ Jesus" (Philippians 2:5, NIV).

JOHN 3:22-36

110 Andrew Murray, *Humility: The Beauty of Holiness,* 2nd ed. (1896), p 50.

OCTOBER 1

BODY AND SOUL

"When I kept silent, my bones wasted away through my groaning all day long. For day and night your hand was heavy upon me; my strength was dried up as by the heat of summer." PSALM 32:3-4

Those who work in the fields of psychology, psychiatry, and social services are often confronted with a strong correlation between what is happening in a person's heart and mind and what is being displayed in that person's body. God's word speaks into this connection and then goes deeper, for it tells us that there is a connection between the state of our body and the state of our soul.

In Psalm 32, David speaks very personally to God, acknowledging the heaviness he experienced when he hid in the shadows and refused to confess his sin against Bathsheba and the murder of her husband, Uriah (see 2 Samuel 11). And through David, the Spirit teaches us that there is a link between a tortured conscience and lack of repentance, and our physical wellbeing. Those who were in David's immediate company may not have been aware of what was going on inside him spiritually, but they could not have avoided the indications of what was happening to him physically.

The description he provides adds to the account he gives elsewhere: "My heart throbs; my strength fails me, and the light of my eyes—it also has gone from me. My friends and companions stand aloof from my plague, and my nearest kin stand far off" (Psalm 38:10-11). It's a quite devastating picture.

David recognized his condition for what it was: a punishment. The Bible makes it clear that there is a natural outcome to lust, excess, and a disregard for the commands of God (see Romans 1:24-25)—all of which David was guilty of. Frailty, weight loss, sleeplessness, a sense of rejection, melancholy, anxiety, and despair often haunt individuals who are seeking to hide their sin from God and deny it to themselves.

What restored David was not a health kick or getting to bed earlier but rather dealing with the root cause—his sin: "I acknowledged my sin to you ... and you forgave the iniquity of my sin" (Psalm 32:5). God kept His hand heavy upon David until David placed his sin into God's hands and asked Him to deal with it. It is a blessing to us when God does not allow us to forget our sin—when we feel physical heaviness because of our spiritual sickness. It is His means of bringing us to do what we most need: to confess it and ask for forgiveness for it.

Are you harboring sin? Do not cloak it; confess it. David experienced liberating relief from his pain and distress when he sought God's forgiveness. You too can know that joy, for the promise of God's word is that "if we confess our sins, he is faithful and just to forgive us our sins and to cleanse us from all unrighteousness" (1 John 1:9).

PSALM 51

OCTOBER 2

THE PROMISE OF RESTORATION

"The mystery of his will, according to his purpose, which he set forth in Christ [is] a plan for the fullness of time, to unite all things in him, things in heaven and things on earth." EPHESIANS 1:9-10

In his essay "On Fairy Stories," J.R.R. Tolkien writes about the reasons why people are drawn to fairy tales. Such stories are often at the opposite end of the emotional spectrum to our daily news: instead of war, financial volatility, pandemic, and heartbreak, fairy tales offer happy endings that reflect the longings of the human heart. Tolkien suggests that at the root of those longings is an ache for Christ to set the world right—to unite all things, restore all things, and make the world as absolutely, perfectly beautiful as it was before Adam's rebellion. Don't you yearn for God to fix it all? Don't you long for the happy ending?

Laced all throughout Scripture, as through our lives, are reminders that we are not there yet. We live in a fallen world, fraught with alienation, frustration, and disintegration. The first Adam sinned, and death and chaos followed. But a second Adam came to undo what Adam had done and to accomplish what no one else could. God will fix it all. In fact, He has already begun to.

Throughout his letters to the first-century churches, Paul recognized their hardships and never downplayed them; but he also always reminded his readers that there would be a day "when sufferings cease and sorrows die," and all our longings are satisfied.[111] He encouraged them to keep their eyes on what was ultimate to help them deal with the immediate challenges.

What they needed then is what we need now. If you focus only on what you see right in front of you and neglect to allow God's promise of restoration to enter your vision, you won't actually be able to deal with the issues you face. They will grow out of perspective. They will come to dominate. They will drain you of hope and happiness. No—whether the problems are global, national, or personal, the best strategy is to keep your eyes on what God's word says about God's plan. There will be a happy ending. There will be a time when all things are united under a perfect King.

What is troubling you today? Bring an eternal perspective to the affairs of time, with the help of the Spirit, and you can find security in His perfect plan. You can't yet know all the details of the story of this world, but you can know that for those who trust in Christ, the final scene is a happy, endless ending—and that it is no fairy story.

ISAIAH 65:17-25

111 Stuart Townend, "There Is a Hope" (2007).

OCTOBER 3

DEVOTED TO THE WORD OF GOD

"'We will devote ourselves to prayer and to the ministry of the word.' And what they said pleased the whole gathering." ACTS 6:4-5

While the Spirit-filled events of Pentecost and the resulting ministry were extraordinary, the apostles and their followers did not begin saying afterward, *Well, now the Spirit of God teaches me; therefore, I don't need to listen to anybody else.* Instead, when filled with the Holy Spirit, they were all ears for the authoritative preaching and teaching of God's word. This teaches us an important lesson: the Spirit of God always leads the people of God to devote themselves to the word of God.

This is why the book of Acts is full of the centrality of preaching. The apostles recognized that God's supreme instrument for renewing His people in the image of His Son was and is through His word, as His Spirit works through it. Here in Acts 6 we see an example of the priority and protection the apostles gave to those called and equipped to teach. The apostles recognized the sobering importance of being entrusted as servants to bring before the people the very words of God Himself.

The Old Testament books refer to the "oracles" of the prophets; this word can also be translated as "burden" (see, for instance, Isaiah 13:1, KJV). It describes a weight upon the heart and mind that comes about because of the awesome responsibility of speaking God's truth to people. Back in the nineteenth century C.H. Spurgeon acknowledged this burden by declaring his pulpit to be more influential than the throne of the king of England, for he brought a message from the throne of God to that pulpit and delivered the truth of Christian doctrine.

We must pray for and protect those called to teach the truths of Scripture, whether to a congregation, or to little children, or in any other context. It is no small thing to stand regularly between a holy God and His people, declaring His word. It is a heavy burden as well as a wonderful privilege.

In addition to praying for our teachers and preachers, we must also be humble and eager to sit and learn under the authoritative teaching of God's word. Such an example of devotion was set by the early church in their dedication to the apostles' teaching (Acts 2:42). Contemporary devotion ought to look the same; we must be committed to teaching that is based on the New Testament truths revealed to the apostles and built upon the foundations of Old Testament doctrine. We must not be spending all our time snacking on the fast food of box sets that soak up our time, TV networks that confirm what we already think, and books or video games that offer escape from the real world. Instead, we need to feast on the word of God. Let that be your spiritual food and you will find each day that the Spirit of God leads you deeper into the truths and the joys within it.

PSALM 119:81-96

OCTOBER 4

THE SHAKY ROCK

"When they had finished breakfast, Jesus said to Simon Peter, 'Simon, son of John, do you love me more than these?' He said to him, 'Yes, Lord; you know that I love you.' He said to him, 'Feed my lambs.'" JOHN 21:15

Jesus' appearance on the beach in John 21 occurred after His resurrection and therefore after His crucifixion and all the events surrounding it—including Peter's cowardly denial of even knowing Christ. We can safely assume that Peter felt shame at his failure of loyalty and faith. We can just imagine him confiding to the other disciples, *I had my chance, and I blew it. I betrayed Him. Here I am, the one who thought he would play the hero, standing as a testimony of the worst cowardice.* So, as Jesus spoke to him, surely Peter wondered, *What will He say? What part do I have in His people now?*

Jesus didn't write off Peter's failure; He acknowledged it. After their meal together, Jesus addressed Peter by his old name, Simon, which means "listen." At the beginning of His ministry, Jesus had changed Simon's name to Peter, which means "rock" (John 1:42). This change symbolized a shift that would occur in Simon Peter's character and calling: he was shaky, but he would become firm like a rock. There on the shore, however, Jesus wanted to remind Peter of his shakiness. Before Peter could become steady, he needed to understand that his behavior had displayed neither a firm faith nor any measurable boldness rooted in Christ's love.

Like Peter, you and I will sometimes feel sidelined by our failures, our backsliding, our unbelief. We will feel the ache of a dislocated faith; we will need the Master Surgeon to reach out and put our love back in place, sometimes painfully but always restoratively. Notice that it is indeed Peter's heart, his love and devotion, that Jesus is most concerned about. Other qualities are desirable and necessary, yes, but it is our love for Christ that is indispensable. Where is *our* love? Is it built on shaky sand or on a firm rock?

Yet even as Christ puts our love back in alignment, He entrusts us with kingdom work. Jesus still chose to use Peter to build His church. How surprising that Jesus entrusted His "lambs" to the disciple who (with the exception of Judas) had most let him down and in whom was the greatest gap between profession and action. But how encouraging for us that Jesus would do so: for if He was willing to use someone like Peter, He will be willing to use someone like me and you. Jesus still chose to give Peter great responsibility, but that responsibility was meant to test Peter as well. The test of love for Jesus is whether a life displays obedience and action. The book of Acts shows how Peter, with the enabling of God's Spirit, responded to the test.

The story of Peter, the shaky rock, stands as a reminder to us that God is a God of grace and second chances. Our weaknesses reveal our need for a strength that is not our own, a measure of might that is found only in our great Rock of Ages. Therefore, knowing that such strength is available to us from the Savior who died for us and commissions us in His service, you can walk into your day and do His bidding out of love for Him.

ACTS 5:17-42

OCTOBER 5

SPIRIT-FILLED BOLDNESS

"But if you are afraid to go down, go down to the camp with Purah your servant. And you shall hear what they say, and afterward your hands shall be strengthened to go down against the camp." JUDGES 7:10-11

It is always easier to hang back in fear than to move forward in faith: easier, but never better.

Gideon knew a lot about fear and the hesitation it birthed. He hesitated when God's angel called him to lead Israel (Judges 6:13, 15). He hesitated when Israel's enemies gathered to oppose him (v 36-40). And, it seems, he hesitated again the night before the battle in which God had promised victory (7:9-10). And into this fear and hesitancy, God spoke. God's grace and patience is clear as He says, "But if you are afraid..." and encourages Gideon to take his servant down to the camp with him. This is a sensitive way to address his fear. It recognizes that, humanly speaking, there was great reason to be afraid! Gideon was about to go into battle against an army that outnumbered his by tens of thousands. God didn't rebuke him for his fear; instead, He gave him a reason to be confident.

Like Gideon, we need such kind words from our Lord. We are often slow to remember that we can cast all our cares on Him (1 Peter 5:7). We can lay down all of our burdens and fears at His feet. We're permitted to come to Him and say that we don't know what to do. And His response is always filled with grace and sensitivity towards us.

What makes this story even more beautiful is Gideon's response to God's gentle suggestion. During his discreet visit to the enemy camp, he overhears two men discussing a dream, which one soldier interprets as meaning that they will fall under "the sword of Gideon" because "God has given into his hand Midian and all the camp" (Judges 7:14). When Gideon hears that and realizes that God has indeed gone before him to do what is impossible for him to do alone, what does he do? "He worshiped" (v 15). There's such wealth contained in that response. Facing impossible odds but assured of God's promise, this fearful, fragile, unlikely leader poured out his heart in praise, and then utilized his God-given courage to rally his troops. His boldness came from a private, secret moment between him and the Lord.

There's a difference between personality-driven schemes for manipulating people and genuine, Spirit-filled boldness. One is produced on a purely human plane and is apt to crumble; the other can be discovered only as we humble ourselves before God, acknowledge our inadequacy, and remember His sufficiency. That is a firm place on which to take our stand. The antidote to fear isn't to think more highly of yourself, as so many claim. It's to think more highly of God. It's to trust in God's enablement, which can grant you a holy, humble boldness beyond compare.

What are you fearful of right now? How are you tempted to hang back even though God is calling you to walk forward in obedience? Bring your fears to God. Ask Him to show you His ability to do what you can't. Then trust Him, worship Him, and obey Him.

JOSHUA 1:1-11

OCTOBER 6

THE DOCTRINE OF SCRIPTURE

"The sacred writings ... are able to make you wise for salvation through faith in Christ Jesus. All Scripture is breathed out by God and profitable for teaching, for reproof, for correction, and for training in righteousness, that the man of God may be complete, equipped for every good work." 2 TIMOTHY 3:15-17

The authority, sufficiency, infallibility, and inerrancy of Scripture are doctrines that are absolutely foundational to the ongoing work of God and His church. We cannot engage a lost and hurting world with the gospel unless we are convinced of its divine origin. As J.C. Ryle wrote, without the Bible as a "divine book to turn to as the basis of their doctrine and practice," Christians "have no solid ground for present peace or hope, and no right to claim the attention of mankind."[112]

Paul addressed this very issue when he reminded Timothy that "all Scripture is breathed out by God." In other words, the Bible is not a human product infused with divinity; it's a divine gift produced through human instrumentality. Its every book, chapter, sentence, and syllable was originally given by God's inspiration.

The doctrine of Scripture, like many other Christian doctrines, can be challenging to grapple with. But the fact that something is difficult to understand does not undermine its truthfulness. Furthermore, when it comes to the doctrine of Scripture, there *are* matters that we can consider objectively. For example, it's easy to see that the Bible is a completely harmonious work. While it was written by more than thirty authors over a period of about fifteen hundred years, all the writers tell the same story, giving the same account of this world, the character of its Creator, and the problem of the human heart, and pointing to the same wonderful way of salvation through the sacrifice of the Lamb of God—all the way from Genesis to Revelation!

The Bible also transcends time, culture, gender, and intellect. Some books may fit a certain person, a certain era, or a certain place, but there is no other book that perfectly stands up to the challenges of every day and every age and to the questions that confront life itself. The brightest minds cannot exhaust the riches of God's word, and yet, at the same time, even young girls and boys can read their Bibles and discover its truth transforming their lives.

The authority, sufficiency, infallibility, and inerrancy of Scripture are the grounds on which we must stand; and we have divine help in order to do so. The same Spirit that inspired the word of God illumines the word of God and convinces us that it *is* the word of God, given to us so that we may believe in Him who is the Word made flesh. It is as the Spirit does this work in you that your belief in the divine authorship of Scripture is undergirded and moves from only being an intellectual assent to a doctrine to an active hunger for more of the word—and more of the one who is both its author and its subject.

PSALM 12

112 *Bible Inspiration: Its Reality and Nature* (William Hunt, 1877), p 6.

OCTOBER 7

A DISTINGUISHED LIFE

"Daniel became distinguished above all the other high officials and satraps, because an excellent spirit was in him. And the king planned to set him over the whole kingdom. Then the high officials and the satraps sought to find a ground for complaint against Daniel with regard to the kingdom, but they could find no ground for complaint or any fault, because he was faithful, and no error or fault was found in him." DANIEL 6:3-4

After being seized and taken away into captivity in Babylon, Daniel became part of a select group of outstanding young Israelite men who were chosen to be part of King Nebuchadnezzar's court. Though he was taken into exile, given a different name, and distanced by many miles from familiarity and family, through it all Daniel purposed in his heart that he would not defile himself with the king's food and drink (Daniel 1:12-16). He stood out as a man of integrity amid the moral decay of his time.

Daniel distinguished himself within the structure of the governments he served by the quality of his life. Over many years, his loyalty proved to be unquestionable. He was a man of consistency, which he displayed through a succession of kingdoms. He had an extraordinary capacity for facing and overcoming difficulties, as well as God-given wisdom which enabled him to provide counsel that would alter the course of human history.

While the governmental positions that Daniel occupied were susceptible to corruption, he distinguished himself by saying no to all kinds of dishonesty. He was neither negligent nor unethical, nor was there a gap between his public activities and his private life. He was blameless in the eyes of his fellow man. Even colleagues who were jealous and despised him because of his distinctiveness could find no ground for complaint.

Filled with envy, these officials eventually decided to plot against Daniel. They didn't like his unswerving commitment to his God or the fact that he occupied a position of power. They couldn't handle the way that he displayed through his life an unshakable conviction regarding the might and purity of God. Holy living often brings that kind of disdain. Daniel was framed not because he was a bad fellow but because he stood for truth. He loved what God loves, and he lived it out.

Is your life marked by a similar conviction? Do your actions declare the truth about your God? Are you prepared to diligently cultivate a passion for integrity? Are you more concerned with obeying God than with what others think of you? Jesus warned His followers that they would be reviled and would experience persecution for His sake (Matthew 5:11) even as they lived in a way that revealed and commended their Father (v 14-16). Live with the kind of devotion that Daniel had; be unequivocal in your commitment to love what God loves, and then live it out.

1 PETER 2:9-17

OCTOBER 8

OVERCOMING FRICTION

"Walk in a manner worthy of the calling to which you have been called, with all humility and gentleness, with patience, bearing with one another in love, eager to maintain the unity of the Spirit in the bond of peace." EPHESIANS 4:1-3

One of the by-products of friction is heat: when two or more objects rub against each other, the temperature increases. Likewise, when you put sinful people together—even in the church, where sin no longer reigns but still remains—there is bound to be friction. We shouldn't be surprised by this. We're not perfectly created bricks that are all beautifully positioned to fit together. We're rough, imperfect people. But equally, we must not allow friction to distract us from our ultimate focus.

Friction will not disappear by being ignored; instead, it is overcome as we focus on Christ and value what He values for the body of believers: priorities like hospitality, bearing one another's burdens, mutual encouragement, prayer, and giving. These values do not push us to ask "What can the body of Christ do for *me*?" but "What can *I* do for the body of Christ?" Only when we work from that perspective will our self-pity, aggravations, and concerns begin to melt away.

While friction should be expected, then, it should not be tolerated. As believers, we should show evidence of humble, repentant hearts. When we don't, it is right for others in the church to help us and, if necessary, lovingly to challenge and discipline us. Church leaders during the Reformation said that for a church to be a true church, there had to be the preaching of God's word, the celebration of the sacraments, and the exercise of church discipline.

Tolerating unrepentant divisiveness in a church not only allows the heat caused by friction to go unchecked but can lead to destruction. We wouldn't let someone sit at our dining-room tables and destroy our families because they had a bad attitude; yet how easy it is to tolerate friction and division in the church for the sake of appearing to be a nice, cozy place. But we must take the harder path. The future of the church depends on it.

Friction will come. We will mess up. So we are going to need to bear with one another in love. We are going to have to be patient toward each other. We are going to need to "make every effort" to maintain the unity the Spirit brings us into when He brings us into God's family by faith (Ephesians 4:3, NIV). In other words, we are going to need to be Christlike, for it is His selfless *agape* love that shows us how to sacrificially love one another and overcome conflict. Unity is a precious gift, and therefore friction needs to be addressed—gently and patiently, but addressed nonetheless. Perhaps there is someone you need to speak with today. Perhaps today there is someone you need to show repentance to, or offer forgiveness to, or walk alongside to help them resolve their friction with another church member.

JAMES 3:13-18

◇ Bible Through The Year: Ezekiel 45–46; John 19:23-42

OCTOBER 9

GUARANTEED WITH AN OATH

"When God desired to show more convincingly to the heirs of the promise the unchangeable character of his purpose, he guaranteed it with an oath, so that by two unchangeable things, in which it is impossible for God to lie, we who have fled for refuge might have strong encouragement to hold fast to the hope set before us. We have this as a sure and steadfast anchor of the soul."

HEBREWS 6:17-19

An oath should carry great weight for both the person making it and the person receiving it. It's a decisive appeal to the highest power available, intended to end all doubt over someone's word and confirm the reliability of the promise being made. Though people have repeatedly made nonsense of oaths through lying and perjury, they are still meant to demonstrate the integrity of one's word.

An oath is, of course, only as good as the character of the individual making it. Therefore, we know that God's promises are trustworthy if for no other reason than the fact that *He* made them. He didn't need to guarantee His promise with an oath; the bare promise of God to His people is sufficient to command our belief. Yet He went a step further, swearing by Himself, since He cannot swear by anyone or anything greater.

God has brought us from the realm of hopelessness into the reality of hope, and the anchor of our souls is secure and certain. It is fixed to an immovable object—the promises of God—and fixed in the unseen heavenly realm by the God who cannot lie. These promises are so secure, in fact, that sharing them with others in evangelism is compelling to them, because we live in a world that is full of desperation and a culture that tries to cover its discontentedness with fake smiles, vacations, and material gain.

How wonderful that we can be people who are grounded in faith, anchored by the promises of our God. Jesus Christ is worthy of our trust, and we can know that "all the promises of God find their Yes in him" (2 Corinthians 1:20), whose life, death, resurrection, and ascension have achieved for us a momentous and eternal victory.

Which promises of God to you do you find hardest to trust and to build your life upon? Remember who made those promises. He is the same God who swore to childless, elderly Abraham that his descendants would be as innumerable as the stars in the sky above him—and who kept His promise. He is the same God who swore to His disciples that He would be rejected and killed, and then after three days rise again—and who kept His promise. Remember who has made the promises you find hard to believe. Remember what He is like. That is the anchor for your soul and the hope for your future.

PSALM 105

OCTOBER 10

UPHELD BY PRAYER

"The people of Israel have forsaken your covenant ... I, even I only, am left, and they seek my life, to take it away." 1 KINGS 19:14

A certain pastors' conference once hosted a seminar that dealt with despair and depression in ministry. In a way that was either phenomenally encouraging or horribly depressing, it was the best-attended seminar of the whole conference, a standing-room-only event. Pastors, some accompanied by their wives, were looking for hope and answers regarding what to do when facing severe discouragement in ministry.

The prophet Elijah would have known how the most afflicted minister in that room was feeling. He experienced hopelessness in his own ministry. He once stood alone in front of 450 armed men—prophets of the false god Baal, who were totally opposed to him—and experienced God coming down in mighty power and vanquishing his enemies. Yet immediately after this, he received a threatening message from Queen Jezebel and ran away to the desert. He spent a dejected night in a cave, convinced he was the only one left who was zealous for God. And in this most dejected state, God met with Elijah and encouraged him, not least with the promise that "I will leave seven thousand in Israel, all the knees that have not bowed to Baal" (1 Kings 19:18).

Your faith and your growth in Christlikeness are of great encouragement to your pastor. The apostle Paul, on hearing that the young congregation in Thessalonica was still standing firm in their faith, wrote that "now we live" and described "all the joy that we feel for your sake before our God" (1 Thessalonians 3:8-9).

God's servants in all areas of ministry are not immune to discouragement. The path of Christian service is full of highs and lows; there are delightful days and disastrous days. When we're disheartened, it can seem difficult to keep going—but God uses His people to uphold pastors and ministry leaders by their faith and growth, and by their prayers. When C.H. Spurgeon showed people around the Metropolitan Tabernacle in London, he would take them downstairs to show them the "boiler room." There was no boiler there; instead, there were seats. Here, several hundred people would gather every Sunday morning to pray for Spurgeon while he preached. He knew that his ministry's effectiveness depended on those who prayed and on the God who answered their prayers.

If you are in ministry (whether paid or not) and are feeling disheartened, consider this: you have impacted lives for eternity. Look back over the past couple of years and among the difficulties you will be able to see evidences of God's work through you. Let that encourage you! And whoever you are, how long has it been since you last wrote a note of encouragement or prayed for those serving in ministry around you? It is vitally important that you do so. Even if these leaders continue to preach and teach the same messages and minister in the exact way they always have, it will be to far greater effect when we simply pray for them in faith. All of us have the responsibility—indeed, the *privilege*—of doing so.

1 THESSALONIANS 2:17 - 3:13

OCTOBER 11

JOY IN OUR TRIALS

"Count it all joy, my brothers, when you meet trials of various kinds, for you know that the testing of your faith produces steadfastness. And let steadfastness have its full effect, that you may be perfect and complete, lacking in nothing."
JAMES 1:2-4

For a long time, I have imagined that I see everybody with a wheelbarrow. I have a wheelbarrow too. We push them around, and inside are our trials, temptations, fears, failures, disappointments, heartaches, and longings. These are the things that wake us and then keep us awake at three o'clock in the morning.

Living in this world places demands upon us, confronts us with challenges, and buffets us in ways that are painful and sorrowful. When we face these difficulties, often we are told to deny them, conceal them, shoo them away, or live above them. All the while, we're tempted to resent our trials and grow more and more bitter.

The biblical perspective on hardship differs greatly from all of these options. James said that it is possible to know pure, complete joy *in* our trials. How can this possibly be? Receiving joy in trials seems to be an absolute contradiction. Most of 21st-century Western life is lived in such a way as to keep trials at bay. It seems obvious that the way to joy is to avoid trials.

James, however, tells us that the way in which we can "count it all joy" is not by moving ourselves into a citadel where troubles are absent but through having our attitudes to those troubles transformed. In saying "for you know," he is reminding us that we have to bring our feelings under the rule of what we *know* to be true. And what do we know? That faith by itself does not develop perseverance. True faith is proven and strengthened when it is tested. The things we seek to avoid are the very things that make us.

We have to be honest about the trials we face. We are not yet in heaven, and so our faith is still being tested. It's not revealed in some blissful, otherworldly experience but in the rough and tumble of everyday life. And the testing of true faith will always produce steadfastness. It will make us more like Jesus. It will make us more able to comfort others. Therefore, we can trust that through all our difficulties God will continue to fashion in us a faith that is perfect and complete. It is as we hold on to that promise that we are able to "count it all joy" as a trial looms ahead or we realize we are deep in one already. We are able to think, "I would not have chosen this path, but the Lord has, and He is going to use it to show me more of Himself and to make me more like Him."

What is in your wheelbarrow today? They are things you would not have chosen. But what would change if you saw them as opportunities for your faith to be tested, strengthened, and perfected? That is the path to deeper, unconquerable joy.

ROMANS 5:1-11

OCTOBER 12

MADE FOR GOOD WORKS

"Let our people learn to devote themselves to good works, so as to help cases of urgent need, and not be unfruitful." TITUS 3:14

You are not here by chance but by God's choosing. You did not invent yourself, nor did you have any part in your own creation. You were intricately knit together in the womb (Psalm 139:13). The hand of God formed you to be the person that you are; He created you at the exact moment that He desired, and He has placed you at this point in history so that you, in Christ, by grace, through faith, might do good deeds—good deeds which He has planned for you to do (Ephesians 2:10).

In other words, you have received grace upon grace that you might do good.

While the concept of "doing good" may not be our first thought when we consider the impact on ourselves of God's transforming grace, it was virtually number one on the apostle Paul's list. In his letter to Titus, he writes that God, in Jesus, "gave himself for us to redeem us from all lawlessness and to purify for himself a people who are *zealous for good works*" (Titus 2:14, emphasis added). This emphasis appears several times throughout the letter, culminating in Paul's closing exhortation: "Let our people learn to devote themselves to good works."

Paul's particular zeal for good works was and is completely countercultural, both in his day and in our own. We live in a world that is full of enticements to pursue self-centered lives of leisure. How, then, are we to imitate Paul and excel in good deeds?

First, we need to be clear that our pursuit of good deeds does not earn God's favor. We do not do good to *be* saved but *because* we're saved. Without grace as its foundation, the call to virtuous living is pure externalism and will either exhaust us or puff us up. Second, we need to remember that our pursuit of good deeds does bring God pleasure; we live "not to please man, but to please God who tests our hearts" (1 Thessalonians 2:4). So, we are to be marked by God-honoring, Christ-exalting goodness as a living testimony to our great salvation.

Our ability to do good is also, Paul says, a learned behavior. We are called to "*learn* to devote" ourselves to goodness. Our actions shouldn't just be the result of an emotional surge or come about only when we feel like it. Instead, we are to endeavor on a daily basis to do the kingdom work that God has planned for each one of us, and do it intentionally and habitually. And we are to look at those further on in their faith who live this kind of life and seek to learn from them.

In Christ, all of your days and all of your deeds may be good for someone and for something. Learn to begin each day asking for His help to do good to others as a response to His grace to you, trusting that He will graciously enable you to give evidence of your beliefs by your actions.

JAMES 1:27 – 2:13

◇ Bible Through The Year: Song of Solomon 6–8; Ephesians 2

OCTOBER 13

DESIRING A BETTER COUNTRY

"Joseph remained in Egypt, he and his father's house. Joseph lived 110 years ... And Joseph said to his brothers, 'I am about to die, but ... God will surely visit you, and you shall carry up my bones from here.'" GENESIS 50:22, 24-25

Roughly 60 years of Joseph's later life are summarized by the phrase "Joseph remained in Egypt." Presumably, these were quieter times than the recorded drama of his early days. But 60 whole years are surely not pointless. Considering these years in the life of Joseph causes us to reflect: What are we living for? What are we planning to do with the time God has given us?

It's far too easy to spend our lives chasing earthbound horizons such as career success, financial stability, or comfortable luxuries. The myth is seductive: that life is about slaving at your job as long as you can in order to line the nest in which you plan to settle down—that the purpose of life is to prepare for retirement. Just at the point when believers are often in a position—financially, emotionally, socially—to free up an incredible amount of time to serve God's kingdom, they start to talk hibernation.

As followers of Jesus, we must not live as though this world is all there is. Yet some of us can't say with integrity, "There is more than just this life," because everything we are doing with our time, talents, and money seems to be saying, "This *is* it! That's why I'm working 60 hours a week. That's why I don't come home or take a vacation. That's why I missed church again last Sunday. That's why I don't make time and take risks to serve and to share the gospel with my neighbors. Because this is it."

It's one thing to have a vibrant and unwavering faith when we're in the middle of a battle; it's a whole new challenge to live a life of steady obedience through daily routine. For a life to be well spent—especially as it relates to our resources and legacy—we must consider not just what we *want* in life but what we *ought to do* with life. We need a vision of the heavenly horizon.

Joseph had a purpose for his life and for those final, quieter years. His vision was set beyond the borders of Egypt. He wasn't focused on himself; he was responsible for ensuring that his children and his children's children did not settle down too comfortably in Egypt but instead remained unsettled enough so that they might truly settle one day in the promised land. God had given him peace, prestige, and prosperity in Egypt—everything that so many of us chase today. Yet he was always looking beyond Egypt. He knew this was not where he, or any of God's people, truly belonged. He was not yet home. We too must live in such a way that we help our loved ones and our own hearts to "desire a better country, that is, a heavenly one" (Hebrews 11:16). Whatever you have or do not have today, you are not yet home. There is more, and better, than this. Be sure that your time, talents, and money reflect that knowledge.

1 THESSALONIANS 5:1-11

OCTOBER 14

UNJUST SUFFERING

"Do not be surprised at the fiery trial when it comes upon you to test you, as though something strange were happening to you. But rejoice insofar as you share Christ's sufferings, that you may also rejoice and be glad when his glory is revealed." 1 PETER 4:12-13

Any true believer will eventually face unjust suffering. If we are genuinely following Christ, there will be seasons when we find ourselves on the receiving end of accusation, slander, or maligning. It may happen in our home, workplace, or school; it may even happen within a church.

These trials are a real challenge. When we objectively lay out the facts before us, we think, "You know what? He had no right to say that! She had no right to think that! They had no right to do that! And yet, here I am. It's just not fair!"

When faced with suffering, our great temptation is to regard it as a strange misfortune—as totally out of step with whatever following Jesus is really about. Deep down, it is easy to think that everything should be easy when we're following Jesus. For a while, in some areas of the world (including much of the West today), we can happily go along with that assumption. But then we face a "fiery trial," and suddenly our life experience proves that being a Christian is not, in fact, easy.

Shepherding the church in his day, Peter encouraged them not to be surprised by difficult trials. Like a parent sitting down to talk with a child before she makes her way in the world, Peter urged believers to anticipate suffering. It wasn't that at some point they would act wrongly and would therefore receive rightful justice. No, it was that they would suffer simply because of their commitment to Jesus Christ. This was, Peter told them, part of the life of the Christian. It should not be a surprise but an expectation.

After all, as Jesus Himself told His disciples on the night before the world's hatred nailed Him to a cross, "A servant is not greater than his master. If they persecuted me, they will also persecute you" (John 15:20). Consider the way Jesus was treated in Pilate's hall. During the interrogation, Pilate said of Jesus—for the first of three times!—"I find no guilt in him" (18:38; 19:4, 6). He was convinced that Jesus' opponents were trying to manipulate circumstances, and he was confident that Jesus wasn't guilty of the accusations. But instead of releasing Jesus, Pilate took Him and had Him flogged before handing Him over to be crucified. Every sorrow and every grief that Jesus experienced was unjust. And when we choose to follow after Christ, therefore, we're called to be willing to suffer as He did.

Are you facing a fiery trial today or reeling from walking through one? Take heart! When the Christian walk is painful, we are suffering in the cause of the one who suffered far, far more for us. We are giving ourselves to the one who gave Himself to us. And we can look forward to the day when the trials are past, when justice is done, and we live in our Savior's glory forever.

JOHN 15:18 – 16:4

OCTOBER 15

ABIDING PEACE

"Finally, brothers, whatever is true, whatever is honorable, whatever is just, whatever is pure, whatever is lovely, whatever is commendable, if there is any excellence, if there is anything worthy of praise, think about these things."
PHILIPPIANS 4:8

We long to know God's peace and feel His presence. But the peace of God, which guards our hearts and minds (Philippians 4:7), does not come about in a vacuum. It will not happen spontaneously. God's abiding peace will only be experienced when we train our minds on that which is pleasing to Him. So to know peace, first ask, "What should be my pattern of thinking?"

This verse gives Paul's answer. He encourages us to build our framework for thinking on the basis of that which is excellent and praiseworthy. To that end, he provides us with a list of six foundational virtues of a Christian thought life.

The first is *truth*. The belt of truth must be fastened before we can benefit from any other aspects of the armor of God (Ephesians 6:14). So here, truth—found objectively in Christ and experienced subjectively as we proclaim the gospel to ourselves and to others—comes first. Second, Paul directs us toward "whatever is *honorable*"—or "noble," as some translations have it. Fastening our minds on that which is majestic or awe-inspiring is the opposite of contemplating that which is immoral and earthly. As believers, we are not to feed our minds on trashy entertainment or similar trivialities, which preoccupy so much of our secular society. Instead, we are to think about that which lifts our souls upward towards God and His great works. Third and fourth, Paul calls us to make decisions based on what is *just* and *pure* instead of what is convenient or gratifying. It was this way of thinking that distinguished Joseph from David in otherwise similar situations, for when Joseph was pursued by Potiphar's wife, he made his decision to run from her on the basis of what was right, not what was easy or instantly pleasing to him (Genesis 39:6-12). David, on the other hand, followed his feelings and committed great injustice in sleeping with Bathsheba and murdering her husband (2 Samuel 11). Being a saved person does not immunize us from ungodliness, which starts in the mind and ends in sinful action. Thinking like a saved person does. Fifth and sixth, we are to think on "whatever is *lovely*" and "whatever is *commendable*"—or, as it is translated in the King James Version, what is "of good report." When we think this way, we will listen to reports that build people up as opposed to reports that tear down, disappoint, and destroy. This is a mindset that promotes brotherly love and accompanies God's grace as it works in our lives.

Tailor your thinking to the pattern Paul provides and make sure you accompany it with prayer (Philippians 4:6-8), and you will have very little room left for anxiety—that peace-disrupting, joy-destroying state of mind which so often creeps into our lives. Instead, train your mind to think God's thoughts after Him, and you can experience an increased measure of His peace and presence.

PSALM 119:97-104

OCTOBER 16

GUARD YOUR LIPS

"Whoever guards his mouth preserves his life; he who opens wide his lips comes to ruin." PROVERBS 13:3

The Puritan Thomas Brooks once wrote, "We know metals by their tinkling, and men by their talking."[113]

Words are seldom neutral. God hears every word we speak—our lives are exposed before Him, and the Bible has the uncanny capacity to probe the recesses even of that which we seek to hide from ourselves and others.

Each of us is marked by memories of words spoken to us. Perhaps we reflect on the joy of a child's first words or still feel the bitterness of a friend's hurtful words. From our earliest days, we learn how to use words both to bring harm and to bring gladness. King Solomon was right: "Death and life are in the power of the tongue" (Proverbs 18:21).

We are all fallen. Therefore, hurtful words easily flow from our mouths. They can be reckless, like the careless swing of a sword, and unguarded during times when we answer before we listen. Sometimes we simply say too much; inevitably, we say things we should have kept to ourselves. Words can destroy a neighbor, crush the feelings of a friend, and set fire to our relationships with others. One wrong word may spoil a person's character, smear a reputation, or mar the usefulness of someone else's life for a very long time. We know all this, yet how hard we find it to guard our mouths. How often we close our mouths too late, only after we have opened them wide and brought damage to ourselves or to others.

If we were truly honest about the failings of our tongues, we would cut each other much more slack. And we would be far more serious in seeking, by God's enabling, to guard our own mouth and banish ruinous words. What a beautiful display of grace that would be to our friends, family, and neighbors! Jesus is the only perfect man; He never sinned with His words (James 3:2). If we seek to be like Him in this way, perhaps we will find more people marveling at the compassionate, tender, and kind words that came from His very lips (Luke 4:22).

Though your words and your works in and of themselves achieve nothing for you before the gate of heaven, they are evidence that your profession of faith in the Lord Jesus Christ is true. What will it look like for you to take seriously these words: "Everyone should be quick to listen, slow to speak and slow to become angry" (James 1:19, NIV)?

JAMES 3:2-12

113 "The Unsearchable Riches of Christ," in *The Complete Works of Thomas Brooks,* ed. Alexander Balloch Grozart (James Nichol, 1866), Vol. 3, p 178.

OCTOBER 17

OUR PATIENT TEACHER

"They did not understand the saying, and were afraid to ask him." MARK 9:32

Imagine a student sitting in a classroom, staring at a formula on the board. The formula's symbols are complete gibberish to her, but she is afraid to raise her hand to ask a clarifying question. Many of us have likely experienced a similar situation, caught in a dilemma: on the one hand we're in fear of being shown up or of where the answer will lead if we ask, but on the other hand we know we'll be impossibly stuck if we don't.

Although the disciples lived in the company of Jesus, regularly listened to His teaching, received His instructions, and saw His miraculous deeds, they still struggled to understand the bigger picture of His ministry. Many times, Jesus spoke plainly with them about all that lay before Him—His betrayal, death, and resurrection. Yet they faced the worst of predicaments: "They did not understand the saying, and were afraid to ask him."

Peter, James, and John had just witnessed Jesus' transfiguration (Mark 9:2-8). They knew He was the Son of God. But the sincerity of the disciples' belief in Jesus as Messiah wasn't matched by their understanding of what it meant for Him to actually *be* the Messiah. Their perception of the Messiah was blurred and incomplete, causing confusion and fear. Perhaps they did not ask Jesus to explain further because they did not want to admit their ignorance; or perhaps because they were unwilling to confront the implications of what He was telling them, both for Himself (v 30-31) and for them (8:34-35).

Even after Jesus' death and resurrection, the two disciples on the road to Emmaus needed Him to take them back through the whole panorama of the Bible in order that they might understand His suffering and put everything together (Luke 24:26-27). Immediately before His ascension to heaven, the disciples were still unsure of the nature of Christ's kingdom. This time, though, they asked Jesus for answers; and Jesus didn't say, *Are you back again with that same question? How many times are you going to ask?* Instead, He graciously explained that His kingdom would not come by the re-establishment of the temple in Jerusalem but would advance through the work of the Holy Spirit in each of the disciples (Acts 1:8).

Maybe you find yourself identifying with the disciples here, finding it difficult to understand all that is taught in God's word or unsure that you really want to confront the implications of what you have begun to understand. But your situation need not be filled with fear. How good that Jesus is such a kind and patient teacher—so kind and patient with His disciples, so kind and patient with you and me. And how good that the Holy Spirit dwells within you, enabling you to do all that your Lord calls you to do (Ezekiel 36:26-27; Galatians 5:16). Today, then, if you find yourself lacking wisdom and understanding, simply ask God, "who gives generously to all without reproach" (James 1:5).

1 CORINTHIANS 2:1-16

OCTOBER 18

PREPARING FOR ACTION

"Preparing your minds for action, and being sober-minded, set your hope fully on the grace that will be brought to you at the revelation of Jesus Christ."

1 PETER 1:13

Training to become a pilot involves hours and hours of intense preparation. Some of this training takes place in simulators where the intensity is high enough to induce sweating and stress. Why are pilots subjected to such rigorous training? So they can learn to make the right decisions when it really matters!

When it comes to purity, it is often the case that people fall into sin because they try to make vital decisions in the heat of the moment. That just won't cut it. If we are going to maintain purity, we need to make choices in advance and on the basis of God's word.

This is why Peter tells us to prepare our "minds for action ... being sober-minded." The King James Version translates this verse, "Gird up the loins of your mind." In other words, we are to keep control of our minds—to get a grip of our thought processes—so that we're able to run after what is good and flee from what is evil.

If we do not prepare our minds for action, then we will be easily seducible and prone to tragedy. We will tend to make difficult, life-altering decisions in the heat of the moment when our emotions are engaged and our desires are shouting at us. But a life of purity does not happen by accident; it is an act of absolute determination prompted by God's Spirit, guided by His word, and enabled by His power.

We need to make a commitment to purity, as the psalmist did when he said, "I have sworn an oath and confirmed it, to keep your righteous rules" (Psalm 119:106). Make your commitment before it's too late.

And here's a suggestion for the kind of commitment to make: determine to live in the *center* of the narrow way, not on the edge. The young man in Proverbs 7 who fell prey to the temptation of a "forbidden woman" was living on the edge; he was "passing along the street near her corner, taking the road to her house in the twilight" (Proverbs 7:5, 8-9). The Bible's lesson is clear: don't get yourself in the wrong place at the wrong time.

There is nothing to be gained from living on the edge when it comes to purity. Make your commitment *before* the temptation confronts you, so that when the evil day comes, you will be ready to say, "No, I already made that decision." Keep your life in the center of the narrow way and determine to stay there. On the day when Christ Jesus returns and by grace His people stand around His throne, none of us will say that the pursuit of holiness was not worth the effort.

PROVERBS 7

OCTOBER 19

SILENCE AND SUFFERING

"Now when Job's three friends heard of all this evil that had come upon him, they came each from his own place ... And they sat with him on the ground seven days and seven nights, and no one spoke a word to him ... Then Eliphaz the Temanite answered and said: 'If one ventures a word with you, will you be impatient? Yet who can keep from speaking?'" JOB 2:11, 13; 4:1-2

Job's friends show us how to respond when someone is going through the depths of pain and sorrow—and then they show us how not to.

Job's friends had front-row seats in witnessing the depth of his suffering, and they struggled to bring him any measure of comfort by their words. Their eventual response was heavily theoretical and quite unhelpful.

There is great danger in commenting on affliction or speaking to someone who is suffering if we have either not experienced something similar or have not taken time to listen to them well and to pray to God humbly. Job 16 describes these same friends as miserable comforters—those who "could join words together" against Job and whose words had no end (16:4).

In search of an instant cure and a quick answer to Job's suffering, his friends piled on the accusations. Zophar in particular reminded Job that he deserved worse than what he was currently experiencing (Job 11:4-6). In the same vein, Eliphaz suggested that maybe Job had been wandering from God and needed to listen more carefully to Him (22:21-23). These men adopted an overly simplistic approach to Job's suffering—an approach which hurt rather than healed. They were quick to the draw and ready with an answer to any and all of Job's laments. When Eliphaz asked, when he first opened his mouth, "Who can keep from speaking?" he should have answered, "Me"!

Job was scathing about their means of counseling him: "You whitewash with lies; worthless physicians are you all. Oh that you would keep silent, and it would be your wisdom!" (Job 13:4-5). And in fact, his friends had done exactly that—to begin with. They had sat with him for a week without speaking.

In the experience of suffering, silence in the sufferer's presence is often a far greater aid than many words. It is quite possible that Job would have experienced greater comfort and companionship had his friends maintained their initial response: joining him on the ground, sitting, not speaking a single word.

Silence is often a missing ingredient in our response to suffering. While it is certainly not the only response that is needed, it is vastly undervalued. If we endeavor, without an agenda, to unplug from all the noise around us and listen to the voices of the suffering, we might make far more progress in that silent contemplation than any of us imagine. And we may then have far more useful things to say, both in what we say and in how we say it. Job certainly thought so. Is there someone whom you could bless with your quiet presence this week?

PSALMS 42 - 43

Bible Through The Year: 1 Samuel 17–18; 2 Peter 2

OCTOBER 20

SUPERNATURAL PATIENCE

"And we urge you, brothers, admonish the idle, encourage the fainthearted, help the weak, be patient with them all." 1 THESSALONIANS 5:14

Patience is a great virtue. It is also a great challenge!

As the apostle Paul wrapped up his first letter to the Thessalonians, he did so with a staccato burst of priceless principles. Each one is like a gem in a necklace, a wise truth to wear around our necks as we chart our way through life (Proverbs 3:3). Standing out among these principles is the command to be patient.

In the Greek, Paul uses the word *makrothumeo*, a word that literally means "long-hearted" and that the Scriptures usually use to describe the character of God (for example, Romans 2:4; 2 Timothy 1:16; James 5:10). Patience is not quick-tempered with those who fail. Paul tells us to have this divine type of patience as we deal with the idle, the fainthearted, and the weak. Encountering each provides us with an opportunity to live out godly patience.

How do we gain this kind of patience? It does not come naturally! So we need, first, to look at God. We have a God who is "gracious, slow to anger [*makrothumeo*] and abounding in love" (Psalm 103:8). He looks upon our rebellious hearts and yet forgives us. He looks upon our repeated failures and yet does not give up on us. He looks upon our doubts and anxieties and yet is gentle with us. We are called to mirror this patience. And so we need, second, to ask God for help. This supernatural patience is something that only God, by His Spirit, can produce within our lives. Paul, for example, prayed that the Colossians would be "strengthened with all power, according to his glorious might, for all endurance and patience with joy" (Colossians 1:11). Every one of us needs someone to pray that prayer on our behalf, as well as to pray it for ourselves. Every one of us ought to be doing the same for others, because it's a prayer God is eager to answer. When God's power is unleashed in our lives, we can endure when we feel like quitting, and so we can extend patience when we feel like flat-out losing it.

How will you respond to the nuisances of everyday life—while waiting in line at the drive-thru, or at the green light when the car in front of you doesn't move? How will you respond to your brothers and sisters who are idle, or fainthearted, or weak? Let your watchword in those situations and with those people simply be *patience*. The people around you won't be particularly impressed by your theological knowledge, but they'll surely notice your impatience, which communicates that you think your time and interests are more significant than theirs. But conversely, they will notice your patience, which tells them that you are prizing the interests and well-being of others above your own (Philippians 2:3)—just as your heavenly Father does.

No doubt you will have opportunities today to show divine patience when you are tempted to display human impatience. In those moments, recognize the immensity of God's patience to you and you will surely grow in your patience for others.

COLOSSIANS 1:9-12

OCTOBER 21

APPROVED BY GOD

"Do your best to present yourself to God as one approved, a worker who has no need to be ashamed." 2 TIMOTHY 2:15

Whose praise are you living for?

By nature, we desire the approval of others. But, as believers, the approval we should long for above all else is the approval of God Himself. It is worth pausing to consider the awesome truth that, today, what we do can bring pleasure to the God who sustains the universe (1 Thessalonians 4:1), and that one day, He will greet those who have lived all out for Him with the wonderful words, "Well done, good and faithful servant" (Matthew 25:21, 23). Just imagine hearing those words, directed to you, from divine lips!

How, then, are we to live "as one approved" by God—as "a worker who has no need to be ashamed"?

First and foremost, we must determine to keep the faith to the very end. Paul, rounding the bend on his final lap, declared to Timothy, "I have fought the good fight, I have finished the race, I have kept the faith" (2 Timothy 4:7). Paul's life was not characterized by short bursts of enthusiasm followed by periods of chronic inertia. He understood that the race of faith was a lifelong marathon to the end.

We don't want to be known for little spurts every now and then. We especially must avoid being those who only do God's work when other Christians are watching us. Instead, we want to run hard every day, remembering that God's eye is always upon us.

As we press on in faith, we can remember that we are promised a "crown of righteousness" that has been "laid up" for us, "which the Lord, the righteous judge, will award" to us (2 Timothy 4:8). And we must remember that we do not run in our own strength. Rather, we are to have every confidence that "he who began a good work in [us] will bring it to completion at the day of Jesus Christ" (Philippians 1:6). God promises never to leave us or forsake us along the way (Hebrews 13:5). If the finish line looks a long way away, we are called not to focus on the tape but to look to Jesus, keeping our eyes fixed on the "founder and perfecter of our faith" (Hebrews 12:2).

Never underestimate the impact of a single life lived to God's glory. Consider the prospect of standing before your heavenly Father as a worker approved and you will come to the place where you say in humility, "Lord, I want to do my best to know Your approval on my life. 'I am only one, but I am one. What I can do, I ought to do. And what I ought to do, by God's grace I will do.'"[114]

MATTHEW 25:14-46

114 Attributed to Edward Everett Hale.

OCTOBER 22

EVERY ANSWER WE NEED

"Now while Paul was waiting for them at Athens, his spirit was provoked within him as he saw that the city was full of idols. So he reasoned in the synagogue with the Jews and the devout persons, and in the marketplace every day with those who happened to be there. Some of the Epicurean and Stoic philosophers also conversed with him." ACTS 17:16-18

When addressing the intellectuals of his day in the city of Athens, Paul discovered that his hearers had been influenced by two fundamental ideas: Stoicism and Epicureanism. Stoicism holds that the events of the world are determined by a merciless, cold, and impersonal fate, while Epicureanism teaches that good is determined by what brings the most pleasure. Neither of these philosophies hold up for the children of Almighty God.

One of the most distinctive features of Christianity is the way in which we are able to articulate our view of the world. In contrast to much of the culture around us, we know that our time is in God's hands (Psalm 31:15)—that we're neither trapped in the grip of blind forces nor tossed about on an ocean of chance. Whether people have been drawn in by Marxism, Hinduism, nihilism, or any one of countless other philosophies and religions, they are all faced with questions and insecurities regarding their beliefs. Have they been caught in a struggle for a classless society or in an endless cycle of birth and death? Perhaps they are convinced that life has no meaning at all. Whatever someone's questions or beliefs are, God provides every answer that they need. Instead of living life caged by a senseless, uncaring fate or endless uncertainty, as believers we now live with unfailing hope. We, like Paul, are now stewards of all the answers God has given us through His word—answers that we must share. He has given us a great confidence, and His name is Jesus.

The question, therefore, is not whether we have a message that can answer the deepest longings of every human and the various objections of every other philosophy and religion: we do. The question is whether we will share that message. When Paul was in Athens, he saw what others did not see. He did not enjoy the impressive sites or stand in awe of the city's intellectual reputation. He saw a city lost in idol-worship, and "his spirit was provoked within him," for every time an idol is worshiped, the Lord Jesus is robbed of the glory that only He deserves. And "so," without regard for his own reputation, Paul reasoned with and proclaimed the gospel of resurrection hope to the inhabitants of that city (Acts 17:18).

Wherever you live, in one way or another you find yourself in a modern-day Athens. What are the idols that those around you are worshiping? Is your spirit provoked by that? You have an answer that satisfies human longing in a way no idol can. You have an opportunity to bring glory to God. With whom can you reason today, saying, "Can you see that what you are worshiping will not satisfy? Can I warn you that you are ignoring the God who brings meaning and hope but who will not be mocked? Can I tell you about the answers I have found in coming to know Jesus Christ?"

1 THESSALONIANS 1:1-10

◇ Bible Through The Year: 1 Samuel 25–26; 1 Timothy 2

OCTOBER 23

THE NEW AND BETTER ADAM

"As by the one man's disobedience the many were made sinners, so by the one man's obedience the many will be made righteous." ROMANS 5:19

Adam, the first man, was made in the image of God. The Lord gave Adam a role unique in all creation, yet he failed to fulfill it and was sent out of Eden. God then made a new start with the Israelites; they were called to be His people. They displayed His character as and when they obeyed His law. Like Adam, though, the Israelites failed in their role and were sent into exile.

Gloriously, when we come to the New Testament, we discover that where Adam and Israel failed, Jesus succeeded. Jesus is what the people of God were meant to be: the new and better Adam, the true Israel. He is descended from Adam, and He identifies with Adam's race. He identifies with us completely, yet unlike Adam, Jesus was tempted and did not sin (Hebrews 4:15).

What we have in the Lord Jesus is the only human being who ever obeyed God perfectly, the only one with whom God is always pleased. He kept every letter of the law. Therefore, Jesus is the one person to have lived who doesn't deserve to be banished from God's presence. But He *was* banished. On the cross, He willingly faced the punishment that sinners deserve—sinners who are bound up in Adam's sin.

All of humanity finds its heritage in Adam, both by nature and by descent. We are born in sin and united with Adam in our rebellion against God. There is no exception. The only answer to humanity's predicament is for men and women to be introduced to the one person who kept the law perfectly and who did not deserve to be banished from God, but who then was obedient to the point of death on the cross so that sinners may, by grace through faith, receive all that He deserves instead of bearing all that Adam deserved.

This truth is at the heart of everything. For believers, all that was formerly true of us found its root in that one act of Adam, while all that is true of us now is a result of the obedience of Christ.

If you lack assurance, perhaps you're guilty of trying to examine your own spiritual life to see if you're doing enough. But you are not saved by anything done by you. As the hymn writer reminds us, we are saved by a work done for us:

Because the sinless Savior died,
My sinful soul is counted free,
For God the just is satisfied
To look on Him and pardon me.[115]

ROMANS 5:6-21

115 Charitie Lees Bancroft, "Before the Throne of God Above" (1863).

OCTOBER 24

SONGS OF DELIVERANCE

"You are a hiding place for me; you preserve me from trouble; you surround me with shouts of deliverance." PSALM 32:7

If you watch old black-and-white Robin Hood or King Arthur movies, you will see queens who ride through battlefields on horseback. They don't go alone on their journeys, but mounted soldiers ride all around them, surrounding them with protection.

On difficult days, we can remind ourselves that God "will command his angels concerning [us] to guard [us] in all [our] ways" (Psalm 91:11), and that He has surrounded us with a band of others who are following Christ's banner—namely, our church. The Christian life is meant to be a corporate journey, not an individualistic one. We have the benefit of rallying together for the cause of Christ. We are to surround ourselves with those who provide "shouts [or "songs," NIV] of deliverance." When we worship together, we experience the benefits of the deliverance that God provides for us.

When we are disoriented by life or acutely aware of our flaws, failings, discouragements, and doubts, the antidote is not to try to pull ourselves up by our bootstraps. Instead, we can look at the wonders of what Jesus has done and make sure we are hearing from brothers and sisters in Christ what Jesus has done. With the help of a simple hymnbook alongside God's word, we can encourage one another through the darkest of days by filling our minds with truth through song and Scripture.

Alec Motyer once wrote, "When truth gets into a creed or hymn-book, it becomes the confident possession of the whole church."[116] With words deeply rooted in theology, we can daily tell ourselves, "He is all I need to get through." Then, in the company of God's people, we can worship together, asking our Lord for grace and peace. A living church will always be a singing church.

You are not meant to worship on an island. This is part of what corporate worship is about: to be surrounded by songs of deliverance. You are wired by your Creator to stand in the assembly of those who affirm to you, as you affirm to them, memorable words like these:

Sing, O sing of my Redeemer!
With His blood He purchased me;
On the cross He sealed my pardon,
Paid the debt, and made me free.[117]

PSALM 147

116 *Look to the Rock: An Old Testament Background to Our Understanding of Christ* (Kregel, 2004), p 222 note 48.

117 P. P. Bliss, "I Will Sing of My Redeemer" (1876).

◇ Bible Through The Year: 1 Samuel 30–31; 1 Timothy 4

OCTOBER 25

A THORN IN THE FLESH

"To keep me from becoming conceited because of the surpassing greatness of the revelations, a thorn was given me in the flesh, a messenger of Satan to harass me, to keep me from becoming conceited." 2 CORINTHIANS 12:7

If you gather many talented musicians who are only interested in their individual parts, you won't have an orchestra. What you will produce is merely discordant noise: an affront to the listening ear. However, when that giftedness is exercised in selflessness and humility, under the headship of a conductor and the rule of a score, you get beautiful, harmonious music.

Just as a musician's desire for individual greatness is the death knell of orchestral usefulness, so it is with our Christian faith. A spiritual gift should never be the source of pride—because, after all, it's a gift! Yet we are often tempted to take God-given gifts and attribute them to ourselves as if we developed or deserve them, or to use them for ourselves as if they were ours. This puts us in danger of cherishing exaggerated ideas about our own importance—and those with the most significant gifts are typically in the greatest danger.

Paul himself had to face this temptation. He was particularly bright, had a strong education, was from the best kind of background, and was influential in many lives (see Philippians 3:4-6). And when taking on the false apostles of the day, who were making elaborate claims about their knowledge of God, Paul honestly described having seen extraordinary visions (2 Corinthians 12:2-4). He was a prime target for an inflated ego. What protected him from that? A thorn in his flesh. He does not specify precisely what it was, and so we would be wise not to speculate. What matters is not what it was so much as what it achieved; for Paul recognized that this thorn in the flesh was a humbling reminder from God of his inherent weakness, given so that he would not boast about his own importance and so that he would continue to rely on God.

Like the false teachers Paul addressed, we are often tempted to allow our influence and apparent success, whether great or small, to serve as the means by which we judge our worth. Eventually, however, such temporary matters will be exposed as temporary and will fade away.

In the providence and goodness of God, Paul's "thorn" helps us to understand our own difficulties such as illness, financial lack, relational challenges, the effort of raising children, and even the ongoing struggle with sin. God knows what He's doing when He allows these necessary, uncomfortable, unrelenting elements in our lives. Better to be a humble believer beset by thorns than a proud, self-reliant no-longer-believer unplagued by anything. We need to know our own weakness in order to continue to rely on God's grace for our eternal salvation and God's power for our daily lives. The question, then, is not whether the thorns will come to you but whether you will allow God to use your "thorns" to remind you that He alone is the source of your gifts and the one who makes you spiritually useful.

2 CORINTHIANS 11:30 – 12:10

OCTOBER 26

THEOLOGY THAT SUSTAINS

"Joseph said to his brothers, 'I am about to die, but God will visit you and bring you up out of this land to the land that he swore to Abraham, to Isaac, and to Jacob' ... So Joseph died, being 110 years old." GENESIS 50:24, 26

That the Bible is filled with accounts of individuals' deaths should cause each of us to confront the reality of our own eventual death. God has not chosen to inform us of the date of our demise, but the psalmist tells us that every day of our lives was written in God's book before one of them came to be (Psalm 139:16). Joseph lived to be 110 years old—but nevertheless, like all of us, he had to come to terms with his mortality.

Joseph understood and accepted his death. Here was no raging against the dying of the light, to use the words of the poet Dylan Thomas,[118] but rather what our Puritan forefathers would have called a "good death." What is it that allows us to die well? A strong theology—a strong understanding of who God was and is. In the end, Joseph strengthened his faith by calling to mind evidence of God's lifelong providential care to Him and His promises to His people. Because of his belief in God's goodness, he could face death straight on. He wasn't scared or selfish; he didn't grasp at shadows or clutch at vain hopes. Instead, his words were brief and focused on his family and God. Such a response can only come from a view of the world framed by divine character and purpose.

Do we believe, as Joseph did, that God will deliver His people? Can we see evidence of this belief in our own lives? Have we looked back at God's faithfulness and discovered that no matter what the distress or brokenness we've been through, we can say with the psalmist, "On God rests my salvation and my glory; my mighty rock, my refuge is God" (Psalm 62:7)? It is good theology, not feelings, that will sustain us in life and comfort us as we wrestle with death. When difficult days come, it is then that we cling to what we know to be true. From Joseph and his life we can learn this amazing truth: the God who knit us together has ordered all of our steps in all of our days, and He weaves our lives into the great story of His sovereign fulfillment of His promises to His people. With faith in this God, we can face death singing:

With mercy and with judgment
My web of time He wove;
And aye, the dews of sorrow
Were lustered by His love;
I'll bless the hand that guided,
I'll bless the heart that planned,
When throned where glory dwelleth
In Immanuel's land.[119]

PSALM 62

118 "Do Not Go Gentle Into that Good Night" in *In Country Sleep, And Other Poems* (Dent, 1952)
119 Anne R. Cousin, "The Sands of Time Are Sinking" (1857).

OCTOBER 27

RECEIVED BY JESUS

"'Let the children come to me; do not hinder them, for to such belongs the kingdom of God. Truly, I say to you, whoever does not receive the kingdom of God like a child shall not enter it.' And he took them in his arms and blessed them."
MARK 10:14-16

In the 21st century, when we think about children, we tend to focus on their subjective qualities; they are cute and cuddly, and at times we mistakenly think they are perfect and the center of the universe. Such contemporary views of children actually hinder our ability to grasp what Jesus meant when he said, "Let the children come to me."

It is the objective characteristics of children that are truly at the heart of Jesus' illustration. Children do not vote. They do not have driver's licenses. Adults don't often ask them to make decisions regarding significant events in their own lives or in the lives of their families. In their infancy, they are entirely dependent on someone else. Put bluntly, little children are small and helpless, without much apparent outward claim or merit.

Isn't it a wonder, then, that children are so warmly received by Jesus? But while it's certainly wondrous, it shouldn't surprise us when we consider how often God uses the meek and lowly in mighty ways. We cannot hope to enter heaven because of our own merit or self-worth. Instead, the kingdom of God belongs to people who are needy, lonely, and helpless, who have no claim or merit on their own—people just like children.

As we come to terms with what it means to be like a child, we start to see that our entrance into the kingdom can only come after we've accepted our own helpless, dependent state. We come to Christ not with hands full of our own abilities or achievements but with empty hands, ready to receive. And remarkably, the gospel tells us that we must look to God Himself, who took on flesh as a helpless babe. It's only fitting, then, that entry into His kingdom would be enjoyed by those who follow His humble example.

Jesus' embrace of the children in these verses both flattens our pride and picks us up in our weakness. Perhaps you regard your work as commendable or your position as noteworthy, and you find yourself desiring to be a benefactor and not a beneficiary. Or maybe you know that others think very little of you (or you think little of yourself), and you are surprised that God would want to give you anything, let alone be looking forward to spending eternity with you. No matter what your character or your circumstances are, come to Jesus each day in childlike trust, aware of your weakness and helplessness. This, and only this, is the way into His kingdom and the way to enjoy the blessing of closeness to Him.

LUKE 11:1-13

Bible Through The Year: 2 Samuel 6–8; 1 John 1

OCTOBER 28

LOOK OUT!

"Look out for the dogs, look out for the evildoers, look out for those who mutilate the flesh. For we are the circumcision." PHILIPPIANS 3:2-3

In all of the apostle Paul's writings, there is perhaps no place where he made a more graphic statement than in this verse. Referring to the false teachers of his day as "dogs" was even more audacious and confrontational then than it is today. But Paul was not using this language merely for effect; he was gravely concerned because there were dangerous people moving around the Philippian church.

Cults and false teachers are almost always joyless, and these evil men in Philippi were no different. They were the opposite of what they claimed to be, insisting that the Old Testament ceremonial law was a necessary qualification for true Christianity. They addressed the Philippian believers, who had discovered joy in the Lord, by asking, in essence, *Are you really a true Christian if you don't pay careful attention to the external rite of circumcision?* This warning from Paul to "look out" was meant to remind the young church that an "augmented" Christianity actually distorts the true gospel. Adding to the gospel always subtracts joy and even salvation from the gospel.

Therefore, when we read the word "dogs" in this verse we shouldn't think of a friendly family pet. Paul was not referring to a golden retriever. Think of a scavenger, a diseased mongrel that roams around garbage cans and could harm you greatly with a bite. Paul was emphatic that these men, in insisting that people meet legal requirements to be qualified for grace, were equally dangerous. They were drawing attention away from Christ, diluting the sufficiency of His death, resurrection, and ascension.

Paul constantly warned of the tragic consequences of false teaching—and, because he loved the people of the Philippian church, describing them as his "joy and crown" (Philippians 4:1), he was opposed to anyone and anything that would reroute them from the only way to glory. He wanted them to remain vigilant.

We, too, could easily forget that the good news is not a message of "Do your best, and be good enough!" but rather "Your best is never enough—but Jesus is."

Here's the good news, though: by faith in Christ alone, we are the true "circumcision"—that is, those who have been set apart as the true people of God, not because we have had some flesh cut off but because Christ was cut off for us. In each generation, there are always those who wish to insist on the outward features of the faith and—implicitly or explicitly—make those observances necessary for salvation. But no external ritual or religious performance can save. Do not place your confidence in your flesh—in your church attendance, your daily Bible reading, your performance as a spouse or parent or worker or evangelist or anything else. Put it all in Christ. He, and He alone, is enough.

GALATIANS 2:11-21

OCTOBER 29

EXTENDING GOD'S KINDNESS

"She told her mother-in-law with whom she had worked and said, 'The man's name with whom I worked today is Boaz.' And Naomi said to her daughter-in-law, 'May he be blessed by the LORD, whose kindness has not forsaken the living or the dead!'" RUTH 2:19-20

Today, you can make the invisible God visible.

When Ruth set out for the fields to glean, she never could have known just how wonderful God's provision would be. She had already taken refuge in God, but through Boaz she discovered that the Lord was able to do far more abundantly than all that she could have asked or thought.

As God established His covenant with Israel, He revealed His own kindness as one who "executes justice for the fatherless and the widow, and loves the sojourner, giving him food and clothing" (Deuteronomy 10:18). He gave His law to His people not to make them legalists but to have them display His character and bring glory to His name through their obedience. Part of that law created a framework to provide for those in difficult circumstances. As Boaz obeyed the law's instruction by extending his invitation to Ruth to come and eat (Ruth 2:14), he did so graciously. He had received God's kindness, and he realized that he could in turn share it with others. He put literal hands and feet to obeying God's commands—and Ruth further discovered God's heart as a result. Further, Boaz's graciousness was paired with generosity: he not only invited Ruth to feast but also offered her a seat among his harvesters. He encouraged her to eat her fill. He allowed her to take from the best sheaves of grain, not just the leftovers. Despite her social and racial differences, he didn't alienate or hold her at arm's length. Quite the reverse: Boaz went beyond what God's law had laid down.

This is but a glimpse of the welcome God extends to us through Christ as He invites us to His heavenly table. And this is the offer that all of us as Christians should embody. If somebody—be they widowed, poor, hurting, or bitter—enters a church gathering or a Christian home, there ought to be a sense of faithful acceptance because of how God's people embody His covenant care.

By the end of the day, Ruth was overwhelmed with the favor Boaz kept extending. When she returned home with her plentiful provision, Naomi rejoiced over the generosity, describing it with the word *checed*—the continual loving kindness and merciful provision of God. Boaz's *checed* caused Ruth's and Naomi's hearts to worship the God who abounds in *checed* (Exodus 34:6-7).

Boaz's kindness overflowed from the gracious, generous, and continual kindness he had received from God. As fellow recipients of the Lord's care, when we extend such kindness to others, they too may come to know Him. The invisible God becomes visible to every generation through the compassion of His people. To whom will you extend gracious, generous, unexpected kindness today?

RUTH 2:14-23

OCTOBER 30

THE COMFORT OF GOD'S PROVIDENCE

"Then Naomi ... said to her, 'My daughter, should I not seek rest for you, that it may be well with you? Is not Boaz our relative, with whose young women you were? See, he is winnowing barley tonight at the threshing floor. Wash therefore and anoint yourself, and put on your cloak and go down to the threshing floor.'" RUTH 3:1-3

God is sovereign, and therefore we can make bold choices.

As any nurturing figure would do, Naomi wanted her widowed daughter-in-law Ruth to be settled and cared for in life. So she urged Ruth to go to Boaz and ask him to assume the role of provider by marrying her.

Of course, we must be careful not to read too much into this Old Testament story, since that era had its own set of customs. However, we must also remember that these were real people in a real Middle-Eastern village meeting a real God and committing their lives unreservedly to Him. As such, there are eternal truths to be learned. Primarily, we can learn that while God's providence rules over our lives, it does not limit our freedom in making decisions. God's overruling sovereignty did not hinder Naomi's reasoning or Ruth's response. The Lord was sovereign over all of it, but not at the expense of their choices.

Ruth's story is also a reminder that even when mistakes alter our lives, God redeems them for our good and His glory. Naomi's husband should not have moved his family from the promised land to Moab, the enemies of God's people; and her sons should not have married Moabite women, since God's law prohibited marrying into other religions. Yet these wrong choices brought Ruth to Naomi, to God, and into the line of redemptive history as an ancestor of Jesus (Matthew 1:1-6). Such redemption is not an excuse for intentional rebellion, but it is an assurance that we need not despair over past mistakes.

Equally, God's sovereignty in weaving His plan of redemption, first in bringing His Son into the world and then in calling His people to faith in Him, is a constant assurance as we face decisions and consider this or that course of action. We trust God through faith-filled action. Naomi didn't just sit in her house waiting on God to act, saying, *Whatever God wills will be.* No, she took action by encouraging Ruth to take the next step in what seemed to be unfolding.

Trusting God's providence does not mean we sit back and wait for the plan to unfold, singing *Que será, será*—whatever will be, will be—for "the future's not ours to see."[120] Instead, we should be quoting Jesus' words: "Not my will, but yours, be done" (Luke 22:42). After Jesus prayed this prayer, He proceeded to live it out in perfect obedience, even to the point of death. The path of life may have many twists and turns, but God's word promises that "for those who love God all things work together for good, for those who are called according to his purpose" (Romans 8:28). Take heart in this promise. Are you facing a decision? Are you wondering what path to take? God is sovereign, and God saves. Whatever you decide, live boldly and live freely within the comfort of God's providence.

ACTS 16:6-15

120 Ray Evans, "Que Será, Será" (1956).

OCTOBER 31

OUT OF THE WAITING ROOM

"Then [Ruth] came softly and uncovered [Boaz's] feet and lay down. At midnight the man was startled and turned over, and behold, a woman lay at his feet!" RUTH 3:7-8

The Christian life is not lived in a comfort zone.

In Ruth 3 we find Ruth taking a great risk as she approached Boaz to request that he care for her as his wife. She, a single woman, went in the middle of the night to a barn filled with men after they had finished celebrating the completed harvest. Once Boaz fell asleep, she went to him under the cover of darkness and uncovered his feet. If she had made a mistake or had been discovered, there is no telling what these men would have done to her or what people might have said regarding her motives.

These events look strange to our 21st-century eyes, but Ruth's unusual actions demonstrate a sincere trust in God's care and protection. God had laid down in His law that Boaz could act as a kinsman-redeemer—a protector and provider—for Ruth. God had providentially led Ruth to Boaz's field, where he had extended favor to her. Her story shows us again and again how God providentially rules over all unforeseeable circumstances for His glory and the well-being of His people.

Like Ruth, we will sometimes face occasions in life when we cannot see much beyond our next step. Many of us are tempted to remain in the waiting room until all of the details are seemingly clear and known. We want to feel safe and in control. Yet if we insist on never moving until we do feel like that, our lives will speak little of spiritual progress and witness little of God's miraculous work. The fear of going in the wrong direction leaves us going nowhere at all.

When we cannot see beyond our next step or when times of uncertainty come in life—and they *will* come!—we have to trust God and act on the basis of the truth of His word and trust in His Spirit's guidance. Ruth's plan was not fail-safe and certain, but she proceeded because she trusted God, who had proven His faithfulness to her time and time again.

Do you need to start thinking this way? Do you need to look above and beyond the borders of your comfort zone to that to which God may be calling you? If Ruth was motivated by trust and obedience, what are you motivated by? What is there about your life right at this moment that speaks of faith? There may be a decision to make, a place to go, a venture to undertake, or a conversation to have about which you don't know all the implications, and all you can say is "I don't have a clue how this is going to go, but it's what God is calling me to do." In these situations, God's word calls you to use wisdom and then proceed in faith, step by step, trusting in the one who died for you and who promises to be "with you always, to the end of the age" (Matthew 28:20). Entrust your life not to the safety of your comfort zone but to the guidance of His providential hand.

RUTH 3

NOVEMBER 1

THE KINSMAN-REDEEMER

"I am Ruth, your servant. Spread your wings over your servant, for you are a redeemer." RUTH 3:9

Here is a truth that makes all the difference: you have a kinsman-redeemer.

The second chapter of Ruth ends with Naomi revealing that Boaz is a distant relative and "one of our redeemers" (Ruth 2:20). Long before Ruth's story took place, God had established practices that would affect not only her but also the people of Israel and all His people throughout redemptive history.

The two longstanding Old Testament practices that we need to understand in order to appreciate the context and joy of this story are the levirate and the *goel*. The levirate process regulated Israelite remarriage customs so that if a man died, his name and family line would not die with him or be vulnerable to the whims of other people (Deuteronomy 25:5-10). *Goel*, meanwhile, is a Hebrew verb meaning "to recover or redeem" and is often (and best) translated "kinsman-redeemer." The Law of Moses lays out this responsibility in Leviticus 25, where it makes provision for a relative who can care and provide for a less fortunate family member under certain circumstances. The kinsman-redeemer had a responsibility to do all that was necessary to secure the land and to support his relative.

Boaz willingly upheld both of these customs, providing and caring for Naomi and Ruth in their vulnerability and need. Not only was Boaz one of Jesus' ancestors but in this he foreshadowed Christ's coming as our own Kinsman-Redeemer.

As Ruth cast herself at Boaz's feet, desperately needy and dependent on his care, so we cast ourselves at the feet of Christ, seeking His mercy. And as Boaz dealt with Ruth, so Christ deals with every sinner who comes to Him in repentance, covering them with the blood of the covenant, by which He welcomes us into all the peace, security, and contentment of being under His wing (Psalm 91:4). He soothes our sorrows, calms our fears, and dries each one of our tears. Ruth came to Boaz as a penniless alien and became enriched by all his blessings. We come to Jesus in spiritual poverty and become fellow heirs with Him (Romans 8:17). As Boaz took Ruth and made her his bride, so Christ takes us and makes us His bride (Revelation 19:7-8).

The Bible is full of examples of God providing for and preserving His people long before they realize they need it. God's redemptive plan for Ruth in Israel, and for all His people throughout history, was laid out not only from the establishment of the role of kinsman-redeemer, but from the very beginning of time (Ephesians 1:3-7).

Today, rest assured that Jesus is the Bridegroom and Kinsman-Redeemer of His church. Rest assured that He has taken the responsibility to do all that is necessary to care for and provide for you and to bring you securely to His eternal promised land. Rest assured that whatever assails you within and without, you are safe under His wing.

PSALM 57

NOVEMBER 2

DETERMINED TO DO RIGHT

"Then Boaz said to the elders and all the people, 'You are witnesses this day that I have bought from the hand of Naomi all that belonged to Elimelech and all that belonged to Chilion and to Mahlon. Also Ruth the Moabite, the widow of Mahlon, I have bought to be my wife.'" RUTH 4:9-10

The question we must ask ourselves every day when faced with various circumstances is "What is the *right* thing to do?"

This is what Boaz considered when he determined to go to the city gate. He wanted to marry Ruth and provide for and protect her as her kinsman-redeemer. But he knew there was a relative closer to Ruth than him, who could choose to take on that role. Boaz was a man of integrity, unable to simply allow himself to rush off in a great swell of emotion when Ruth proposed to him on the threshing floor. His vision was set clearly on winning Ruth legitimately. In doing so, Boaz prioritized doing the right thing over his reputation. He went to the most public place—the city gate—in order to pursue a marriage with a foreigner, which potentially could have harmed his reputation and legacy. The closer relative was not willing to take this risk (Ruth 4:6). This man isn't even given a name in Scripture. This is a lesson to us: we shouldn't strive to make and safeguard a name for ourselves. Let someone else make a name for us and praise us. We should simply strive to do right.

Boaz's words reveal that one of his motivations was to "perpetuate the name of the dead in his inheritance" (Ruth 4:10)—to preserve the name of Elimelech, Naomi's deceased husband, by continuing his family. That's selfless. That's impressive. If Boaz had only been concerned for himself and his desires, he could have whisked Ruth away as his wife. Instead, he carried out his responsibility and publicly owned the situation. At the time, the passing of the kinsman-redeemer title was customarily sealed with the public exchange of a sandal (v 7). This exchange symbolized something greater—namely, Boaz's commitment, love, and personal sacrifice for Ruth. Similarly, the cross stands in public view, and there we see Christ's commitment, love, and sacrifice on our behalf. It cost Boaz financially to marry Ruth. It cost Christ His very *life* to redeem us and make us His beloved bride.

Both of these sacrifices—Boaz's and Christ's—won great rewards and legacies, providing a future and a hope: one for a young Moabitess and her mother-in-law, the other for all of humanity. Boaz's pursuit of rightness resulted in a marriage that played an integral part in all of history by continuing a lineage that eventually led to the birth of our Savior (Matthew 1:5). And because of Christ's sacrifice, we now look forward to the day when we will stand in glory, see His face, and praise His name forever. Our Bridegroom came and rightfully won us at great cost to Himself. Imagine Ruth's joy when she heard that Boaz had given his sandal and confirmed that he would marry her. A similar joy should be ours as we look at the cross and know we are Christ's. And the example of Boaz should be ours as we look at our day's decisions and difficulties and learn simply to ask, "What is the right thing to do?"

RUTH 4:1-12

NOVEMBER 3

A COVENANT OF COMMITMENT

"All the people who were at the gate and the elders said, 'We are witnesses...' So Boaz took Ruth, and she became his wife. And he went in to her, and the LORD gave her conception, and she bore a son." RUTH 4: 11, 13

In biblical times, the city gate was the main hub of local activity, serving as both a marketplace and civic center. Merchants, beggars, city officials, religious leaders, and a host of others gathered there to conduct business, administer the law, receive alms, shop, and socialize. It was to that crowded place that Boaz went to declare publicly his commitment to marry Ruth. Their marriage helpfully leads us to consider the biblical definition of marriage.

First, biblical marriage is to involve *committed love*. Such love is not based purely on emotion or circumstances but remains deeply rooted and unconditional through all of life's seasons and situations. This is reflected in the vows the church uses today in marriage ceremonies—commitment for better or worse, for richer or poorer, in sickness and in health.

Second, marriage involves *committed witnesses*. When a man and a woman marry, they become one unit under a covenant of love and care. As fallible humans, we need others to hold us accountable to this commitment. This is why wedding ceremonies must have at least one witness to attest to the forming of a new union, a new family. Boaz put this into practice at the city gate, where a crowd of people and the elders of the town witnessed his pledge to take Ruth's hand in marriage. They were then able to hold him to his word.

Third, godly marriage must have *committed communion*. God intends marriage to reflect the growing depth of intimacy that we experience with Him as His pursued bride. The personal relationship between husband and wife should deepen within marriage through, among other things, sexual intimacy. Such physical union should only take place within the context of a committed, loving, publicly recognized relationship. To try and isolate the physical commitment of marriage from the emotional, psychological, spiritual, and intellectual aspects makes a mockery of God's design.

Much of the world's perception of love and marriage pales in comparison with the beauty and benefit of a reliable, faithful, committed monogamous heterosexual union. When we see each facet of this covenant lived out, we are seeing a glimpse of the riches of our heavenly Bridegroom's commitment to His church (Ephesians 5:22-27). Christian marriage is a blessing itself, and a portrait of that even greater reality. No marriage but that greater one is perfect, but every marriage between believers is to strive to picture it. In how you think of, speak about, pray for and behave towards marriage (whether your own or the marriages around you), be sure to uphold the biblical definition and to live it out.

SONG OF SOLOMON 6:4-12

NOVEMBER 4

GLORY IN THE ORDINARY

"The women said to Naomi, 'Blessed be the LORD, *who has not left you this day without a redeemer, and may his name be renowned in Israel! He shall be to you a restorer of life and a nourisher of your old age...' Then Naomi took the child and laid him on her lap and became his nurse."* RUTH 4:14-15, 16

A new baby being introduced to a beaming grandparent is not an unusual scene. But Naomi's history and the future of this little family make this scene quite extraordinary.

Naomi had returned to Bethlehem having buried her husband and sons, empty-handed and sorrowful. Now her life and lap were full again with joy and hope. Here was a future generation of her family to bring life and nourishment in her old age. In this sense, the child brought her freedom—redemption. But as we look back on this ordinary scene from this side of the incarnation, we also know that it declares extraordinary news: because of God's gracious care for two defenseless widows, all of Israel—indeed, all of mankind—was helped. Through Ruth, God continued a family line that would later lead to King David, and then on to Jesus Christ Himself.

Even Jesus, this King of kings and Lord of lords, was found among the ordinary things of life. He had ordinary earthly parents. He was born in an animal stable, not a great palace. His victory came through a criminal's cross, not a conquered throne. This is not what most would expect of the incarnate God Almighty—yet, just as the wise men looked for Jesus first at the palace (Matthew 2:1-3), so we often start looking for Him in the wrong places. And when we do, we are in danger of ending up as a "Mara" rather than a "Naomi" (Ruth 1:20), feeling bitter rather than enjoying contentment.

God's eternal plans unfold in the midst of the ordinary—ordinary people in ordinary places doing ordinary things. If you lead an ordinary life, this should encourage you! Very few of us will even be a footnote in history. Whether you are an ordinary mother raising ordinary kids doing ordinary things day in and day out, an ordinary grandpa telling the same old ordinary stories, or an ordinary student going about your ordinary routine homework and activities—whatever sort of ordinary you are—the glory of God can be found all around you. And your faithfulness in the midst of the ordinary may, by His grace, become the means of extraordinary impact for the sake of the gospel.

When you are tempted to feel like you're not doing much—to believe the devil's lie that you cannot make a difference or are outside of God's purposes—remember this: long after human achievement, words, and wisdom fade, the faithfulness, kindness, integrity, love, and gentleness that God works in and through you will be seen to have had a more dramatic impact on the lives of men and women than you could ever imagine. This is the wonder of Naomi's story and the wonder of all of history—that God's extraordinary glory is at work in the ordinary. That truth can change the way you feel about and go about your day.

RUTH 4:13-21

NOVEMBER 5

THE MYSTERY OF HISTORY

"The women of the neighborhood gave him a name, saying, 'A son has been born to Naomi.' They named him Obed. He was the father of Jesse, the father of David." RUTH 4:17

History matters. *Your* history matters.

You are who you are, to some significant degree, because of who your parents were, who your grandparents were, and so on. Inevitably, you and I are products of our lineages—and as a result, we are living proof of God's providence, which has brought us to this place in this moment.

As Ruth gave birth to Obed, Naomi's grandson, she could not have known what the narrator tells the reader: Obed would be the grandfather of the great King David—and, therefore, he would be the ancestor of Jesus. But God knew, of course; and so here we see God's redemptive plan at work. Ruth and her family were neither held in the grip of blind forces nor swept along on a sea of chance. The birth of Obed was yet another reminder that God cares, God rules, and God provides, and that He is always at work behind the scenes of human choices and the twists and turns of life, working out His purposes.

This is the mystery of all of history: that God has stitched together all of the elements of our past, separate and distinct as they are, to nudge and guide us to who and where we are right now. Before our infant hearts could ever conceive what was happening, God was graciously, mercifully providing for us—in mothers who fed us, in family friends who looked after us, or in grandparents who came around us.

Since you were conceived, God has guarded and guided you, through even the darkest days. You and I are not random collections of molecules. We are divine creations, and God is caring for each of us. Not only that but we are divinely redeemed. From the very beginning, God has worked through individuals and families, putting together a people that are His very own. From Genesis all the way to Revelation, we get glimpses of this redemptive, eternal purpose. The very engrafting of Ruth, a Moabitess, into this redeemed family testifies of God's sovereign, comprehensive mercy, in which He used her unlikely marriage to Boaz to produce the lineage for King David and Christ Jesus.

Examples like that of Ruth should strengthen our faith in what God can do. They should embolden us to say to our friends and neighbors that the glories and tragedies that happen in our nation, the joys and sorrows in our own lives, and the pains and disappointments of family life find their ultimate meaning not in human history or personal biography but as a part of God's plan. He has made Himself known as loving and holy, personal and infinite, Creator and Redeemer, Sustainer and Ruler. He has brought us into the great story of redemption—the only story that will last eternally.

This is good news! This is food for our souls when days get dark and doubts get real. This is assurance that God will never quit on us. This brings meaning to life.

MATTHEW 1:1-18

NOVEMBER 6

SEARCHING FOR ASSURANCE

"Behold, a man came up to him, saying, 'Teacher, what good deed must I do to have eternal life?' ... Jesus said to him, 'If you would be perfect, go, sell what you possess and give to the poor, and you will have treasure in heaven; and come, follow me.' When the young man heard this he went away sorrowful, for he had great possessions." MATTHEW 19:16, 21-22

Observing religious rules in an attempt to gain acceptance into heaven doesn't produce a sense of security or assurance of forgiveness. Nor does it gain eternal life.

It was a lack of assurance of forgiveness that drove this young man to approach Jesus and boldly ask his question. He was rich; Luke adds the detail that he was a ruler, powerful and influential (Luke 18:18)—the kind of person the world looks up to and considers blessed. Not only that, but he was serious about keeping God's commands (Matthew 19:20). We are supposed to look at him and think, "If anyone would make it to eternal life, surely it is this man." So this man probably expected Jesus to pat him on the back for his extensive rule-following and assure him of his heavenly reward. But instead, Jesus gently pointed out that he had not kept God's law perfectly. Indeed, the young man had broken the very first commandment: instead of loving God with all his heart, soul, strength, and mind, he had worshiped his wealth, as was evidenced by the fact that he "went away" from Jesus when asked to choose between his Master and his money. Jesus showed this man that God's commandments are not a ladder we climb to reach His acceptance but a mirror revealing our true spiritual condition.

At his core, the rich young ruler had a heart problem. That's our problem too. The Bible says we are born at odds with God and are unable to put ourselves in right relationship with Him. We *haven't* loved God with all of our heart, for we have loved other things more than Him. The young ruler's inability to obey God's law and love God as he should have is our inability as well. No one has, no one can, and no one will ever love God and keep His commands perfectly, except Jesus Himself. But this is actually good news! Salvation does not depend on us and what we do. Rather, peace, security, forgiveness, and right standing before God come when we cast ourselves on His mercy: when we accept His offer of salvation as a free gift that cannot be earned or bought and when we bow down in humility and gratitude before the provision that Jesus made by His atoning death on the cross.

This man did not have to walk away in sadness from his encounter with Jesus. He could have given up his pride and self-sufficiency. He could have known the joy of placing Jesus first rather than the nagging sorrow of trusting to his own goodness and clinging to his wealth. Self-reliance will always prove futile and induce anxiety, for us no less than for him. But if we will go before our Savior in childlike faith and trust, we can experience true peace and the assurance of eternal life. So enthrone Jesus in your heart and be prepared to place all that you are and have in His service. Come to Jesus with empty hands, and know the joy and life He gives.

MATTHEW 19:16-30

NOVEMBER 7

THE HOLY CITY

"I saw the holy city, new Jerusalem, coming down out of heaven from God."
REVELATION 21:2

In Jesus, God has come from heaven and reached down to us—and at the end of all things, the holy city, the new Jerusalem, will also come down out of heaven from God.

God is putting together a new Jerusalem that will comprise believers from all the ages and from all places—people like you and me. We will be city dwellers living in perfect harmony with one another; God's face will be before us, and we will be marked as His own (Revelation 22:4). This company will be a multitude so vast and magnificent that no one can count it, with citizens coming from every nation, tribe, people, and language (7:9).

The description of this vast multitude was intended as a source of hope and encouragement for the church in the apostle John's day, and it should also be so for us. The early church was very, very small in numbers—quite insignificant by human standards, just as it has been in many eras throughout history. But John tells us that the church is actually far greater, vaster, and more significant than we can ever imagine, for its members are citizens of the new Jerusalem, journeying as pilgrims ever onwards until they stand in its streets.

One day, in that city, innumerable believers will worship together, and we will witness the final fulfillment of God's promise to Abraham: "He brought him outside and said, 'Look toward heaven, and number the stars, if you are able to number them ... So shall your offspring be'" (Genesis 15:5).

For now, creation is marked by division and discord. We are separated by language, nationality, and culture—by ancient enmities and recent suspicions. One day, though, all of that is going to be reversed. God is putting together a new community—a multiracial, multicultural city under His reign and rule. When we are finally all brought together as heaven comes to earth and Christ's people are raised to dwell in it, we will be united by the gospel of the Lord Jesus Christ because the gospel is for all nations.

Can you imagine such a day? No, not fully, of course—but yes, sufficiently to pull you onwards through the trials and pressures of this life and to cause you to fling off all that would hold you back (Hebrews 12:1-2). This world is not your home; but one day, the heavenly city will come down, and it will be. One day you will see for real what John saw in this vision, and you will be home.

REVELATION 22

NOVEMBER 8

THE WAR AGAINST TEMPTATION

"Sin will have no dominion over you, since you are not under law but under grace." ROMANS 6:14

In this life, we will never be exempt from temptation. In fact, the older we get, the more we discover that the same old temptations—often in new guises—are right there behind us, biting at our heels and seeking to bring us down. And if that were not bad enough, they're often joined by a whole batch of new ones!

Yes, temptation is a reality, and it is unavoidable. But why is this the case?

The first reason is that the same grace which reconciles us to God also opposes us to the devil, who, Scripture tells us persuaded us that he was our friend before we came to trust in Christ. When God's grace makes us *His* friend instead, it simultaneously makes us enemies of His great enemy. And although the Evil One cannot prevent God from saving His people, he can bring all of his endeavors—namely, temptation—to bear upon us once we have been saved.

Secondly, when we are born again, sin no longer masters us, but it does continue to wage a war against our souls—and temptation is among its greatest weapons. We are tempted by the world: all that is out there that says to us, "If you can obtain this, you will be happy and will enjoy life." We are also tempted by our flesh. Our old sinful nature—which still lingers in us in this present life, even after we trust in Christ—wages a fierce rearguard battle against our new selves.

Yet as strong as the appeals of the Evil One may be—and they *are* strong—they do not in themselves have the power to compel us to yield to temptation. The devil has the power to bring the world to us, but he does not have the power to make us sin.

Do not be paralyzed by fear, then, or complacent about the temptations you face. In your war against temptation, you do not need to wonder if you'll win or lose. God has already declared checkmate, for, as John writes, "he who is in you is greater than he who is in the world" (1 John 4:4). The war is over, and victory is assured. Battles may still go on, but they cannot affect the war's ultimate conclusion.

What temptations are you currently struggling with or giving in to? Take a moment to name them. And then take comfort in this today: as powerful as those temptations may be, the devil is a defeated foe, and Jesus Christ reigns victorious! His power in you is sufficient to enable you to fight temptation, and His death for you is sufficient for God to forgive you!

ROMANS 6:1-14

NOVEMBER 9

FAITH TO MOVE MOUNTAINS

"Jesus answered them, 'Have faith in God. Truly, I say to you, whoever says to this mountain, "Be taken up and thrown into the sea," and does not doubt in his heart, but believes that what he says will come to pass, it will be done for him. Therefore I tell you, whatever you ask in prayer, believe that you have received it, and it will be yours.'" MARK 11:22-24

In reading our Bibles, we will come across verses that seem straightforward and easy to understand immediately. On the other hand, there are also verses like this one!

"Whatever you ask in prayer, believe that you have received it, and it will be yours," says Jesus. We are tempted essentially to sidestep what these words say. We try to bury them under a hundred qualifications. The misapplication of such verses has scared some of us so much that we hardly give any attention to the encouragement and the challenge they contain.

In this bold command, Jesus reminded His followers to trust God, because it is actually faith's foundation *in* God that gives that faith significance. We should not have faith in faith or faith in ourselves, but faith in God alone.

The metaphor that Jesus employed—that of someone commanding a mountain to be thrown into the sea—was perhaps familiar to the disciples; it was similar to a common rabbinic figure of speech for accomplishing something that was seemingly impossible.[121] The disciples would not have misunderstood Jesus as suggesting that they *literally* hurl the Mount of Olives into the Dead Sea over 4,000 feet below them. They would have understood his words as a proverbial statement indicating that God wants to do extraordinary things for His children.

We discover vivid proof of Jesus' teaching on faith and prayer throughout the book of Acts. Early on, when a lame beggar asked Peter and John for money, Peter told him instead to stand up and walk (Acts 3:6). Perhaps as he spoke to this man, Peter was remembering Jesus' words and thinking to himself, "Whatever you ask... believe..."

When God is the object of our faith, we can have an audacious faith—a faith that believes the impossible to be possible with Him. We can know that we are speaking to someone who is able to do far more than we can even imagine (Ephesians 3:20-21). Jesus essentially says to us, *I want you to pray in a way that says you actually believe in a God who is too wise to make mistakes, who is too kind to be cruel, and who is too powerful to be subdued by the normal forces of the universe.*

Do not set aside these verses with a hundred qualifications. Just let them sit there for a minute. Enjoy the truth that God is able to do things beyond anything you can imagine. Rest in the reality that He knows no impossibility. And then pray.

EPHESIANS 3:14-21

---

121 Alfred Edersheim, *The Life and Times of Jesus the Messiah* (Longmans, Green, and Co., 1898), Vol. 2, p 376 (footnote).

NOVEMBER 10

THE REALITY OF EVIL

"The heart is deceitful above all things, and desperately sick; who can understand it? 'I the LORD search the heart and test the mind, to give every man according to his ways, according to the fruit of his deeds.'" JEREMIAH 17:9-10

The Bible is very clear about the reality of evil—and it is equally clear about the personality of the one who is *behind* the evil in the world. Satan, the Evil One, is completely opposed to the spiritual well-being of his victims. He is a ferocious lion, and (though not outside of God's sovereign control) he is the ruler of this world. He is behind all sin; and before anyone is born again of the Spirit of God, they actually belong to his domain, and their evil actions give proof of his ownership.

Of course, the idea of an actual Evil One is laughed at by most of our contemporaries. They say, "Oh, you can't possibly believe in the existence of an evil spiritual force called the devil, can you?" But at the same time as they downplay the idea of a personal devil, such people are at a loss to explain why we're able to make such great technological advances and yet are unable to control the sinful impulses of our own lives any better than previous generations. Why is this?

The Bible teaches that when Adam followed his wife in placing himself under the influence of the deceiver and sinning, he took the whole of humanity down with him. In other words, when Adam sinned, we *all* sinned. Each of us was born fallen. Therefore, our hearts—the core of our being, the source of our feelings, our longings, our decisions—are "deceitful above all things, and desperately sick." Jeremiah anticipates what Jesus would say to the Pharisees: "There is nothing outside a person that by going into him can defile him, but the things that come out of a person are what defile him ... For from within, out of the heart of man, come evil thoughts, sexual immorality," and all other sorts of wickedness, both blatant and discreet (Mark 7:15, 21).

While these truths provide a compelling explanation of what we see in the world, they also confront us with a very challenging view of ourselves. The truth is that we are not good people who make mistakes; we are sinful people in need of mercy. Because it requires humility to accept what our hearts are truly like, those same hearts will tend to prefer to be deceived by preachers of self-esteem and self-confidence rather than listen to prophets such as Jeremiah.

The truth is that everyone is born in need of a heart transplant—not a physical one but a spiritual one. Only God can accomplish such a transformation. Just as God charged us with Adam's guilt, by grace He credits believers with the righteousness of the Lord Jesus Christ. As believers in Jesus, we have been changed from the inside out. Today, as with every day, the only antidote for your deceitful heart is to come humbly and sincerely before the Lord, praying, "Create in me a clean heart, O God, and renew a right spirit within me" (Psalm 51:10).

MARK 7:1-23

NOVEMBER 11

THE PROMISE AND THE BLESSING

"I will make of you a great nation, and I will bless you and make your name great, so that you will be a blessing. I will bless those who bless you, and him who dishonors you I will curse, and in you all the families of the earth shall be blessed." GENESIS 12:1-3

Children have a way of getting underfoot as dinner is being prepared. Sometimes parents feel like shouting, "Listen, why don't all of you get out of the kitchen? Just go!"

At the Tower of Babel, the people did more than get underfoot; they turned their backs on God. Determined to have their own kingdom, they built their tower and tried to reach up to the heavens to see what they could do by their own might. As a result of this rebellion, God brought judgment by diversifying their languages and scattering them all over the world (Genesis 11:1-9).

Being far more justified than an exasperated parent, God could have sent the people away and been done with them. But He didn't.

To demonstrate His grace, in the very next generation God began to repair what was broken. He spoke to a childless, elderly pagan man named Abram, whose name ironically meant "exalted father," and He promised to reverse the effect of His judgment at Babel. People there had aimed to make their name great. God would make Abram's great. They had sought to build their own kingdom. God would make Abram's people a great nation. They had planned to find blessing in a world without God. God would bring blessing to the earth through Abram's family. Sin would be unwound and its effects undone by God's intervening grace.

In this very covenant God took Abram and made him Abraham, "the father of a multitude," as He promised to extend His grace to this chosen servant and to future generations scattered throughout the earth.

God's promise to Abraham is an early expression of the gospel promise. He made a promise to Abraham, and Abraham's descendants later received the blessing. They would eventually realize, though, that the promise and blessing encompass all who believe in Jesus: "For in Christ Jesus you are all sons of God, through faith ... And if you are Christ's, then you are Abraham's offspring, heirs according to promise" (Galatians 3:26, 29). So, while the promises that God made to Abraham were partially fulfilled in the Old Testament nation of Israel, they were ultimately fulfilled in the gospel of Jesus Christ and in His people.

Catch just a tiny glimpse of the immensity of this fulfillment and your life will be forever changed. If you are in Christ today, the promise that God made to Abraham has your name on it. You are a citizen of heaven and serve a King descended from Abraham called Jesus. What God began as He spoke to Abram has come to encompass you as God calls people back into His kingdom, to enjoy Him face-to-face forever. Whatever else is true of you today, by faith you are a child of God, a member of Abraham's people, and an heir to these glorious promises.

GENESIS 11:1-9; 12:1-9

NOVEMBER 12

THE REASON WE FORGIVE

"Be kind to one another, tenderhearted, forgiving one another, as God in Christ forgave you." EPHESIANS 4:32

God's forgiveness is not merely an expression of His heart (although it is certainly that)but also a promise from His word. Our experience of God's forgiveness is therefore directly tied to our willingness to take Him at His word.

The author of Hebrews explains that our assurance of forgiveness rests on nothing but the atoning blood of Jesus (Hebrews 10:19-22). Furthermore, when we come to God in repentance, He promises to remember our sins no more (v 17). God has pledged Himself not to keep a record of our iniquities (Isaiah 43:25). In other words, if we try to go back to God with issues that He has already dealt with, we'll find Him saying, in effect, *My dear child, I have no recollection of what you're talking about. I promised not to bring that up ever again—and so neither should you.*

God's example is meant to be the model for how we forgive others. Forgiving others is not about a feeling; it's about a promise and obedience. When you or I forgive someone, we are essentially making a three-point pledge: first, that we will not bring the matter up with that individual again; second, that we will not bring it up with anyone else; and third, that we will not bring it back up to ourselves. A genuine expression of forgiveness says, "I want to do for you as God in Christ has done for me."

This does not mean forgiveness is merely in our minds and an act of the will only. We are clearly meant to forgive from the heart (Matthew 18:35). It does mean, however, that our expressions of forgiveness are most genuine when they flow out of an awareness of and sense of gratitude for our own forgiveness from Christ, paired with obedience to God's command to forgive.

Is there someone you need to forgive? You may not feel like extending forgiveness to another today—but that is not the issue. As a recipient of God's forgiveness in Christ, you are called to forgive as He has forgiven you. That is not easy, but it is possible. God's Spirit can enable you to make and keep your promise to do so. When you forgive by making that three-fold pledge in obedience to God's command, He can and will make the feelings follow.

MATTHEW 18:21-35

NOVEMBER 13

AGREEING IN THE LORD

"I entreat Euodia and I entreat Syntyche to agree in the Lord. Yes, I ask you also, true companion, help these women, who have labored side by side with me in the gospel together with Clement and the rest of my fellow workers, whose names are in the book of life." PHILIPPIANS 4:2-3

Divisions corrode churches from within.

This is why Paul took seriously reports that two women in the Philippian fellowship had fallen out. He made space in his letter to "entreat" them to "agree." And in his approach to addressing the disagreement between Euodia and Syntyche, the apostle gives us a helpful model of reconciliation. He makes it clear that we must remember we are bound together with our brothers and sisters "in the Lord." This phrase explains who we are at our core: we are not our own; we belong to Christ.

So Paul pleads with Euodia and Syntyche to remember their unity "in the Lord" and to submit to God's instruction as it came through the apostles, just as we submit to God's word now in the Scriptures. The Bible is clear that as Christians, we must first love and serve God. Then, as we seek to please God, He will so work in our hearts that we desire to serve our neighbors for their good, to build them up (Romans 15:2).

When we forget that we belong exclusively to Christ, we will very quickly begin to champion our own agendas, establish our own causes, fight for our personal rights, and get on our high horses to dispute with anybody who doesn't agree with us. Dissension among believers can cause us to grow distracted by petty and often peripheral concerns, sapping the energy of the arguers as well as all who are caught up in the dispute. Instead of reaching out, the church then becomes inwardly focused. It is utterly incongruous for us to insist on our own way when we belong to a Savior who never did so. If Jesus had thought of Himself in the way we so often and so easily think of ourselves, then there would have been no incarnation, there would have been no cross, there would be no forgiveness, and there would be no hope of heaven for us.

We should not pretend that dissent doesn't exist among believers. It does. But as a company of the redeemed, we are to *work through* our disagreements on the strength and foundation of our unity in the Lord. Our focus cannot remain on ourselves. In the healing and mending of fractured relationships, we must imitate Christ by initiating reconciliation.

This is a call to all of us. If you find yourself today in the shoes of Euodia and Syntyche, then the call to you is clear, though challenging: "Agree in the Lord." Whatever else divides, your unity with other Christians is stronger. And if you find yourself today in a church with a Euodia and a Syntyche, then you are called to act in the way Paul commanded his "true companion" to act: to help those who are divided to reconcile. True love takes the initiative. True love gets involved. True love does not allow division to corrode; instead, it pursues the unity that builds up.

JOHN 17:1-26

NOVEMBER 14

RADICALLY CHANGED

"Neither the sexually immoral, nor idolaters, nor adulterers, nor men who practice homosexuality, nor thieves, nor the greedy, nor drunkards, nor revilers, nor swindlers will inherit the kingdom of God. And such were some of you. But you were washed, you were sanctified, you were justified in the name of the Lord Jesus Christ and by the Spirit of our God." 1 CORINTHIANS 6:9-11

The proof of Christianity lies in its power. Only the power of Christ can take men and women, lost to shame, and make them sons and daughters of God. There is no depth of guilt to which someone can plummet or degree of humiliation someone can feel that puts them beyond God's forgiving grace.

As he concludes a long, ugly list, Paul states, "Such were some of you." This statement is a shout of triumph, not of remorse. It is past tense, not present. Why? Because of Jesus' transforming power. No man can change himself; no woman can change herself—but Jesus can change them!

Do we actually believe a total personal transformation can happen? We are tempted to offer people cosmetic fixes but tell them they must now limp through the rest of their lives as a result of former sins, or to assure them that they are saved by grace but must now work hard to change themselves. Where did we get these messages? Did Jesus tell people, *I'll touch your life and change you, but I want you to know that you'll only be changed a wee bit—now it's up to you*? No! He said, *I'll make you brand-new from the inside out. I'll transform you, liberate you, change you.* That's Jesus' message. And that was the testimony of these Corinthian Christians. They were one kind of person—sinful, facing judgment. But then they were transformed. Now they were different. So how does this transformation begin? With a clear view of our own sin. If I don't know myself to be sinful, how could I ever know myself to be saved? We must each face the depths of our own depravity so that when God's word tells us that Jesus came to rescue people from every trial and entanglement of life and give them His Spirit to change them from inside out, we will reach out for Him with both hands. That's salvation! That's transformation!

Every Christian is living evidence that God changes lives. There are men and women everywhere who are living proofs of Christ's re-creating, life-transforming power. Are we prepared, then, to have a church full of people who were once sexually immoral, adulterers, drunks, and swindlers? And are we prepared to acknowledge that this is what we ourselves were but no longer are, and all by grace? Or do we just want churches of people properly put together—fairly acceptable individuals who really believe they have no need of Jesus?

Jesus saves, and Jesus transforms. By faith, you are not what you were, and you will be able to say that again next month and next year. Who seems to you to be too steeped in sin ever to come to Christ? Pray for divine transformation. What part of your own life feels too resistant to change ever to please Christ? Pray for divine transformation. You cannot change anyone, including yourself. But Christ is powerful to do what you cannot.

2 CORINTHIANS 3:17 – 4:6

NOVEMBER 15

THE FATHER'S TENDER CARE

"Do not be anxious, saying, 'What shall we eat?' or 'What shall we drink?' or 'What shall we wear?' For the Gentiles seek after all these things, and your heavenly Father knows that you need them all. But seek first the kingdom of God and his righteousness, and all these things will be added to you."
MATTHEW 6:31-33

As creatures in God's world, we are not at the mercy of fate or chance. We are not driven along by blind and impersonal forces, nor do we need to be concerned about horoscopes, the motions of the planets, or similar distractions.

But for those who don't know and trust God as their heavenly Father, this is how the universe appears. So, as Scripture makes clear, "the Gentiles"—meaning here those with no interest in God—"seek after all these things." Such individuals are uncertain that there ever really was a Creator—and if there was, they suppose, He's had His hands off creation since it was established. In their minds, every up and down, every ebb and flow of human history, is down to chance, with all of us caught up in the grip of a vast, faceless mechanism.

It's a grim picture. Thankfully, the Bible tells us otherwise. According to Scripture, all things were created through Christ and for Christ, and He remains intimately involved in His creation (Colossians 1:16-17). In light of this, God the Son essentially says in Matthew 6:26-33, *Why should you be worrying about food, clothing, or anything else? The pagans worry. But you? You just keep your eyes on Me, and I'll take care of you. There's not a bird in the sky I do not know. The very grass of the field is clothed by My mighty power, and I'm going to look after you too.*

Indeed, Christ's promise that He and His Father care for us is a truth echoed wonderfully in Romans 8:28, that "for those who love God all things work together for good, for those who are called according to his purpose." If we are in Christ, all of our days and our desires, our hopes and our heartaches, our fears and our failures are being worked out according to the wise, gracious, loving will of God.

If you are alone today, or you spent last evening alone, or you are fearful of the prospect of another week of fractured or difficult relationships, allow the word of God to come in and warm and fill your heart with an intimate awareness of the Father's love and presence. If you are burdened by financial worries, allow Jesus to calm your fears by telling you that He will provide for you what you truly need. If you are struggling with health problems—be they physical or emotional—be assured that He knows, and cares, and will bring you through. No matter what happens or how difficult life becomes, God Himself will look after you, because He cares for you.

MATTHEW 6:19-34

NOVEMBER 16

A CALL TO PURPOSEFUL WORK

"Whatever you do, work heartily, as for the Lord and not for men, knowing that from the Lord you will receive the inheritance as your reward. You are serving the Lord Christ." COLOSSIANS 3:23-24

Work is part of God's creative design and therefore part of our purpose in life. Work existed before the fall: God gave Adam and Eve the garden "to work it and keep it" (Genesis 2:15). We were not fashioned to sit around and do nothing! Rather, we were made in the image of a God who loves to work and create.

The New Testament writers expect believers to work—not only to imitate our Creator but also to "help cases of urgent need, and not be unfruitful" (Titus 3:14). This call to "work heartily" is not beyond our grasp; it is not an exhortation to be superhuman. Instead, it is an invitation to live quietly, mind our own affairs, and work with our hands (1 Thessalonians 4:11) so that we may provide not only for ourselves but also for those who are in particular need. Life's routine activities are divine providences for us to "work heartily, as for the Lord and not for men." In all our everyday responsibilities and commitments—whether they involve investing millions or changing diapers, working on a factory assembly line or plowing a field or sitting in a boardroom—we can view them as the very instruments God will use for His purposes and to glorify His name.

Working hard within the bounds God has ordained for us eliminates worry concerning the work of the person next to us. After all, we're not the ones keeping the score, and neither are they! God, who is pleased when we work diligently on the tasks He has appointed us for, is the one who will give the rewards on the day we stand before Him. It is His approval of our work and how we think about it and conduct ourselves in it that matters, not primarily that of our boss, our colleagues, or ourselves.

In Paul's instruction we find no loophole. It is a straightforward exhortation to work, and to work hard. Elsewhere in Scripture, Paul encourages Timothy also to command fellow believers to provide for their relatives, especially for members of their own households, "so that they may be without reproach" (1 Timothy 5:7). The implication is clear: when grace is at work in our lives, we will be committed to meeting the needs of our dependents and those who are in need.

You were made in the image of God and created for good works. No matter what your station in or stage of life, you have work to do today in God's creation. Be sure to do it heartily, to the best of your ability. Be sure to do it with godliness, caring for God's good opinion more than anyone else's. And be sure to do it joyfully, however mundane, repetitive, or challenging it may be, for, in doing so, you are serving Christ and bringing glory to His name. That is enough to transform any task into something glorious!

PROVERBS 24:30-34

NOVEMBER 17

BLESSINGS AND CURSES

"All these blessings shall come upon you and overtake you, if you obey the voice of the Lord your God … But if you will not obey the voice of the Lord your God or be careful to do all his commandments and his statutes that I command you today, then all these curses shall come upon you and overtake you." DEUTERONOMY 28:2, 15

On the plains of Moab by the River Jordan, the Israelites were on the brink of finally entering the land God had promised them. Moses addressed the people for the last time, trying to ensure that they would not spoil their relationship with God by their disobedience, as the previous generation had done. He reminded them of what God had said and done in the past, and he exhorted them, on the basis of God's great intervention and covenant-keeping faithfulness, to be a people set apart for God.

Through Moses' instructions, God set before His people two striking alternatives—and the stakes were high. He gave them a promise of blessing and then a word of warning. He presented them with a simple question: How were they going to live? Would they keep the covenant and enjoy blessing in the land, or would they disobey and be expelled from the land?

The people who were gathered on the edge of the land must have heard God's word and said, *Oh, no, disobedience like that will never happen to us!* Yet fast-forward a few hundred years and where do we find them? "By the waters of Babylon, there we sat down and wept, when we remembered Zion … How shall we sing the Lord's song in a foreign land?" (Psalm 137:1, 4). Captives of a foreign people, the Israelites look back and wonder how they ever ended up where they are.

As creatures living in a fallen world, you and I are so vulnerable, so tempted, so tested. We are always only a single decision away from disobedience and from walking away from God. We are desperately in need of God's sustaining grace. Tragically, many who once appeared to be devoted, committed, and headed towards the promised land have not simply tripped; they have tumbled down into disbelief. And the worst mistake we can make is to think, "Oh, no, that will never happen to me!"

The Evil One loves to come and tell us that the reason that God has given us His law and established His commands is because He wants to sour our lives, deprive us of fun, and fill our days with heartache and pain. That is the absolute lie of all lies. God gives His word for our good! All the warnings of Scripture are there to corral us and sting us when we are on the verge of ruin, and all the promises of Scripture are there to pick us up when we are timid and unsure, and all the commands of Scripture are there to lead us into the blessing of life lived God's way, in His presence, in His world. His commitment to our good is seen most supremely in His Son coming to bear the curse of our disobedience so that we can enjoy the blessing that He, and He alone, deserves.

Do you love God? Do you know that God loves you? Then take heed of His warnings, obey His commands, and cherish the comforts of His promises.

GALATIANS 3:10-14

NOVEMBER 18

THE HEART OF THE MATTER

"Just as it is appointed for man to die once, and after that comes judgment, so Christ, having been offered once to bear the sins of many, will appear a second time, not to deal with sin but to save those who are eagerly waiting for him."
HEBREWS 9:27-28

The ultimate statistic is that one out of one will die. Death is the only certainty of life. As Christians, while we may fear the event, we need not fear the outcome.

We need not fear for this reason: Jesus did not come merely to add to the sum total of our happiness or to offer us a leg up in life or worldly riches, but to save sinners and to rescue us from judgment.

The Bible teaches that God's judgment and eternal punishment will fall on those whose names are not included in the Book of Life (Revelation 20:11-15). How, then, can we be sure that *our* names will be found in its pages? There is only one way: by believing in the Lord Jesus. We must look to Christ, who will freely pardon and justify those who come to Him in repentance and faith. And to come to Jesus is about more than mere intellectual assent, necessary though that is. It is not enough to be cerebrally tuned in to Christian doctrine. We must recognize our failure to treat God properly. We have denied and defied Him. We must surrender our lives to His loving authority and rely entirely on what Christ accomplished on the cross that we might find acceptance before God.

The heart of the matter is not whether we believe certain facts about Jesus or the Bible, or whether we've cleaned up our lifestyle. The question is, have we ever gotten so spiritually thirsty that we have said, "Lord Jesus Christ, give me Your living water so I may thirst no more"?

But what if Jesus turns us away? What if we're not supposed to be in the Book of Life? Jesus addressed this fear Himself with a promise, saying, "Whoever comes to me I will never cast out" (John 6:37).

Do you realize the kindness of God's invitation to you? Have you heard God's call to take refuge in Jesus? Do you hear it afresh each day and take refuge in the shadow of His wings (Psalm 57:1)? May we say with the hymn writer:

I came to Jesus as I was,
Weary and worn and sad;
I found in Him a resting place,
And He has made me glad.[122]

For if we have taken refuge in the Son, we can know with certainty that He has borne our sins in His own death, and that when He returns, we will face not a fearful condemnation but a glorious welcome. And then we can hear the truth that "it is appointed for man to die" and find our hearts still at rest.

PSALM 49

122 Horatius Bonar, "I Heard the Voice of Jesus Say" (1846).

NOVEMBER 19

A WARNING AGAINST COMPLACENCY

"There is no one who has left house or brothers or sisters or mother or father or children or lands, for my sake and for the gospel, who will not receive a hundredfold now in this time, houses and brothers and sisters and mothers and children and lands, with persecutions, and in the age to come eternal life. But many who are first will be last, and the last first." MARK 10:29-31

Jesus' priority is not that we would be comfortable.

When a conversation with Jesus about inheriting eternal life ended with a rich young ruler leaving the scene sad because he was unwilling to part with his wealth in order to follow Him, Jesus told His followers that "it is easier to go through the eye of a needle than for a rich person to enter the kingdom of God" (Mark 10:25). In response, Peter, who liked to blurt things out on such occasions, pointed out the sacrifices that he and the other disciples had made to follow Jesus (v 28).

Presumably, Peter was trying to elicit a reassuring word that he and the other disciples were "safe" from Jesus' warning since they had left behind their possessions. And indeed Jesus replied by offering the encouragement that whoever sacrifices much for His sake and for the gospel will surely receive plenty in return. In other words, God will care for them both in this life and in the age to come. But Jesus wasn't concerned with simply making His disciples feel good about themselves. So He followed these words with a sting in the tail: "Many who are first will be last, and the last first."

We can imagine Peter, on hearing those words, comparing himself to the rich young ruler and feeling reassured. But that does not seem to be the point Jesus was making. He had already dealt with riches. Rather, it seems that Jesus was warning His disciples, *Be careful that complacency doesn't get to you.* There are those who assume they are "first"—many who are told, by the world or by the church, that they are "first"—who will one day be shocked by Jesus' assessment of them. It will be those who gave all they had for Him, often in ways unnoticed by others, for whom Jesus reserves the highest praise.

Perhaps we, like Peter, feel protected from Jesus' challenges about wealth and being "first," either because we don't have riches in the first place or because we have sacrificed so much for Jesus already. We can always find someone wealthier than us or who has given up less than us, and base our sense of security on that comparison. But Jesus isn't concerned with making us feel comfortable. Instead, He calls us from our complacency and into devotedly following Him. Relative poverty is no more a virtue than relative wealth. He has promised to care for us, and He has called us to find our security in His finished work for us, not in what we are doing for Him. Do not give in to complacency born of comparison with others. Instead, hear Jesus' call to Peter when, on a later occasion, Peter asked his Lord whether John's life would play out differently from his: "You follow me!" (John 21:22).

PSALM 73

NOVEMBER 20

OVERFLOWING WITH THANKFULNESS

"Walk in him, rooted and built up in him and established in the faith, just as you were taught, abounding in thanksgiving." COLOSSIANS 2:6-7

If we walk around with a full glass and someone bumps into us unexpectedly, whatever is inside it will come out. The same principle also applies to our character: if we are filled with bitterness, ingratitude, envy, or jealousy, then it won't take much of a "bump" for what is within us to overflow.

As Paul wrote to the Colossian Christians, he encouraged them instead to be marked by a grateful heart—a key characteristic of the Christian life. The word Paul uses to describe this thankfulness, "abounding," comes from a fairly common Greek word, *perisseuo*. In other places in Scripture and in other English translations, its root is translated as "overflowing." Paul's meaning is clear: when people "bumped into" these believers, the overspill, he instructed, was to be thankfulness.

When men and women have not been transformed by Christ, ingratitude—along with its resulting bitterness, complaining, anger, and malice—often marks their lives. In Christ, however, believers trade ingratitude for thanksgiving, bitterness for joy, and anger for peace. Having heard of God's grace in all its truth and having turned to Him in repentance and faith, we have our sins forgiven. We have the Spirit dwelling in us. We have a new family in the church of God. We have eternal life ahead of us. We have access to the heavenly throne room in prayer. In other words, we have much to be grateful for. Thankfulness becomes the song, the overflow, of the Christian.

This kind of gratitude has significant effects. It turns our gaze to God and away from ourselves and our circumstances. It defends us against the devil's whisper, which incites us to despair and to distrust what God has said. It also protects us from pride, eradicating from our vocabulary phrases like "I deserve more than this" or "I don't deserve this." And it allows us to rest in the knowledge that God works out His loving purpose not only in pleasant and encouraging experiences but also in unsettling and painful ones. It is only by grace that we learn to "give thanks in *all* circumstances" (1 Thessalonians 5:18, emphasis added).

The antidote to thanklessness is found only in union with Christ. Do you see in yourself any lingering ingratitude over what God has chosen not to give you? Bring it to the foot of the cross, seek Christ's forgiveness, and ask for His help to see all that you have been freely given in His gospel. Set aside a time each day to write down and recount to yourself the blessings from God you have received. Then you will truly overflow with thankfulness.

PSALM 103

NOVEMBER 21

BE SILENT AND LISTEN

"Woe to him who says to a wooden thing, Awake; to a silent stone, Arise! Can this teach? Behold, it is overlaid with gold and silver, and there is no breath at all in it. But the LORD is in his holy temple; let all the earth keep silence before him."
HABAKKUK 2:19-20

The world around Habakkuk was in a state of turmoil and appeared to be past the point of recovery. His own heart was deeply unsettled, prompting him to ask God why He was permitting all that was happening (Habakkuk 1:2-3). The prophet longed for something to be done. He longed for answers. He longed for change. And God said to Habakkuk, *Remember that I still reign. Remember who I am, and who you are.* God was still present "in his holy temple," sovereignly ruling over all the earth. He had already ordained the means by which His will would be achieved. Recognizing this was a call to humility and silence for Habakkuk. Though he had his questions and complaints, and though he was permitted to raise those with God, most of all he needed to choose to listen to what God said and think about His words.

We see this call to silence throughout Scripture. God says through the psalmist, "Be still, and know that I am God" (Psalm 46:10). In the New Testament, when Jesus stood before Peter, James, and John on the Mount of Transfiguration in His heavenly glory and Peter, in his fear, said the first thing that came into his head, this was the divine call the disciples heard: "This is my beloved Son, with whom I am well pleased; *listen to him*" (Matthew 17:5, emphasis added).

When times are hard, some of us by character respond as activists: the problem needs to be overcome, and so we throw ourselves into working for a solution. Others of us respond as pessimists: the problem cannot be overcome, so we simply buckle under it or waste time on activities to escape it. In both cases, our response is prompted by an absence of being still before God to listen to and think about His words. We live in a world of constant noise: words, words, words—the babble of the pundits, professors, and politicians. But if we will not listen to God, we will end up relying on an idol that cannot speak (Habakkuk 2:18-19). Idols cannot truly speak about our lives or the circumstances in our world.

When days of difficulty are upon us, Habakkuk reminds us, "Let all the earth keep silence before him." We do not have all the answers, and neither do the experts. It is not wrong to ask questions or pursue solutions, but it *is* wrong if this comes at the expense of simply being still and hearing God's word to listen to God's voice. Whatever is going on around us, what we most need is to remember that the Lord is in His holy temple, directing history from His throne for the good of His people. That is the foundation upon which we can build a framework for understanding what God is doing in the world around us. Do you feel as though the nations are raging and the kingdoms tottering? Are the mountains moving and the waves mounting up (Psalm 46:2-3, 6)? Be still, know that God is God, and listen to Him.

PSALM 46

NOVEMBER 22

A PICTURE OF HEAVEN

"I looked, and behold, a great multitude that no one could number, from every nation, from all tribes and peoples and languages, standing before the throne and before the Lamb, clothed in white robes, with palm branches in their hands, and crying out with a loud voice, 'Salvation belongs to our God who sits on the throne, and to the Lamb!'" REVELATION 7:9-10

Many of our ideas and songs about heaven have more to do with Victorian-era Christianity and views of the universe based on the teaching of the Greek philosopher Plato than they do with a rigorous, thoughtful consideration of what God has revealed in His word. We will not spend our eternity just sitting on clouds and playing harps, as heaven is often depicted in art. We will do something far better. Scripture shows us that we will sing God's praises and worship the Lamb.

The book of Revelation calls us to notice the ever-expanding circles of praise that surround the Lamb. In the first circle, we see four living creatures and twenty-four elders offering incense and singing a new song of praise (Revelation 5:8-9). The second circle, in verses 11-13, then consists of tens of thousands of angels giving Him honor, joined by every creature in all creation. Next, Revelation highlights those who have been redeemed by the blood of the Lamb (7:4, 9). They are described both as 144,000 in number and as a company beyond counting. They are portrayed both as the twelve tribes of Israel and as people from every nation and language. These descriptions may seem mutually contradictory, but this makes perfect sense from God's perspective. The exact number represents perfection and completion; but from a human perspective, the crowd is so vast that you can't count it when you see it before you. In God's eyes, the people that are redeemed are His chosen sons and daughters, representatives of every tribe. He knows every single individual. Yet His people are drawn from all peoples. Here is a picture of God's absolute, total triumph—and of God's people exalting Him and exulting over His triumph.

So, while this scene opens with the four creatures and the twenty-four elders, it progresses to these thousands upon thousands, reflecting Paul's declaration that, eventually, "at the name of Jesus *every* knee should bow, in heaven and on earth and under the earth" (Philippians 2:10, emphasis added). Our praise will join that of the countless multitudes, and we will all declare that Christ is the Lamb that was slain, that by His blood our sins have been cleansed, that with His righteousness we are clothed, and that in His company we will live for all of eternity.

One day we will get to join the ever-expanding circle of praise around Christ, who will step forward as the conquering Lion and the humble Lamb, our beloved Bridegroom. But we do not need to wait until then, for we can, even now, join the song of worship with our eyes fastened on Him. One day you will stand before Him and see Him! And day by day, you walk toward that day.

REVELATION 7:1-17

NOVEMBER 23

THE QUESTION OF SUFFERING

"Cursed is the ground because of you; in pain you shall eat of it all the days of your life." GENESIS 3:17

No one is a stranger to suffering. Whether it's the death of a loved one, a painful diagnosis, a conflict at work, a broken relationship, or anything similar, trials are not exclusive to any one person. Throughout Scripture, we see numerous accounts of suffering. As we live life and as we read our Bibles, it becomes unarguably apparent that suffering is a part of human existence. And once we accept this reality, one of the most critical questions we find ourselves asking is "Why?" Why do people suffer? All worldviews and religions offer their attempts at answers: "Pain is just an illusion." "There is no God; pain is meaningless." "Pain is out of God's control." "Pain is payback for past deeds in your present or previous life." All those answers have something in common: they offer no hope. But God Himself offers us a better answer.

While He could have stopped Satan from deceiving, or stopped Adam and Eve from being deceived, or even stopped suffering altogether. God instead chose to use suffering to teach men and women the meaning of willing love and genuine obedience, and of their need for a Savior. It is our very freedom that makes learning this lesson a possibility. God did not make us to be automatons. He wanted us to serve Him freely and lovingly, not out of force or obligation. Tragically, though, in that freedom, humanity chose life apart from Him—with dreadful consequences. And whenever we sin, we show that we are no different than our first ancestors.

God knew that men and women needed to be confronted by the truth that rebellion against Him is folly. That is why He banished them from the tree of life in Eden (Genesis 3:22-24). That is why the world no longer works as it was created to—and neither do our bodies (v 16-19). Like a rebellious child realizing the folly of their choice, willingly returning home and appreciating their family all the more, we can freely return to God, longing for His love. God allowed sin to come into the world in all its horribleness so that we could feel the consequences of our choices and learn to love Him all the more as He displays the beauty of His own love in a world of evil.

C.S. Lewis famously put it this way: "God whispers to us in our pleasures, speaks in our conscience, but shouts in our pain. It is His megaphone to rouse a deaf world."[123]

God is not the author of evil, but He is sovereign over evil. Therefore, we can have this hope: there will be a day when God will bring all evil to an end. Meanwhile, He determines to leave things as they are in order that through our trials we might cling to the Suffering Servant as our Savior. Do not let your disappointments over life in a fallen world persuade you that God is not there or He does not care. Rather, let them drive you again and again to your Savior, who promises one day to make an end of all that is wrong and stretches before you an eternity in which all is right.

LUKE 15:11-32

123 *The Problem of Pain* (Harper Collins, 2001), p 91.

NOVEMBER 24

COME, YE THANKFUL PEOPLE

"Give thanks in all circumstances ... May the God of peace himself sanctify you completely, and may your whole spirit and soul and body be kept blameless at the coming of our Lord Jesus Christ. He who calls you is faithful; he will surely do it." 1 THESSALONIANS 5:18, 23-24

Thanksgiving is not always easy, even when, as a nation, the US sets aside a holiday for the express purpose of doing so. During this holiday, many of us become keenly aware of life circumstances that don't stir up feelings of thankfulness. Some of us may be facing our loneliest days, while others are overwhelmed by the crushing burden of a loved one wandering from the gospel. Still others enter this season greatly disappointed as a result of various failures—a lost job, a broken relationship, another missed promotion. We sometimes find ourselves absolutely stuck, unable to pull ourselves out of despondency and feeling as far from gratitude as the east is from the west.

When we're facing such situations and we read "Give thanks in all circumstances," we often wonder how we're supposed to respond. Yet the Bible never offers exhortations without also offering aid.

The answer for how we can show constant gratitude lies in God's sanctifying work in us. The word "sanctify" means "to set apart for God." When the Lord Jesus Christ comes to rule and reign in our lives, the Holy Spirit enters us in order to produce the ongoing cleansing necessary for spiritual growth. It is the work of God that enables us to be what Jesus desires for us to be, "for it is God who works in you, both to will and to work for his good pleasure" (Philippians 2:13). When we abide in Christ, "rooted and built up in him" (Colossians 2:7)—studying our Bibles, learning to pray, fellowshipping with God's people, telling others about Him—we are reminded of all that He is for us and all that He has done for us and in us. We learn to sing with the psalmist, "We give thanks to you, O God; we give thanks, for your name is near. We recount your wondrous deeds" (Psalm 75:1). Whatever our own regrets and disappointments, we are able to overflow with thankfulness as we remember His wondrous deeds—His cross, His resurrection, His ascension, and His work in us by His Spirit to bring us to faith and keep us in faith.

Our trials may be tough and gloomy. We may not *feel* thankful in every moment. That's ok, because that's not the point. God enables us to be grateful regardless. He provides the strength for us to fulfill Paul's instruction.

If you are experiencing an absence of thankfulness in your life right now, then you need to turn your attention away from your circumstances, at least for a moment, and reflect on God's gift of love for you. As you abide in Christ and allow God's Spirit to continue His sanctifying work, He will quicken you from within, so that even through tears, pain, and disappointment, you'll be able to respond when He bids us, "Come, ye thankful people, come."[124]

PSALM 149

124 Henry Alford, "Come, Ye Thankful People, Come" (1844).

NOVEMBER 25

LIVING THE TRUTH

"If you know these things, blessed are you if you do them." JOHN 13:17

Can you recall a time when a stranger approached you out of the blue and asked what you believe about Jesus Christ and the Christian faith? I imagine that you have had very few, if any, experiences like that. We ought to be prepared for such encounters, to be sure; the apostle Peter tells us to be ready to give a reason for the hope we have (1 Peter 3:15). But opportunities to explain what we believe most often result not from random encounters with strangers but from the way we live day in and day out before those who know us well.

How we live and what we believe ought to reflect our attachment to Christ. This is one reason why Peter says Christians are "a people for [God's] own possession" (1 Peter 2:9). Our connection to Jesus as those who are in Him and belong to Him is comprehensive. That means we are not at liberty to *believe* whatever we want; we are not free to form our own views of marriage, of sexuality, of finance, or of anything else. Our view is now to reflect that of our Messiah and Teacher, Jesus. But He is not content with His disciples simply knowing the truth. They also need to be living the truth: "If you *know* these things, blessed are you if you *do* them." Believing must lead to doing. We are not free to *behave* in any way we like either, then. Our conduct is to reflect that of our sacrificial Savior, Jesus.

Many contemporary religions and secular creeds require nothing from you; they leave you free to live as you please. (In fact, many make their guiding principle that you do what seems right to you.) But the call to Christian discipleship is utterly different, for at its heart it is a call to follow a King who is not you. The call is not merely to believe the gospel but to "let your manner of life be worthy of the gospel of Christ" (Philippians 1:27).

We all fall short. Do you have someone helping you, and whom you can help, in seeing areas of behavior that are not yet worthy of the gospel? Lock arms with a brother or sister in Christ, shine the light of God's word on one another, and seek to bring the truth to life!

The church is God's primary appointed means of reaching His world. You are part of that. But do not expect those around you to ask about the gospel—still less to repent and believe the gospel—if you are not living out that gospel:

You are writing a gospel,
A chapter each day,
By deeds that you do,
By words that you say.
Men read what you write,
Whether faithless or true,
Say! What is the gospel
According to you?[125]

JOHN 13:31-35

125 Commonly attributed to Paul Gilbert.

NOVEMBER 26

WHY GIVE?

"You will be enriched in every way to be generous in every way, which through us will produce thanksgiving to God." 2 CORINTHIANS 9:11

God is not a cosmic killjoy. He doesn't ask us to bear with some disappointing existence in which we sit around and fake happiness. Instead, He richly provides for us. We don't have to apologize for what He gives us; but we do have to *share* it.

The reason why God gives us all that we need (and oftentimes more!) is so that we can in turn give to others. When we are "enriched in every way," Paul tells us, it is in order "to be generous in every way, which through us will produce thanksgiving to God." What we have received as a gift from God we are to give as a gift from God. James picks up this idea in challenging form when he asks, "What good is it ... if someone says he has faith but does not have works?" (James 2:14). The answer is clear: it's no good at all! In fulfilling our responsibility to help those in need, we not only prompt praise for God, but we give evidence of the reality of our faith in God.

God supplies us not only with resources but also with the grace we need to be truly generous—to go without ourselves so that others may be blessed (2 Corinthians 8:1-3). He is the one who "is able to make all grace abound to you, so that having all sufficiency in all things at all times, you may abound in every good work" (9:8).

A generous heart protects us from selfishness and the desire to amass significant wealth for ourselves. The joy of God's blessing isn't found in laying up a firm financial foundation so that we can retire to somewhere fantastic, pass on a greater monetary inheritance, or find comfort in a savings account. Rather, we are called to share the wealth He gives us now so that as others enter into its enjoyment, they'll find true satisfaction in God the Provider.

If we're honest, the very reason we often hold back from sharing generously is that we think God might just leave us high and dry after we give stuff away. Yet Scripture assures us that the same God who cared for us in our infancy will provide for us in our old age (see Isaiah 46:4).

Joy is to be found in unshackling yourself from enslavement to what you own. It is your privilege and your responsibility to be rich in deeds and eager to share, whether you've been given much or only a little. Ask God for the grace to cheerfully give without reluctance, and remember this: you cannot outgive God.

2 CORINTHIANS 9:6-15

NOVEMBER 27

THROUGH HIS MERCY

"It depends not on human will or exertion, but on God, who has mercy."
ROMANS 9:16

God is not tied to man-made customs, and He is under no obligation to fit in with our expectations.

Perhaps this is nowhere better seen than in the lives of Esau and Jacob. Esau was the firstborn of Isaac, whose father, Abraham, had been chosen by God to be the bearer of His promises to make Himself a people and bring blessing to His world (Genesis 12:1-3). As the customary heir, Esau typically would have received Isaac's blessing and inheritance, just as Isaac had inherited these from his father, Abraham.

Instead, God chose Esau's brother, the younger twin, Jacob, to receive both.

Not only was Jacob younger, but he was also an unpleasant character whose name essentially means "he cheats." It seems unbelievable that he would be chosen—yet the line of promise was to flow through Jacob, and his descendants became Israel, the people of God.

I sometimes struggle with this concept, wondering why God would select Jacob. It seems unfair! Yet the Bible tells us that although Jacob was an unlikely choice, God determined in advance to fulfill His promises through Jacob instead of Esau: "… though they were not yet born and had done nothing either good or bad—in order that God's purpose of election might continue, not because of works but because of him who calls" (Romans 9:11). In choosing Jacob, God was fulfilling His purposes from all of eternity. He was also teaching this principle: *God does not choose on the basis of merit.* None of us deserve to belong to Him.

This is where we sometimes get things turned upside down. We look at Jacob and wonder why he was chosen, when we should really look at God and wonder at His graciousness. He says, "I will have mercy on whom I have mercy, and I will have compassion on whom I have compassion" (Romans 9:15). And God mercifully calls us, too, though we are undeserving.

When we fully realize our predicament before we became children of God—our rebellion, which is deserving of condemnation, wrath, and death—we can begin to understand the greatness of God's love and mercy for us. We stop asking why God does not show mercy to some; we start wondering why God does show mercy to any. It becomes a matter of deep gratitude that He has made us His heirs, children of God.

You didn't do a single thing to earn the King's favor. You made absolutely no restitution for your rebellion. There is only one basis on which you have been adopted into His family: His mercy, freely given and never deserved. In the words of the hymn writer, "Jesus paid it all."[126] This truth will keep you humble when days are good, and hopeful when you see your sin; salvation is never about your merit but always and only about His mercy.

ROMANS 9:1-18

126 Elvina M. Hall, "Jesus Paid It All" (1865).

NOVEMBER 28

THE PATHWAY TO HAPPINESS

"Blessed is the one whose transgression is forgiven, whose sin is covered." PSALM 32:1

Several years ago, the BBC conducted a survey of some 65 countries in the world and reported on which were the most and least happy. When individuals were asked what contributed to their joy, there was no clear consensus. The path to happiness was elusive.[127]

In the ESV, Psalm 32 begins with the word "blessed," but "happy" may be the more evocative and more fitting translation. Indeed, the same Hebrew word that is used here is often translated into the Greek word for "happy" elsewhere, both in the Septuagint (the Greek translation of the Old Testament) and in the New Testament. The word is used at the beginning of the Sermon on the Mount, where Jesus began to speak to His followers by telling them, "Blessed [that is, happy] are the poor in spirit" (Matthew 5:3).

Many of us would like to be happier than we are. But how? Some think that if they could travel more, they would be content. Some think in more grandiose terms: for instance, that by establishing justice in their part of the world, they would be happier. Others reason there is joy to be found in appreciating the beauty of creation or exploring spirituality. Yet we are continually confronted by the fact that something spoils our ventures and settles like dust upon all our dreams. Happiness derived from these things is always brittle; it is easily broken and it cannot last. The chase after happiness or the attempt to hold on to happiness becomes a burden. So our search remains futile for as long as we fail to look where the psalmist says it is fundamentally to be found: in a relationship with our Creator God, which begins with forgiveness. It seems like an oxymoron that we would find happiness by first considering the seriousness of our transgressions and our need for forgiveness. But the Hebrew word for "forgiven" actually means "lifted" or "removed." The happiness and peace we desire comes only when the burden of sin is taken away. And then we are free to enjoy all that life offers, without asking created things or people to bear the weight of being the source of our ultimate joy.

This truth was Augustine's experience. He spent the first part of his life in an untrammeled commitment to indulgence. Then, after reading the Bible and meeting God in His word, he emerged from his haze, later writing, "O God, our hearts are restless until they find their rest in You."[128] Do you believe what Augustine believed? The basis for his statement is found in the opening verse of this psalm. You do not need to walk through life encumbered by sin and sorrow, because God has offered you forgiveness and a relationship with Him through Jesus. You do not need to chase after happiness the way the world does. When your burdens are lifted and you know that God knows the worst of you and loves you anyway, you experience phenomenal, lasting happiness.

PSALM 32

127 Michael Bond, "The Pursuit of Happiness," *New Scientist,* October 4, 2003, https://www.newscientist.com/article/mg18024155-100-the-pursuit-of-happiness/. Accessed April 13, 2021.

128 *Confessions* 1.1.

NOVEMBER 29

WORSHIP IN UNITY

"I appeal to you, brothers, by the name of our Lord Jesus Christ, that all of you agree, and that there be no divisions among you, but that you be united in the same mind and the same judgment." 1 CORINTHIANS 1:10

A church united in the gospel will be a healthy church. And nothing corrodes a church as fast as division.

It has always been like this for God's people. In their greatest moments, we see great unity. For instance, after returning from exile in Babylon, we're told in Nehemiah 8, the Israelites gathered expectantly, "as one man," to hear the public preaching of Ezra the priest from the Book of the Law (Nehemiah 8:1). In that moment, nearly 5,000 men and women went to the public square before the Water Gate in a spirit of unity and mutual commitment to worship. Their focus was not simply "What am I *receiving* from this teaching?" but "What am I *contributing* to my brothers and sisters who have gathered with me?"

This is the way God's people must always come to worship if there is to be unity among us.

When we are truly walking with Christ, we will long to worship corporately with the people who love Christ. Though our motivation may sometimes run dry, with the help of the Holy Spirit it is possible to share the psalmist's spirit of worship: "I was glad when they said to me, 'Let us go to the house of the Lord!'" (Psalm 122:1). Gathered church worship is far more than an event for you to attend or endure; it is a declaration of shared loyalty to our King and a powerful reminder of the deep unity God's people enjoy.

Within our congregations, we don't and won't always agree. We all have individual preferences and convictions. But at the very center of membership in God's family there is to be unanimity regarding core issues of our faith—issues like the authority of the Bible, the centrality and preeminence of Jesus, the necessity of evangelism, and the priority of prayer and worship in our daily lives. These shared convictions allow God's people to gather together in unity. Therefore, while humor from the pulpit, beautiful music, and meaningful programs for families may be gifts from the Lord, they should not be our priority. Instead, we ought to be in prayer for our fellow saints as we seek to worship together in unity, asking that revival may come from our own desire to hear God's word preached in truth. For when a congregation is prayerfully expectant, God will surely do what He has pledged to do through His word. It is easy to have a "me-first" approach to church and to be quick to criticize—easy, but corrosive. Be sure next Sunday that you are not there only for yourself but for others, and that you are quick to build up and undergird your shared unity in how you sing and speak.

NEHEMIAH 8:1-12

◇ Bible Through The Year: 2 Chronicles 21–22; Luke 9:1-17

NOVEMBER 30

GOD HEARS OUR CRIES

"The people of Israel groaned because of their slavery and cried out for help ... And God heard their groaning, and God remembered his covenant." EXODUS 2:23-24

The promise of food had encouraged Jacob and his family to leave their famine-stricken land and relocate to Egypt with Joseph. For a time, everything was terrific. But their experience took a turn for the worse when a new king came to power. He didn't like the idea of Israel's people growing in stature and number, so he put them to work, ruthlessly enslaving them. Their lives were filled with tears and bitterness.

The people of God still had His promises, but those promises seemed empty. It had been easy to trust God when they were free and well-fed. It was far less easy when they were enslaved. In the long, long years of oppression, some must have said to themselves, *I think that God has forgotten His promise. I am not at all sure that He is really going to do what He said.* Yet despite this, they called out to God, desperately seeking rescue.

God had not forgotten, and His answer came. God heard their cry; He heard their groaning, and in response He implemented a rescue operation. God would not leave them in their misery. He was going to fulfill His purposes for His people and set them free from slavery. He "remembered his covenant"—which is not to say that His promises to Abraham had slipped His mind but that now, at exactly the right moment (though no doubt not as soon as His people would have chosen), He moved to keep His covenant to His people.

This is what God's people need to be reminded of now, just as they did then: God hears our groaning, God knows our circumstances, and He *will* act. Not one of His promises will fail. Indeed, when we are at a loss for words in our distress, we discover that the Holy Spirit even intercedes for us through our prayerful groanings (Romans 8:26-27). That's the level of God's concern for each of us and the depth of His determination to do eternal good for His people.

When your soul's cries seem to go unheard—when you begin to wonder if anyone truly cares—recall who God has revealed Himself to be, in Egypt and supremely in His Son:

Why should I feel discouraged,
Why should the shadows come,
Why should my heart be lonely
And long for heav'n and home,
When Jesus is my portion?
My constant friend is He:
His eye is on the sparrow,
And I know He watches me.[129]

Keep crying out for deliverance. God hears, He cares, and He works on your behalf.

MARK 5:21-43

129 Civilla D. Martin, "His Eye Is on the Sparrow" (1905).

DECEMBER 1

THE PRE-EXISTENT WORD

"In the beginning was the Word, and the Word was with God, and the Word was God. He was in the beginning with God." JOHN 1:1-2

Most of our mental pictures of Jesus owe more to artistic creativity than to biblical theology. The Bible gives us no physical description of Christ other than that He "increased … in stature" (Luke 2:52). It's extremely unhelpful for us, then, to imagine Him with blond hair and striking blue eyes, as many in Western culture have done. Such a picture not only fails to remember that He was a Middle-Eastern Jew; it also prevents us from understanding and enjoying the awesome way in which the Gospel of John introduces Him.

From the very first verse, John tells us of Christ's eternality, His personality, and His deity. No matter how far back we consider the beginning of time to be and no matter what model we may have in our minds of how time began, there we will find the preincarnate Son of God. He was not created, for He is the Creator. The child in the manger was the very same person who put the stars in the sky—including the very star which led the wise men from the east to come and worship Him.

In His eternality, this Word, Jesus, is distinct from the Father and from the Spirit, not in essence but in person. He "was with God," yet He "was God." Though it may sound puzzling, John wasn't writing in abstractions. He was presenting a person he had met, seen, heard, and touched. The stage is set for readers to say with the apostle, "The life was made manifest, and we have seen it" (1 John 1:2), because that's the power of God's living Word.

In asserting the reality that Christ was not only *with* God but *was* God, John wants us to read his whole Gospel with Jesus' deity in mind. When we turn each page, read Jesus' words, and observe His deeds, we are supposed to see that they're the very words and deeds of God Himself.

If Jesus was simply a good man, then what we read in John's Gospel is ultimately blasphemous. But He is more than a man. He was, is, and forever will be one with the God of all creation. We need to understand John's opening verses in order to truly grasp who Jesus is so that we can, in the words of Bruce Milne, "worship him without cessation, obey him without hesitation, love him without reservation, and serve him without interruption."[130] If you are finding it hard to worship, obey, love, or serve the Lord today, here is the answer: look at Him. For the better we understand that the Word who lay in the manger was the Word who was with God and was God from the beginning, the more naturally we will find our Christian duties turning to joys.

JOHN 1:1-18

130 *The Message of John,* The Bible Speaks Today (IVP Academic, 2020), p 21.

DECEMBER 2

KNOWING THE CREATOR

"The true light, which gives light to everyone, was coming into the world. He was in the world, and the world was made through him, yet the world did not know him." JOHN 1:9-10

While each of the Gospels takes a different approach to detailing Jesus' life, their purpose is the same: that, as John puts it, "you may believe that Jesus is the Christ, the Son of God, and that by believing you may have life in his name" (John 20:31). Those words come near the end of his Gospel and were intended to remind even his earliest readers that God graciously took the initiative to pursue His people in order that we might know and love Him.

Although Jesus was the Creator of the world He entered into, the world did not recognize Him. He came down from heaven in the form of a man, navigating city streets and moving among us so that we could live with Him in the light rather than have to live in darkness for all of eternity. Yet today, not unlike 2,000 years ago, many don't understand the immensity of the gift of life in this world that Christ has given us, and therefore they forfeit the gift of eternal life that Christ was born to offer us, because they don't know Him.

In his great treatise in the book of Romans, Paul wrote that God's "invisible attributes, namely, his eternal power and divine nature, have been clearly perceived, ever since the creation of the world, in the things that have been made." In other words, as a result of God's common grace, the creation displays enough evidence to at least bring us to the point of becoming theists. Because of this, men and women "are without excuse" (Romans 1:20).

Even with that context, however, Paul goes on to say that although men and women "knew God, they did not honor him as God or give thanks to him, but they became futile in their thinking, and their foolish hearts were darkened" (Romans 1:21). They knew of God's existence but, suppressing that knowledge, they refused to know Him as Lord and Savior.

This is a humbling warning to us. If we should neglect to give God the honor and praise He is due, we risk forgetting the glorious ways He continues to pursue us, even today.

The word, truth, and story of Jesus have been made available in the Western world for hundreds of years—but still, so often men and women go about their weeks without any recognition of who Jesus truly is. Believers are not immune from living lives that, Sunday mornings or morning devotions apart, bear no mark of a knowledge of and relationship with Jesus as Lord and Savior. Imagine the difference it would make if we lived each moment calling to mind the truths that He is the light and the new life within us, that He makes it possible to live with God for all of eternity, that He is our great Lord and gentle Savior, and that He is surely worth knowing.

1 CORINTHIANS 1:18-31

DECEMBER 3

CHALLENGING GOD'S AUTHORITY

"He came to his own, and his own people did not receive him." JOHN 1:11

Many actors think they're fit to play the role of Hamlet. In many instances, though, they're simply not. They just don't have the ability and experience to do it—though, of course, that doesn't necessarily stop them trying!

Similarly, all men and women are at some point tempted to challenge God's authority over their lives, wrongly believing that they can play a role for which He alone is suited. We often fail to trust His divine hand in our circumstances. Instead, we question His sovereign will. We try to steal the part for which only the Creator God is fit.

Resistance to God's authority is nothing new. While Jesus came down to earth in fulfillment of Old Testament prophecies, throughout His ministry He was unwelcomed by His own people. Israel had been waiting for the Messiah—but once He arrived, they questioned His authority and rejected His identity. They knew these prophecies, yet they were blind to their fulfillment.

Days before He died at the hands of Jewish religious leaders as well as Gentile rulers, Jesus told His parable of the wicked tenants who rejected the vineyard owner and killed his son. The Lord was graciously and boldly pointing out the blindness of the chief priests, scribes, and elders, who were demanding that He justify His actions (Mark 12:1-12). They understood that Jesus was claiming to be God's Son. Yet having just been warned by Jesus that they were acting like the tenants who had seized the owner's son, these men then (with tragic irony) immediately wanted to arrest Him.

It is tempting to think, "How presumptuous of those religious leaders to confront the King of the universe and challenge His authority!" But each of us was once no different from them. In our own sinful nature, we didn't want to receive the Son whom God sent. We were inclined to live in darkness. Actually, we quite liked the darkness! John captures it well when he says that light has come into the world, but people love darkness instead of light because their deeds are evil (John 3:19). People by nature are not by sitting and waiting for the light of the gospel to come into their hearts. Yet by His grace, God opens blind eyes to see the identity of His Son so that people trust and worship Him.

That is why the Bible always speaks in the "now." There is no day better than today to live for Christ. Even as believers, we are called to continual repentance and restoration in our walk with the Lord rather than choosing to play God in our own lives. As our hearts grow more sensitive to our sin and we experience His continued patience towards us, His kindness will lead us to holiness. And when you live with God at the center of your life, with Him playing the part that only He can, you find that you are able joyfully and confidently to fulfill the role He has given you—to live out the life He has gifted you and the purpose for which He invited you onto the "stage": a life spent enjoying, knowing, and serving Him.

MARK 12:1-12

DECEMBER 4

CHILDREN OF GOD

"To all who did receive him, who believed in his name, he gave the right to become children of God, who were born, not of blood nor of the will of the flesh nor of the will of man, but of God." JOHN 1:12-13

In some churches, it's routine to speak of the universal fatherhood of God and the resulting brotherhood of man. But we ought to be mindful of the limits of such claims. While in one sense it is true that we are all God's children by virtue of creation, the New Testament reminds us that we are also "children of wrath" who are lost and need to be adopted into God's family (Ephesians 2:3).

We don't become God's children by any natural process. It is not the result of human genetics or even human effort. No one is born into God's kingdom—which is why Jesus told Nicodemus, a religious man with an impeccable Jewish lineage, that he had to be born again (John 3:3). Becoming a child of God is a *spiritual* process—something that God, in His mercy and grace, does on our behalf.

Think about your physical birth. You didn't have any control over it. It wasn't something you achieved. The same is true of our new birth in Christ. When God causes someone to be born again, the new life that follows is only possible because of His authority. He alone can give us the right to become His children.

It has been said that the emperor Napoleon was once nearly unseated from his horse when he dropped the reins in order to read some papers he was carrying with him. When the horse started to rear up, a young corporal quickly intervened by grabbing the horse's bridle. Napoleon turned to him and said, "Thank you, Captain." "Of what company, Sire?" the soldier asked. "Of my guards," answered Napoleon.[131]

In an instant, the man was promoted, received access to the headquarters of the general staff, and took his place among the emperor's officers. When asked by others what he was doing, he could respond that he was the captain of the guard by the authority of the emperor himself.

If you have received Jesus as your Lord and Savior, you are a child of God. God has stamped your life with a new identity, and nobody can dispute it. You can live with the great assurance that Jesus, the King of Kings and the captain of your salvation, has made it possible for you to be numbered among God's children. That is the great reality that is now the heart of your identity, whoever you are and whatever is going on in your life. That is the great reality that enables you to go into each day with your head up, confident that whatever happens, you are a child of God.

1 JOHN 2:28 – 3:3

131 James Montgomery Boice, *The Gospel of John: An Expositional Commentary* (Zondervan, 1975), Vol. 1, p 89.

DECEMBER 5

HE HUMBLED HIMSELF

"The Word became flesh and dwelt among us, and we have seen his glory, glory as of the only Son from the Father, full of grace and truth ... from his fullness we have all received, grace upon grace." JOHN 1:14, 16

The actor Steve McQueen led an amazing, albeit sometimes sordid, life. He died in 1980, but before illness claimed him, a faithful pastor shared the gospel with him, and he bowed down and trusted in Christ. After his conversion, he had a faithful routine of Bible study and Sunday worship that went unnoticed by the public. He remained in awe of the truth that though his life was messy with divorces, addictions, and poor moral choices, God would show him such love.

McQueen grew to understand that God had made him nothing so that in the discovery of his nothingness, he might then become something. God does the same with us as well.

In this, we are called to follow the pattern of Jesus Himself. From the day of His birth, Christ set aside His previously uninterrupted glory in order to come to this fallen, helpless world on our behalf. He came not on a chariot but to a manger; He came not with a scepter but to a stable. Jesus was as much an earthly servant as He is the heavenly sovereign.

To say that He made Himself nothing, however, doesn't mean that He transitioned from being God to being man, and then back to being God again. When we read that "the Word became flesh and dwelt among us," we should reflect on the awe-inspiring paradox that our marvelous Savior poured Himself into His humanity without giving up His deity. He is fully God and fully man!

Our finite human minds sometimes focus on Christ's deity so much that we don't remember that He was no less human than you or me; and at other times we can become so preoccupied with His humanity that we lose sight of His divinity. The Scriptures hold Christ's two natures in perfect tension: although He was found in human form (Philippians 2:8), He was not merely who He appeared to be.

There is more to Jesus than meets the eye. He may have looked just like any other man, but no other man can stand in a boat during a storm and calm the sea. Only God can heal the lame or restore sight to the blind. This man alone deserves the worship of angels and the praise of all creation. Yet Jesus didn't approach the incarnation asking, *What's in it for Me?* Instead, He arrived knowing that He "came not to be served but to serve, and to give his life as a ransom for many" (Mark 10:45). He was willing to leave everything and become nothing so that those who acknowledge their nothingness can be given everything. He became flesh so that He might serve, and He beautifully modeled humility to all who might follow Him. How will you look to His example in your tasks and responsibilities today?

PHILIPPIANS 2:1-13

DECEMBER 6

STAYING AWAKE

"The hour has come for you to wake from sleep. For salvation is nearer to us now than when we first believed ... Let us walk properly as in the daytime, not in orgies and drunkenness, not in sexual immorality and sensuality, not in quarreling and jealousy." ROMANS 13:11, 13

"Careless talk costs lives," proclaimed a campaign by the British Government during the Second World War. The government wanted people to be aware of the danger around them: that listening enemy ears were ready to pounce on any slip of the tongue.

Here, Paul gives us a similar warning for our Christian lives: carelessness can cost lives. Carelessness makes us susceptible to danger. So many of us live carelessly when it comes to our spiritual lives, walking about in a kind of moral dream, failing to stay awake and alert to the dangers around us. That leaves us vulnerable. Consider just two reasons why it is vital that we stay awake and alert in our pursuit of purity.

First, the apostle Peter tells us, "Your adversary the devil prowls around like a roaring lion, seeking someone to devour" (1 Peter 5:8). Let's not kid ourselves: sin is predatory. The enemy is a lion. Recall the way the Lord spoke to Cain when he was angry with his brother: "Sin is crouching at the door. Its desire is contrary to you, but you must rule over it" (Genesis 4:7). Do you know who makes for easy prey? An isolated Christian. When we're isolated, we're vulnerable and without accountability. We "walk properly" most easily in godly company. As children of the daytime, we must not be lured by the darkness, because darkness creates isolation. A passion for purity demands that we walk in the light and with the children of light.

Second, we must stay awake and stay alert because eternity awaits. What is it that made the heroes of Hebrews 11 worthy of the title "heroes"? They were looking for a city beyond them. They looked for a city whose foundation and builder was God (Hebrews 11:10).

Moses, for example, did not succumb to the lure of instant gratification. He did not sell his soul for the moment. He did not give up his ministry, future, and family for comfort and privilege. He chose instead a more difficult course. And what was the explanation? "He considered the reproach of Christ greater wealth than the treasures of Egypt, for he was looking to the reward" (v 26). Moses was not without blemish, and neither are we. But that must not excuse us from living for the sake of Christ in matters of purity. After all, our salvation is drawing ever closer, and we want to be found ready for the Lord Jesus when He appears.

Whatever your past has been, whatever your recent mistakes and disappointments, it's not too late to wake up and stay alert. The enemy will not sleep, and eternity will be worth it. Ask God today to write a commitment on your heart to a life of purity, so that today you would walk properly and carefully, with your head up and your eyes fixed on that glorious future day of your salvation.

EPHESIANS 6:10-20

DECEMBER 7

WALKING WITH GOD

"Enoch walked with God after he fathered Methuselah 300 years ... Enoch walked with God, and he was not, for God took him." GENESIS 5:22, 24

Genuine faith is no flash in the pan. It's both a decisive act and a sustained attitude.

Enoch, we are told, "walked with God"—but this wasn't always the case. It is clear from Genesis 5 that there was a time in Enoch's life when faith began. In fact, we're told that "Enoch walked with God after he fathered Methuselah." Perhaps, as with many life-altering experiences, the responsibilities and challenges of parenting quickly revealed Enoch's inadequacies to him. Whatever the case, there appears to have come a moment in Enoch's life when he stopped believing in himself, stopped depending on himself, and started believing in and depending on God.

But not only was Enoch's faith a deliberate choice; it was also a sustained relationship. Faith begins with and continues as a decisive act. Enoch "walked with God" until "he was not." And as a result of his enduring faith, Enoch was taken by God. He didn't taste death.

Enoch's almost-unique end-of-life experience anticipates the glorification of the body, which will be the experience of all believers when Jesus Christ returns. Paul explains that "the trumpet will sound, and the dead will be raised imperishable, and we shall be changed. For this perishable body must put on the imperishable, and this mortal body must put on immortality" (1 Corinthians 15:52-53). When we walk with God, remembering that every dimension of our lives is under His control and constraint, then being gathered into our eternal future will change our bodies and our setting but it will not change our company.

Enoch's sustained relationship with God has culminated in his enjoyment of God's presence forever. If we are going to spend all of eternity in worship of our God, then in worshiping Him on earth we are simply beginning what will never end. If we are going to spend all of eternity in fellowship and in adoration, then our experience here is preparation for what happens there. So walk with Him today. Be aware of His presence. Be dependent on His grace and power. Be quick to ask for His forgiveness. Be alert to His guiding. Walk with Him today, until today is the day you see Him face-to-face.

1 THESSALONIANS 4:13-18

DECEMBER 8

GROWING IN CONTENTMENT

"In any and every circumstance, I have learned the secret of facing plenty and hunger, abundance and need." PHILIPPIANS 4:12

The elusive nature of contentment is not new to our age. Back in the 17th century, the issue of contentment was pressing enough that the Puritan Jeremiah Burroughs wrote a whole book about it, *The Rare Jewel of Christian Contentment*, which remains a classic of Christian devotion. Yet most bookshelves today don't carry that book. Instead, we're much more likely to find titles feeding the fantasy that our satisfaction depends upon worldly concerns, such as the abundance of our possessions or the indulgence of our desires.

If we're honest with ourselves, we must admit that we are too easily swept along by the tides of covetousness, bombarded by a discontented spirit that is directly tied to our circumstances. Like young children, we are often displeased with what we are given or frustrated that our friends have more. As a result, we become determined to do whatever it takes to "fix" our circumstances financially, socially, or physically.

It's easy to believe that either self-denial or indulgence is the answer to covetousness. Out of a sense of false humility, for example, I could say I have no interest in cashmere sweaters, but only in horribly scratchy sweaters that cause me to break into a rash—but that would just breed pride in my own false view of apparent holiness. On the other hand, I could just buy up all the sweaters I could find in hopes of ridding myself of my desire for more!

Neither of these approaches glorifies the Lord. Instead, what glorifies the Lord is to hope in Him, the one who richly provides us with gifts for our enjoyment. While we don't put our hope in material riches, Christians recognize that every gift from God is the result of His gracious providence and that we glorify Him by enjoying what He gives in the way that He calls us to in His word. We are free to enjoy things—but we are not to make those things into gods, chasing and serving them as though they will supply our needs and satisfy our longings. Contentment is gained by remembering that Christ is Lord, and that nothing else is.

This does not come naturally. You and I, like Paul, have to learn it as we mature in faith. Whether it's your attitude on a gloomy day, or your response to getting passed over for a promotion, or anything else, the question you should ask remains the same: What is it about Christ's all-sufficiency that means He is enough for me to find contentment in this circumstance? Contentment is a rare jewel and a precious thing to find.

PSALM 16

Bible Through The Year: Esther 6–8; Luke 13:1-21

DECEMBER 9

AN INSIDE JOB

"Each person is tempted when he is lured and enticed by his own desire. Then desire when it has conceived gives birth to sin, and sin when it is fully grown brings forth death." JAMES 1:14-15

Every sin is an inside job.

As creatures made in God's image, we have all kinds of desires, and our desires are not necessarily bad. As a result of the fall, though, all of our longings have an amazing potential for evil. Even God-given desires can be distorted and used for wickedness.

We are masters at explaining away our propensity for evil as the fault of the devil, our peers, our heredity, or our environment. Scripture, though, says that we are tempted by our own desires. For all of us, the temptation to disobey God and indulge our desires, whether those desires are evil or distorted, emerges from within.

The devil may come and entice us, but only we make the decision to disobey. Jesus made this perfectly clear: "What comes out of a person is what defiles him" (Mark 7:20). Every temptation comes to us when we are dragged away and enticed by our own desires. And temptation, when succumbed to, eventually leads to death.

Temptation's allure is seen so clearly in the folly of fish. They see bait; it shines and it sparkles; they go for it—and they get hooked! If the bait is attractive and appealing enough, fish cannot ignore the hook.

Are we really much brighter than fish? If the bait looks pleasing, we try to convince ourselves that there is no hook there. But the hook is there. "Sin when it is fully grown brings forth death." The road of sin leads to the destination of judgment, and on the way it marks our lives in ways that time will never erase—though, in His mercy, God can redeem even these.

As long as we live on this earth, we will never be exempt from temptation. In Genesis, God warns Cain, "Sin is crouching at the door. Its desire is contrary to you, but you must rule over it" (Genesis 4:7). This is a telling picture: sin is always waiting inside us, ever ready to pounce upon us.

Be determined, then, to deal with every encroaching advancement of sin. It's a daily battle. Today, refuse to allow your eyes to wander to, your mind to contemplate, or your affections to run after anything which draws you away from Christ. How? By learning to question your desires, asking, "Is this a godly desire I should feed or a sinful desire I should fight?" And learn to wear the armor of God: to "take up the shield of faith, with which you can extinguish all the flaming darts of the evil one" (Ephesians 6:16). For it is in your faith in God's Son as your Ruler and your Rescuer that you find both power to stand firm and forgiveness when you fall.

1 CORINTHIANS 10:1-13

DECEMBER 10

DON'T TIRE OF WHAT'S GOOD

"Let us not grow weary of doing good, for in due season we will reap, if we do not give up." GALATIANS 6:9

If you are anything like me, you can remember studying subjects in school that caused you to stare at your homework with a feeling of hopelessness. Perhaps you felt that the teacher had determined you were a lost cause. That's a difficult environment in which to learn. John Calvin once noted something similar, writing, "There is nothing that can alienate us more from attending to the truth than to see that we are deemed to be past hope."[132]

It's easy to feel hopeless in our Christian walk—to "grow weary of doing good." Perhaps many of our contributions to the needs of God's people have been abandoned simply because we grew discouraged about their effects or discouraged by our own ongoing inability to get to grips with defeating sin and growing in holiness. We must stick with it! As we work at obeying the Lord in the Christian life, God works in us to change and grow us (Philippians 2:12-13). And John assured the believers of his day about their faith in Christ when he said, "We know that we have passed out of death into life, *because we love the brothers*" (1 John 3:14, emphasis added). How many of us would finish that sentence in that way? Yet even Jesus Himself said, "By this all people will know that you are my disciples, if you have love for one another" (John 13:35).

So, do not give up. When the apostle Paul wrote to the Thessalonians, he recognized their exemplary "work of faith and labor of love and steadfastness of hope in our Lord Jesus Christ" (1 Thessalonians 1:3). What was true for the church in Thessalonica could be true for us: our expression of faith can, like theirs, be practical, tangible, and persistent. They were not a flash in the pan followed by enthusiasm fizzling out; their acts of Christian kindness were consistent over time.

Doing good is tiring, but we must be careful not to tire of it. For one day the King of Glory will say to the righteous, "As you did it to one of the least of these my brothers, you did it to me" (Matthew 25:40). Until that time comes, we have the privilege of obeying and serving Christ with unwavering hope. So, how are you showing tangible expressions of Christian kindness toward the wanderer, the stranger, the prisoner in affliction, the widow, the destitute? Is it time to ask God for strength and purpose to be about His work and to get started, or restarted, in "doing good"?

ACTS 6:1-7

132 *Commentaries on the Epistle of Paul the Apostle to the Hebrews,* trans. John Owen, Hebrews 6:9.

DECEMBER 11

GROWING UNDER GOD'S WORD

"Repent and be baptized every one of you in the name of Jesus Christ for the forgiveness of your sins." ACTS 2:38

If you've been a Christian for any length of time, you have probably noticed that it is easy to go through the motions in your study of God's word, whether individually or on Sundays in church. The gospel can seem so straightforward that we put ourselves in danger of missing it—but in our weakness, we always need to hear its truth preached to us. We need to hear the same thing today that we did the first day we believed. We cannot disconnect our Christian walk from "the word of truth, the gospel of [our] salvation" (Ephesians 1:13) because God ordained the two to be connected. The Spirit of God works through the word of God to sustain the people of God.

Therefore, the first thing Peter did after receiving the Spirit on the day of Pentecost was to stand up and preach a long sermon; then, as more and more people heard and listened to the word of God, they grew as individuals and as a whole (Acts 2). Alternatively, when the word of God is not heard, the church does not grow. Why not? Because the Spirit works as the word is heard, and the word is heard as the Spirit works. The sermon of Acts 2 is in your Bible not only to show you how those men and women came to faith but also to bolster and encourage you in yours.

Here is what the word produces when the Spirit is at work. When Peter preached on that day, his hearers "were cut to the heart, and said to Peter and the rest of the apostles, 'Brothers, what shall we do?'" (Acts 2:37). In other words, there was *conviction*. Peter replied, "Repent and be baptized every one of you in the name of Jesus Christ for the forgiveness of your sins, and you will receive the gift of the Holy Spirit" (v 38). And they did. So there was also *commitment*. Finally, the new believers gathered together to hear the apostles' doctrine, break bread, and pray (v 42). So there was *community*. Conviction, commitment, and community—and it all started with a Spirit-prompted sermon!

Growing in our faith involves both heart and mind. We have the responsibility to place ourselves under biblical teaching and pursue the study of God's word individually, asking God's Spirit to show us Christ on the pages of our Bibles and cause us to love Him more. If you are going through the motions somewhat in your reading of Scripture or in your Christian life more broadly, come back to how you first started. Read the gospel in God's word. Be convicted by your sin, and commit to trusting and serving your Savior. Immerse yourself in the community of believers that God has given you for your good. And ask Him to work in you through His Spirit, so that the commitment and excitement that suffused that Jerusalem church might be your experience too.

ACTS 2:22-41

◇ Bible Through The Year: Joshua 1–3; Luke 14:25-35

DECEMBER 12

PERFECT JUSTICE

"If when you do good and suffer for it you endure, this is a gracious thing in the sight of God. For to this you have been called, because Christ also suffered for you, leaving you an example." 1 PETER 2:20-21

C.H. Spurgeon once said to his congregation in London, "If, my dear friend, you make it a rule that nobody shall ever insult you without having to pay for it, nor treat you with disrespect without meeting his match, you need not pray God in the morning to help you carry out your resolve."[133] His point was simple: defending our reputations and getting even with those who cross us come naturally to us. Enduring suffering and leaving the enacting of judgment to God, on the other hand, does not.

Yet enacting judgment is a responsibility for which we are totally incompetent. When we hit back, we never know how hard to hit, and when somebody says something hurtful, we often respond with something much worse. Deep down, we tend to think we will overcome hatred by more of the same; instead, we magnify the wickedness. Clearly, evil *should* be punished, and evil *will* be punished. But it must not be punished by us.

Only God is perfect in His judgments and His justice. He will right every wrong. There is a higher throne than any this world has seen, and one day at that throne, all the corrupt jurisdictions, failures of judgment, and miscarriages of human justice will be righted.

This should not be a cloak for our own vindictiveness, though. We must not wish for anything other than the salvation of our enemies. To those who have reviled us, who have worked against us, or who have undermined us, our responsibility is clear: we are to bless and pray for them (Matthew 5:44; Luke 6:28).

Jesus is our example: "When he was reviled, he did not revile in return; when he suffered, he did not threaten, but continued entrusting himself to him who judges justly" (1 Peter 2:23). You will not suffer greater injustice than Him; so in every situation, you are called to respond like Him.

In what situations and with which people are you tempted to hit back hard instead of meeting wrong with right? These three things will help you please God by doing good to those people. First, *fix your eyes on Jesus.* It is difficult to look at Christ upon the cross saying, "Father, forgive them, for they know not what they do" (Luke 23:34), and then proceed to execute vengeance, in whatever form. Second, *let the grace of God amaze you.* Remember who you are by nature and who you have become by grace. It is impossible to be amazed by grace and wish ill to others. And third, *focus on eternity and God's higher throne.* Your earthly situation is not the complete picture, and you do not need to see justice done in the here and now. So, ask God to help you to do good and endure, even when you are met by evil. He is ready to help you accomplish something that's entirely in line with what He has commanded.

TITUS 2:11-14; 3:1-7

133 "Overcome Evil with Good," *The Metropolitan Tabernacle Pulpit* 22, no. 1317, p 556.

DECEMBER 13

A RANSOM FOR MANY

"Even the Son of Man came not to be served but to serve, and to give his life as a ransom for many." MARK 10:45

I like paying bills. I may not like the size of the bills or the frequency with which they come, but it's wonderful once they've actually been paid. Back in the days when bills were often paid in person, I found it especially satisfying to pass my bill across the counter with my payment and then receive it back marked "PAID."

In these verses, Jesus references His death with the little phrase "a ransom for many." A few Old Testament examples provide context for Jesus' use of the word "ransom" here.

Jewish law stated that when a man's ox killed someone, both the ox and the owner were to be put to death. However, if a ransom was imposed upon the owner, then he could pay it to redeem his life (Exodus 21:29-30). In other words, the owner of the ox could purchase his own life by paying a sum of money. The same was true of setting a relative free from servitude or releasing a field or piece of property from a mortgage (see Leviticus 25). In each case, the ransom involved a decisive and costly intervention to release someone from a form of captivity.

All of these situations in the Old Testament were material plights. What Jesus was referring to, however, was a moral predicament. We are enslaved by sin and have offended God. Jesus explained that only His decisive intervention—this costly purchase of our life—could set us free and make us whole. As the hymn writer puts it, "He took my sins and my sorrows, He made them his very own."[134]

Christ is our ransom. He "redeemed us from the curse of the law by becoming a curse for us" so that we may be released from our bondage when we place our trust in Him (Galatians 3:13). By His death, Jesus settled the judgment against all who believe in Him. When He cried, "It is finished," He used the Greek word *tetelestai*, which was written on a bill to declare that it had been paid (John 19:30). In His Son's resurrection, the Father provided the receipt of the payment. The debt, which was justifiably leveled against us and too great for us to pay, is now stamped unmistakably: "PAID."

At times, the Evil One will antagonize us and our own hearts will accuse us. "Are you really forgiven? Surely this is one sin too many! Does God really love you? Do you really have a place in glory for all eternity?" When you hear these whispers, remind yourself that Christ strode up to the very bar of justice and settled the account that stood against you. The Father raised Him from the dead; therefore, you can find total security in the fact that He will never again demand payment for any of these accusations. Your account has been settled once and for all. You have been ransomed.

COLOSSIANS 2:8-15

---

134 Charles H. Gabriel, "My Savior's Love" (1905).

DECEMBER 14

THE QUALIFIED SAVIOR

"When the fullness of time had come, God sent forth his Son, born of woman, born under the law, to redeem those who were under the law, so that we might receive adoption as sons." GALATIANS 4:4-5

One of the best ways to get a sample of a culture's beliefs is to talk to children. Once, for instance, when asked who Jesus was, a British child replied, "He was the one who took from the rich and gave to the poor"! (It seemed he was mixing up Jesus and the disciples with Robin Hood and his Merry Men!) When asked, "What is a Christian?" another child responded, "Aren't they the people who grow their own vegetables?"

At this time of year, many who do not spend time thinking about God much for the other eleven months find themselves reflecting on the reason for Jesus' birth. Countless friends, colleagues, and relatives would likely say that Jesus is, at best, something of a mystery. These responses are a sobering reminder that Christianity's message is not as obvious to our neighbors as we may think. Who Jesus is must first be clear in our own minds and dear to our own hearts if we are going to articulate that to others.

Jesus stands out among other figures of religion, history, and humanity since He alone possesses the qualifications to be the Savior of our world. His coming isn't regarded by the apostle Paul as an accidental intervention; it was a divine appointment. When Paul says, "God sent forth his Son," he implies that He was sent out from a previous state of existence. Jesus' life didn't begin when He was "born of woman" as a child in Bethlehem; He was before time itself began (John 1:1-3). Without ceasing to be what He was—namely, God—He became what He was not—namely, a man, "born under the law," owing the Father full and perfect obedience—which He, alone in the great mass of humanity through the ages, achieved.

If God would save, then the Savior must be God. If man must bear the punishment because man sinned, then the Savior must be a man. If the man who bears the punishment of sin must himself be sinless, then who other than Jesus Christ meets these qualifications? Jesus was uniquely qualified to accomplish God's plan of salvation.

There was no other good enough
To pay the price of sin;
He only could unlock the gate
Of heav'n and let us in.[135]

Who is Jesus? He is God the Son, born as a man. He is the perfect law-keeper, who died to free those who had not kept the law. What is a Christian? It is someone who has been freed from the penalty of sin and adopted into the family of God. That is a message we should preach to ourselves daily and should pray for an opportunity to share with someone else daily. For it is the most surprising and the most glorious message in all of history.

GALATIANS 3:23 - 4:7

135 Cecil Frances Alexander, "There Is a Green Hill Far Away" (1848).

DECEMBER 15

WHY THE RIGHTEOUS SUFFER

"Before I was afflicted I went astray, but now I keep your word … It is good for me that I was afflicted, that I might learn your statutes." PSALM 119:67, 71

When we come face-to-face with suffering, whether in our own lives or in the lives of others, we often wonder why those of us who profess belief in God still suffer. Doesn't God love us? What could His purpose be in our suffering?

When the Bible addresses the issue of pain and suffering, it does so within the framework that God is good and all-powerful and has an eternal plan to create a people who are His very own, to make them into the image of His Son, and to bring them safely to glory (Titus 2:14; Romans 8:29; 2 Timothy 4:18). He will do whatever it takes to achieve those objectives—even if it means permitting temporary sorrows.

Here are some examples of what suffering can achieve:

- *Suffering brings commonality.* Most suffering is actually just the reality of living in a fallen, imperfect world. We all experience pain, sickness, and grief. The righteous and the unrighteous alike see the sun and feel the rain (Matthew 5:45). The righteous and the unrighteous alike live with the effects of suffering.
- *Suffering is corrective.* As a father disciplines his children in order for them to know and do the right thing, so God sometimes uses suffering to get us back on the right path when we are going astray (Hebrews 12:5-13).
- *Suffering is constructive.* Not only can suffering correct us, but it can also build character within us (James 1:2-5). Have you ever looked at people and wondered, "How did she become so hopeful? How is he so empathetic with my brokenness?" It's likely because they've gone through suffering, grown from it, and learned to care for others through it.
- *Suffering is glorifying.* God always works through suffering to bring Himself glory, even years, decades, or generations later. As with the blind man in John 9, God can use a life of pain or disappointment to eventually display a miraculous example of His own power. We may question why we are going through a difficult experience, but somewhere along the journey of our days, we may realize, "Oh, that's why I went through such pain; it is for this exact moment, that God may be glorified."
- *Suffering is cosmic.* While not all suffering is part of a great spiritual drama, some suffering certainly is. Job is perhaps the most profound example of this, as God used him to demonstrate before Satan that a person can love and trust God for who He is and not merely for what someone can get out of Him (Job 1).

The truth is, you will suffer in life. But you do not have to suffer without hope. You can remember God's greater purposes through suffering. The question you and I ultimately need to ask ourselves is not "Why?" but "Will I…?" Will I believe God's promises? Will I cling to God's purposes? Will I trust Him?

JOB 1

◇ Bible Through The Year: Joshua 13–15; Luke 17:1-19

DECEMBER 16

MERCY THERE WAS GREAT

"For we ourselves were once foolish, disobedient, led astray, slaves to various passions and pleasures, passing our days in malice and envy, hated by others and hating one another. But when the goodness and loving kindness of God our Savior appeared, he saved us, not because of works done by us in righteousness, but according to his own mercy." TITUS 3:3-5

You don't need a fire brigade to come to your house if your house isn't on fire; neither would you want a doctor administering an IV drip when you're perfectly healthy. It's pointless! Similarly, until we are truly aware of our need for forgiveness, God's story of grace and mercy doesn't really mean much to us. We will think it irrelevant.

From time to time, we are all guilty of looking around and recognizing that others are dreadfully in need of forgiveness while turning a blind eye to our own need. "Thankfully," we say to ourselves (though we don't like to admit this), "I'm not like *them*." By God's grace, though, we soon realize that we too have been unkind, have said and done things we shouldn't have, or have failed to do what we should have. In such moments of conviction, we are aware of our need for forgiveness, and we are grateful when it's extended by those we've offended.

We can't have all the upside of forgiveness, in other words, without the downside of recognizing our sin. First, we need to see ourselves rightly: by nature as lost sheep, rebels against God, empty vessels needing to be filled. We need to accept that however long we go on in the Christian life and however much the Spirit changes us in this life, we never outgrow our need for grace because we never outrun our own sinfulness. We need to realize what we deserve for our sins before we will bow down in wonder at the realization that a perfect Savior died in our place and paid all that we owe so that we might receive God's forgiveness.

Our great need is to continue to turn to Christ in faith and repentance. Every one of us, no matter where we are in our walk with Christ, needs to pray that God would show us the truth both about ourselves and about our Savior. Then, as we grow in our understanding of all that we deserve, we will adore that very Savior more and more each day. We will stand in awe of God's love and all that Jesus has done for us. Pause now, therefore. Ask God, "Show me myself," and reflect on your own sin. Then ask Him, "Show me my Savior," and bask in the reality and joy of His mercy. Then His kindness and mercy in saving you will consume your affections so that you joyfully join the chorus:

Mercy there was great, and grace was free;
Pardon there was multiplied to me;
There my burdened soul found liberty
At Calvary.[136]

EPHESIANS 2:1-10

136 William R. Newell, "At Calvary" (1895).

DECEMBER 17

NECESSARY TRIALS

"We rejoice in our sufferings, knowing that suffering produces endurance."
ROMANS 5:3

Whatever the realm of experience, perspective is always crucial. In art, it helps the artist create an image so that a cup appears ready to be filled or a chair seems firmly planted on the ground rather than suspended in the air. Similarly, in life's trials the right perspective is required if we wish to make the right response. Unless we think correctly about them, we cannot respond properly.

Trials are the means by which our trust in Jesus as our only hope is tested. They help determine whether the faith we profess is genuine or false. When everything is going smoothly, it's fairly easy to feel confident. But when the wheels fall off—when family life begins to disintegrate, when body or mind fails, when our hopes for this life are dashed—we begin to discover whether our faith is sincere. And when it is proved by testing to be genuine, there is joy, for that kind of faith is "more precious than gold that perishes though it is tested by fire" (1 Peter 1:7).

Difficulties also help us measure the growth of our faith—whether we are stagnant or flourishing. Disappointments and tears often bring more progress and growth in our faith as we put God's word into practice in ways we hadn't before and learn Christ's all-surpassing value in ways we hadn't appreciated before. As one writer puts it, "The wind of tribulation blows away the chaff of error, hypocrisy, and doubt, leaving that which survives the test ... the genuine element of character."[137]

Testing develops staying power. The Christian life is not a few hundred-yard sprints; it's a cross-country run that lasts throughout our lives. Marathon runners go through miles that feel difficult and exhausting, but they keep on going. They are not surprised that it hurts. They expect it to. But they know that beyond the hardships lies the finish. The trials we face along our way similarly call for and produce the endurance we need to run our spiritual race well.

Look at the life of any Christian who has soft eyes and a tender heart and you will almost certainly find that they came to that kindness through the experience of trials. It's easy to want results without effort. Yet this is not how it works. God usually grows our faith in the soil of affliction.

The question to ask yourself is, "Do I believe this?" If you do, it will dramatically change your perspective and your response to life's difficulties. Trials may still fill you with pain, fear, and uncertainty—but you will at the same time be able to consider them with joy, knowing that your spiritual endurance is being developed and therefore your ability to reach the finish line is being enhanced.

1 PETER 1:3-9

137 James B. Adamson, *The Epistle of James,* The New International Commentary on the New Testament (Eerdmans, 1976), p 54.

DECEMBER 18

LISTEN TO HIM

"Peter said to Jesus, 'Rabbi, it is good that we are here. Let us make three tents, one for you and one for Moses and one for Elijah.' For he did not know what to say, for they were terrified. And a cloud overshadowed them, and a voice came out of the cloud, 'This is my beloved Son; listen to him.'" MARK 9:5-7

For Peter, the days leading to Jesus' transfiguration had been a roller-coaster ride. One minute he was declaring, "You are the Christ, the Son of the living God" (Matthew 16:16), and the next minute Jesus was saying to him, "Get behind me, Satan! You are a hindrance to me. For you are not setting your mind on the things of God, but on the things of man" (v 23). Peter had risen to the heights of declaring the true identity of the man who had called him to become a fisher of men; then he had fallen to the depths of being told by the Son of the living God that he was being influenced by the Evil One and was an obstacle to the Son's mission. He would fall even further, and yet rise still higher (26:69-75; Acts 4:5-20). If you, like me, have found that your Christian life is a series of highs and lows, let Peter's example be an encouragement to you.

In Matthew 17, Peter suddenly found himself on a mountain with the transfigured, radiant Jesus conversing with Moses and Elijah. Understandably, Peter "did not know what to say" because he and his two friends "were terrified" (Mark 9:6). He didn't know what he was saying (Luke 9:33)—but that didn't stop him!

The glimpse of majesty Peter received left him stunned. He was in the midst of suggesting that he put up some shelters for the Lord and these two great Old Testament prophets when suddenly, in a moment reminiscent of Jesus' baptism, a voice from heaven came to tell him the correct response to what he was seeing: *That's enough, Peter! It's time to listen to Jesus. This is My Son, whom I love. Listen to Him.*

This is the insistent call of God at all times, for all people, in all places. God's word is as alive and active today through Scripture as it was when Peter heard it on the Mount of Transfiguration. When we read our Bibles, we have the opportunity to see the same glimpse of majesty and experience the same foretaste of glory as Peter, James, and John did, as the Spirit works in our hearts.

We, like Peter, may find our Christian walk "chequered in its course ... Today, it is a depth almost soundless; tomorrow, a height almost scaleless."[138] But when the unrelenting, eternal word of God breaks into our lives, we are redirected to Jesus, the beloved Son of God, the one who was always pleasing to the Father, and who comes to reveal Himself to us. The question is: will we listen to Him?

2 PETER 1:16-21

138 Octavius Winslow, *Soul-Depths and Soul-Heights* (Banner of Truth, 2006), p 1.

DECEMBER 19

FUTURE GLORY

"By faith Joseph, at the end of his life, made mention of the exodus of the Israelites and gave directions concerning his bones." HEBREWS 11:22

The book of Genesis ends with Joseph's death, but that was nowhere near the end of the story. It marks just the beginning of the story of God's provision and deliverance, which carries on throughout the rest of the Bible and into our lives today.

Joseph took great care over what was to happen to his remains after his death, not because of some morbid interest but to offer a symbol of God's provision in the past and the promise of a future deliverance. Joseph's bones pointed future generations of Israel forward to promises that were then yet to be fulfilled.

Despite all the extraordinary trials and experiences that defined Joseph's life—being betrayed by his brothers, wrongfully accused by Potiphar's wife, favored by Pharaoh, positioned within the Egyptian royal court, reunited with his family, and so on—the author of Hebrews chose to highlight none of those things but rather Joseph's faith for what was to come. Why? Because it was so phenomenally significant.

Joseph did not want his family to settle their roots too deeply in Egypt. He knew the promised land was coming. Instead of an elaborate funeral, then, he only asked for his body to be embalmed, placed in a coffin, and left in Egypt (Genesis 50:22-26). Why? He didn't want his bones to be buried. He wanted his body to be ready to be moved when it was time to travel to the promised land. He recognized that the coffin itself would be a memorial of the fact that the hope of the promised land was as certain as any promise God had ever made. When difficult days would come for the future generations of this growing refugee family, as he surely imagined they would, he wanted them to be able to look to the promise. They could look at his coffin, standing at the ready, and say, *Joseph was sure we would leave. If he hadn't been sure, he wouldn't have us carting his bones around like this.*

Today, you do not have Joseph's coffin full of bones to look to. Instead, you have an empty tomb to remind you of God's provision in the past and your promised hope for the future. Christ is "our help in ages past, our hope for years to come." He is "our eternal home."[139] Because of Him, you can live through difficult days, and die on your final day, secure in your hope of heaven, our great promised land.

LUKE 23:32-43

139 Isaac Watts, "O God, Our Help in Ages Past" (1719).

DECEMBER 20

CONFESSION AND RELIEF

"David sent and brought [Bathsheba] to his house, and she became his wife and bore him a son. But the thing that David had done displeased the LORD ... And the LORD sent Nathan to David." 2 SAMUEL 11:27; 12:1

If we stop seeking to cover up our sin, God is willing to cover it over.

David's sin of adultery with (or very possibly even rape of) Bathsheba was compounded by his cover-up of it, arranging for her husband, Uriah, to be killed. But the plan seemed to have worked masterfully. David married Bathsheba, and no one was any the wiser. A time of deceit and silence followed. David believed he had it covered. Sin frequently deceives us into thinking that. But what others think of us and what God says of us are often very different.

God knew what others did not. He sent a prophet to the king. Yet Nathan didn't show up at David's door to jump straight to bold accusations. He simply told him a story about a rich man with many flocks and herds unjustly taking a poor man's only lamb, which drew out David's sympathy for the wronged man and rage over the rich man's actions. Then Nathan delivered the devastating punchline: "You are the man!" (2 Samuel 12:7).

"The LORD sent Nathan to David." Those six words are words of amazing grace! Yahweh would not allow His servant David to settle down comfortably in his sin. As unpleasant and difficult as it may have been for the king to face his sin, the reason why God sent the prophet to David was because He loved him. God granted David something he did not deserve, and David responded to Nathan's words with humility and repentance. Because God intervened and David confessed, the story ended not with despair and guilt but with deliverance and grace (see Psalm 32:5-6). As Derek Kidner writes, "The relief of climbing down, and the grace which meets it ... altogether outweigh the cost."[140]

That is true for us no less than it was for David. We may fear that if we quit our own cover-up games with sin, then our reputations will suffer. But if you are accommodating immorality in your life, it doesn't matter how well you can conceal it from the watching world. Ultimately, the watching world is irrelevant: God knows your heart. It is on account of God's faithfulness that He pursues us and won't let us remain comfortable in our disobedience and rebellion. While we may not have a prophet like Nathan sent to us, we do have God's word to open in front of us; it is "living and active, sharper than any two-edged sword ... discerning the thoughts and intentions of the heart. And no creature is hidden from his sight" (Hebrews 4:12-13)—including both the creature writing these words and the one reading them. God exposes our sin that we might bring it to Him to cover it over with the blood of His Son.

What is He pointing out to you right now? Are you seeking to excuse or justify or hide it? It's time to climb down and stop covering it up. The cost of sin is far outweighed by the benefits of forgiveness.

2 SAMUEL 11:1 – 12:25

140 *Psalms 1–72,* Kidner Classic Commentaries (1973; reprinted IVP, 2008), p 151.

DECEMBER 21

SUBMISSION AND HUMILITY

"[Give] thanks always and for everything to God the Father in the name of our Lord Jesus Christ, submitting to one another out of reverence for Christ."
EPHESIANS 5:20-21

When people take part in an orchestra, they lose something of their own individuality. A symphony is not a solo performance. Although the musicians do not lose their identities, they're nevertheless subsumed into the orchestra itself. The group is more significant as a whole than an individual is on their own, and the collective produces something that no individual musician could create.

Paul expresses a similar idea when he writes of "submitting to one another"—though here, of course, the group is not an orchestra but the church.

While we may have a variety of responses to the concept of submission, we must acknowledge that the Bible uses it straightforwardly and frequently. For Paul, the unity and health of the church depended on Christians understanding submission rightly and putting that into practice among one another.

What does it look like to take the matter of believers' mutual submission seriously? In part, it means each of us realizing that we don't have the slightest reason to feel overly pleased with ourselves or superior to somebody else. In other words, we demonstrate mutual submission by putting on humility. This is made difficult, of course, by our pride—a great challenge we all face, and one that is intensified by living in a culture that is constantly pressuring us to push ourselves to the front.

Yet the church ought to stand out in and from that kind of environment. As God's people, we understand that we cannot even wake in the morning without His enabling. The fact of the matter is that we are entirely dependent on Him (Acts 17:24-25). The gospel is the key to true humility because the gospel reminds us that God has done for us in Jesus the thing that we most need, and the thing that we are utterly unable to do for ourselves.

Real humility is not self-deprecation; it is freedom from ourselves. It's the freedom to be ourselves and forget ourselves. It's the freedom that comes from knowing that we are not the center of the universe. When you keep such humility in sight, you will be prepared to submit to others—to bring all that you are and use it to serve the greater good, under the direction of others, with the interests of others as your priority. Then your church can produce something beautiful—a gospel-displaying community. So do not wait for others in your church to be that kind of Christian. Today, humbly resolve that you will be that Christian.

EPHESIANS 4:1-16

DECEMBER 22

A WARNING AGAINST IDLENESS

"I passed by the field of a sluggard, by the vineyard of a man lacking sense, and behold, it was all overgrown with thorns; the ground was covered with nettles, and its stone wall was broken down ... A little sleep, a little slumber, a little folding of the hands to rest..." PROVERBS 24:30-31, 33

Imagine driving down the road and coming to a house that is broken down and overgrown with weeds. First, you assume that no one lives there. But then you see someone through a broken window. You wonder if the owner is sick and unable to care for the property. Then they wander outside and they look full of health. It turns out that they are simply lazy.

That, of course, is the scene described in this proverb: a sluggard lives on the land, and his vineyard is a testimony to his laziness.

Sluggards don't set out with the desire to live in poverty and disgrace. Rather, when challenged with work, their attitude is marked by key characteristics that many of us may find in our own lives if we are willing to gaze into the mirror of God's word.

A sluggard doesn't merely enjoy his bed; he is hinged to it, making a lot of movement but no progress towards anything substantial (Proverbs 26:14). He never flat-out refuses to do anything. Rather, he just puts off tasks bit by bit, moment by moment, and deceives himself into thinking he will get around to them.

A sluggard is also masterful at making excuses. Possessing no mind to work, she always finds reasons to continue in her idleness. There is nothing difficult about taking out the overflowing trash bag, but the sluggard will rationalize her failure to follow through on even the simplest of duties.

Sluggards will, quite ironically, always be hungering for fulfillment, because, by virtue of their posture of heart, they never find it. It's always "out there somewhere," but it's never realized. The souls of sluggards crave and gets nothing, not because they can't but because they won't. In their overabundance of rest, they are restless.

When laziness comes to mark our existence, we may convince ourselves that we really are prepared to run ten miles, start writing that paper, or finish that project—but we are only living in the realm of imagination until our reality is changed by God's power and grace.

Beware of looking at idleness as some sort of minor detail or small problem. Laziness is not an infirmity. It is a sin. Little by little it can affect the whole of our lives, growing with unperceived power—and Satan is longing to lull us into defeat. In what ways are you tempted to be lazy? What are you putting off or making excuses for, and why? Will you confront this sin and ask God to help you deal with it ruthlessly, immediately, and consistently?

2 THESSALONIANS 3:6-15

DECEMBER 23

LORD, YOU KNOW

"He said to him the third time, 'Simon, son of John, do you love me?' Peter was grieved because he said to him the third time, 'Do you love me?' and he said to him, 'Lord, you know everything; you know that I love you.'" JOHN 21:17

The heart of Christianity isn't found in doing a course on systematic theology or in memorizing doctrines to be regurgitated. The focal point for the Christian is a relationship with Jesus—to be known and loved by Him, and to love Him in return.

We see this illustrated firsthand when, after sharing a meal on the beach with His disciples, the risen Jesus initiated a private conversation with Peter. This talk resulted in both Peter's conviction and calling. Supremely, though, it displays Christ's intimate knowledge and care for those who love Him. Christ's greatest concern was Peter's response to His question, "Do you love me?"

In this exchange, Jesus asked Peter this question repeatedly. The question was not meant to provoke mere sentimentalism; it demanded a decision. The repetition served as a stark reminder of Peter's three denials of knowing Christ (John 18:15-18, 25-27), and forced Peter to recognize that his recent actions had failed to show his love for Christ. He couldn't point to his own works to justify himself.

We will come to the same realization as we consider times when we have stumbled. When Christ asks us the same question, there is nothing we can say or do in our defense to prove our love. The only thing that Peter could plead before the Father, before Christ, was God's own omniscience: "Lord … *you know* that I love you." Likewise, our only appeal is to the understanding heart of Jesus.

Our actions may discourage us, our circumstances may have buffeted and beaten us, and our love for God may be weak—but we can take comfort in the truth that Jesus knows our hearts! He knows our hearts will fail. He knows our faith can be weak. But our failings are the very reason why He came into this world, died on the cross, and rose again.

If we find ourselves needing restoration but having nothing to say in our defense, the wonderful hope we have is that we can say, "Lord, *You know*." And if we find ourselves needing our love to be rekindled but having nothing within us to spark it, the wonderful truth is that we can look to our Lord hanging on a cross out of love for us: for "we love because he first loved us" (1 John 4:19).

Take a moment and reflect upon the immensity and the intimacy of God's grace and love for you. Jesus bore all of your failures on the cross so that you might die to sin and live for Him (1 Peter 2:24), and He continues to pursue relationship with you despite all your imperfections. He knows you utterly, and yet He loves you perfectly.

Do you love Him? For surely there is none more worthy.

1 JOHN 3:16-24

DECEMBER 24

THE CHRISTMAS SERVANT

"I will give you as a covenant for the people, a light for the nations, to open the eyes that are blind, to bring out the prisoners from the dungeon, from the prison those who sit in darkness." ISAIAH 42:6-7

At Christmas, many of us feel tremendously cozy as we think about the familiar Nativity story. Filled with all kinds of sentimentalism, it is entirely possible for us to completely disengage from the whole panorama of God's purpose: to allow familiarity with the scene to blind us to the awe-inspiring truth that as we look at the baby in a Bethlehem manger, we are looking in on the Servant of God.

This Servant, Jesus, had a mission. Even Mary and Joseph had only an inkling about all He would accomplish—yet hundreds of years before Jesus arrived, God had announced what He would do to fulfill His purpose (Isaiah 42:1-4).

Jesus came to open the eyes of the spiritually blind. During His earthly ministry, He gave a wonderful illustration of this by granting physical healing to the blind. The greatest issue, however, concerned not the body but the soul. He came to open the eyes of men and women who were blind to God's truth.

The Servant also came to free captives from prison. Many of us have felt the captivity of our guilt, trying countless hoped-for solutions to wash it all away. But nothing works except Jesus. He breaks our chains and sets us free. Once slaves of sin, we have now been rescued. Our Savior releases from the dungeon those who sit in darkness, if only they see His light.

The story of the Servant is a story not about what we must do but about what Jesus has done. He came down into the dungeon, into our enslavement, into our blindness, and said, *You've failed and broken the law, and you are entirely unable to rectify your condition. But I save sinners. I open blind eyes. I release captives. I bring light. I have done everything required for you. Turn to Me in simple faith and childlike trust and you will see. You will be free, and your darkness will give way to sunshine.*

The one who has done all this is the one you are gazing at as you consider that familiar Nativity scene. Never let it fail to move and inspire you to praise and worship of the divine Son, who came as our Servant.

LUKE 1:26-56

DECEMBER 25

COME, ADORE ON BENDED KNEE

"'Let us go over to Bethlehem and see this thing that has happened, which the Lord has made known to us.' And [the shepherds] went with haste and found Mary and Joseph, and the baby lying in a manger." LUKE 2:15-16

Come to Bethlehem and see
Him whose birth the angels sing;
Come, adore on bended knee,
Christ the Lord, the newborn King.[141]

When we sing these kinds of words in our Christmas carols, not many of us physically kneel. We understand that this carol's invitation is metaphorical. Yet if we wish to actually behold Christ, then we must be ready to accept the invitation to come on bended knee in terms of the posture of our hearts. What does that mean? It means to come humbly and expectantly, and in recognition that this person is worthy of such homage.

Much like the shepherds, we are compelled and enabled to go to God because He is a seeking God. At the Nativity, He wonderfully took the initiative, sending His Son to the world as a helpless baby, and speaking to the shepherds through the angel: "Fear not, for behold, I bring you good news of great joy that will be for all the people. For unto you is born this day in the city of David a Savior, who is Christ the Lord" (Luke 2:10-11). God took the initiative in grace, and the shepherds responded in faith. They believed the angelic message and eagerly began seeking the manger. Prioritizing their search above their livelihood and all they knew, they immediately sought to know for themselves the Redeemer of the world. What a wonderful illustration of how we ought to respond to God's message!

Some may view the shepherds with ridicule, deeming them foolish in their simple belief and response. What prevents a man or woman from trusting God's message like they did? One word: pride. Pride would have kept the shepherds in the fields, in possession of the angelic announcement but not of a relationship with the Christ. Pride will keep us from coming to Christ on bended knee and blind us to the truth that to know God truly requires of us a contrite spirit and a humble heart (Psalm 51:17).

At the Church of the Nativity in Bethlehem, it's impossible to just stroll in. The door is too low. If you want to enter the place that represents the birth of the Lord Jesus, there is only one way to get in: stoop, bow down, and kneel. This is a beautiful picture—and it moves us to ask: Am I prepared to humble myself before Christ? Am I willing, like those shepherds, to give up my prior assumptions and previous plans to know and follow this Redeemer? Check your heart this Christmas Day: let its posture forever be one that bows before God's glory and adores the one who first humbled Himself by coming to us as an infant King.

LUKE 2:1-20

141 James Chadwick, "Angels We Have Heard on High" (1862), trans. from the traditional French carol "Les Anges dans Nos Campagnes."

DECEMBER 26

CHRISTMAS ACCORDING TO CHRIST

"When Christ came into the world, he said, 'Sacrifices and offerings you have not desired, but a body have you prepared for me; in burnt offerings and sin offerings you have taken no pleasure.'" HEBREWS 10:5-6

The Gospels of Matthew and Luke introduce us to a whole cast of Christmas characters with whom we've grown quite familiar: Joseph, Mary, the shepherds, the wise men, and so on. Sometimes we even consider those who are less known, such as Zechariah, Elizabeth, Anna, and Simeon. With each passing Christmas season, we have probably been treated to sermons and studies from the perspective of just about every cast member. Yet there is one notable exception: surprisingly few of us have pondered Christmas from Jesus' vantage point.

In this verse, the author of the letter to the Hebrews tells us that when Jesus stepped onto the stage of history, He took the words of Psalm 40 upon His lips. Just as Cinderella's glass slipper fit only her foot, these words fit nobody but Jesus.

God was preparing for the first Christmas throughout the centuries of the Old Testament, for all the Old Testament sacrifices were mere shadows of the reality to which they pointed. Those sacrifices involved the death of animals that had to be prodded to the altar. They had no choice in the matter; they were simply pressed into service. But before He even experienced humanity, Jesus knew His role—His sacrifice—would be different. He willingly consented. In the humblest of forms and in an unexpected setting, God the Son took on a body that was prepared for Him—prepared "as a ransom for many" (Matthew 20:28). He looked at this broken world and its sinful people, and He said to His Father, *Yes, I will go there. I will become one of them, and I will die for them.*

Peter grasps the weight of Christ's death when he writes, "He himself bore our sins in his body on the tree, that we might die to sin and live to righteousness. By his wounds you have been healed" (1 Peter 2:24). Jesus, being fully God and fully man, entered this world to do in His body what no animal sacrifice could do: He has borne our punishment, cleansed our consciences, and held out divine mercy. He perfectly accomplished all that is necessary for sinful men and women to enter into fellowship with God.

This is very different from the promise of mere religion, in which rules and effort become futile mechanisms for trying to climb into heaven. In contrast, the manger's message is one of liberating mercy. God has wonderfully taken the initiative and come to rescue us through Jesus. We don't need to make a long journey to find God, because Christ, the newborn King, knew His role. What is the right response? Simply to bow before Him humbly, praise Him wholeheartedly, and wait for Him expectantly all of our days.

PSALM 40

DECEMBER 27

THE FRAILTY OF LIFE

"Come now, you who say, 'Today or tomorrow we will go into such and such a town and spend a year there and trade and make a profit'—yet you do not know what tomorrow will bring. What is your life? For you are a mist that appears for a little time and then vanishes. Instead you ought to say, 'If the Lord wills, we will live and do this or that.'" JAMES 4:13-15

The Bible does not condemn business acumen or future planning. What the Bible does condemn, however, is a prideful, self-centered way of thinking that, whether intentionally or unintentionally, leaves God out of our decisions and future plans—a mindset that assumes certainties that are never promised to us.

James confronts us in no uncertain terms with the reality of our finite knowledge and understanding. Indeed, he reminds us that we need to accept what we do not know. Do we want to be able to plan weeks and months in advance? Of course we do! But James points out that we don't even know what will happen tomorrow. It is pride that leads us to assume that our next breath is a given.

He then goes on to remind us of our frailty. The fact is that our lives are each "a mist that appears for a little time and then vanishes." Like an early-morning fog that hovers over the grass and is gone at the first touch of the sun's rays, our lives are transient; eventually, they seemingly vanish, without even a trace left to be seen by future generations.

In light of our frailty and limitations, how are we then to think about the future? James not only calls out our presumptuous thinking and planning, he also supplies the antidote. Very simply, we need to learn to make plans in humility, recognizing our complete dependence on God's providential care. Nothing in the entire universe—including us—would continue to exist for one fraction of a second apart from God. As Alec Motyer writes, "We receive another day not as a result of natural necessity, nor by mechanical law, nor by right, nor by the courtesy of nature, but by the covenanted mercies of God."[142]

Tomorrow is not promised. We may plan for it, but we may not assume we can control it. God's mercy alone enables us to awaken to each new day. The sin of presumption is exposed as folly when we realize that our very life is grounded in God's sustaining gifts. We cannot ignore our limitations and life's brevity, but we can allow these realities to shape and transform our thinking and our decisions for the sake of His glory. So consider your plans for today, for tomorrow, for next year, and for further on in your life. Did you pray about them? Have you acknowledged that His plans are sovereign and that all of yours are contingent on His? Lift your plans up to Him now and place them in His hands. You cannot control the future. But you do not need to, for you know the one who does.

MATTHEW 6:25-34

142 *The Message of James,* The Bible Speaks Today (IVP Academic, 1985), p 162.

DECEMBER 28

THE ANTIDOTE TO PRIDE

"Beware of the leaven of the Pharisees and the leaven of Herod." MARK 8:15

It is sobering to consider how many people saw the Lord Jesus, heard His teaching, and witnessed His miracles—and yet refused to believe. The same day that they saw Him feed 4,000 with a few loaves and fishes—revealing Himself to be the God who provides for His people in the wilderness (Mark 8:1-10; see Exodus 16)—the Pharisees asked Him for a "sign from heaven" (Mark 8:11). In response, Jesus cautioned His followers, "Beware of the leaven of the Pharisees and the leaven of Herod."

The Pharisees were marked by hypocrisy: Herod by hostility. The Pharisees wished to hold on to their self-righteous assumptions that they merited blessing from God, and so they had no place for a Savior. Herod wished to hold on to the power he wielded over the people, so he had no place for the King. Therefore, they were committed to a blindness to truth. Their approach refused to believe or understand who Jesus was. They were essentially saying, *I really don't want to find out what Jesus means, and I certainly will not accept that He is my Savior or my King.* Jesus warned against taking on that same attitude, because even a trace amount of leaven—of unbelief—can make a significant difference.

When pride rears its ugly head, it can lead us to judge the Scriptures rather than learning from them. When we stand in judgment over God's word, though, what we might regard as trivial and insignificant tweaking of truth will actually be the leaven—the yeast—which spreads throughout the entire bread of our convictions.

Jesus' challenge to us is to humbly accept Him as who He is—to allow Him to save us of our sins and to rule over our whole life. He patiently reminds us again and again of who He is. His challenge is prophetic and parental, direct and loving.

We need the work of Christ to overcome the effects of the leaven of pride. It takes divine intervention to understand Christ's work in our lives. That's why people can read the Bible and see nothing—can listen to the gospel story and hear nothing. Until the eyes of understanding are opened and our ears are unplugged, we will remain unaffected. But every day that God's Spirit shows us the beauty of Jesus, and reminds us of our desperate need for Him, our hearts and minds can sing:

I know not how the Spirit moves, convincing men of sin,
Revealing Jesus through the word, creating faith in Him.
But I know whom I have believed, and am persuaded that He is able.[143]

The antidote to the leaven of the Pharisees and Herod is the work of the Spirit. Do not be so proud as to assume you do not need Him. Pray that He would show you Jesus afresh in His word today, so that you might worship your Savior and King with every part of your life.

LUKE 18:9-14

143 Daniel Webster Whittle, "I Know Whom I Have Believed" (1883).

DECEMBER 29

SEASONS OF WAITING

"[God] brought [Abraham] outside and said, 'Look toward heaven, and number the stars, if you are able to number them.' Then he said to him, 'So shall your offspring be.' And he believed the L*ORD, and he counted it to him as righteousness."* GENESIS 15:5-6

If our faith is to remain steadfast in seasons of prolonged waiting, then we must be confident of these truths: first, that God has the power to do what He promised to do; and second, that God Himself is sufficient to meet all of our needs, in every season.

Abraham's faith was tested in the waiting room of life. For years he lived in a foreign land, waiting for his "very own son" to come into the world as God had promised (Genesis 15:4). And it was his trust in God's promises while he waited that God "counted … to him as righteousness."

Paul, when he writes of Abraham's faith during this time, says, "No unbelief made him waver concerning the promise of God, but he grew strong in his faith as he gave glory to God, fully convinced that God was able to do what he had promised" (Romans 4:20-21). In other words, Abraham believed that nothing and no one could stand in the way of God fulfilling His spoken word—even when he could not begin to see how God would keep His promises. His faith wasn't a blind leap in the dark. Rather, it was a belief based on God's character.

Fast-forward to today, and one of the great promises to which we cling is that the Lord Jesus has promised to prepare a place for us and that He will come to take us to Himself (John 14:3). Therefore, when we take Him at His word, we are filled with the hope of heaven. We can be certain beyond any shadow of a doubt that Jesus is coming back personally, He is coming back visibly, and He is coming back for His own. These promises to us are as sure as the promise God made to Abraham, for which he waited 25 years before it was fulfilled.

Furthermore, through Abraham's experience we see that it is God alone who is sufficient to bring us through seasons of waiting. In Genesis 17, God appears once more to Abraham in order to strengthen his faith. How? By revealing *who He is*: "When Abram was ninety-nine years old the LORD appeared to Abram and said to him, 'I am God Almighty [*El-Shaddai*]; walk before me'" (17:1). This Hebrew term, *El-Shaddai*, can mean "God who is sufficient." God, in other words, affirmed His promises to Abraham on the strength of His character.

The Christian life is a life of waiting. And all of God's "hold ons" and "not yets" are part and parcel of His purpose. Every season of waiting is an opportunity for you to take God at His word. And while you wait, you can surely trust Him to meet your every need. Rest in this: the God in whom you believe is able to do all that He has promised.

GENESIS 17:1-8

DECEMBER 30

ALL THINGS MADE NEW

"God himself will be with them as their God. He will wipe away every tear from their eyes, and death shall be no more, neither shall there be mourning, nor crying, nor pain anymore, for the former things have passed away."
REVELATION 21:3-4

The whole idea of a new heaven and a new earth is hard to comprehend. But we can say with absolute certainty that God is going to take what is present and transform it, and He's determined that no one and nothing will be capable of destroying His perfected kingdom. We can say this with such certainty because He is the God who is powerful to keep His promises, seen most gloriously of all at a wooden cross and an empty tomb. Right now, behind the scenes of what we call history, God is preparing to bring His kingdom in all its fullness—and it is, in fact, something He has been preparing from all of eternity. When Christ returns, He will usher in this new kingdom, a new heaven and earth in which righteousness dwells.

When God's perfected kingdom is finally established, sin will have been punished, justice will have been satisfied, and evil will have been destroyed. There will be no more death, mourning, crying, or pain. Those will all be merely "the former things" that will have "passed away." When God brings His kingdom to fruition, when His perfect plan unfolds, no one and nothing will be able to spoil it.

The word "new" as it is used to describe the new heaven and new earth in Revelation is not describing time or origin; it's describing *kind* and *quality*. In other words, God is going to transform creation so that it reflects all the glory and magnificence that He originally intended for it. Satan will not get the satisfaction of watching God destroy His creation. Rather, God is going to use fire to purify it, just as He once used water in the days of Noah (2 Peter 3:5-7).

So the new earth will still be earth. It will be a physical place inhabited by physical people, but now it "shall be full of the knowledge of the Lord as the waters cover the sea" (Isaiah 11:9). No wonder, then, that the whole of creation stands on tiptoe, longing to be liberated from its bondage to sin and decay (Romans 8:19-22)!

This new creation is worth waiting for. It is worth living for and even dying for. God is going to renew all things—our souls, our minds, our bodies, and even the environment in which we live. None of the things which currently spoil life on earth will be present, and all that is hoped for, all that is anticipated, will find its fulfillment.

So "we wait eagerly" (Romans 8:23). There is never a need to despair, no matter how dark life may become—for the day God wipes your tears away lies ahead. And "we wait for it with patience" (v 25). There is never a need to seek to seize all you think you need now, no matter how tempting that may be—for the day when God brings all the joy and satisfaction you could imagine lies ahead. Let eagerness and patience be your watchwords today.

ROMANS 8:18-25

DECEMBER 31

THE BREVITY OF LIFE

"As for man, his days are like grass: he flourishes like a flower of the field; for the wind passes over it, and it is gone ... But the steadfast love of the L*ORD is from everlasting to everlasting on those who fear him."* PSALM 103:15-17

Life passes us by a lot more quickly than we imagine. I vividly remember the birth of my first child—and then it seemed that he was a teenager only a few weeks later. When we were children, just the time between December 1 and December 25 stretched out for years; now the years race by ever more quickly. Suddenly, we wake up older or we hear of the death of someone who was our age, and we realize that life really is very brief. We flourish for a time, but not forever.

As we age, our physical and mental abilities fade, old friends pass away, familiar customs which have been routine disintegrate, and our long-held ambitions lose their potential or appeal. These realities, though, shouldn't drive us into despair but rather stimulate us. Like grass, we have a limited number of days, but there is opportunity in every one of them! As the Bible scholar Derek Kidner writes, "Death has not yet reached out to us: let it rattle its chains at us and stir us into action."[144] With the minutes that remain in our lives, we can lift up our eyes and look at the "fields"—at those who live and work around us and who do not yet know Jesus as their Lord and Savior, who are not enjoying the steadfast and everlasting love of the Lord. As Jesus said, those fields are already "white for harvest" (John 4:35).

The Bible doesn't encourage us to wait until we graduate or get married or settle down or sort ourselves out or retire before we start to serve Christ. Rather, it calls us to do so today. The wise person knows that we have limited time and that the best way to spend it is on the Lord's errands.

So whether you are at the start of life, or feel you are in the prime of life, or are looking back at life, before the strength in your hands fails you and your teeth, eyes, and ears grow weak, will you choose to live all out for Jesus Christ? If you wait until tomorrow, tomorrow may be too late. As C.T. Studd once put it, there is...

Only one life,
'Twill soon be past.
Only what's done
For Christ will last.

Therefore, look at your days in this life as the "grass" that they are. Spend them in awe of the God who will love you eternally—and spend them not building your own empire of sand but on the work of the only kingdom that endures forever. And pray that as you do so, the Lord will "establish the work of [your] hands" (Psalm 90:17), both today and throughout the year that tomorrow will bring.

PSALM 90

144 *The Message of Ecclesiastes,* The Bible Speaks Today (IVP UK, 1976), p 104.

ACKNOWLEDGMENTS

Long before the phrase "Truth For Life" became the title of this daily devotional, it was the name of both a daily Bible teaching program and a ministry organization based in Northeast Ohio. If it were not for the team at Truth For Life, this project never would have seen the light of day. I'm especially indebted to Alyssa Scheck, Constance Brannon Boring, Kate Nees, Katie Tumino, and Matt Damico for their help with the writing; Adam Marshall for his expertise throughout the entire editorial process; and Ryan Loague for getting this project off the ground and for helping to ensure its theological precision. Lastly, I'd be remiss if I did not mention Bob Butts. He has long encouraged me to make something like this happen, and, well, here we are. He reviewed every one of these entries and provided helpful feedback all while leading the day-to-day operations at Truth For Life.

My thanks also go to my publisher, The Good Book Company, and in particular my editor, Carl Laferton. It has, as ever, been a joy to work with these brothers and sisters.

SCRIPTURE INDEX

Entries in **bold** refer to the main verse or passage for that date's devotional